ENGLAND
AND WALES

Signpost
Guides

Titles in this series include:

- Andalucía and the Costa del Sol
- Bavaria and the Austrian Tyrol
- Brittany and Normandy
- Burgundy and the Rhône Valley
- California
- Canadian Rockies, Alberta and British Columbia
- Catalonia and the Spanish Pyrenees
- Dordogne and Western France
- England and Wales
- Florida
- Ireland
- Italian Lakes and Mountains with Venice and Florence
- Languedoc and South-west France
- Loire Valley
- New England
- New Zealand
- Provence and the Côte d'Azur
- Scotland
- Tuscany and Umbria
- Vancouver and British Columbia
- Washington DC and Virginia, Maryland and Delaware
  and

- Selected Bed and Breakfast in France (annual edition)

For further information about these and other Thomas Cook publications,
write to Thomas Cook Publishing, PO Box 227, Units 19–21, The Thomas Cook Business Park,
Coningsby Road, Peterborough PE3 8XX, United Kingdom.

Signpost
Guides

ENGLAND AND WALES

The best of England and Wales,
from the national parks of the
Yorkshire Dales and Snowdonia to the
bird-filled marshes of East Anglia, and
from the rural delights of the
Cotswolds to the big-city attractions
of York, Oxford, Cambridge and Bath,
with suggested driving tours

Lindsay Hunt

The
Globe
Pequot
Press

Thomas Cook
Publishing

Published by Thomas Cook Publishing
A division of Thomas Cook Holdings Ltd
PO Box 227, Units 19–21
The Thomas Cook Business Park
Coningsby Road
Peterborough PE3 8XX
United Kingdom

Telephone: +44 (0)1733 416477
Fax: +44 (0)1733 416688
E-mail: books@thomascook.com

For further information about
Thomas Cook Publishing, visit our website:
www.thomascook.com

ISBN 1-841573-35-3

Published in the USA by
The Globe Pequot Press
PO Box 480
Guilford, Connecticut 06437
USA

ISBN 0-7627-2650-4

Text: © 2003 Thomas Cook Publishing
Maps and diagrams: © 2003 Thomas Cook Publishing
Road maps and London city map supplied by Lovell Johns Ltd, OX8 8LH, © Lovell Johns Ltd, 2000
Maps prepared by Polly Senior Cartography

Head of Publishing: Donald Greig

Written, researched and updated by: Lindsay Hunt
Series Editor: Edith Summerhayes
Project Editor for second edition: Sarah Hudson

About the author

Lindsay Hunt travels widely in Europe, North America, Asia and the Middle East to write for various magazines and many hotel and destination guides. Periodically rediscovering the British Isles remains a constant pleasure. Over the past 20 years she has ground the dust of urban streets and country lanes into her boots, written a book on Ireland and completed a Grand Tour of the entire coastline of England and Wales. Encapsulating the best of England and Wales within the scope of these pages has been a formidable challenge. The UK offers a tantalisingly rich variety of scenery and places to visit. What follows is necessarily selective. Researching this book has reconfirmed yet again that these isles are every bit as absorbing, exhilarating and even exotic as any far-flung destination.

Acknowledgements

The author would like to thank all the staff of the English Tourism Council, the Welsh Tourist Board and many regional tourist offices, museums, hotels and attractions (too numerous to mention individually) who have co-operated in the preparation of this guide. Special thanks also to: Anne Copp of Johansens, the *Good Britain Guide*, and *Holiday Which?* magazine, whose publications have been invaluable.

Below
Chipping steps, in Tetbury

Contents

About Signpost Guides

Thomas Cook's Signpost Guides are designed to provide you with a comprehensive but flexible reference source to guide you as you tour a country or region by car. This guide divides England and Wales into touring areas – one per chapter. Major cultural centres or cities form chapters in their own right. Each chapter contains enough attractions to provide at least a day's worth of activities – often more.

Symbol key

ⓘ Tourist Information Centre

🔄 Advice on arriving or departing

🅿 Parking locations

🔄 Advice on getting around

🔟 Sights and attractions

🍴 Eating

🅒 Accommodation

🛍 Shopping

⚽ Sport

🎭 Entertainment

Star ratings
To make it easier for you to plan your time and decide what to see, every sight and attraction is given a star rating. A three-star rating indicates a major attraction, worth at least half a day of your time. A two-star attraction is worth an hour or so of your time, and a one-star attraction indicates a sight that is worth visiting, but often of specialist interest. To help you further, individual attractions within towns or theme parks are also graded, so that travellers with limited time can quickly find the most rewarding sights.

Chapter contents
Every chapter has an introduction summing up the main attractions of the area, and a ratings box, which will highlight its appeal – some areas may be more attractive to families travelling with children and others to wine-lovers visiting vineyards, while others will appeal to those interested in finding castles, churches, nature reserves, or good beaches.

Each chapter is then divided into an alphabetical gazetteer, and a suggested tour. You can select whether you just want to visit a particular sight or attraction, choosing from those described in the gazetteer, or whether you want to tour the area comprehensively. If the latter, you can construct your own itinerary, or follow the author's suggested tour, which comes at the end of every area chapter.

The gazetteer
The gazetteer section describes all the major attractions in the area – the villages, towns, historic sites, nature reserves, parks or museums that you are most likely to want to see. Maps of the area highlight all the places mentioned in the text. Using this comprehensive overview of the area, you may choose just to visit one or two sights.

One way to use the guide is to find individual sights that interest you, using the index, overview map or star ratings, and read what our authors have to say about them. This will help you decide whether to visit the sight. If you do, you will find practical information, such as the address, telephone number for enquiries and opening times.

Practical information

The practical information in the page margins, or sidebar, will help you locate the services you need as an independent traveller – including the tourist information centre, car parks and public transport facilities. You will also find the opening times of sights, museums, churches and other attractions, as well as useful tips on shopping, market days, cultural events, entertainment, festivals and sports facilities.

Alternatively, you can choose a hotel, with the help of the accommodation recommendations contained in this guide. You can then turn to the overall map on page 10 to help you work out which chapters in the book describe the cities and regions closest to your touring base.

Driving tours

The suggested tour is just that – a suggestion, with plenty of optional detours and one or two ideas for making your own discoveries, under the heading *Also worth exploring*. The routes are designed to link the attractions described in the gazetteer section, and to cover outstandingly scenic coastal, mountain and rural landscapes. The total distance is given for each tour, and the time it will take you to drive the complete route, but bear in mind that this indication is just for driving time: you will need to add on extra time for visiting attractions along the way.

Many of the routes are circular, so that you can join them at any point. Where the nature of the terrain dictates that the route has to be linear, the route can either be followed out and back, or you can use it as a link route, to get from one area in the book to another.

As you follow the route descriptions, you will find names picked out in bold capital letters – this means that the place is described fully in the gazetteer. Other names picked out in bold indicate additional villages or attractions worth a brief stop along the route.

Accommodation and food

In every chapter you will find lodging and eating recommendations for individual towns, or for the area as a whole. These are designed to cover a range of price brackets and concentrate on more characterful small or individualistic hotels and restaurants. In addition, you will find information in the *Travel facts* chapter on chain hotels, with an address to which you can write for a guide, map or directory.

The price indications used in the guide have the following meanings:

£	budget level
££	typical/average prices
£££	de luxe

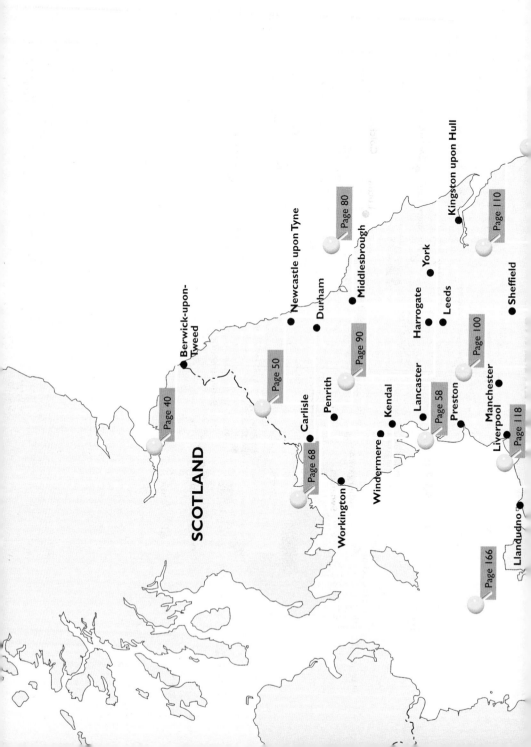

SCOTLAND

Berwick-upon-Tweed

Newcastle upon Tyne

Durham

Middlesbrough

Carlisle

Penrith

Kendal

Windermere

Lancaster

Preston

Workington

Liverpool

Manchester

Llandudno

Harrogate

Leeds

York

Sheffield

Kingston upon Hull

Page 40

Page 50

Page 68

Page 90

Page 80

Page 58

Page 100

Page 110

Page 118

Page 166

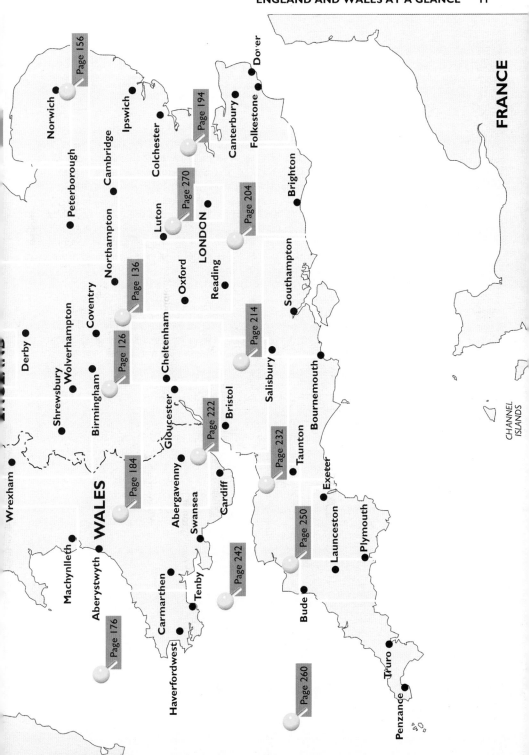

Above
Lincoln Cathedral

Introduction

England and Wales account for about two-thirds of the total land mass of Great Britain, and for the vast majority of its population. It's not a huge area. A crow setting off from Dover Docks (as many visitors do), would be unable to fly in a straight line for more than 400 miles without reaching the sea again. Within these limited confines, however, there are enormous diversions of scenery and character, and this is the key to the enduring attraction of these two neighbouring countries. Despite intense urbanisation in certain areas – indeed, there is little true wilderness left even in wild Wales – and a dense network of roads, England and Wales retain an extraordinary mosaic of different landscapes, the result of an exceptionally variable climate and geological structure. Just as stimulating as its natural phenomena are its man-made features. The visitor is never far from evidence of human activity – even well away from cities, towns or villages, there will be some castle, mill, church or stately home, a prehistoric monument, or sign of countryside management. And these constitute the 'heritage' that most visitors come to see in England and Wales.

A bird's-eye view

Flying westwards from Dover above the white cliffs and chalk downlands of southern Britain, our crow might pinpoint the tall spire of Salisbury Cathedral and Stonehenge's mysterious megaliths, then spy the sweeping moorland contours of Exmoor and Dartmoor on its port and starboard wings before running out of English air space over the churning surf of the Hartland coast. If it were to head northwest from Dover, it would see a sharply contrasting landscape of estuarial mudflats, flat fenlands and rugged Pennines, crossing Hadrian's Wall somewhere near Corbridge. If it started from Penzance, it might set a course through Wales, buoyed by thermals above the magnificent coastline of Pembrokeshire and the wild massifs of Snowdonia, then over England's highest mountains in Cumbria and the lonely foothills of the Northumbrian Cheviots.

A green and pleasant land?

The pressures of new housing and ever-increasing traffic congestion are eating remorselessly away at what is left of Britain's unspoilt countryside, especially in the southern counties. The itineraries described in this book focus mainly on the less densely populated upland and coastal regions of England and Wales, with particular emphasis on the dozen or so National Parks. Coverage is inevitably selective – for example, the industrial Midlands or the textile towns of Yorkshire and Lancashire may be missing, not because they lack interest, but because touring such built-up regions by car is more difficult, and overall, less rewarding.

Towns and villages

The brightest and best of Britain's museums, nightlife, restaurants and cultural events, in the major cities, including London, can be more easily enjoyed on public transport. More enticing for many visitors, though, are the smaller towns, some of them university or cathedral cities, which are perfect as 'base camps' for tours. Salisbury, Winchester, Durham, York, Lincoln, Oxford and Cambridge, among many others, are redolent with historic associations and monumental architecture. Neither town nor countryside, but a mixture of both, are the thousands of hamlets and villages which form the backbone of Britain's rural life. Some are large and complex, others no more than a pub and a few cottages or outlying farms. More than merely photogenic, many form a fascinating and often under-rated archive of social history and architecture dating back centuries.

Below
Chipping Campden

Above
Lavenham, Suffolk

Travel facts

Accommodation

Good places to stay

Most parts of England and Wales (and certainly all the main tourist areas) offer attractive places to stay, whatever your budget level. Dire establishments also abound, but standards everywhere are generally improving as a result of competition and more rigorous safety and hygiene inspections.

Many tourist offices offer reservation services (ask about the 'Book-a-bed-ahead' scheme), but operate simply on a listing system. In other words, they will book a room for you within any given budget or location, but are not allowed to offer any opinion or recommendation. To be sure of a pleasant stay at a specific location in high season, always book in good time. Remember that in the UK a hotel reservation, even one made by telephone, constitutes a formal contract. You will often be asked to quote your credit card number when booking and may be charged a penalty if you cancel or fail to turn up.

At the top end of the range, you'll find every last luxury and facilities such as golf courses, fitness centres, gourmet restaurants and swimming pools. Less expensively, there is a whole range of country-house hotels, historic conversions (abbeys, castles, mills), quaint inns and pubs, restaurants-with-rooms, purpose-built motel-style blocks, chain hotels, and a bewildering assortment of guesthouses, bed-and-breakfast establishments, farmhouses and family homes. Not to mention all kinds of self-catering property, serviced apartments, budget hostel and campus accommodation, and camping and caravanning sites.

Increasingly, hotels now offer *en-suite* rooms (with bathroom attached), TV and direct-dial telephone as a matter of course. Older, more personal places (inexpensive guesthouses, farmhouses or B&Bs, for instance) may well lack these facilities, so check when you book. Single rooms can be hard to find – hoteliers often regard them as unprofitable. They tend to be smaller and less well equipped or attractively sited than larger rooms, and disproportionately expensive. Expect to pay about three-quarters of the standard rate for single occupancy of a double or twin room. Tariffs in the UK are generally quoted inclusive of tax (VAT) and service, although this may not be the case in expensive city hotels (especially in London) – check carefully when you book. Check also whether the rate quoted is per person or per room, and whether it includes breakfast (continental or 'full English', in other words, a classic fry-up).

For more personal accommodation, **Wolsey Lodges** is a group of privately owned country houses that take paying guests. The rooms are often in delightful family homes, some of considerable historic or architectural interest, with very welcoming hosts. Many offer an excellent home-cooked dinner as well as a good breakfast, and you may eat in house-party style around a single table. Not all accept dogs or children. **Wolsey Lodges** *9 Market Place, Hadleigh, Ipswich, Suffolk IP7 5DL; tel: 01473 822058; fax: 01473 827444; www.wolsey-lodges.co.uk.*

Camping and caravanning are very popular in the UK; sites are listed and graded according to the quality of their facilities, which vary widely. Free camping (not on an authorised site) without permission constitutes trespass, and is illegal anywhere in national parks, nature reserves and protected sections of coastline. For more information, ask any tourist office or contact camping/caravanning organisations for advice.

- **Camping and Caravanning Club** *Greenfields House, Westwood Way, Coventry CV4 8JH; tel: 02476 694995; www.campingand caravanningclub.co.uk.*
- **Caravan Club** *East Grinstead House, London Road, East Grinstead RH19 1UA; tel: 01342 326944; www.caravanclub.co.uk.*

Hotel chains and groups

Best Western, *tel: 08457 747474; www.bestwestern.co.uk*
Corus and Regal Hotels, *tel: 0845 300 2000; www.corushotels.co.uk*
Days Inn, *tel: 0800 0280 400; www.daysinn.com*
De Vere Group, *tel: 01928 712111; www.devereonline.co.uk*
Grand Heritage Hotels, *tel: 0800 056 0457; www.grandheritage.com*
Hilton, *tel: 08705 90 90 90; www.hilton.co.uk*
Holiday Inn, *tel: 0800 40 50 60; www.6c.com*
Innkeeper's Lodge, *tel: 0870 243 0500; www.innkeeperslodge.com*
Macdonald Hotels, *tel: 0870 400 9191; www.macdonaldhotels.co.uk*
Marriott Hotels, *tel: 0800 221 222; www.marriott.com*
Novotel, *tel: 020 8283 4500; www.novotel.co.uk*
Premier Lodge, *tel: 08702 01 02 03; www.premierlodge.co.uk*
Pride of Britain, *tel: 01666 824 666; www.prideofbritainhotels.com*
Savoy Group, *tel: 00800 7671 7671; www.savoy-group.co.uk*
Thistle, *tel: 0870 333 9292; www.thistlehotels.co.uk*
Travel Inn, *tel: 0870 242 8000; www.travelinn.co.uk*
Travelodge, *tel: 08700 850 950; www.travelodge.co.uk*

Above
Clovelly, Devon

Children

Britain has not in the past had much of a reputation for child-friendliness, especially in hotels and restaurants, but the situation is improving. Most regions list attractions which, even if not specifically targeting younger visitors, at least make some provision for them. Ask local tourist boards; many produce good ideas for families with young children.

Grades and guides

A rating system for English hotels and guesthouses first introduced in 2000 aims to merge the confusing systems previously operated separately by the English Tourist Board (now the English Tourism Council), the AA (Automobile Association) and the RAC (Royal Automobile Club). All three publish long-established hotel guides, and now grade hotels in the same way, from 1–5 stars (the more, the merrier) on their standard of facilities and service; guesthouses and B&Bs are graded on quality from 1–5 diamonds. Hoteliers are charged a substantial fee for an inspection and listing in each of the relevant guides, and some highly recommendable places may choose not to be listed. The Scottish and Welsh Tourist Boards operate their own star grading system based on quality rather than facilities.

Other well-respected independent hotel guides such as the *Which? Hotel Guide* or the *Good Hotel Guide* give detailed (often critical) descriptions of places to stay rather than star ratings, based on anonymous inspections or guest feedback. In Alastair Sawday's sprightly accommodation guides, listed establishments pay a fee for inclusion, but inspection standards are rigorously selective. The 'special places to stay' are chosen with a real eye for character and individuality.

Climate

At the mercy of prevailing westerly ocean winds, Britain is renowned for its changeable and often inclement weather. While England and Wales don't generally suffer the rigours and extremes found, say, in the Scottish Highlands, long spells of settled weather can never be guaranteed. In general terms, the further south you go, the warmer it is, and the further east, the drier. Western coastal regions have a mild, equable climate influenced by the Gulf Stream. Some of the itineraries described here are not recommendable in icy or misty conditions. 'Breathable' outdoor gear, including something to cover your head, is a better bet in the countryside than an umbrella, which takes up a spare hand and may well blow inside out in a gust of wind. For recorded weather information, *tel: 09003 444 900.*

Currency and credit cards

Britain's currency is based on the pound sterling (£), a decimal unit divided into 100 pence (p). Bank notes are issued in denominations of £5, £10, £20 and £50, and coins in 1p, 2p, 5p, 10p, 20p, 50p, £1 and £2 units. Banks generally give a better rate of exchange than most *bureaux de change*, but Thomas Cook's Foreign Exchange Bureaux, located in towns throughout the UK, provide a full range of financial services for visitors, and will change TC travellers' cheques commission-free. They can also offer emergency assistance if any cheques get lost or stolen.

Cashpoint (ATM) machines, found in most sizeable towns, often provide the most convenient way of obtaining cash quickly, using a credit or debit card. Before you leave home, make sure your PIN works in Britain. If you're a UK resident, try to stick to your usual bank's ATMs while travelling to avoid extra charges. Most hotels, restaurants, petrol stations and large stores accept major credit or charge cards. Cafés, B&Bs, newsagents and smaller shops may be unwilling to accept anything but cash, and may levy an extra charge or insist on a minimum spend for plastic transactions.

Entry formalities

EU citizens need valid identity documents to enter the UK. Passports, and sometimes visas, are required for other nationalities. Check with your embassy before arrival. Innoculations and vaccinations are not compulsory, but a health certificate may be required if you are travelling from certain parts of the world, for example where yellow fever is endemic.

Below
Llanberis Pass, Snowdonia

Customs regulations

Duty-free allowances for goods imported to the UK from outside the EU are:
- 200 cigarettes or 100 cigarillos or 50 cigars or 250g tobacco
- 2 litres still table wine
- 1 litre spirits, or 2 litres fortified or sparkling wine or other liqueurs
- 60cc/ml perfume
- 250cc toilet water
- Other goods, gifts or souvenirs to a maximum value of £145.

Within the EU, duty-paid goods can be imported in much larger quantities, but if you exceed the 'guidance levels' permitted for your own use, you may be suspected of smuggling. Random checks are made on incoming travellers to search for prohibited or restricted items (narcotics, firearms, explosives, obscene publications, counterfeit goods, endangered species, unlicensed pets, etc). Use the special EU blue channel as you enter the UK. For more advice, *tel: 0845 010 9000.*

Travellers with disabilities

For more advice, contact **RADAR** 12 City Forum, 250 City Road, London EC1V 8AF; tel: 020 7250 3222; www.radar.org.uk; **Holiday Care** 2nd Floor, Imperial Buildings, Victoria Road, Horley, Surrey RH6 7PZ; tel: 01293 771500, fax: 01293 784647; holiday.care@virgin.net; www.holidaycare.org.uk.
Disability Wales Wernddn Court, Caerphilly Business Park, Van Road, Caerphilly CF83 3ED; tel: 029 2088 7325; fax: 029 2088 8702; info@dwac.demon.co.uk; www.dwac.demon.co.uk.

Travellers with disabilities

Facilities for disabled visitors are gradually improving in Britain. There's still a long way to go, but many public places (museums, cinemas, restaurants, etc) provide easier access for wheelchair users or special equipment for visitors with visual or hearing difficulties. Ask local tourist offices for publications giving practical advice, such as hotels with specially adapted bedrooms, or public transport for travellers with mobility problems. Modern, purpose-built chain hotels generally have wheelchair-accessible facilities.

Drinking

Beer and tea are Britain's traditional national drinks, and the pub and the teashop are two of the most enduring and endearing of British institutions. 'Real ales' are sold on draught in many typical pubs, while cider and perry (made from apples and pears) are made in the West Country. England and Wales produce limited quantities of home-grown wine. All imported wine is subject to high taxation, making it more expensive than in most of Europe. Many restaurants now pride themselves on their adventurous and carefully chosen wine lists; sadly, pubs able to produce a decent glass of well-kept wine are still in a minority. Good coffee, once a rarity in Britain, is now available in hotels, restaurants, bars and cafés. Bottled mineral water is increasingly popular, but often ludicrously expensive to drink with a meal in restaurants, or from hotel minibars. Get your own stocks from supermarkets.

Below
Brighton café

Eating out

The range of eating places is enormous, with restaurants of many different ethnic types. Most communities of any size have a Chinese or Indian restaurant, and a pasta/pizza place, while larger cities can offer you almost any kind of meal, at virtually any time. Fast-food places and cafés stay open throughout the day (sometimes most of the night as well), offering easy ways of satisfying hunger pangs. Few sizeable attractions lack some sort of coffee shop or snack bar these days, and the best serve excellent food. Takeaways and picnics are an enjoyable alternative for touring or walking holidays, while pubs increasingly provide appetising, inexpensive bar food and non-alcoholic drinks, including coffee, for drivers. Tea-time is a traditional part of the day, perhaps with scones and jam, and clotted cream in the West Country. A traditional Welsh tea will probably include Welsh cakes (drop scones) or *bara brith*, a delicious kind of fruit loaf.

Electricity

Voltage in the UK is pitched at 240v, 50Hz. Plugs are of the square three-pin type; you will need an adaptor for foreign appliances. Hotel bathrooms have two-pin sockets for shavers only. More expensive business hotels provide suitable gadgetry (ISDN lines, modem points, etc) for computer users.

Organisational abbreviations and websites

CADW: Welsh Historic Monuments; www.cadw.wales.gov.uk

EH: English Heritage; www.english-heritage.org.uk

HHA: Historic Houses Association; www.hha.org.uk

NP: National Park; www.anpa.gov.uk

NT: National Trust; www.nationaltrust.org.uk

RHS: Royal Horticultural Society; www.rhs.org.uk

RNLI: Royal National Lifeboat Institution; www.rnli.org.uk

RSPB: Royal Society for the Protection of Birds; www.rspb.org.uk

Festivals

Hundreds of festivals take place in England and Wales throughout the year. Contact local tourist offices for listings of regional events. Some of the most interesting are the arts festivals held in Chichester, Buxton, Brighton, Bath, Aldeburgh, Cheltenham, Glyndebourne, Harrogate, and many other towns and cities. Music lovers head for the hugely popular Glastonbury Rock Festival, the Huddersfield Contemporary Music Festival and the more highbrow Festival of the Three Choirs, which rotates between the cathedrals of Hereford, Gloucester and Worcester.

From mid-July, the Proms (promenade concerts) are staged at the Royal Albert Hall, London. London's other great spectacles of pageantry include the Lord Mayor's Show and the Trooping of the Colour, magnificent flower shows at Chelsea and Hampton Court, and the annual International Boat Show, Crufts Dog Show, the Summer Exhibition at the Royal Academy and the Ideal Home Exhibition. The best-known festivals in Wales are its two Eisteddfods, the Royal National, held annually in a different location, and the Llangollen International, a celebration of Welsh culture in music, dance and poetry. The Hay Festival of Literature (and its associated Children's Festival) at Hay-on-Wye also attracts a large number of visitors during the last weeks of May and the first days of June.

Health

Britain has no particular health hazards. All EU citizens are entitled to free medical treatment at National Health Service hospitals, but other nationals with no reciprocal agreement will be charged for anything other than emergency treatment. Chemists (pharmacists) such as Boots can dispense a limited range of drugs over the counter, but for many drugs a doctor's prescription is needed. After normal shop hours, one chemist in the neighbourhood will be open for emergencies. If you have a minor accident, ask your hotel to direct you to the nearest hospital with a casualty department; in an emergency, dial 999 for an ambulance.

Information

Most towns in Britain have a tourist office (TIC), usually marked with the 'i' symbol. Some are seasonal, generally open daily from Easter to October, but closed, or with restricted opening hours, in winter. You will also find information points in car parks or lay-bys on popular touring routes or in National Parks. Tourist offices can book accommodation, organise tickets for local events and arrange tours, guided walks or sporting activities. Before you set off, contact regional tourist boards for useful information, or a local holiday guide.

Regional tourist boards

Cumbria Tourist Board *Ashleigh, Holly Road, Windermere, Cumbria LA23 2AQ; tel: 015394 44444; fax: 015394 44041; www.golakes.co.uk*
East of England Tourist Board *Toppesfield Hall, Hadleigh, Suffolk IP7 5DN; tel: 01473 822922; fax: 01473 823063; www.eetb.org.uk*
Heart of England Tourist Board *Woodside, Larkhill Road, Worcester WR5 2EZ; tel: 01905 763435; fax: 01905 763450; www.heartofengland. com*
London Tourist Board *6th Floor, Glen House, Stag Place, London SW1E 5LT; tel: 020 7932 2000; fax: 020 7932 0222; www.londontown.com*
North West Tourist Board *Swan House, Swan Meadow Road, Wigan Pier, Wigan WN3 5BB; tel: 01942 821222; fax: 01942 820002; www.visitnorthwest.com*
Northumbria Tourist Board *Aykley Heads, Durham DH1 5UX; tel: 0191 375 3010; fax: 0191 386 0899; www.ntb.org.uk*
South East Tourist Board *The Old Brew House, Warwick Park, Tunbridge Wells, Kent TN2 5TU; tel: 01892 540766; fax: 01892 511008; www.seetb.org.uk*
Southern Tourist Board *40 Chamberlayne Road, Eastleigh, Hants SO50 5JH; tel: 023 8062 5400; fax: 023 8062 0010; www.southerntb.com*
Wales Tourist Board *Brunel House, 2 Fitzalan Road, Cardiff CF24 0UY; tel: 029 2049 9909; fax: 029 2048 5031*
South West Tourism *Woodwater Park, Exeter, Devon EX2 5WT; tel: 01392 360050; fax: 01392 445112; www.swtourism.co.uk*
Yorkshire Tourist Board *312 Tadcaster Road, York YO2 2HY; tel: 01904 707961; fax: 01904 701414; www.ytb.org.uk*

Insurance

Health insurance is recommended for all non-EU visitors to Britain, and more general insurance is advisable for any traveller, to cover theft or loss of belongings, travel delays, or the cost of having to cancel or curtail accommodation bookings, etc. Check your home contents policy to see whether your property is insured while you're in transit.

Maps

The best-known UK maps are those produced by the Ordnance Survey. The bright pink 'Landranger' series is very useful for detailed exploration, at a scale of 1:50 000 (2cm = 1km, or 1.25in = 1 mile); smaller-scale OS 'tourist maps' of popular areas include helpful information for visitors. For more general touring, you may find a national road atlas of the type produced by the motoring organisations (AA or RAC) adequate. If you plan to explore wilderness terrain on foot, make sure you have good detailed maps and preferably a compass.

National Parks

England and Wales now have about a dozen National Parks between them, as well as controversial areas of specially protected countryside in the Norfolk Broads, the New Forest and South Downs. The other, longer-established parks are: Brecon Beacons, Dartmoor, Exmoor, Lake District, Northumberland, North York Moors, Peak District, Pembrokeshire Coast, Snowdonia, Yorkshire Dales.

Opening times

Core business hours for banks, shops and tourist offices are Mon–Fri 1000–1700, though there are plenty of variations on this. Shops may open at weekends, or until late in the evening in cities, or close one day or half-day a week. Some banks are open on Saturday mornings. Many tourist attractions have longer hours in summer, but close completely between October and Easter, or for one or two days a week (often Sun–Mon) in winter. Pubs may now open 1100–2300 Mon–Sat and 1200–2230 on Sun, but most take a break at some point in the afternoon. In general, restaurants are open for lunch from 1200–1430, and for dinner from 1900–2100, or later. Check when you book.

Postal services

Post offices generally open Mon–Fri 0900–1700 and on Saturday mornings. Some are located in newsagents or other shops, but should be clearly marked with the post office livery (usually red and yellow, sometimes green). Some smaller branches close at lunchtime.

Packing

Be prepared for Britain's changeable weather with warm, waterproof clothing and sensible footwear, especially if you plan to get to grips with any upland or coastal regions. Peelable layers are the best way of dealing with variable temperatures. Britain's popular 'outdoor' areas (Lake District, Snowdonia, Pembrokeshire) are excellent places to buy suitable weatherproof clothes or walking boots. Unless you are staying in exceptionally ritzy hotels you won't need very formal clothes, although most restaurants expect something reasonably smart for the evenings. Take adaptors/transformers for foreign electrical devices, any prescribed medicines you may need, and binoculars and identification guides if you are keen on wildlife. Don't forget your driving licence if you plan to hire a car locally. If you belong to an organisation like the National Trust or English Heritage, the Royal Society for the Protection of Birds or the Royal Horticultural Society, take your membership cards along for free entrance to their sites.

Telephones

International operator:
155

International directory enquiries: 153

International: *dial 00 plus destination country code*

Public holidays

England and Wales have eight official public or 'bank' holidays, most of which fall on a Monday. Most businesses, shops and banks close, but you can usually expect tourist attractions and many restaurants to be open, even if they generally close on a Monday. At Christmas and New Year, almost everything shuts, and public transport is severely restricted.

Safety and security

Take the usual sensible precautions when travelling. Leave unnecessary valuables at home; don't carry large amounts of cash; never leave anything tempting visible in your car. Keep documents and spare cash in hotel safes. If you are unlucky enough to lose something, enquire at the local police station, and contact the relevant authorities as soon as possible (your embassy, airline, bank or credit card company, etc). Directory Enquiries (dial *192*) can give you the numbers. In a genuine emergency, dial *999*. You will need to make a statement to the police if you plan to make an insurance claim. Most foreign embassies are in central London. If you plan to explore wilderness areas on your own, make sure someone knows where you're heading, and what time you expect to return.

Opposite
Portobello Road market

Below
Belstone village stocks, Dartmoor

Shopping

Clothing and fashion, especially the rugged outdoor type, is an especially good buy in Britain. Wales, like Scotland, has a thriving textile industry. The cloth industry in England, much depleted of late, centres around Bradford, and you can still find high-quality tweeds, woollens and waxed cottons in local mill shops. For Britain's celebrated bespoke tailoring industry, you'll have to go to London's Savile Row; near by, Aquascutum, Austin Reed and Jaeger sell suits, while Burberry does the last word in raincoats. China from the Potteries (Wedgwood, Minton, Royal Doulton, Coalport), English perfumes and soaps (Floris, Woods of Windsor), antiques, tea (Twinings or Jacksons), conserves and books are other good buys, while many rural parts of England and Wales have thriving craft industries. (For more information on the very best contemporary craftspeople, contact the Crafts Council, *44a Pentonville Road, London N1 9BY; tel: 020 7278 7700; www.craftscouncil.org.uk.*) Markets, antique fairs, factory outlets (sometimes clustered in village-like malls), and farm shops are less conventional venues for shoppers. Many museums and other attractions offer a good range of themed merchandise.

Telephones

Public phone boxes take phonecards (sold in post offices and shops – look for the phonecard logo), coins (minimum 20p), or credit or charge cards. Most are operated by British Telecom (BT); other companies may use different phonecards. Most public telephone boxes contain instructions in several languages. Hotels often charge a significant premium for direct-dial facilities in bedrooms. Beware of premium rate lines (beginning with the prefix 09). Some larger tourist authorities provide visitors with expensive recorded information rather than attempting to deal with personal calls. If you need to make lots of international calls from the UK, contact an independent telephone company and set up a credit card account. Most sizeable towns have libraries or cybercafés providing e-mail and internet access.

Time

Britain is on Greenwich Mean Time (GMT) during the winter (5 hours ahead of Eastern Standard Time, or 10 hours behind Sydney). From mid-March to mid-October, clocks go forward one hour to British Summer Time (same as Central European Time). Dial *123* for the Speaking Clock service.

Toilets

There are public conveniences all over Britain, conditions varying from exemplary to unspeakable. Some are free; others may charge 20p or so (but are often better maintained). Coin-operated 'superloos' can be found in some places.

Driver's guide

Automobile clubs

For emergency rescue
services, call:
AA *0800 887766*
RAC *0800 828282*

Accidents

If you have an accident, you are obliged by law to stop and give your name, address and car registration number to anyone involved. If anyone is injured, the police must be notified within 24 hours. Exchange insurance details with other relevant drivers, and do not admit fault or liability. If you can find any independent witnesses, ask for their details. To avoid having accidents in the first place, keep alert by taking sensible rest breaks and don't allow yourself to be distracted by the scenery. If you are unfamiliar with driving in Britain, take it steady, but pull over and allow other drivers to pass you whenever possible. A line of frustrated motorists stuck behind a slow-moving vehicle is a recipe for disaster.

Breakdowns

Try to park as safely as possible; alert other drivers with hazard lights or a warning triangle if you have one. SOS telephones are located at regular intervals on the 'hard shoulder' (verge-side lane) of motorways, which you should use only in an emergency. Car-hire companies will provide you with a contact number to ring. Motoring organisations like the Automobile Association (AA) and the Royal Automobile Club (RAC) have reciprocal arrangements with similar clubs overseas, and may provide a free rescue service or advice.

Below
Kersey, Suffolk

Caravans and camper vans

During the summer months, it can seem as though half the UK population loads itself into a caravan and sets off for the West Country with the specific aim of delaying and annoying the other half. Some of the lanes and minor roads in rural areas are entirely unsuitable for towed or large vehicles, so plan your route carefully and watch for warning signs.

Car hire

To hire a car in Britain you must be aged at least 21 (some companies have different age limits), and have held a full valid driving

Car hire

Avis *0870 60 60 100;*
www.avis.co.uk
Hertz *08708 44 8844;*
www.hertz.co.uk
Budget *08701 56 56 56;*
www.budget.co.uk
Europcar *0870 607 5000;*
www.europcar.co.uk

licence for over one year. Major international rental companies are well represented in the UK, but a smaller local company may be cheaper. If you book before you leave home, you stand a good chance of getting a discounted deal. Check your contract very carefully; most hire agreements include insurance, unlimited mileage and all taxes, including VAT. Specify all drivers before setting off. Damage to tyres, or the vehicle interior, may not be covered. As well as your driving licence, you will almost always be required to produce a credit card when hiring a car, and your passport or ID if you are not resident in the UK.

Driving conditions

The main problem on UK roads is traffic congestion. Popular holiday routes and urban areas can be very slow-moving at times. Road maintenance varies from region to region, but overall is generally good in Britain.

Documents

An overseas driving licence is valid for use in the UK for stays of up to a year. If you bring your own car, you'll need a green card (showing you have adequate insurance) as well as the registration documents for your car.

Drinking and driving laws

Penalties are severe for driving with more than the legal limit of blood alcohol (currently 80mg/100ml), or driving while under the influence of any drugs. If you have an accident while in such a condition, you will automatically be considered at fault.

Fuel

Most modern vehicles in the UK run on unleaded petrol, available in virtually all petrol stations (look for the green hoses) along with diesel. Some petrol stations stay open 24 hours a day, but you will need to plan more carefully in rural areas. Fuel costs in Britain are among the most expensive in the world. The most reasonable rates can be found at large supermarket petrol stations such as Tesco; motorway service areas tend to be more expensive.

Information

The rules and regulations on driving in Britain can be found in the current edition of *The Highway Code*, available from bookshops, newsagents and motoring organisations.

Left
Net stores and fish shops in
Hastings, East Sussex

Lights

Dipped headlights should be used in rain or whenever weather conditions reduce light levels, as well as after the official 'lighting-up' time, when street lamps are switched on. Use fog-lights only when visibility falls below 100 yards. If you are driving a vehicle designed for right-hand drive roads, don't forget that your headlights will need to be adjusted. Simple beam adjusters are available at ferry terminals, or from motoring organisations.

Parking

Parking is a serious problem in many urban areas. Traffic wardens lie in wait with expensive tickets for illegally parked vehicles; worse, your vehicle may even be immobilised or towed away. If you are fined, you will generally get a discount for prompt settlement. Parking is always prohibited on double yellow lines, or on single lines during business hours (check the sign beside the road). Larger towns may have metered or pay-and-display zones, or require you to display a time disc or purchase a voucher before parking. Keep some coins handy for parking meters. Many urban areas contain zones restricted to residents' parking only. The safest bet is to head for a designated parking area, usually marked by the letter 'P'. NCP car parks can be expensive, but you can stay as long as you like and you pay for your time when you leave. Park-and-ride facilities are useful on the outskirts of popular tourist cities, while National Trust members will find their parking spaces in rural areas invaluable. Never obstruct farm gateways, or passing bays on single-track lanes. Whenever you park and leave your car, remove all valuables from sight or you may return to find a smashed window and your possessions missing.

Police

To contact the police in an emergency, dial 999. Local police stations are listed in telephone directories, or ask directory enquiries (dial *192*). Drivers unfortunate enough to find the police contacting them (via flashing blue lights or wailing sirens) should pull over as soon as it's safe to do so.

Road signs

Most regions of Britain conform to the standard style of road signage used in the rest of the EU. Generally, signing is clear, though city suburbs can be confusing. Distances are still shown in miles in Britain. Motorways are marked in blue, major trunk routes in green, minor routes in white. Visitor information is indicated by brown signs with white lettering. Advisory or warning signs are usually triangular, in red

Seat belts

The use of seat belts is compulsory in the UK, including those in the rear seats if they are fitted. Small children should not sit in the front seats, but should be properly restrained in a child seat in the back of the vehicle.

Tolls

Most roads in Britain are still toll-free, although various new schemes to reduce traffic congestion are being debated. Several river crossings incur tolls: the Severn suspension bridges into (but not out of) South Wales, the Humber Bridge, and various car ferries in Cornwall. A few old-fashioned tollgates still remain, and may charge you a small fee.

and white. Watch out for overhead electronic messages on motorways indicating road works, accidents, fog or other hazards, and the advised speed limit. Level crossings over railway lines have manually operated gates or more often automatic barriers. If the lights flash *you must stop* to let a train pass.

Security

It seems the British are no longer the well-mannered drivers of the halcyon days of early motoring. 'Road rage' is an alarming phenomenon exacerbated by the stresses of congested roads. You'll see plenty of aggressive driving in Britain, especially on motorways. Don't react to it, and give yourself room to avoid the consequences. In Britain, flashed headlights are habitually used both as a warning (an alternative to the horn), and an invitation to take priority over another driver. You will simply have to use your judgement to decide what is meant – flashed headlights do not officially form part of the Highway Code. Elementary courtesy includes raising your hand to thank a driver who has given way to you. If you break down or need roadside assistance, take special care when getting out of your vehicle. Always lock your car if you leave it, even for a moment or two, and never leave valuables on view inside.

Speed limits

Unless otherwise stated, speed limits are 30mph/48kph in urban areas; 60mph/96kph on single carriageways; 70mph/112kph on dual carriageways or motorways. Camper vans or cars towing caravans are restricted to 50mph/80kph on normal roads or 60mph/96kph on motorways. Always make allowances for adverse conditions (rain, fog, ice, etc), when braking distances increase dramatically.

Getting to England and Wales

By air

Air travellers to Britain have a wide choice of carriers from North America, Australasia and Europe. Most intercontinental flights land at one of London's two main international airports, Heathrow or Gatwick, but it is possible to plan a direct route from some destinations to a regional airport, such as Birmingham, Manchester or Cardiff, as well as the smaller London airports of Stansted, Luton or even London City.

The internet is now a major source of information on last-minute flights. A departure tax is levied on flights from UK airports.

Airports

Heathrow: 15 miles (24km) west of London, linked by fast rail/Underground links to central London, and by Airbus and taxi. *Flight information: 0870 0000 123; www.baa.co.uk.*
Gatwick: 24 miles (40km) south of London, linked most efficiently by rail to central London. *Flight information: 0870 000 2468; www.baa.co.uk.*
Stansted: Modern airport northeast of London, with direct train services to London's Liverpool Street station (40 mins) and bus/rail links to other UK destinations. *Flight information: 0870 0000 303; www.baa.co.uk.*
Luton: Mainly holiday charter and budget scheduled flights. Regular 45-min rail service to London King's Cross/St Pancras stations. *Flight information: 08706 000 000; www.london-luton.co.uk.*
London City: Business airport in London's Docklands, serving European and domestic destinations. Now linked to central London by Underground. *Flight information: 020 7646 0088; www.london cityairport.com.*
Birmingham: 8 miles (13km) southeast of Birmingham. Courtesy bus to railway station, with fast nationwide intercity links. *Flight information: 0121 767 5511; www.bhx.com.*
Manchester: 10 miles (16km) south of Manchester. 20-min rail

ⓘ **Eurostar**, tel: 08705 186 186 in UK; +44 1233 617575 from elsewhere; sales.enquiries@eurostar.co.uk; www.eurostar.com. **National Rail Enquiry Service**, tel: 08457 484950. **Brittany Ferries**, tel: 08703 665 333; www.brittany-ferries.co.uk. **Hoverspeed**, tel: 0870 240 8070; www.hoverspeed.co.uk. **P&O European Ferries**, tel: 0870 2424 999; www.poportsmouth.com. **Stena Line**, tel: 08705 707070; www.stenaline.co.uk. **SeaFrance**, tel: 0870 571 171; www.seafrance.co.uk. **Eurotunnel**, tel: 08705 353535; www.eurotunnel.com.

journey to city centre; intercity links. *Flight information: 0161 489 3000; www.manairport.co.uk.*

Cardiff: 12 miles (19km) east of Cardiff. Bus link to city centre. *Flight information: 029 20 711111; www.cardiffairportonline.com.*

By rail

Eurostar services link Britain with France and Belgium via the Channel Tunnel. Trains terminate at London's Waterloo station, with onward routes all over the UK. The BritRail Pass (available only to overseas visitors outside Britain through offices of BritRail/Rail Europe or specialist rail agents) permits unlimited travel anywhere on the railway system for specified periods of up to a month; *info@britrail.net; www.britrail.com.*

By sea

Cross-Channel ferry services arrive from over 20 continental destinations at a dozen UK ports. Shortest hop is between Calais and Dover. Book ahead during peak holiday periods, especially if you plan to bring a car. Reserve a cabin for an overnight crossing.

By car

You can bring a car to Britain by ferry or hovercraft, or by Eurotunnel trains through the Channel Tunnel, a 40-min journey. The terminal on the French side is near Sangatte, south of Calais; the UK terminal is near Folkestone, with easy access to London or other parts of Britain via the M20. Advance booking is advisable at busy holiday times. If your final UK destination is the West Country or Wales, consider taking one of the longer European ferry crossings to Plymouth, Poole or Portsmouth.

Below
Tetbury Market Hall

Setting the scene

Britain's chief geographical characteristic – the fact that it is an island – has shaped the whole of its history, and to a large extent the outlook of its people. This natural fortress in the sea was successfully invaded only once in the last millennium. Even after the establishment of a permanent Euro-link, the Channel Tunnel, the English still see themselves as a race apart, eccentric and in many ways different from their Continental neighbours. In fact, the English are a hotchpotch of many European races who began arriving long before the Dark Ages, mixed with the genes of thousands of subsequent settlers and colonial imports from all over the world.

In recent years, England has been forced to remember that the lands just over its borders are two entirely separate countries. The Scots and the Welsh have grown tired of the Act of Union melting pot, and have been demanding that Westminster take notice of their cultural and political identity. With the dawning of the new millennium, the Welsh, like the Scots before them, at last achieved their dream of an independent assembly. Where does it all leave the English? The answer is, rather puzzled. In the last decade or two, the nation has become uncharacteristically self-analytical, and the phrase 'identity crisis' has been bandied about at every turn. Do they still live in Great Britain, or in any sort of United Kingdom? Or will they simply revert to Little Englandism, and rattle the standard of St George again in the face of all-comers?

Origins

The Roman colony known as *Britannia* roughly equalled the territory now covered by England and Wales, but it wasn't until well after the Romans left that Britain assumed anything resembling its present political divisions. New waves of invaders from Central Europe appeared, bringing strange Teutonic gods like Woden and Freya whose names are still reflected in the days of the week. They pushed the native Celts north and west into Scotland and Wales. During this period, Christianity reached Britain, in the hands of an enthusiastic missionary called Augustine. One tribe, which settled predominantly in the east, gave its name to a new nation. The territory occupied by the Angles (East Anglia, Mercia and Northumbria) became known as Angle-land, or England.

Other kingdoms belonging to Saxons and Jutes gradually assimilated into a coherent political unit, forced into alliances despite their natural quarrelsomeness by continual attacks on the east coast from Viking raiders. One powerful leader, Alfred of Wessex (AD 871–

901) emerged to defeat the Danes, and at least confine them by treaty to the area around York, known as the Danelaw. During the new, if uneasy, peace that followed, the foundations of the English state were laid. Strip-farming methods were introduced, and the manorial feudal system established. A Witan, or council, was set up to advise the king, a vital rein on absolute power that has played a part in the English constitution ever since. In 1066, the Normans achieved the last successful invasion of British shores, and thereby changed the direction of England and Wales decisively and permanently.

Subsequent dynasties busied themselves with expansionist policies in Europe, and tightened their grip on the recalcitrant Celts in Scotland and Wales. The Plantagenet kings spent over a century and vast quantities of resources and manpower in attempting to claim the French throne; ultimately it was a futile adventure, despite Henry V's famous victory at Agincourt. The darkest hour of these medieval times came in the mid-14th century, when the Black Death reduced Britain's population from about 4 million to under 2 million within 50 years.

Under the colourful Tudors (the Golden Age of Shakespeare and Elizabeth I), England developed as a powerful maritime nation. The defeat of the Spanish Armada in 1588 was crucial in confirming England's naval superiority in Europe. The Stuart dynasty, however, suffered as a result of the religious controversy begun by Henry VIII during the Reformation, when England split away from the Church of Rome and established the Protestant Anglican faith. The climax of these internal struggles was the Civil War, when a monarch lost his head and for a few years England became a republic under Oliver Cromwell.

Below
Shrewsbury

The Restoration brought back the monarchy, but with the restraining forces of political parties in place, kings and queens were never again allowed to rule the roost as they had in the past. The Glorious Revolution ousted the unpopular James II and replaced him with his son-in-law, the Dutch prince, William of Orange, who finally defeated James at the Battle of the Boyne. Queen Anne's reign was marked by an important political change – the Act of Union, which united England, Wales and Scotland under a new name, Great Britain. As the later Jacobite rebellions proved, this 'union' was more nominal than real. However, it did serve to establish a measure of internal security that enabled the British empire to continue its expansion under the Hanoverian dynasty. The Industrial Revolution got under way in earnest from the 1770s onwards, creating untold wealth, and untold misery. Despite the embarrassing loss of the American colonies in 1783, Britain was still 'top nation' by the end of the Napoleonic Wars in 1815. By the end of the Victorian age, the British Empire stretched across vast tracts of the world.

The 20th century's main events were the two world wars and their aftermath. Though victorious, Britain's influence as a world power gradually waned. Its colonies gained independence as Commonwealth nations. Britain is still adjusting to its revised status within Europe, and to the effects of devolution in Wales and Scotland, which now have their own separate parliamentary assemblies.

Milestones

Prehistory

8000 BC The glaciers of the last Ice Age begin to retreat, followed by cave-dwelling hunter-gatherers who find a route across the land bridge then connecting Britain with Europe.

6000 BC Rising sea levels sever Britain from the Continent.

5000 BC Neolithic settlers arrive from Mediterranean areas, a small dark race of farmers, potters and sophisticated stone-workers. Their flint factories can be seen in Norfolk, and their burial places are scattered over the chalklands of southern Britain. The first stone circles, or henges, are built.

2000 BC Bronze Age peoples such as the Beaker Folk, arrive – traders with a knowledge of metal-working.

500 BC Celtic peoples arrive from somewhere around the Rhine, bringing with them the art of iron-smelting. They are miners, traders, stock rearers, builders of hillforts and tellers of tales.

150 BC Gaulish tribes displace the Celts into the uplands of west Britain.

Below
Stonehenge

Romans and Anglo-Saxons

AD 43 The Romans arrive and subjugate the resident tribes, including Boadicea's Iceni. Britain becomes a Roman colony. The Roman legacy survives in roads, camps, forts and Hadrian's Wall across northern Britain.

410 Decline and fall – the Romans withdraw, leaving Britain to successive waves of invading Angles, Saxons and Jutes from Germany and Scandinavia. The Anglo-Saxons settle in southeast Britain and set up kingdoms.

597 St Augustine is sent to convert the English to Christianity.

779 King Offa builds a dyke to keep out the Welsh.

878 Alfred the Great defeats the Vikings and begins reconquering the Danelaw.

1017 Canute, a Dane, seizes the crown.

Above
Gloucester Cathedral

The Middle Ages
1066 The Norman Conquest.
1086 The Domesday Book is completed.
1154 Henry II becomes the first Plantagenet king.
1167 Oxford University is founded.
1170 Murder of Thomas à Becket.
1215 King John signs the Magna Carta.
1283 Edward I conquers Wales and begins building fortresses. Llewellyn ab Gruffydd is killed.
1348–9 The Black Death ravages Europe, killing roughly half the population
1381 The Peasants' Revolt after the imposition of the poll tax.
1387 Chaucer's *Canterbury Tales* published.
1415 The Battle of Agincourt, and the death of Owain Glyndwr, the charismatic Welsh leader.
1453 End of the Hundred Years War in France.
1476 Caxton's first printing press.

Tudors and Stuarts
1485 Henry VII becomes the first Tudor king.
1535 Henry VIII becomes head of the Church of England; Act of Union with Wales.
1536–40 Dissolution of the Monasteries.
1558 Elizabeth I is crowned.
1580 Sir Francis Drake circumnavigates the world.
1588 Defeat of the Spanish Armada.
1603 James VI of Scotland becomes James I of England, uniting two kingdoms and ushering in the Stuart dynasty.
1605 Guy Fawkes fails to blow up parliament in the Gunpowder Plot.
1620 Pilgrim Fathers set sail for America.
1642–9 Civil War between Royalists and Roundheads. King Charles I is beheaded.
1653–8 Cromwell rules as Lord Protector.
1660 The Restoration of the monarchy under Charles II.
1665–6 The Great Plague and the Great Fire of London.
1688 The Glorious Revolution: James II is deposed and replaced by William of Orange.
1694 The Bank of England is established.
1700 St Paul's Cathedral is completed.
1707 The Act of Union with Scotland.

Georgian Britain
1714 George I succeeds Queen Anne and becomes Britain's first Hanoverian monarch.
1721 Robert Walpole becomes the first Prime Minister.
1746 Bonnie Prince Charlie is defeated.
1757 Britain's first canal begins the Industrial Age.

Above
Civil War re-enactment

1775 James Watt's first steam engine is built.
1776 American Declaration of Independence.
1783 The first steam-powered cotton mill appears.
1805 The Battle of Trafalgar ends Napoleon's maritime ambitions, and Admiral Nelson's life.
1807 Abolition of the slave trade.
1811 The Prince Regent takes on the duties of monarchy during George III's madness.
1815 The Battle of Waterloo: Wellington defeats Napoleon.
1825 Stockton to Darlington railway opens.
1829 Catholic Emancipation Act is passed.

Victorian Britain
1832 The Reform Bill extends the vote to all male property owners.
1833 The Factory Act reduces the exploitation of children as cheap labour.
1834 The Tolpuddle Martyrs are transported for forming a union.
1837 Queen Victoria ascends the throne, aged 18.
1851 The Great Exhibition, a celebration of industry and empire, devised by Prince Albert.
1854–6 The Crimean War, and the focus on health care provided by Florence Nightingale.
1863 The London Underground opens.
1870 Compulsory education is introduced up to age 11.
1877 Queen Victoria becomes Empress of India.
1899–1902 The Boer War.
1901 Queen Victoria dies.

The 20th century
1903 The Suffragette Movement founded.
1908 Old-age pensions are introduced.
1914–18 World War I
1919 Women over 30 get the vote.
1924 The first Labour government.
1926 The General Strike.
1929 Stock Market crashes.
1936 Edward VIII abdicates; television services begin.
1939–45 World War II.
1948 The National Heath Service is introduced.
1951 The Festival of Britain.
1953 Coronation of Elizabeth II.
1962 The Beatles burst on the scene.
1973 Britain joins the European Community.
1975 Drilling begins for North Sea oil.
1976 Concorde begins commercial service.
1979 Margaret Thatcher becomes Britain's first woman Prime Minister.

1981 Prince Charles marries Lady Diana Spencer.

1982 The Falklands War.

1991 Canary Wharf emerges as the centrepiece of London's revitalised Docklands.

1994 Channel Tunnel opens; oil discovered off the Scottish coast.

1997 Tony Blair elected as head of a Labour government; Diana, Princess of Wales, dies.

1999 Scottish and Welsh assemblies exercise devolution from Westminster.

2000 National Lottery cash funds ambitious tourist projects and charities throughout the UK.

Remembrance of things past...

Nostalgia is a central plank in Britain's tourist industry. The English love to dwell on past victories and triumphs, and bask in the reflected glory of heroes and heroines like Alfred the Great, Henry V, Elizabeth I, Francis Drake, Horatio Nelson, the Duke of Wellington and Winston Churchill. The Welsh recall with pride the feisty resistance of Llewellyn ab Gruffydd or Owain Glyndwr in the face of the oppressive control of the English monarchy (which historically claims the Principality for its own heir to the throne, who holds the title 'Prince of Wales').

Britain is no longer a great military world power, nor such a dominant industrial or economic force. But the folk memories live on, and they are for sale. The British monarchy and aristocracy, and the pageantry that goes with them, are as popular as ever, however much their real powers are curtailed. The last remnants of Britain's former industrial past are revamped as tourist attractions, with ex-miners playing the part of tour guides. Whatever you might think of it, the heritage industry is on a roll, and here to stay.

Below
Oxford

As well as selling these images of the true past, the British tourist industry also repackages fictional history, allocating chunks of countryside to different themes. Visitors are thus invited to discover 'Catherine Cookson Country' or 'Thomas Hardy's Wessex', or to go in search of Compo and his friends from the television series *Last of the Summer Wine*, based and filmed in and around Yorkshire's Holmfirth. Glorious Welsh countryside is seemingly prized more as the recognisable backdrop to a recent film than for its own intrinsic value, and the film of *The French Lieutenant's Woman* did more than any tourist board publicity to put Lyme Regis on the map.

Highlights

A selection of some of the best things to see in England and Wales:

- **Architecture:** The Rows (Chester); Christ Church College (Oxford); Royal Pavilion (Brighton); Royal Crescent (Bath); Covent Garden Piazza (London); Tower Bridge (London); Houses of Parliament (London); Portmeirion
- **Art galleries:** Tate Gallery (St Ives); National Gallery (London); Tate Britain/Tate Modern (London); Sainsbury Centre (Norwich)
- **Beauty spots:** Borrowdale; Teesdale; Lindisfarne; Malham Dale; Wensleydale; Dovedale; Thames Valley; Wye Valley/Symond's Yat; Cheddar Gorge; Dart estuary; South Hams; St Michael's Mount
- **Castles:** Windsor; Arundel; Tower of London; Caernarfon; Beaumaris
- **Cathedrals:** Durham; Ely; Lincoln; Peterborough; Gloucester; St Davids; Hereford; Canterbury; Winchester; Salisbury; St Paul's (London); Westminster Abbey (London); York Minster
- **Churches and abbeys:** Rievaulx Abbey; York Minster; Fountains Abbey; King's College Chapel (Cambridge); St George's Chapel (Windsor); Holy Trinity (Long Melford); Tintern Abbey
- **Cities:** London; Durham; York; Cambridge; Lincoln; Chester; Oxford; Norwich; Hereford; Canterbury; Chichester; Winchester; Salisbury
- **Coastline/beaches:** Northumberland; Yorkshire; North Norfolk; Suffolk; Barafundel Bay; Pembrokeshire; Beachy Head/Seven Sisters; Chesil Beach; Poole Harbour; Hartland Point; Woolacombe Bay; Blackpool Sands (Devon); Babbacombe Bay; Kynance Cove (Cornwall)

Below
The magnificent landscape of mid Wales

- **Excursions:** Steam Yacht Gondola (Coniston Water); Settle–Carlisle Railway; Ffestiniog Railway (Snowdonia); London Eye
- **Gardens:** Harlow Carr (Harrogate); Bodnant (Conwy Valley); Sissinghurst (Kent); Stourhead (Wilts); Powis Castle (Wales); Rosemoor (Devon); Kew (London); Eden Project (Cornwall)
- **Lakes:** Windermere; Buttermere; Derwent Water; Ullswater
- **Mountains:** Langdale Pikes; Great Gable; Snowdonia; Helvellyn
- **Museums:** Beamish Open-Air Museum; Centre for Life (Newcastle); Tullie House (Carlisle); Fitzwilliam (Cambridge); Ironbridge Gorge; Ashmolean (Oxford); Big Pit Mining Museum (Blaenavon); National Motor Museum (Beaulieu); Portsmouth Historic Dockyard; British Museum (London); V&A (London); National Maritime Museum (London)
- **Prehistoric monuments:** Stonehenge; Avebury; West Kennet long barrow; Uffington White Horse
- **Roman sites:** Hadrian's Wall/Housesteads Roman fort; Roman baths (Bath); Fishbourne Palace (near Chichester)
- **Stately homes:** Cragside; Hampton Court; Levens Hall; Muncaster Castle; Castle Howard; Chatsworth House; Haddon Hall; Burghley House; Blenheim Palace (Woodstock); Blickling Hall; Audley End (Suffolk); Leeds Castle (Kent); Hever Castle; Knole; Cotehele House; Eltham Palace (Kent); Erdigg (Wales)
- **Towns:** Brighton; Bury St Edmunds; Buxton; Chipping Camden; Colchester; Greenwich; Harrogate; Ludlow; Rye; Saffron Walden; Shrewsbury; Stamford; Stratford-upon-Avon; Windsor

Northumberland and Hadrian's Wall

Ratings

Beaches	●●●●●
Scenery	●●●●●
Castles	●●●●○
Heritage	●●●●○
Outdoor activities	●●●●○
Wildlife	●●●●○
Children	●●○○○
Eating/shopping	●●○○○

The Romans drew the northern line on their empire between the estuaries of the Solway and the Tyne, and built Hadrian's Wall to keep out the barbarians. Now, the national boundary stretches diagonally from just north of Carlisle as far as Berwick-upon-Tweed. This invigorating border country has plenty of wild scenery and grim history, but it certainly isn't barbaric. The milecastles and waystations on Hadrian's Wall tell the story of everyday Roman folk. In the Northumberland National Park, majestic, sweeping moorland combines with dense conifer forests. Northumberland's Heritage Coast scrolls past romantic castles, magical islands and gloriously unspoilt beaches that are a treat for walkers and naturalists. At either end of the journey stand the sturdily fortified towns of Carlisle and Berwick. This is a landscape strewn with defensive pele towers and bastle houses, and grand estates belonging to long-established aristocratic families.

ALNWICK CASTLE❖❖

ⓘ Tourist Information
2 The Shambles; tel: 01665 510665.

ⓗ Alnwick Castle £££
Tel: 01665 510777.
Open Apr–Oct 1100–1700.

Alnwick Gardens ££
www.alnwickgarden.com.
Open daily 1000–2000. The gardens are being redesigned with a modern composition of sounds, sight, texture and smell.

Right
The Percy lions at Alnwick

This grand **castle❖❖** has been in the Percy family since the early 14th century. It was famously described by the Victorians as the 'Windsor of the North'. In the pleasant market town of Alnwick (pronounced 'Annick'), monumental Percy lions prowl around. Medieval gatehouses, remnants of the old town walls, survive in the centre.

BERWICK-UPON-TWEED✧✧

ⓘ Tourist Information 106 Marygate; tel: 01289 330733.

ⓗ Berwick Barracks ££ The Parade; tel: 01289 304493. Open Apr–Sept daily 1000–1800, Oct 1000–1700, Nov–Mar Wed–Sun 1000–1600; EH.

Now England's most northerly town, Berwick changed hands on over a dozen occasions in medieval times. In Tudor times it reverted permanently to English possession. Its sturdy **ramparts✧✧** are remarkably intact, and give splendid views over the multi-arched **Royal Border Railway Bridge✧**. Several museums occupy the 18th-century **Barracks✧✧**.

Accommodation and food near Berwick and the Border

Tree Tops ££ The Village Green, East Ord; tel: 01289 330679; fax: 0870 0549818; john@treetops-jn.demon.co.uk. Comfortable B&B in well-kept grounds near Berwick. Spotless rooms and splendid dinners.

The Coach House £ Crookham; tel: 01890 820293; fax: 01890 820284; thecoachhouse@englandmail.com; www.coachhousecrookham.com. Farm guesthouse near the Border with wholesome home cooking and good-quality bedrooms.

CARLISLE❖❖

ℹ **Tourist Information** *Old Town Hall, Greenmarket; tel: 01228 625600; tourism@carlisle-city.gov.uk.*

🏰 **Carlisle Castle ££** *Castle Way; tel: 01228 591922. Open Apr–Sept daily 0930–1800, Oct 1000–1700, Nov–Mar 1000–1600; EH.*

Guildhall Museum *Greenmarket, tel: 01228 534781. Open Apr–Oct Tue–Sun 1200–1630.*

Tullie House Museum and Art Gallery ££ *Castle Street; tel: 01228 534781; enquiries@tullie-house.co.uk; www.tulliehouse.co.uk. Open Apr–Oct Mon–Sat 1000–1800, Sun 1100–1800; rest of year Mon–Sat 1000–1600, Sun 1200–1600.*

The Cumbrian capital is a cathedral city with a formidable **castle❖❖** and a well-preserved core of red sandstone buildings. The drum-towered gateway, market cross and timber-framed **Guildhall❖❖** make handsome centrepieces. The **cathedral❖❖** is relatively small; its East Window has some of the finest surviving 14th-century glass. The **Tullie House Museum and Art Gallery❖❖❖** explains the exploits of the feuding 'Reiver' families who controlled the border country until the 17th century.

Accommodation and food in Carlisle

Number Thirty-One ££ *31 Howard Place; tel/fax: 01228 597080; bestpep@aol.com; www.number31.freeservers.com.* Award-winning townhouse accommodation; very stylish décor and super cooking. Friendly, cheerful hosts.

The Beeches £ *Wood Street; tel: 01228 511962.* Cottage charm in a Georgian building just a few minutes off the M6. Friendly, helpful B&B.

CRAGSIDE❖❖❖ AND WALLINGTON❖❖

🏰 **Wallington £££** *Cambo; tel: 01670 773600. Open Apr–Sept Wed–Mon 1300–1730 (1630 in Oct); gardens all year; NT.*

Cragside House £££ *Rothbury; tel: 01669 620333. Open Apr–Oct Tue–Sun 1300–1730 (1630 in Oct); gardens same days 1030–1900 and Nov–Dec Wed–Sun 1100–1600; NT.*

Wallington❖❖, near Cambo, dates from 1688. Elegantly designed in local sandstone, it was remodelled in the mid-18th century, with fine plasterwork and panelling. Other attractions include a pretty walled garden. Victorian **Cragside❖❖❖**, just outside Rothbury, is memorable for its extravagant mix of neo-Tudor and Arts and Crafts styles. Described as 'the Palace of a Modern Magician', it was the first house in the world to be lit by hydroelectricity. The 900-acre grounds have artificial lakes (to power the lighting system), giant rock gardens, and millions of trees.

The great landscaper **Lancelot 'Capability' Brown** was born just over a mile down the road from Wallington. At 16 he became a gardener's boy at nearby Kirkharle Tower.

HADRIAN'S WALL❖❖❖

🏛 Heading east from Carlisle, these are some of the best sites along the Wall:

Birdoswald Roman fort❖ **££** *Gilsland; tel: 01697 747602. Open Mar–Oct daily 1000–1730; EH. Every stage of the Roman defensive system.*

Greenhead Roman Army Museum❖ **££** *Carvoran; tel: 01697 747485. Open Mar–Oct 1000–1800 (1000–1600 off season). Life on duty; next to a possibly pre-Hadrianic fort.*

Once Brewed National Park Centre❖❖ *Military Road, Bardon Mill; tel: 01434 344396. Open Mar–Oct 0930–1700 (Nov–Feb weekends 1000–1600). Useful visitor centre with exhibitions and good access to the Wall.*

Vindolanda❖ **££** *Chesterholm Museum, Bardon Mill; tel: 01434 344277; www.vindolanda.com. Open Mar–Nov daily 1000–1700 (later in summer, some winter weekends). Exhibition on daily life in a Roman garrison town.*

Housesteads Roman Fort and Museum❖❖❖ **££** *Haydon Bridge; tel: 01434 344363; open Apr–Sept daily 1000–1800, Oct 1000–1700, Nov–Mar 1000–1600; NT/EH. Probably the most impressive fort, at a well-preserved section of the Wall. Communal latrines attract plenty of attention!*

Begun on the orders of Emperor Hadrian in about AD 122, this spectacular relic of Roman Britain once spanned the north-western frontier of the empire for a distance of 73 miles between the Solway Firth (Bowness) and the Tyne Estuary (Wallsend). For 250 years, it defended the British province against the ungovernable tribes from the north. 'Milecastles' were built at Roman-mile intervals along its length; turrets or larger forts every 5 miles or so acted as barracks, supply depots and signalling stations. About 15,000 cavalry and infantry troops (many recruited locally) defended the wall. The structure consisted of a 15-ft battlemented wall erected over high ground, flanked by deep ditches on either side. Hadrian's Wall was abandoned towards the end of the 4th century. Despite subsequent damage and much dismantling for roadstone in the 18th century, various sections of the wall can clearly be seen striding across the Northumbrian hills. The course of the wall is a popular walking route, and the B6318 follows it for much of the way. The Tullie House Museum is a good place for an overview of the Wall.

Carrawburgh Temple of Mithras * *Hexham; open at any reasonable time.* Replica altars from a 3rd-century Mithraic shrine on view outside the Roman fort of Brocolitia.

Chesters Roman fort⁺⁺ **££** *Chollerford; tel: 01434 681379. Open Mar–Sept daily 0930–1800, Oct 1000–1700, Nov–Mar 1000–1600; EH.* Well-preserved cavalry fort and bath-house; museum.

Low Brunton⁺⁺ *Near Wall, Hexham; open at any reasonable time.* One of the best-preserved sections of wall and turret.

Corbridge Roman site⁺⁺ **££** *Northwest of Corbridge; tel: 01434 632349. Open Apr–Sept 1000–1800 (closes earlier off season); EH.* Granaries, columns, aqueduct of a major legionary stronghold; museum.

Opposite
Hadrian's Wall at Steelrigg

Right
Lindisfarne Castle on Holy Island

Accommodation and food near Hadrian's Wall

General Havelock Inn £ *Ratcliffe Road, Haydon Bridge; tel: 01434 684376.* Popular stone-clad pub in peaceful setting. Hearty menu favourites to stoke up for Hadrian's Wall.

Abbey Bridge £ *Lanercost; tel: 01697 72224; info@abbeybridge.co.uk; www.abbeybridge.co.uk.* Close to Hadrian's Wall and Lanercost Priory, this attractive riverside inn produces enterprising food in interestingly decorated surroundings. Simple bedroom accommodation.

LINDISFARNE⁺⁺⁺

Lindisfarne Priory and Museum ££
Holy Island; tel: 01289 389200. Open daily Apr–Sept 1000–1800, Oct 1000–1700, Nov–Mar 1000–1600; EH.

Lindisfarne Castle ££
Holy Island; tel: 01289 389244. Open Apr–Oct Sat–Thu 1200–1500 (depending on tides); NT.

Twice a day, the sea retreats sufficiently to allow access to this windswept, low-lying stretch of dunes, beaches and quiet grazing land. Holy Island, as it is often called, was one of Europe's primary centres of Christianity in Celtic times, and is still a place of pilgrimage. The richly illuminated Lindisfarne Gospels created in about AD 700 were carried away for safe-keeping in AD 875. The island's main sights are the 11th-century **priory**⁺⁺, built on the site of the Celtic monastery, with arches and columns of weathered red sandstone, and the 16th-century **Lindisfarne Castle**⁺⁺⁺. In 1903 it was imaginatively converted into an idyllic residence by Edwin Lutyens.

NORTHUMBERLAND HERITAGE COAST✦✦✦

ⓘ Tourist Information *Craster car park; tel: 01665 576007 or Seahouses car park; tel: 01665 720884.*

Islands, volcanic crags, bays, winding estuaries and several splendid castles create continual interest along the scenic stretch of Northumbrian coast north of Amble. Swathes of pale, tide-washed, dune-backed sand are completely unsullied by beach huts or ice-cream kiosks. It is often too cold to swim, and some beaches have dangerous currents, but the area is ideal for coastal walks and wildlife spotting. Many sections are designated nature reserves, or Areas of Outstanding Natural Beauty.

NORTHUMBERLAND NATIONAL PARK✦✦

ⓘ Tourist Information *Otterburn Mill Visitor Centre, Otterburn; tel: 01830 520093; enquiries@ otterburn-mill.demon.co.uk or Northumberland National Park Centre, Church House, Church Street, Rothbury; tel: 01669 620887 or Fountain Cottage, Main Street, Bellingham; tel: 01434 220616; bellinghamtic@ btconnect.com or Kielder Castle Forest Park Centre, Kielder Castle, Kielder; tel: 01434 250209 or Tower Knowe Visitor Centre, Kielder Water; tel: 01434 240398.*

ⓟ Kielder Bikes Cycle Centre *The Cyclery, Castle Hill, Kielder; tel: 01434 250392; kenbone@ kielderbikes.dabsol.co.uk; www.kielderbikes.dabsol.co.uk. Open daily 1000–1800 in school holidays, closed Fri in term-time.*

ⓒ Kielder Water Cruises *Kielder Water; tel: 01434 240398; lake trips Apr–Oct daily 1015–1650.*

Remote, empty moorland of bilberry and bracken rises in glacier-rasped contours to the Cheviot watershed – the National Park and the adjoining Border Forest Park cover 400 square miles. Settlements and visitor facilities are sparse, and there are few easy walks, but over a million people visit each year. Deep in the forest, Kielder Water, Europe's largest man-made lake at over 9 miles long, offers leisure facilities. The Pennine Way crosses the more scenic areas of the park before tracking a rugged stretch of the border through the grassy Cheviot Hills to its Scottish terminus near Kirk Yetholm.

Right
Dunstanburgh Castle on the Northumberland coast

Suggested tour

Billy Shiel's Farne Island Boat Trips £££ *Seahouses harbour; tel: 01665 720308; www.farne-islands.com; sailings Apr–Oct from 1000; winter trips by appointment, weather permitting.*

Warkworth Castle ££ *Warkworth; tel: 01665 711423; open Apr–Sept daily 1000–1800, Oct 1000–1700, Nov–Mar 1000–1600; EH.*

Dunstanburgh Castle £ *Coastal footpath from Craster or Embleton; tel 01665 576231. Open Apr–Sept 1000–1800, Oct 1000–1700, Nov–Mar Wed–Sun 1000–1600; EH.*

Farne Islands ££ *Tel: 01665 721099; landings permitted on Inner Farne and Staple Island Apr–Sept daily 1030–1800; restricted access during breeding season.*

Marine Life Fishing Heritage Centre £ *8–10 Main Street, Seahouses; tel: 01665 721257; www.marinelifecentre.co.uk. Open Mar–Oct daily 1030–1700.*

Bamburgh Castle ££ *Bamburgh; tel: 01668 214515; www.bamburghcastle.com. Open Apr–Oct daily 1100–1700.*

Grace Darling Museum *Radcliffe Road, Bamburgh; tel: 01668 214465. Open Easter–Oct Mon–Sat 1000–1700, Sun 1200–1700; donations for RNLI welcome.*

Total distance: 250 miles (400km). Add 20 miles (32km) for the National Park detour.

Time: A very long day – take a weekend at least to see Hadrian's Wall and the National Park.

Links: Use Carlisle as a springboard for the Lakes (*see pages 58 and 68*), and Hexham/Corbridge for the North Pennines (*see page 50*).

Route: From **CARLISLE** ❶, take the A69 east to **Brampton**. Turn off through the attractive town centre (with its octagonal Moot Hall) and follow signs on minor roads to the Augustinian sandstone ruins of **Lanercost Priory***. From here, pick up the course of **HADRIAN'S WALL** ❷ and follow signs to Gilsland, site of the Roman fort of **Birdoswald***. Join the B6318 and keep to it, stopping at signed forts and attractions on the way. At Wall, a brief detour down the A6079 enables you to visit **Hexham** (*see page 54*) and **Corbridge** (*see page 52*) before heading north up the A68 and turning right after 7 miles on the B6342 past **WALLINGTON** ❸. This twisty but pretty road passes wooded valleys, lakes and the heathery sandstone flanks of the Simonside Hills. Turn right on to the B6341 at the stone town of **Rothbury***, calling at **CRAGSIDE** ❹, 1 mile east. Continue up the B6341 to **ALNWICK** ❺, then head for the **NORTHUMBERLAND HERITAGE COAST** ❻, hugging it as closely as possible on minor roads. Near Amble, **Warkworth**'s fine medieval castle dominates the mouth of the River Coquet, spanned here by a rare example of a fortified bridge. Traditional oak-smoked kippers are a speciality at **Craster*** – track them down at Robson's famous smokery. From here, or Embleton further north, a good walk begins to the evocative coastal ruins of **Dunstanburgh Castle***. **Low Newton*** is a picturesque hamlet of white fishing cottages with RSPB and marine nature reserves. Offshore lie the treeless, rocky **Farne Islands****, haunt of puffins and seals, reached in summer from **Seahouses*** harbour, a lively little fishing resort. Photogenic **Bamburgh**'s** principal landmark is a magnificent castle on a basalt crag overlooking the beach; still lived in, it has interesting contents. A small museum in the village is dedicated to Grace Darling, heroine of a dramatic Farne Islands sea rescue in 1838. Return to the A1 at Belford. Head up the A1, deviating right at Beal towards **LINDISFARNE** ❼.

Getting out of the car: Several companies offer seasonal trips to the **Farne Islands** from Seahouses harbour. Access is restricted during the breeding season to avoid disturbing wildlife. A landing fee is payable in addition to the boat fare. Choose calm weather.

Lindisfarne*** is a 3-mile walk across tidal flats past marker poles, and easily explored in two or three hours. Check the tide-tables, posted on

Chillingham Castle ££ *Chillingham, Wooler; tel: 01668 215359; enquiries@chillingham-castle.com; www.chillingham-castle.com. Open May–Sep Wed–Mon 1200–1700 (daily in Jul–Aug).*

L Robson & Sons Ltd *Craster; tel: 01665 576223; enquiries@kipper.co.uk; www.kipper.co.uk.* Kippers and smoked fish traditionally prepared on tenterhooks over oak shavings.

Fisherman's Kitchen *2 South Street, Seahouses; tel: 01665 721052; wilkin@swallowfish.co.uk; www.swallowfish.co.uk.* A traditional smokehouse; postal deliveries.

boards by the causeway, or in local papers, *carefully*. The island is cut off for about five hours a day.

Retrace your route to the A1 and continue north towards **BERWICK-UPON-TWEED 8**. For the return leg of this tour, skirt close to the **NORTHUMBERLAND NATIONAL PARK 9** through ancient border battlegrounds. From Berwick, take the B6354 southwest via the model estate villages of **Etal*** and **Ford***, which boast several small visitor attractions. Four miles west of Ford, a monument near Branxton commemorates 'The Brave of Both Nations' who fought at the Battle of Flodden in 1513. From Ford, join the A697 near Crookham and head southeast to the grey stone moorland town of Wooler, a good walking base. Sixteen miles further south, turn right on the B6341 past Cragside (briefly retracing the outward journey but this time continue on the same road through Rothbury where the Coquet squeezes through sandstone ravines, sculpting the rocks into fantastic shapes) towards Hepple and **Elsdon***, a classic Northumbrian village with earthwork remnants of a Norman motte-and-bailey castle and an excellent example of a pele tower from about 1400. Turn right on the A696 to **Otterburn*** (site of another famous Anglo-Scottish battle), and take the B6320 via **Bellingham**, to rejoin the Hadrian's Wall route at Chollerford. Head west on the B6318 back to Carlisle, or take the A69 through Haltwhistle.

Detours: The scenic Upper Coquetdale road passes the attractive stone villages of **Holystone** and **Alwinton***; the A68 and its side-turnings from **Otterburn** and the road via Bellingham towards **Kielder Water** both allow some exploration of the interior of the park. Near Otterburn, extensive areas of the park are used as army firing ranges. Red flags indicate no-go areas. Walkers will need waterproof footwear as many forest tracks are very boggy.

Also worth exploring: A short drive east of the A697 near Wooler lies the ancient estate of **Chillingham****. The restored castle and its gardens can be visited, but the main interest is a herd of unique white cattle, descendants of wild oxen. They are shy but can be fierce, so see them in the company of a warden. Nearby **Ros Castle*** , an Iron Age hillfort, is the most spectacular vantage point in Northumbria.

Accommodation and food on or near the route

Olde Ship Hotel ££ *9 Main Street, Seahouses; tel: 01665 720200; fax: 01665 721383; theoldeship@seahouses.co.uk; www.seahouses.co.uk.* Fine old pub in salty setting overlooking bustling fishing harbour. Lots of character, good fish cooking and real ales. Comfortable bedrooms.

Farlam Hall £££ *Brampton; tel: 01697 746234; fax: 01697 746683; farlamhall@dial.pipex.com; www.farlamhall.co.uk.* Tranquil country house with top-notch cooking. Lovely grounds and period interest.

Pathhead
Cranshaws
Ellemford
Ayton
Burnmouth
B6358
Longformacus
Preston
Chirnside
Berwick-upon-Tweed 8
Oxton
Carfraemill
Duns
Allanton
Paxton
Tweedmouth
Westruther
Polwarth
Swinton
Norham
Haggerston
Beal
Lauder
Greenlaw
Leitholm
Holy Island
Lindisfarne 7
Gordon
Eccles
Birgham
Coldstream
Etal
Lowick
Northumberland Heritage Coast 6
Galashiels
Earlston
Nenthorn
Stichill
Branxton
Crookham
Ford
Belford
Bamburgh
Farne Islands
Melrose
Newtown St.Boswells
Kelso
Sprouston
Mindrum
Pawston
Akeld
Bellshill
Seahouses
Selkirk
St. Boswells
Roxburgh
Sunlaws
Wooler
Chillingham
Ros Castle
Adderstone
Low Newton by the Sea
Midlem
Nisbet
Eckford
Town Yetholm
Middleton Hall
Hepburn
Dunstanburgh Castle
Ashkirk
Lilliesleaf
Minto
Morebattle
Langleeford
Wooperton
Embleton
Craster
Hawick
Jedburgh
Oxnam
Hownam
Chatto
Powburn
Longhoughton
Kirkton
Bonchester Bridge
Chesters
Whittingham
Alnwick 5
Lesbury
Ainmouth
Hobkirk
Carter Bar
Blindburn
Alnham
Lorbottle
Newton-on-the-Moor
Warkworth
Dodburn
Alwinton 9
Holystone
Rothbury
Cragside 4
Swarland
Amble
NORTHUMBERLAND NATIONAL PARK
Hepple
Longframlington
East Thirston
Broomh
Saughtree
Rochester
Longhorsley
Widdrington
Hermitage
Kielder
Otterburn
Elsdon
Netherwitton
Ulgham
Falstone
Gatehouse
West Woodburn
Cambo
Hartburn
Ashington
Kershopefoot
Bellingham
Ridsdale
Wallington 3
Kirkharle
Morpeth
Bedlington
Nook
The Flatt
Wark
Colwell
Whalton
Belsay
Dinnington
Cramlington
Catlowdy
Roughsike
Butterburn
Nunwick
Ryal
Ingoe
Great Whittington
Stamfordham
Darras Hall
Ponteland
Kirkcambeck
West Hall
Gilsland
Bingfield
Chollerford
Low Brunton
NEWCASTLE UPON TYNE
Hethersgill
Lanercost
Greenhead
Haltwhistle
Henshaw
Bardon Mill
Newbrough
Wall
Horsley
Corbridge
Prudhoe
Ryton
Blaydon
Smithfield
Brampton 2
Halton Lea Gate
Langley
Haydon Bridge
Hexham
Riding Mill
Painshawfield
Whickham
Gateshead
Crosby-on-Eden
Hallbankgate
Catton
Slaley
Ebchester
Wetheral
Cumwhinton
Castle Carrock
Knarsdale
Slaggyford
Ninebanks
Sinderhope
Consett
Stanley
Wreay
Cumrew
Ayle
Edmundbyers
Castleside
Waskerley
High Hesket
Ainstable
Alston
Allendale Town
Allenheads
Rookhope
Satley
Leadgate

0 — 5 miles
0 — 5 km

North Pennines

Ratings

Scenery	●●●●●
Castles	●●●●○
Churches	●●●●○
Heritage	●●●●○
Industrial archaeology	●●●●○
Walking	●●●●○
Wildlife	●●●○○
Shopping	●●○○○

The rugged uplands west of Durham are perhaps as close as England gets to true wilderness. These peaty moorlands, scattered with whitewashed farms and crisscrossed by stone walls, reach a height of over 2000ft on the Pennine vertebrae. England's highest metalled road runs through them, to its highest town of Alston. The Pennine Way long-distance footpath snakes north–south over the highest summits. Be prepared for some hostile weather here. Huge tracts of hills are virtually inaccessible by road or path, and rare alpine plants colonise the limestone soils. In medieval times, these lonely places were the domain of the Prince Bishops of Durham, who fended off turbulent tribes from the north. It is an extraordinary area, redolent with history, and full of astonishing scenery. The cathedral and university city of Durham is one of the most enjoyable places in Britain.

ALSTON✣

ℹ **Tourist Information** Alston Moor, Town Hall, Front Street; tel: 01434 382244; alston.tic@eden.co.uk.

🚂 **South Tynedale Railway ££** Tel: 01434 381696; www.strps.org.uk. Trips Apr–Oct (ring for timetable).

Right
The Alston town crier

This tidy little market town is the highest in England, meeting point of several important trans-Pennine road links and terminus of the narrow-gauge South Tynedale Railway. The surrounding views are tremendous.

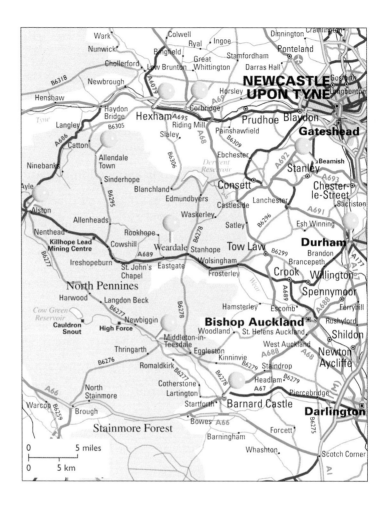

ALLENDALE✦✦

🛈 **Allenheads
Heritage Centre £**
*Allenheads; tel: 01434
685325. Open Apr–Oct daily
1000–1700.*

Some of England's largest and wildest expanses of moorland stretch to either side of the B6295, which follows the East Allen valley. **Allendale Town** is Britain's geographical centre (the sundial on the church marks its longitude and latitude). Upstream, the model village of **Allenheads** prospered on the proceeds of the East Allen Mine, once the most important source of lead in Europe. Streams cut through the heather into scattered, huddled stone villages. Defunct lead-mining shafts and tunnels bestrew the area, which is now better known for trout fishing and walking.

BARNARD CASTLE***

ℹ️ **Tourist Information** *Flatts Road; tel: 01833 690909; tourism@teesdale.gov.uk.*

🏛️ **Bowes Museum ££** *Tel: 01833 690606; info@bowesmuseum.org.uk; www.bowesmuseum.org.uk. Open daily 1100–1700.*

Rokeby Park ££ *Southeast on A66; tel: 01833 637334. Open Jun–Sept Mon and Tue 1400–1700.*

Egglestone Hall Gardens *Egglestone; tel: 01833 650115; www.celmisia.20m.com. Open daily 1000–1700.*

Barney's most striking building is a grand French-style château, built in 1860, to house the prestigious **Bowes Museum***. The town takes its name from a much older Norman ruin, built to guard a strategic crossing of the River Tees. **Rokeby Park*** nearby has Walter Scott associations. An attractive riverside walk from the town centre goes to ruined **Egglestone Abbey*** (1195), on the banks of the Tees, and **Egglestone Hall Gardens***.

Accommodation and food in Barnard Castle

Market Place Teashop £ *29 Market Place; tel: 01833 690110.* Appetising teas and snacks in 17th-century building. Friendly service.

Morritt Arms ££ *Greta Bridge; tel: 01833 627232; fax: 01833 627392; relax@themorritt.co.uk; www.relaxatthemorritt.co.uk.* Traditional coaching inn with comfortable accommodation and open views.

BEAMISH****

🏛️ **North of England Open-Air Museum £££** *10m north of Durham; tel: 0191 307 4000; museum@beamish.org.uk; www.beamish.co.uk. Open Apr–Oct daily 1000–1700, closed Mon and Fri off season.*

🚂 **Tanfield Railway ££** *Tanfield; tel: 0191 388 7545; tanfield@ ingsoc.demon.co.uk; www.tanfield-railway.co.uk for timetable.*

This blockbusting open-air exhibition spreads over a 300-acre site, re-creating life in the northeast during the 18th and 19th centuries. One engine shed contains a full-scale working replica of Stephenson's Locomotion No 1. Just north of Beamish, the **Tanfield Railway***, built in 1725 to carry coal to the Tyne, is claimed as the oldest still in existence. Steam trains operate along the route under **Causey Arch***, a remarkable single-span bridge dating from 1727.

CORBRIDGE*

ℹ️ **Tourist Information** *Hill Street; tel: 01434 632815. Seasonal opening.*

Right
Roman column

The Roman garrison town of *Corstopitum* was an important station along Hadrian's Wall. Excavations of the settlement have revealed forts, temples, fountains, a granary and an aqueduct; the **Corbridge Roman site and museum*** (*see page 45*) explains all. A few later buildings are noteworthy: a part-Saxon church (St Andrew's) and a fortified tower house dating from the 14th century.

DURHAM✧✧✧

ⓘ Tourist Information
Millennium Place; tel: 0191 384 3720;
touristinfo@durham.gov.uk.

Ⓟ Prince Bishop River Cruiser ££
Browns Boat House, Elvet Bridge; tel: 0191 386 9525; sailings all year; ring for schedule.

ⓘ Durham Cathedral
The Chapter Office, The College; tel: 0191 386 4266; enquiries@durhamcathedral.co.uk; www.durhamcathedral.co.uk. Open June–Sept daily 0930–2000 (1800 off season); donation requested, charges for tower and treasury.

Durham Castle ££
Palace Green; tel: 0191 374 3863; ja.marshall@durham.ac.uk; www.durhamcastle.com. Open July–Sept daily 1000–1700; tours Mon, Wed and weekends 1400–1600 in term-time, usually daily out of term.

Durham Heritage Centre £ St Mary-le-Bow, North Bailey; tel: 0191 384 5589; open July–Aug 1100–1630, June and Sept 1400–1630, weekends Apr–May, Oct.

Durham University Oriental Museum £ Elvet Hill; tel: 0191 374 7911; oriental.museum@durham.ac.uk; www.dur.ac.uk/oriental.museum. Open Mon–Fri 1000–1700, Sat–Sun 1200–1700.

Botanical Garden £
Hollingside Lane; tel: 0191 374 7971; www.dur.ac.uk. Open Mar–Oct daily 1000–1700, Nov–Feb 1100–1600.

Enclosed on three sides by a meander of the River Wear, Durham has a remarkable defensive location. The historic centre is hilly but compact and best explored on foot (congestion charges have been introduced for motorists). The sturdy towers of Durham's Norman **cathedral**✧✧✧ rise above the wooded sandstone crag. Completed in 1133, it is one of the finest examples of the Romanesque style in Britain. The **castle**✧✧ guards the citadel's narrow isthmus. Contemporary with the cathedral, this superb Norman fortress now provides handsome premises for Durham's prestigious **university**✧. In the lower town, a good starting point is the Heritage Centre. The university's **Botanical Garden**✧ makes a change from historic buildings, and a river trip provides an interesting perspective on this visually delightful city.

Accommodation and food in Durham

Bistro 21 ££ *Aykley Heads; tel: 0191 384 4354; fax: 0191 384 1149.* Imaginative, wide-ranging menus served in former farmhouse to the north of the city.

Georgian Town House £ *10 Crossgate; tel/fax: 0191 386 8070; enquiries@georgian-townhouse.fsnet.com.* Pretty, cottagey B&B within easy reach of the cathedral.

The Prince Bishops of Durham

After the Norman Conquest, William the Conqueror conferred extensive powers and huge tracts of land on the Bishops of Durham, entrusting them to provide an impregnable bulwark against Scottish raiders who still made periodic incursions. These powerful prelates raised their own armies, minted their own coinage, levied taxes and held private courts. They could ennoble barons, grant charters and conduct peace negotiations with the Scots. The castles, churches and palaces of the Prince Bishops have left an unmistakable mark on County Durham.

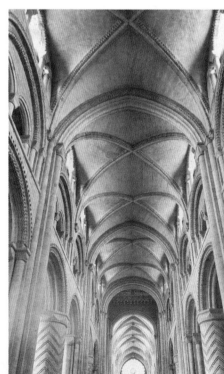

Right
Durham Cathedral

HEXHAM❖❖

ℹ️ Tourist Information
Wentworth Car Park; tel: 01434 65220; hexham.tic@tynedale.gov.uk.

🏛️ Hexham Abbey
Beaumont Street; tel: 01434 602031; hexhamabbey@ukonline.co. uk; www.hexhamabbey.org.uk. Open daily 0930–1900 (1700 in winter); donation welcome.

Hexham Moot Hall and Gallery *Market Place; tel: 01434 652351; museum@tynedale.gov.uk. Open Mon, Tue, Thu, Fri 1000–1500, closed lunchtime.*

Hexham's present size seems modest in comparison with its splendidly atmospheric **abbey❖❖** founded in 674 by St Wilfrid, when it was claimed to be largest church north of the Alps. (It is strictly speaking a priory church, but is now always referred to as an abbey.) Vestiges of Saxon work survive, including the crypt and the bishop's throne (known as St Wilfrid's Chair), but the monastery was looted by the Vikings and most of the existing building dates from the 12th century. Points of interest include a 16th-century rood screen, several Dance of Death panels from the 15th century, and the 'night stair', a rare pre-Dissolution survival which once linked the church with the monks' dormitory. Other medieval buildings in Hexham are the **Moot Hall** and the **Old Gaol**.

Accommodation and food in Hexham

Dene House £ *Juniper; tel/fax: 01434 673413; margaret@denehouse-hexham.co.uk; www.denehouse-hexham.co.uk.* Welcoming stone farmhouse offering homely B&B amid peaceful grazing land. Log-burning stove and meals from the Aga.

East Peterel Field Farm £ *Yarridge Road; tel: 01434 607209; fax: 01434 601753; bookings@petfield.demon.co.uk.* Smart but friendly farmhouse accommodation in rolling countryside.

Langley Castle £££ *Langley-on-Tyne; tel: 01434 688888; fax: 01434 684019; manager@langleycastle.com; www.langleycastle.com.* Imposing medieval setting for luxury stays. Popular with wedding parties.

Dipton Mill £ *Dipton Mill Road; tel: 01434 606577; www.vizual4n.co.uk/diptonmill.htm.* Charming, simple country pub with good home-cooked food.

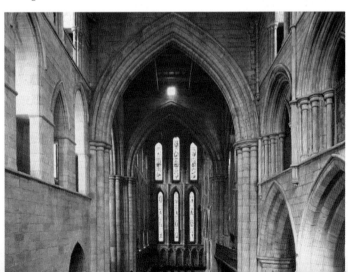

Opposite
The fells in snow

Right
Hexham Abbey

TEESDALE❖❖❖

ⓘ Bowlees Visitor Centre £ *Bowlees, Middleton-in-Teesdale; tel: 01833 622292; www.wildlifetrust.co.uk/ durham. Open Apr–Oct daily 1030–1700, Nov–Mar weekends 1030–1600.*

ⓘ High Force Waterfall £ *Forest-in-Teesdale; tel: 01833 640209; teesdaleestate@ rabycastle.com; www.rabycastle.com. Open daily 1000–1700; parking charge.*

Widdybank Fell National Nature Reserve famed for its rare limestone flora, including the Teesdale violet.

🄲 Rose & Crown ££ *Romaldkirk; tel: 01833 650213, fax: 01833 650828; hotel@rose-and-crown.co.uk; www.rose-and-crown.co.uk.* Characterful coaching inn with excellent restaurant in pretty Teesdale village.

In and around the Teesdale valley, the countryside steals the show, and becomes quite wild. **Cotherstone** is famed for its crumbly sheep's cheese. **Romaldkirk**❖ is especially picturesque, with stone houses around neatly kept greens, a fine Norman church of St Romald and a splendid coaching inn (the Rose & Crown). **Middleton-in-Teesdale**❖'s terraced cottages were originally built by benevolent Quaker mine-owners for their workers. **Newbiggin**, further up the valley, has the world's oldest surviving Methodist chapel, dating from 1759. A couple of miles beyond Newbiggin is **High Force**❖❖, a 70-ft cascade pouring over a ridge of dark rock in lacy froth.

WEARDALE❖❖

ⓘ Tourist Information *Durham Dales Centre, Castle Gardens, Stanhope; tel: 01388 527650.*

🄷 Killhope Lead Mining Museum ££ *Cowshill; tel: 01388 537505. Open Apr–Sept daily 1030–1700, Oct weekends.*

Weardale Museum £ *Ireshopeburn; tel: 01388 537417. Open Easter–July Wed–Sun 1400–1700 (daily in Aug).*

The austere moorland landscapes of upper Weardale are scarred with lead- and iron-ore workings. One of the biggest mines, near Ireshopeburn, is now the **Killhope Lead Mining Museum**❖❖. The 34-ft waterwheel which powered the crushing equipment is in working order. A small **museum**❖ in Ireshopeburn's manse charts the often gruesome history of the industry. **Stanhope**, further downstream, is Weardale's main centre, and a good base for moorland walks. A local curiosity is a large fossilised tree stump in the churchyard. The next village, **Frosterley**, is famous for its black marble-like limestone, used in many local churches, including nearby Eastgate, and Durham Cathedral. Most of the stone has long since been used up.

Suggested tour

Tourist Information *Town Hall, Market Place, Bishop Auckland; tel: 01388 604922.*

Auckland Castle ££ *Market Place, Bishop Auckland; tel: 01388 601627; www.auckland-castle.co.uk. Open Apr–Sept Mon and Thu 1230–1700, Sun 1400–1700.*

Escomb Saxon Church *Escomb; tel: 01388 662265. Open daily 0900–1600 (2000 in summer); donation requested.*

Total distance: 140 miles (225km). Add 24 miles (39km) for the Beamish detour.

Time: 6 hours. Allow a half-day each for Beamish or Durham.

Links: From Hexham, you can pick up the Northumberland and Hadrian's Wall tour (*see page 40*). An easy drive west along the A66 from Barnard's Castle links with Penrith for the Lakeland tours (*see pages 58 and 68*). Or strike south from Barnard's Castle to link with Swaledale (*see page 90*).

Route: From **DURHAM** ❶ , head southwest on the A690 via Brancepeth (with its imposing mock castle), turning off at Willington towards **Bishop Auckland***, where **Auckland Castle*** was the official residence of the Bishops of Durham. (Three miles northwest of the town is a fascinating Saxon church, at **Escomb***.) Continue on the A688 via Staindrop (see **Raby Castle*** here), to **BARNARD CASTLE** ❷. Head northwest on the B6277 via **Romaldkirk** and **TEESDALE** ❸ as far as **ALSTON** ❹, through lovely villages and grand scenery. Note: the high, unfenced moorland may be treacherous in bad weather.

From Alston, take the A689 southeast through **WEARDALE** ❺ past the **Killhope Lead Mining Museum** and Ireshopeburn. All around, the remains of tall chimneys and deserted cottages litter the landscapes. At **Eastgate**, a minor road leads left across lonely moorland towards Rookhope and **Allenheads***. From here, turn right on the spectacular B6295 loop road via **ALLENDALE** ❻. Turn off at Langley on the B6305 for a look at the historic settlements of **HEXHAM** ❼ and **CORBRIDGE** ❽. Return to the B6306 and proceed south via the exquisite model village of **Blanchland****, built of honey-coloured stone around the remains of a medieval abbey. The road is especially picturesque here, curling round the Derwent Reservoir through Edmundbyers before joining the B6278 to **Stanhope**. Turn left along the A689 and continue back to Durham via Crook.

Detour: From Durham, take the B6532 through Sacriston and Stanley, following signs for **BEAMISH OPEN-AIR MUSEUM** ❾ from the B6076 to the north.

Getting out of the car: North of Allendale Town, the East Allen river runs through a dramatic wooded gorge near Langley (park at High Staward station and walk). Other good walks follow old packhorse routes across the moors of Allendale Common, which once carried lead ore to Tyneside smelters.

In Teesdale, keen walkers can track down two spectacular waterfalls. **High Force**** is easy to find, a short walk from the car park a mile beyond the Bowlees Visitor Centre near Newbiggin. **Cauldron Snout****

Manor House Inn
££ *Carterway Heads,
Shotley Bridge, 3m west of
Consett; tel: 01207 255268;
fax: 01207 255268;
www.scoot.co.uk/manor.house.*
Stone-built inn with fine
views and even better
cooking. Simple bedrooms.

Lord Crewe Arms £££
*Blanchland; tel: 01434
675251; fax: 01434
675337; lord@
crewearms.freeserve.co.uk.*
Historic inn (once part of
medieval Blanchland
Abbey) in one of
Northumbria's most
picturesque villages.

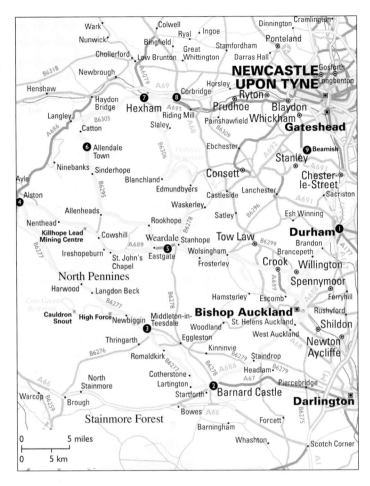

MetroCentre
*Gateshead; tel: 0191
493 0219. Open Mon–Sat
from 0900, Sun from 1100.*

Centre for Life £££
*Times Square,
Newcastle; tel: 0191 243
8210. Open Mon–Sat
1000–1800, Sun
1100–1800.*

National Glass Centre
££ *Liberty Way, Sunderland;
tel: 0191 515 5555. Open
daily 1000–1700.*

entails a nature trail walk from the Cow Green reservoir, signed to the
left beyond High Force. This impressive cataract crashes 200ft down a
rocky staircase near the dam. Near by, **Widdybank Fell✦✦** is a rare
geological habitat supporting unusual sub-arctic plants.

Also worth exploring: There are many reasons to visit Newcastle
upon Tyne – apart from football and hard drinking. It has a good
transport system, vast shopping centres and several excellent free
museums. Besides the Norman fortress which gave the city its name,
and the great bridges over the Tyne (including the dazzling
Millennium Bridge), the **Centre for Life✦✦✦** is a major exhibition based
on the biological sciences. Don't miss the amazing **Glass Centre✦✦** in
Sunderland. If you're travelling past Newcastle via the A1, you *can't*
miss Antony Gormley's huge modern roadside sculpture called *The
Angel of the North*.

East Lakes: Windermere and Ullswater

Ratings

Landscape/geology	●●●●●
Mountains	●●●●●
Outdoor activities	●●●●●
Food interests	●●●●○
Heritage	●●●●○
Children	●●●○○
Museums	●●●○○
Wildlife	●●●○○

The spectacular area of glaciated lakes and mountains in England's northwest corner encompasses an astonishing variety of landscapes within just a 30-mile radius. Easily accessed from the M6, the eastern sector of the Lake District National Park is much visited, and Windermere and Ullswater can get very crowded. However, it is always possible to find the kind of solitude Wordsworth wrote about in his poem *Daffodils* ('I wandered lonely as a cloud ...') at the secretive lake of Haweswater. The best way to do this, as anywhere in the Lakes, is to get out of the car and on to your feet. If the weather is bad, there are plenty of undercover attractions for the whole family, plus some splendid shops, pubs, cafés and restaurants. National Trust members benefit from free access to many Lakeland sights, tracts of countryside and useful parking spaces.

KENDAL✦✦

ⓘ Tourist Information *Town Hall, Highgate; tel: 01539 725758; kendaltic@ southlakeland.gov.uk.*

ⓟ If you have a car, head straight for the **Abbot Hall** at the south end of Kendal's main street, where patrons of the **art gallery** and museum park free of charge.

Visitors stream through this attractive limestone market town, home of the famous Kendal mint cake, for emergency rations on the fells. At the south end of the main street are an excellent **Art Gallery✦✦** (good coffee shop) and the **Museum of Lakeland Life and Industry✦✦**. Further up the main street, the **Kendal Museum✦** provides background on the Lakes, including an exhibition on the great fell-walker and pictorial guide-writer Alfred Wainwright, who spent much of his life in Kendal. The ruined hilltop castle – birthplace of Katherine Parr, Henry VIII's only surviving wife – commands fine views from the opposite bank of the River Kent.

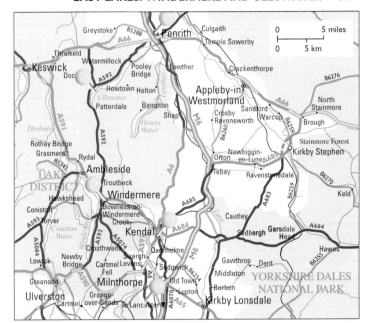

Accommodation and food in Kendal

Low Jock Sear £ Selside; *tel/fax: 01539 823259; ljs@armail.co.uk.*
Friendly, peaceful guesthouse 5 miles north of town. Good home-cooking; extensive, well-kept gardens.

Moon ££ *129 Highgate; tel: 01539 729254.* Enterprising wholefood bistro in stylish surroundings.

LANCASTER✦✦

Lancashire's county town had its origins as a Roman camp (*castrum*), and later became a prosperous port in slave-trading days. Today it is a lively university city. In its attractive historic centre stand a Norman **castle✦✦** (formerly a prison, now used as a crown court and a museum), the priory church of **St Mary✦** and the **Judges' Lodgings✦✦**, a 17th-century house containing furniture by Gillow. On the waterfront, the **Maritime Museum✦✦** is based in the handsome Georgian custom house.

PENRITH✤

ℹ **Tourist Information**
Robinson's School, Middlegate; tel: 01768 867466; pen.tic@eden.gov.uk.

🏛 **Wetheriggs Country Pottery**
2m south off A6; tel: 01768 892733; info@ wetheriggs-pottery.co.uk; www.wetheriggs-pottery.co.uk. Open Apr–Sept daily 1000–1730, Oct–Mar Wed–Sun 1000–1700.

Brougham Castle £ *Off A6 south; tel: 01768 862488. Open Apr–Oct daily 1000–1800 (1700 in Oct).*

Brougham Hall Craft Centre *Tel: 01768 868184; donation requested.*

Rheged – The Village in the Hill ££ *Off M6, J40 on A66; tel: 01768 868000; enquiries@rheged.com; www.rheged.com. Open daily 1000–1800.*

Penrith has a pleasant old centre of warm red sandstone. A ruined castle stands on the outskirts, and there are several old-fashioned shops on the main market square, including Grahams, a traditional grocer. Nearby are the family attractions of the **Wetheriggs Pottery✤✤**, **Brougham✤**, with its romantic waterside castle, and **Rheged – The Village in the Hill✤**, a grass-covered visitor attraction built into the hillside.

ULLSWATER✥✥✥

ⓘ Tourist Information *Finkle Street, Pooley Bridge; tel: 01768 486530 or Main Car Park, Glenridding; tel: 01768 482414.*

ⓐ Ullswater Steamers *Glenridding Pier; tel: 01768 482229; www.ullswater-steamers.co.uk. Sailings all year.*

ⓣ Dalemain House ££ *Dacre; tel: 01768 486450; www.dalemain.com. Open Apr–Oct 1100–1600 (grounds 1030–1700).*

Gowbarrow Fell, near Aira Force on the northern shore, is where Wordsworth and his sister Dorothy first enjoyed those famous daffodils.

ⓒ The lakeshore settlements (Pooley Bridge, Glenridding and Patterdale) are often overrun, but several **country-house hotels**, tucked away in secluded waterfront enclaves, provide peaceful overnight stays and gargantuan Lakeland teas.

ⓒ Sharrow Bay £££ *Ullswater, Pooley Bridge; tel: 01768 486301; fax: 01768 486349; enquiries@sharrow-bay.com; www.sharrow-bay.com.* Exemplary food, service and luxury accommodation in Britain's first country-house hotel – still one of the best. Dazzling lakeshore location. Try it for tea, if you can't afford to stay.

Right
Aira Force

Snaking over 7 miles, Ullswater is often rated the most beautiful of all Cumbria's lakes. It carves through a complex geological layer cake, which give its surroundings great variety. Victorian pleasure 'steamers' ply a triangular course around the lake in summer, while countless sailboats, kayaks and windsurfers battle with the unpredictable wind. Near Ullswater's northern end is **Dalemain**✥✥, a mainly Elizabethan house with fascinating Georgian rooms; its gardens are full of blue poppies in early summer.

WINDERMERE✦✦✦

ℹ Tourist Information *Glebe Road, Bowness Bay; tel: 01539 442895; bownesstic@lakeland.gov.uk or Victoria Street, Windermere; tel: 01539 446499.*

📍 Windermere Lake Cruises *Tel: 01539 531188; www.windermere-lakecruises.co.uk.*

Lakeside & Haverthwaite Railway ££ *Lakeside; tel: 01539 531594. Open Apr–Oct daily services.*

🏛 The World of Beatrix Potter ££ *Bowness-on-Windermere; tel: 01539 488444; www.hop-skip-jump.com. Open daily 1000–1730 (1630 in winter).*

Steamboat Museum ££ *Rayrigg Road, Bowness-on-Windermere; tel: 01539 445565. Open Mar–Oct daily 1000–1700.*

Brockhole Visitor Centre *On A591; tel: 01539 446601. Open Apr–Oct daily 1000–1700; grounds open all year; free to boat or bus passengers, but hefty parking charge.*

Fell Foot Park *Newby Bridge; tel: 01539 531273. Open daily 0900–1900 or dusk; NT; parking charge for non-NT members.*

Blackwell Arts and Crafts House ££ *Storrs Park, Bowness-on-Windermere; tel: 01539 446139; www.blackwell.org.uk. Open Mar–Dec daily 1000–1700, rest of year 1000–1600.*

Both the lake and the Victorian resort on its eastern shoreline share the same name. The town is really two separate communities: the railhead development at Windermere and its lakeshore extension, **Bowness**. In Bowness, prime attractions include the splendidly restored **Blackwell Arts and Crafts House**, **The World of Beatrix Potter✦** and the **Steamboat Museum✦✦**. In Windermere, the showroom of mail-order houseware company **Lakeland Limited✦✦** has an amazing range of kitchen gadgets on sale, and a popular café.

The lake of Windermere is the largest in England (over 10 miles long), and a giant holiday playground all summer. Steamers and launches link Bowness with **Ambleside** (*see page 68*) and **Lakeside** at opposite ends of the lake. Much of the wooded shoreline is in private hands, concealing villas and mansions once owned by wealthy industrialists. One of these is now the **Brockhole Visitor Centre✦✦**, a palatial country mansion with grounds sweeping to the lakeshore. A stunning viewpoint of the lake can be seen from **Orrest Head**, northeast of Windermere town. At the southern end of Bowness, a chain-ferry acts as a floating bridge for vehicles and foot passengers.

At the southern tip of Lake Windermere, a short steam-train ride on the **Lakeside & Haverthwaite Railway✦** links with a lake cruise from the Victorian station at Haverthwaite; **Fell Foot Park✦✦** is a splendid

Lakeland Limited
Windermere Station;
tel: 01539 488100;
www.lakelandlimited.com
Mon–Fri 0800–1900, Sat
0900–1800, Sun
1100–1700.

**Aquarium of the
Lakes ££** *Newby
Bridge;* tel: 01539 530153;
www.aquariumofthelakes.co.uk.
Open daily 0900–1700
(1800 in summer).

Stott Park Bobbin Mill
££ *Finsthwaite, on the
Hawkshead road;* tel: 01539
531087. Open Apr–Sept
daily 1000–1800, Oct
1000–1700; EH.

Below
Dusk on Lake Windermere

waterfront stretch of landscaped scenery; the **Aquarium of the Lakes**✦✦ is an enjoyable introduction to the wildlife of the lake. Just to the northwest of the lake is **Stott Park Bobbin Mill**✦✦, still powered by steam and water.

Accommodation and food in or near Windermere

The Samling £££ *Ambleside Road, Windermere; tel: 01539 431922; fax: 01539 430400; info@thesamling.com; www.thesamling.com.* Luxurious retreat with stylish contemporary décor. Inventive menus and lake views.

Gilpin Lodge £££ *Crook Road, Windermere; tel: 01539 488818; fax 01539 488058; www.gilpin-lodge.co.uk.* Beautifully furnished Edwardian hotel in extensive grounds. Superb cooking.

Old Vicarage £££ *Church Road, Witherslack; tel: 01539 552381; fax: 01539 552373; www.oldvicarage.com.* Tranquil, elegant hotel-restaurant in tiny lanes near Grange-over-Sands. Excellent food.

Lightwood £ *Cartmel Fell; tel/fax: 01539 531454; www. lightwoodguesthouse.co.uk.* Charming 17th-century farmhouse accommodation in unspoilt countryside. Pretty bedrooms and landscaped grounds. Dinner on request.

Above
High Wray, near Windermere

Queen's Head ££ *Troutbeck; tel: 01539 432174.* Upbeat Mediterranean menus in Tudor country inn. Glorious views. Comfortable bedrooms.

Miller Howe Café ££ *Alexandra Buildings, Windermere Station; tel: 01539 442255; www.duttoncuisine.co.uk.* Stylish café-restaurant in the Lakeland Limited showroom near Windermere Station.

Porthole ££ *3 Ash Street, Bowness-on-Windermere; tel: 01539 442793.* Reputable Italian fare in a quaint old building.

Uplands ££ *Haggs Lane, Cartmel; tel: 01539 536248; fax: 01539 536848; enquiries@uplands.uk.com; www.uplands.uk.com.* Tranquil country house restaurant overlooking distant coastal views. Elegant furnishings and superb cooking.

Mason's Arms £ *Strawberry Bank, Cartmel Fell; tel: 01539 568486.* Popular walkers' pub renowned for home-brewed ales and adventurous food, including vegetarian specialities. Terrific views.

Suggested tour

Village Bakery
Melmerby, on A686 Penrith–Alston road; tel: 01768 881515. Open Mon–Sat 0830–1700, Sun 0930–1700. Award-winning bakery, supplying specialist breads to supermarkets throughout the UK. On-site restaurant, craft gallery.

Below
Eskdale

Total distance: 87 miles (140km), or 72 miles (116km) if you omit the Cartmel section. Add 29 miles (47km) for the Lancaster detour, and 21 miles (34km) for Eden Valley.

Time: Half a day, but allow time also for a walk or lake trip. In wintry weather, the high passes of Shap and Kirkstone are among the first to be blocked by snow.

Links: This tour merges almost seamlessly with the Western Lakes tour (*see page 68*). Join it via the A591 from Windermere, or the A66 from Penrith. From Penrith it's a short, fast hop up the M6 to Carlisle for the Northumberland and Hadrian's Wall tour (*see page 40*). From the Eden Valley route (optional detour), join the Northern Pennines tour (*see page 50*) from the A66 (Barnard Castle) or via the A686 at Alston (see Long Meg and Her Daughters (an ancient stone circle) on the way). The Yorkshire Dales tour (*see page 90*) can be joined from Kirkby Stephen (B6270 Birkdale road) or Kendal (A684 via Sedbergh).

Morecambe Bay
Shoreline walks give good views of this huge area of tidal sand and mudflats – one of Britain's most important breeding and feeding grounds for wading birds. Alternatively, take the West Cumbrian Line railway from Arnside, perched on viaducts and miles of sea wall. Many have tried to take short-cuts across the estuary, but some have never made it. The tides gallop in and out, and quicksand and sea fogs make the journey immensely hazardous. Today, experienced local guides offer summer escorted walks over the crossing. Never try this unaccompanied.

Morecambe Bay Walks *Cedric Robinson, Guide's Farm, Cart Lane, Grange-over-Sands: tel: 01539 532165.*

Route: From central **KENDAL** ❶, two exit routes lead to the A591. If you're short of time, head straight to Windermere (10 miles northwest). To see something of the Cartmel peninsula, head south on the A6. The southern Lakes are often overlooked, but they make lovely touring country, through gentle pastoral scenery. Pick a route through a web of tiny lanes and find a quiet picnic spot. Head south on the A591 for 3 miles to **Sizergh Castle**❖❖, a 14th-century pele tower with lovely gardens. Less than 2 miles further on is **Levens Hall**❖❖❖, an Elizabethan mansion with superb topiary gardens.

Detour: At Levens Hall, turn south on the A6 down to **LANCASTER** ❷. Halfway down, **Leighton Hall**❖❖ is an ancient estate owned by the Gillow furniture-making family. The present building is mostly 19th-century neo-Gothic, with a wonderful array of antiques made by master craftsmen.

Follow the A590 west, turning left for Grange-over-Sands, a sedate Victorian resort overlooking Morecambe Bay. **Cartmel**❖❖ (2 miles northwest) is an exceptionally pretty village in lush meadows, dominated by a magnificent priory church. Nearby is **Holker Hall**❖❖, a lavishly furnished house with beautiful formal gardens and a motor museum (special exhibition on the Campbell speed records). Continue north along the B5278 and turn right on the A590 to **Newby Bridge**❖❖, where you can enjoy the southern lakeshore. Take the eastern shore road (A592) via **WINDERMERE** ❸, continuing north to historic **Troutbeck**, surrounded by rolling fells. The National Trust property **Townend**❖❖ is a yeoman's house dating from 1626. The road beyond Troutbeck climbs steeply towards the bleak Kirkstone Pass (1 489ft). The grand fells in the distance belong to the Helvellyn range, rising to over 3 000ft.

The single through road along the northern shore of **ULLSWATER** ❹ has gorgeous lake vistas through the trees. At busy holiday times it is nearly always crowded, and parking is difficult.

Getting out of the car: One of the best places to stop for a walk near Ullswater is **Aira Force**❖, a 70-ft mare's tail waterfall tumbling though mossy rocks (*National Trust; parking charge for non-members*). For even quieter views, head for Pooley Bridge and take the minor road leading along the southern shore. The views and walks between Martindale Common and Patterdale are wonderful. Combine a walk with a boat trip.

Near **PENRITH** ❺, Rheged – **The Village in the Hill**, and the **Lakeland Bird of Prey Centre** are popular attractions for families. Continue south on the A6 over Shap Fell (sometimes impassable in winter). Pause in Shap village to track down **Keld Chapel**, a tiny pre-Reformation building (*key available from a nearby house; National Trust*). Return to Kendal via the A6.

Sizergh Castle ££ 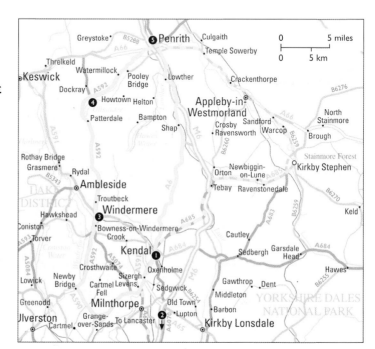 *Off A590; tel: 01539 560070; www.nationaltrust.org.uk. Open Apr–Oct Sun–Thu 1330–1730 (gardens 1230–1730); NT.*

Levens Hall £££ *On A6; tel: 01539 560321; www.levenshall.co.uk. Open Apr–Oct Sun–Thu 1200–1700 (gardens 1000–1700).*

Leighton Hall ££ *Off A6, 3 miles N of Carnforth; tel: 01524 734474; www.leightonhall.co.uk. Open May–Sept Tue–Fri, Sun and Bank Hol Mon 1400–1700 (Aug 1230–1700).*

Holker Hall and Gardens/Lakeland Motor Museum £££ *Cark-in-Cartmel; tel: 01539 558328; www.holker-hall.co.uk. Open Apr–Oct Sun–Fri 1000–1800.*

Townend ££ *Troutbeck; tel: 01539 432628; www.nationaltrust.org.uk. Open Apr–Oct Tue–Fri, Sun and Bank Hol Mon 1300–1700.*

Acorn Bank Gardens ££ *Temple Sowerby; tel: 01768 361893; www.nationaltrust.org.uk. Open Apr–Oct Fri–Wed 1000–1700.*

Lakeland Bird of Prey Centre ££ *Lowther; tel: 01931 712746. Open Apr–Oct 1030–1700; displays at 1100, 1400 and 1600.*

Low Sizergh Barn Farm Shop *On A590 4 miles S of Kendal; tel: 01539 560426. Open daily 0900–1730 (0930–1700 in winter).*

Detour: To see the rich green farmland of the **Eden Valley**, take the A66 heading east of Penrith. Continue through Westmorland's former county town, **Appleby-in-Westmorland**✦✦, where the imposing Norman castle was restored in 1653, following the Eden along the B6259 (turn right at Sandford) to join the A685 at Kirkby Stephen. Turn right again, and return to Kendal via **Ravenstonedale**✦, an attractively wooded touring and walking centre with good pubs, and Newbiggin-on-Lune. Keep on the A685 as it embraces the M6 motorway for a brief waltz along the same course at Tebay (J38).

Also worth exploring: From the B5320 near Pooley Bridge, or the A6 between Penrith and Shap, a number of twisty minor roads meander through farming communities to the remote reservoir lake of **Hawes Water**✦✦. It's a long dead-end drive, but an oddly memorable one, with some serious walks on the fells of High Street. You may even spot a golden eagle.

Accommodation and food on the route

Royal Oak Inn ££ *Bongate, Appleby-in-Westmorland; tel: 01768 351463; www.mortalmaninns.co.uk/royaloak.* Cosy old coaching inn with exceptional food and real ales, and comfortable bedrooms.

Black Swan ££ *Ravenstonedale; tel: 01539 623204; fax: 01539 623604 www.blackswanhotel.com.* Traditional inn serving imaginative menus in the village centre; well-furnished bedrooms.

West Lakes

Ratings

Outdoor activities	●●●●●
Scenery	●●●●●
Walking	●●●●●
Children	●●●●○
Eating out	●●●●○
Literary associations	●●●●○
Heritage	●●●○○
Shopping	●●●○○

This Lakeland tour strikes beyond the beaten Wordsworthian tracks, into the wilder heart of the National Park, past England's highest mountain, deepest lake, wettest valley, steepest pass… Hard Knott is a difficult drive in any weather conditions, but the rewards are the dramatic, ice-carved landforms that inspired the Romantic poets, and countless artists and photographers since. Autumn and winter colouring can be even more spectacular than spring or summer. The tougher fells may be too taxing for short legs, but there is plenty for children to enjoy: walks and climbs for all levels of ability, boat trips on Derwentwater, and the delightful little Ravenglass & Eskdale Railway. And there are many attractive shops, restaurants, pubs and 'heritage' sites en route. Stick to the interior, though – Cumbria's west coast, overshadowed by the ominous hulk of Sellafield's nuclear reprocessing plant, is a less than enticing stretch of seaside.

AMBLESIDE❖❖

ℹ Tourist Information Central Buildings, Market Cross; tel: 01539 432582; amblesidetic@southlakeland. gov.uk.

🏠 Stagshaw Garden £ On A591, half a mile south of Ambleside; tel: 01539 446027. Open Apr–June 1000–1830 (July–Oct by appointment); car access and parking tricky – best to walk from Ambleside.

Strategically placed at the Windermere lakehead, with some of the Lake District's most glorious fells on its doorstep, this little Victorian town stays lively all year round. It lacks any exceptional architecture, but its appealing shops and places to eat and stay make it a thoroughly enjoyable base. It caters for serious walkers and climbers, with specialist outdoor stores, and keeps others happy with stylish crafts and clothes, cafés and cultural events. Its few sights include vestiges of the Roman fort of *Galava*, dating from AD 79, the 90-ft cascade of Stockghyll Force, and the quaint little **Bridge House**❖ built over the stream. Beatrix Potter devotees track down her beautifully detailed fungi paintings in the Armitt Library. The **Stagshaw Garden**❖❖ is a fine sight in spring.

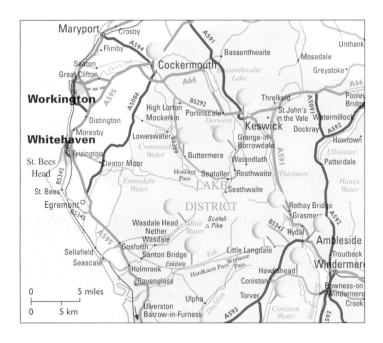

Accommodation and food in Ambleside

Drunken Duck ££ *Barngates; tel: 01539 436347; fax: 01539 436781; info@drunkenduckinn.co.uk; www.drunkenduckinn.co.uk.* Popular, characterful country inn, serving excellent bar and restaurant food. Attractive bedrooms.

Rowanfield ££ *Kirkstone Road; tel: 01539 433686; fax: 01539 431569; email@rowanfield.com; www.rowanfield. com.* Immaculately kept farmhouse in beautiful location, serving super food.

Glass House ££ *Rydal Road; tel: 01539 432137; www.theglasshouserestaurant. co.uk.* Stylish décor and imaginative modern cooking in a working 16th-century mill, with glass-blowing in the studio next door.

Zeffirelli's £ *Compston Road; tel: 01539 433845.* Enterprising combination of wholefood pizzeria and daytime café in shopping and cinema complex.

BORROWDALE***

🛈 **Tourist Information** *Seatoller Barn; tel: 01768 777294; seatollertic@lake-district.gov.uk. National Park exhibition in a converted barn.*

Rugged Borrowdale, with its volcanic crags, waterfalls and lush vegetation, is genuinely spectacular. One of the most scenic stretches lies near the picturesquely bridged hamlet of Grange, where the valley sides constrict to form the awesome 'Jaws of Borrowdale'. Besides lovely views of Derwentwater (best seen from Castle Crag), Borrowdale's points of interest include the **Bowder Stone****, a 2000-ton, delicately poised glacial erratic, and the **Lodore Falls****, a 100-ft cascade. The typical stone villages of Rosthwaite and Seatoller lie on the main road; side trips lead to the remote but much-visited hamlet of **Watendlath*** (National Trust) and **Seathwaite**, England's wettest valley, starting point for walks to Scafell and Great Gable.

Right
Borrowdale

Accommodation and food in and around Borrowdale

Seatoller House £ *Seatoller; tel: 01768 777218; fax: 01768 777189; enquiries@seatollerhouse.co.uk; www.seatollerhouse.co.uk.* Welcoming, friendly guesthouse popular with outdoor types. Hearty suppers served house-party style.

Borrowdale Gates ££ *Grange-in-Borrowdale; tel: 01768 777204; fax: 01768 777254; hotel@borrowdale-gates.com; www.borrowdale-gates.com.* A gorgeous location and excellent cooking in a comfortable Victorian hotel.

BUTTERMERE✤✤✤

Wainwright's ashes

Buttermere church contains a window plaque commemorating the great fell-walker. The fell called 'Haystacks' is visible through the window on a clear day. This is where Alfred Wainwright's ashes were scattered after his death in 1991, in accordance with his final wishes.

A necklace of watery jewels forms one of the Lake District's best-loved scenes between Lorton Vale and the Honister Pass to the northwest of the National Park. With a magnificent setting, amid awesome fells, Buttermere is one of the prettiest of all the lakes. Linked with **Crummock Water**✤✤ and **Loweswater**✤, the three once formed a single lake, but were separated by glacial debris washed from the surrounding hills. The stone village of Buttermere makes a popular starting point for family walks; easy footpaths fringe the waterline. **Scale Force**✤ near Crummock Water is the Lake District's highest waterfall, plunging 120ft in a single drop. Loweswater lies in quieter, gentler scenery.

Accommodation and food in and around Buttermere

Bridge Hotel ££ *Buttermere; tel: 01768 770252, fax: 01768 770215.* Recently refurbished, this popular inn near the shores of Buttermere provides elegant accommodation and filling food for walkers.

Yew Tree Country Restaurant ££ *Seatoller; tel: 01768 777634; www.borrowdale.com/yew-tree.htm.* Interesting fare served in a couple of old miners' cottages at the foot of the Honister Pass.

COCKERMOUTH✤✤

ℹ **Tourist Information** The Town Hall; tel: 01900 822634.

🏠 **Wordsworth House** ££ Main Street; tel: 01900 824805. Open Apr–Oct Mon–Fri 1030–1630 (and Sat June–Aug); NT.

Lakeland Sheep and Wool Centre ££ Off A5086 S of town; tel: 01900 822673. Show times Mar–Oct 1030, 1200, 1400, 1530 except Fri–Sat; free access to exhibitions, shops 0930–1730.

Wordsworth was born in 1770 in this lively little market town. **Wordsworth House**✤✤ is a handsome Georgian building on the main street, open to visitors, with an appealing café and garden. A ruined castle stands at the top of the town. On the main Keswick exit road, the **Lakeland Sheep and Wool Centre**✤✤ presents an entertaining sheep show.

Accommodation and food in or near Cockermouth

Quince & Medlar ££ *13 Castlegate, Cockermouth; tel: 01900 823579.* Accomplished vegetarian restaurant with friendly, relaxing service.

New House Farm ££ *Lorton; tel/fax: 01900 85404.* Stylish farm guesthouse in rural location near Cockermouth. Excellent home cooking.

CONISTON WATER**

Tourist Information *Ruskin Avenue; tel: 01539 441533.*

Gondola *££ Coniston Pier; tel: 01539 441288; sailings Mar–Oct; phone for timetable; NT (but fares apply to members as well).*

Ruskin Museum *££ Yewdale Road, Coniston; tel: 01539 441164. Open Apr–mid-Nov daily 1000–1730 (Wed–Sun 1030–1530 in winter).*

This slender strip of water, set among lowish fells, is best seen from the quieter eastern side, or from the restored National Trust steam yacht *Gondola***. To the northwest, the Old Man of Coniston is scarred by the remains of old copper-mine workings and slate quarries. The **Ruskin Museum** in the green-slate village of Coniston has interesting displays. Coniston Water is associated with Donald Campbell's tragic assault on the world water-speed record in 1967. Happier memories are shared by devotees of Arthur Ransome, whose *Swallows and Amazons* stories were set on Coniston and its islands. The Victorian writer, aesthete and philosopher John Ruskin spent his last years in **Brantwood** (*Coniston Water; tel: 01539 441396; www.brantwood.org.uk. Open Mar–Nov daily 1100–1730 (Wed–Sun 1100–1630 in winter); ££*) on the eastern shore. His house is now an interesting museum, with a good café.

ESKDALE❖❖

 **Ravenglass &
Eskdale Railway ££**
*Dalegarth or Ravenglass
stations; tel: 01229 717171;
www.ravenglass-
railway.co.uk. Operates daily
end Mar–Oct 0800–1700
(restricted service in winter);
phone for timetable.*

Eskdale Corn Mill £
*Boot; tel: 01946
723335. Open Apr–Sept.*

**Muncaster Castle,
Gardens and Owl
Centre ££** *Ravenglass; tel:
01229 717614;
www.muncaster.co.uk. Open
Mar–Oct Sun–Fri
1200–1700 (gardens and
owl centre all year daily
1030–1800); owl shows at
1430 Mar–Oct (weather
permitting).*

From the top of Hardknott Pass, the vale of Eskdale stretches west, its
U-shaped sides smoothed by ancient glaciers and its surface
embroidered with a tracery of stone walls. Small hamlets and scattered
farms stud the landscape of grazing land, pines and rhododendrons.
The valley road follows the River Esk, joined near the pretty village
of Boot by the miniature **Ravenglass & Eskdale Railway❖❖**
(affectionately known as La'al Ratty). Local sights include a couple of
old corn mills restored to working order and some minor Roman
remains (a fort at the top of the pass and a bath-house in Ravenglass).
Muncaster Castle❖❖❖ is the best destination for a family day out, with
its entertaining owl centre.

GRASMERE AND RYDAL**

❶ Tourist Information *Red Bank Road, Grasmere; tel: 01539 435235.*

❶ Dove Cottage and Wordsworth Museum ££ *Grasmere; tel: 01539 435544; www.wordsworth.org.uk. Open daily 0930–1730 (except Jan); discount scheme with Rydal Mount and Wordsworth House in Cockermouth.*

Rydal Mount ££ *Rydal; tel: 01539 433002. Open daily 0930–1700 (1600 in winter).*

The glorious countryside around here inspired the Lake poets. The Wordsworths lived first at **Dove Cottage**** in postcard-pretty Grasmere from 1799–1808, then in **Rydal Mount****, until William's death in 1850. Both houses are now museums, invaded by admirers from all over the world. Sarah Nelson's gingerbread shop near Grasmere's St Oswald's Church (Wordworth's last resting place), is an obligatory stop. Each year, Grasmere holds a traditional rush-bearing ceremony, and a festival of traditional Lakeland sports. Fairfield, Hart Crag and Loughrigg Fell provide some enjoyable walks away from the crowds.

Accommodation near Rydal

White Moss House £££ *Rydal Water; tel: 01539 435295; fax: 01539 435516; sue@whitemoss.com; www.whitemoss.com.* Splendid cooking in a delightful small hotel with Wordsworthian associations.

HAWKSHEAD**

❶ Tourist Information *Main Car Park; tel: 01539 436525; hawksheadtic@lake-district.gov.uk.*

❶ Hill Top ££ *Near Sawrey; tel: 01539 436269; www.nationaltrust.org.uk. Open Apr–Oct Sat–Wed; numbers limited to 800 visitors per day; NT.*

Beatrix Potter Gallery ££ *Main Street; tel: 01539 436355; www.nationaltrust.org.uk. Open Apr–Oct Sun–Thu 1030–1630; timed tickets at busy periods; NT.*

Old Grammar School £ *Tel: 01539 436735. Open Easter–Oct Mon–Sat and Sun pm.*

This showcase village, where Wordsworth went to school, is devoted to the memory of children's author Beatrix Potter, who lived in the neighbouring village of Near Sawrey on the shores of **Esthwaite Water***. **Hill Top****, her quaint 17th-century farmhouse home, is one of the National Trust's most popular tourist attractions. Her exquisite animal illustrations are on display in a timbered house on Hawkshead's main street (no cars in village centre). Restored Tudor buildings line other cobbled streets and squares. A short drive north of Hawkshead takes you to the beauty spot of **Tarn Hows****.

Accommodation in Hawkshead

Queen's Head ££ *Main Street; tel: 01539 436271, fax: 01539 436722; www.queensheadhotel.com.* Masses of character and good cooking in this fine 16th-century inn. Showpiece surroundings. Comfortable bedrooms.

KESWICK AND DERWENT WATER✧✧✧

ℹ Tourist Information *Moot Hall, Market Square; tel: 01768 772645; keswicktic@lake-district.gov.uk.*

🏛 Cumberland Pencil Museum ££ *Southey Works; tel: 01768 773626; www.pencils.co.uk. Open daily 0930–1600 (sometimes longer hours in high season).*

Keswick Museum and Art Gallery £ *Fitzpark, Station Road; tel: 01768 773263; www.allerdale.gov.uk. Open Apr–Oct daily 1000–1600.*

🎭 Theatre by the Lake *Lakeside; tel: 01768 774411; www.theatrebythelake.com. Repertory productions Mon–Sat June–Sept; open all year for events and exhibitions.*

🛍 George Fisher *2 Borrowdale Road; tel: 01768 772178; www.georgefisher.co.uk. Open Mon–Sat 0900–1730, Sun 1030–1630. This long-established shop has a tremendous range of specialist outdoor equipment, a handsome façade and an excellent teashop.*

Keswick, on Derwent Water, is the main centre for the Northern Lakes, ideal for exploring Borrowdale or the smooth slatey fells of Skiddaw and Blencathra. It is an excellent place to look for outdoor gear. A mostly Victorian town of grey slate, it prospered on textiles and leatherworking, then on local graphite deposits. The Derwent pencil factory houses an entertaining **Pencil Museum✧✧**. The **Keswick Museum✧** has a varied collection of Victorian memorabilia. Northeast of the town, the neolithic **Castlerigg Stone Circle✧** stands etched against a backdrop of distant fells. Keswick's main attraction, **Derwent Water✧✧✧**, is picturesque from any direction, from Friar's Crag and Walla Crag to Castlerigg Fell. The Keswick Launch *(www.keswick-launch.co.uk)* chugs round the lake in summer.

Accommodation and food around Derwent Water

Fredericks ££ *1 New Street, Keswick; tel: 01768 775222.* Good-value menus in an attractive old building in the centre of town.

Swinside Lodge ££ *Grange Road, Newlands; tel/fax: 01768 772948; www.swinsidelodge-hotel.co.uk.* Ultra-smart guesthouse with top-notch cooking in secluded and glorious scenery.

Right
Castlerigg Stone Circle

LANGDALE✧✧✧

Britannia Inn £
Elterwater; tel: 01539 437210; fax: 01539 437311; info@britinn.co.uk; www.britinn.co.uk.
Traditional historic inn in picturesque village setting. Small, simple but attractive bedrooms.

Right
Langdale

This gorgeous double valley, ringed by spectacularly glaciated fells with names like Crinkle Crags, Pavey Ark and Pike o'Stickle, attracts serious walkers and climbers. **Great Langdale✧✧✧** has more striking scenery, but **Little Langdale✧✧** is quieter and has some excellent walks. The swan-haunted lake of **Elterwater✧✧** is a pretty spot for a pub lunch or a picnic. From Little Langdale, the steep **Wrynose Pass✧✧** clambers to the Three Shires Stone, an old county-boundary sign marking the meeting point of Cumberland, Westmorland and Lancashire.

WASDALE✧✧✧

The remote location entails a special effort, but Wasdale is definitely on the must-see list. A dead-end single-track road runs along the western shore of England's deepest lake, the mysterious **Wast Water✧✧✧**. From a height of 2000ft, the sheer walls of **The Screes✧✧** plumb Wast Water's icy depths 260ft below. Above the lakehead looms the perfect pyramid of **Great Gable✧✧✧**. The view of the three peaks at the head of the valley (Yewbarrow, Great Gable and Lingmell) is the Lake District National Park's logo. The road ends at a rugged, whitewashed inn, base camp for England's highest mountains. The little church at Wasdale Head commemorates lost climbers.

Accommodation and food around Wasdale

Wasdale Head Inn £££ *Wasdale Head; tel: 01946 726229; fax: 01946 726334; wasdaleheadinn@msn.com; www.wasdale.com.* Rugged walkers' pub in remote but stunning dalehead location. Lots of character and climbing history.

Above
Derwent Water

Suggested tour

Total distance: 104 miles (167km). Add 50 miles (80km) for suggested detours.

Time: 5 hours, but you'll want a walk or lake trip as well.

Links: From Ambleside or Keswick, it's easy to link with Windermere and Ullswater (*see page 58*). Straightforward roads from Cockermouth (A595) or Maryport (A596) lead to Carlisle (*see page 40*). To see more of the National Park, pick one of the minor roads through the Northern Fells to Caldbeck and take the B5299 to Carlisle.

Route: From **AMBLESIDE ❶**, take the scenic but much-used A591 north. By making an early start on **RYDAL** and **GRASMERE ❷**, you will beat some of the Wordsworthian fans. Continue north past the quiet wooded reservoir lake of **Thirlmere**✴ (good views of the Helvellyn range on the right-hand side). The A591 heads straight to

ℹ Tourist Information *Lowes Court Gallery, 12 Main Street, Egremont; tel: 01946 820693.*

ℱ Florence Mine Heritage Centre *£££ On A595 just W of Egremont; tel: 01946 820683; www.florencemine.com. Open Apr–Oct; pit tours 1100 weekends; visitor centre open Mon–Fri 0900–1600 (1000–1600 at weekends).*

☻ Kirkstone Galleries *Skelwith Bridge; tel: 01539 434002; www.kirkstone-galleries.com. Open Apr–Oct daily 1000–1800, Nov–Mar 1000–1700.*

Cumbrian sports

The traditional sport of Cumberland wrestling can be seen in the Lakes during summer, especially at gatherings like the August Grasmere Sports. The opponents try to topple each other over by a skilful application of strength and balance. Another popular pastime is fell running, which must count as one of the most masochistic pursuits ever devised.

KESWICK ❸ ; a slightly longer dogleg via the B5322 takes you along a very pretty road past white farms and green fells. Turn off on a minor gated road through **St John's in the Vale**∗∗, which has a beautiful, simple church in a wonderful setting. Take the A66 into Keswick, then follow the B5289 south through the romantic scenery of BORROWDALE ❹ .

Detours: Take a left-hand turning 2 miles south of Keswick up the **Watendlath**∗∗ road. Pause at Ashness Bridge for a fine view of Derwent Water, then continue to the exquisite tarnside hamlet at the end of the road (best enjoyed on foot; NT parking charge). At Seatoller, another cul-de-sac leads off the B5289 to **Seathwaite**, England's wettest valley, and the starting point for some excellent walks – try going via Sourmilk Ghyll to **Great Gable**∗∗∗ and through the Styhead Pass to the **Scafell**∗∗∗ range.

From **Seatoller**, the road begins a sharp ascent past old green-slate quarries to the **Honister Pass**∗∗. The road now passes along one of the most scenic routes, past BUTTERMERE ❺ and **Crummock Water**∗∗. A sharp left turn beyond Crummock Water gives you a choice of tracking down **Loweswater**∗ and joining the A5086 beyond Mockerkin, or continuing through the lush landscapes of **Lorton Vale**∗ towards COCKERMOUTH ❻ . Take the A5086 heading south for the mining town of Egremont (visit the restored **Florence Mine**∗∗, the last working iron-ore mine in the area).

Detour: Minor roads left off the A5086 take you to the secretive pine-clad lake of **Ennerdale**∗ – a good place for a quiet walk or picnic. Make for Bowness Point on the northern shore.

From Egremont, join the A595 heading south as far as **Gosforth**∗ (10th-century cross in the churchyard), then turn left for Nether Wasdale and follow the road along **Wast Water**∗∗∗ to WASDALE Head ∗∗∗ ❼ (good place for a picnic). Retrace your steps via Santon Bridge towards ESKDALE ❽ . A brief detour here takes you to **Ravenglass**∗ and **Muncaster Castle**∗∗∗.

Getting out of the car: An enjoyable way of seeing Eskdale is on the narrow-gauge steam **Ravenglass & Eskdale Railway**∗∗, which you can pick up at several points between Ravenglass and Dalegarth.

From Eskdale, the road climbs increasingly steeply to the top of Hardknott Pass beside Harter Fell. Stop at the top of the pass for a panoramic backward glance at Eskdale, and the clearly visible remains of the **Roman fort**∗ of *Mediobogdum* to the left of the road. On a clear day you can see as far as the Isle of Man. Continue over the pass (*caution:* it is a very steep descent – give way to oncoming traffic, which will be in first gear round the 1-in-3 bends), and wind down to Cockley Beck and Wrynose Bottom, where mountain streams hurtle over glacial boulders.

ℹ Tourist Information
Coronation Hall, County Square, Ulverston; tel: 01229 587120 or Forum 28, Duke Street, Barrow-in-Furness; tel: 01229 894784 or Maryport Maritime Museum, 1 Senhouse Street, Maryport; tel: 01900 813738.

🏛 Senhouse Roman Museum £ *The Battery, Sea Brows; tel: 01900 816168; www.senhousemuseum.co.uk. Open July–Oct daily 1000–1700, Apr–June, Tue–Thu and Sun, weekends only in winter.*

Laurel and Hardy Museum £ *4c Upper Brook Street, Ulverston; tel: 01229 582292. Open Feb–Dec daily 1030–1630.*

Furness Abbey ££ *Near Dalton, Barrow-in-Furness; tel: 01229 823420. Open Apr–Sept daily 1000–1800, Oct 1000–1700, Nov–Mar Wed–Sun 1000–1600.*

Dock Museum *North Road, Barrow-in-Furness; tel: 01229 894444; www.dockmuseum.org.uk. Open Apr–Oct Tue–Fri 1000–1700 (Wed–Fri 1030–1600 in winter), Sat–Sun 1100–1700 (1130–1630 in winter).*

Detour: For an enjoyable variant (or to avoid Hardknott in bad weather), take the Dunnerdale triangle: follow signs for Ulpha southeast from Eskdale Green, then turn northeast along the **Duddon Valley✦✦** to Cockley Beck. This road leads through gorgeous open moorland scenery. There are good walks and picnic spots at Devoke Water and Birks Bridge.

Wrynose Pass✦✦ is slightly less high and steep than Hardknott, but still very spectacular. Turn left at **Little LANGDALE✦✦ ❾** and follow the loop past Blea Tarn (good walk) through **Great Langdale✦✦✦** and **Elterwater✦✦**. Pause at Skelwith Bridge to see the **Kirkstone Galleries✦** (stylish green-slate crafts showroom; good coffee shop). Return to Ambleside on the A593.

Also worth exploring: The West Cumbrian coast has limited appeal compared with the National Park, but **Maryport✦** has a charmingly revitalised waterfront, and the **Senhouse Roman Museum✦✦** on its outskirts.

The southern peninsulas of Cumbria are excluded from the National Park, but they offer some interesting sightseeing. **Ulverston✦** has a delightful historic centre and an extraordinary collection of Laurel and Hardy memorabilia. The former shipbuilding town of **Barrow-in-Furness✦✦** has well-preserved abbey ruins on its outskirts and a fascinating **Dock Museum✦✦**.

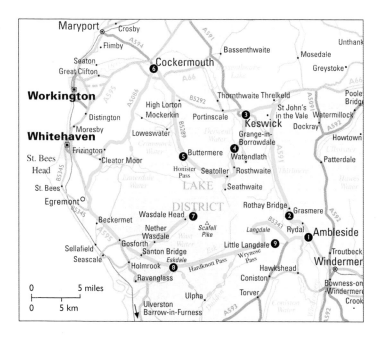

Yorkshire Moors

Ratings

Churches and abbeys	●●●●●
Heritage	●●●●●
Outdoor activities	●●●●●
Scenery	●●●●●
Archaeology	●●●●○
Beaches	●●●●○
Castles	●●●●○
Children	●●●●○

This area of Yorkshire has a National Park, several slabs of Heritage Coast, York (one of Britain's most enjoyable cathedral cities), a host of abbeys, castles, stately homes and picturesque stone villages, and one of England's longest and best 'nostalgia' rail routes. The emerald valleys are called 'dales', but are different from (and less visited than) the officially designated 'Dales' of Yorkshire's other National Park. Consider tackling the area as two separate trips, one concentrating on the coast and wolds, the other exploring the National Park interior. The best inland scenery is accessible only via a maze of minor roads through sheep-strewn pastureland. Just about any lane reveals an unexpected view or point of interest: clouds of spring daffodils; an ancient stone cross; or the kilns and trackbeds of Rosedale's old ironstone industry. Some of the roads are hair-raisingly steep.

CASTLE HOWARD✧✧✧

Castle Howard £££
Malton; tel: 01653 648444;
www.castlehoward.co.uk.
Open Apr–Oct daily 1100–1700, gardens from 1000.

The façade of this most palatial of country houses, best known from the TV serialisation of *Brideshead Revisited*, represents the summit of Sir John Vanbrugh's achievement. His ambitious design of 1699 dominates the formal grounds and ornamental lake. The **Great Hall**✧✧ is topped by a gilded dome, and the **Long Gallery**✧ is hung with family portraits. Other highlights are the **Temple of the Four Winds**✧, designed in 1724, the chapel✧ and the **Costume Galleries**✧.

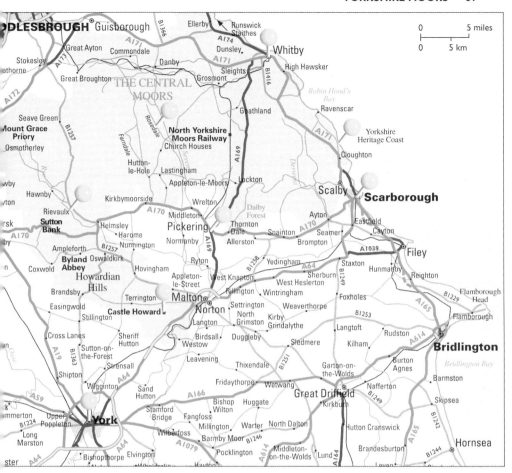

THE CENTRAL MOORS❖❖❖

ℹ️ **Tourist Information** Old Town Hall, Market Place, Helmsley; tel: 01439 770173; helmsley@ytbtic.co.uk or Moors Centre, Lodge Lane, Danby; tel: 01287 660654; moorscentre@ytbtic.co.uk.

England's largest expanse of heather moorland is sparsely populated, but shows many signs of earlier occupation: prehistoric burial mounds, Roman roads, old mine-workings and medieval stone crosses. The long-distance footpath of the Cleveland Way crosses the southern sector of the National Park. The most rewarding of the lush dales for motorists are **Rosedale**❖❖, **Farndale**❖❖, **Ryedale**❖❖ and **Eskdale**❖❖. Farndale is famous for its wild daffodils in spring, protected in a 2000-acre nature reserve (best seen near Low Mill). Rosedale's scenery is steeper and more austere. The Stape–Goathland road is one of the wildest moorland routes, leading past the Roman earthwork training grounds of the Cawthorn Camps to a clearly preserved mile-long trackway known as Wade's Causeway or the **Wheeldale Moor Roman Road**❖. To see it, you must take to your feet.

Accommodation and food on the Central Moors

Mallyan Spout ££ *The Common, Goathland; tel: 01947 896486; fax: 01947 896327; mallyan@ukgateway.net. Heartbeat* fans will recognise the location, but this well-loved hotel was dispensing hospitality long before the TV series existed, from one of the National Park's most glorious moorland villages.

White Horse Farm ££ *Rosedale Abbey; tel: 01751 417239; fax: 01751 417781; sales@whitehorsefarmhotel.co.uk.* Solid, traditional inn with a marvellous location overlooking some of the best scenery in the North York Moors. Dog owners get a special welcome.

PICKERING*

ⓘ Tourist Information *The Ropery; tel: 01751 473791.*

Attractive Pickering is something of a 'gateway', overlooking the broad clay Vale of Pickering, which separates the wolds from the moors. A ruined castle guards the town, and the church of St Peter and St Paul contains some intriguing 15th-century frescos. Pickering's main attraction is the splendid **North Yorkshire Moors Railway**** (Moorsrail), built by Stephenson in 1835 (*daily services Apr–Oct; tel: 01751 472508*).

RIEVAULX ABBEY***

ⓘ Rievaulx Abbey ££ *2 miles NW of Helmsley; tel: 01439 798228; open Apr–Sept daily 1000–1800 (0930–1800 in July–Aug, earlier off season); visitor centre; EH.*

Rievaulx Terrace and temples ££ *Off B1257; tel: 01439 798340; www.nationaltrust.org.uk. Open Apr–Oct daily 1030–1800 (dusk if earlier); NT.*

These evocative monastic ruins stand serenely in the wooded valley of the River Rye. Founded in 1131, Rievaulx was one of the earliest and grandest Cistercian foundations in England, and soon became one of the wealthiest, by exploiting local ironstone deposits and farming sheep. The abbey's prime splendour is the choir, dating from about 1225. **Rievaulx Terrace**, to the east, gives an excellent overview.

Right
Rievaulx Abbey

Opposite
Whitby harbour

SCARBOROUGH✢✢

ⓘ Tourist Information *Pavilion House, Valley Bridge Road; tel: 01723 373333.*

🏛 Scarborough Art Gallery ££ *The Crescent; tel: 01723 374753. Open June–Sept Tue–Sun 1000–1700 (reduced times in winter). Seascapes and views in an Italianate villa. Joint admission to two local museums.*

A civilised seaside town, with a Georgian conservation area and elegant Regency terraces, Scarborough lies around two fine sandy bays to either side of a castle-crowned headland. The town pioneered sea-bathing as early as 1660, and is still a popular resort. Its varied amenities include a lively theatre. The castle hill gives splendid views.

Accommodation and food in Scarborough

Interludes £ *32 Princess Street; tel: 01723 360513; fax: 01723 368597; interludes@ntlworld.com; www.interludeshotel.co.uk.* Attractively renovated townhouse B&B in conservation area near harbour. Theatre breaks.

Lanterna ££ *33 Queen Street; tel/fax: 01723 363616.* Family-run restaurant serving well-prepared Italian fish dishes.

WHITBY✢✢

ⓘ Tourist Information *Langbourne Road; tel: 01947 602674.*

🏛 Whitby Abbey ££ *East Cliff; tel: 01947 603568. Open Apr–Sept daily 1000–1800, Oct 1000–1700, Nov–Mar 1000–1600; EH.*

Captain Cook Memorial Museum ££ *Grape Lane; tel: 01947 601900; www.cookmuseumwhitby. co.uk. Open Easter–Oct daily 0945–1700. The great explorer stayed in this house while apprenticed to John Walker, a Quaker ship-owner.*

Whitby Museum £ *Pannett Park; tel: 01947 602908; www.durain.demon. co.uk. Open May–Sept Mon–Sat 0930–1730, Sun 1400–1700 (closed Mon, Tue pm and Sun am in winter).*

Whitby Abbey✢✢ and St Mary's Church✢ high on the East Cliff guard an attractive huddle of pastel-washed houses and tiny streets around the mouth of the River Esk. Whitby is a popular tourist destination, but remains a busy net-strewn fishing port. Its sea-faring traditions are remembered in several interesting museums and a curious Norwegian whalebone arch, which overlooks the harbour from the West Cliff. The abbey was founded in 657, but the present atmospheric ruins date mainly from the 13th century. A carved cross commemorates its best-known monk, Caedmon, author of the earliest surviving English poem, the *Song of Creation*. Climb the 199 steps from the old town to enjoy the magnificent views.

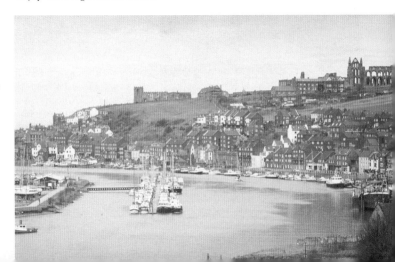

YORK✧✧✧

ⓘ Tourist Information
Exhibition Square; tel: 01904 621756 or Railway Station, Station Road.

② York Minster ££
Deangate; tel: 01904 557216; www.yorkminster.org. Open daily 0900–1830 (2030 June–Sept, 1800 Oct–Mar) (closed for sightseeing Sun am and during services); donation requested; charges for museum, treasury, chapterhouse, crypt and tower.

York Castle Museum
££ Tower Street; tel: 01904 653611; www.york.gov.uk. Open daily 0930–1700 (1630 in winter).

Jorvik – the Viking City
£££ Coppergate; tel: 01904 543403; www.vikingjorvik.com. Open Apr–Oct daily 0900–1730, Nov–Mar daily 1000–1630. A 'time car' whizzes visitors through a reconstructed riverside Viking village.

Right
York Minster

York's significance far outweighs its status as a county town. Two thousand years of history have turned it into something of an open-air museum, and its quaint, traffic-free streets, including Saxon Whip-ma-whop-ma-gate, recall the past at every turn. The Romans founded the city in AD 71, naming it *Eboracum* (the Archbishop of York still adds 'Ebor' to his official signature). The Vikings called the thriving inland port *Jorvik*, and made it the foremost city of the Danelaw. Fortified with walls and castles by the Normans, York continued to prosper in medieval times on the back of its wool trade. Now, chocolate and tourism are the town's major concerns.

At **York Castle**✧✧, little survives of the two original fortresses built by the Normans in York except a keep, known as **Clifford's Tower**✧. Immediately beside it stands the **Castle Museum**✧✧, a splendidly eclectic social history museum. England's best-preserved **city walls**✧✧ ramble over 3 miles around the centre, making a popular promenade. The four '**bars**' or gatehouses, are still intact.

The **Shambles**✧✧, a narrow thoroughfare of overhanging, half-timbered houses, typifies York's medieval charm. **York Minster**✧✧✧, which took two centuries to build, is the largest Gothic church in northern Europe. The present structure was begun in 1220, and additions continued until the central tower was completed in 1470. The building has a stupendous array of medieval glass.

Accommodation and food in York

Easton's £ *90 Bishopthorpe Road; tel: 01904 626646; fax: 01904 626165.* Elegant, comfortable B&B a short stroll from the city walls.

Middlethorpe Hall £££ *Bishopthorpe Road; tel: 01904 641241; fax: 01904 620176; info@middlethorpe.com; www.middlethorpe.com.* Immaculately restored historic country house hotel near the racecourse. An expensive but enjoyable treat. Renowned restaurant.

Mount Royale Hotel ££ *The Mount; tel: 01904 628856; fax: 01904 611171; info@mountroyale.co.uk; www.mountroyale.co.uk.* Good service and comfortable rooms at this long-established family-run hotel.

Melton's ££ *7 Scarcroft Road; tel: 01904 634341; greatfood@meltonsrestaurant.co.uk; www.meltonsrestaurant.co.uk.* Informal, unpretentious restaurant serving interesting, monthly-changing menus at reasonable prices.

The Treasurer's House £ *Minster Yard; tel: 01904 624247.* Home baking in atmospheric medieval National Trust tearooms right opposite the Minster.

CONSTANTINE THE GREAT
A.D. 274–337
PROCLAIMED ROMAN EMPEROR
AT YORK A.D. 306

YORKSHIRE HERITAGE COAST✦✦✦

ℹ️ Tourist Information *John Street, Filey; tel: 01723 518000.*

🏛️ Filey Museum £ *8–10 Queen Street; tel: 01723 515013. Open Apr–Oct Sun–Fri 1100–1400, Sat 1400–1700, July–Aug Tue 1900–2100 (ghostwalk).*

Bempton Cliffs ££ *Bempton; tel: 01262 851179. Open Mar–Nov 1000–1700, Dec–Feb weekends only 0930–1600, parking charge (free for RSPB members). Boat trips from Flamborough and Bridlington.*

North of Bridlington, most of Yorkshire's seaside is Heritage Coast. In the south, at **Flamborough Head**✦✦, resilient chalk has been gnawed by the waves into caves and stacks. The 400-ft white cliffs at **Bempton**✦✦ are the highest, and provide a home for Britain's biggest colony of seabirds. At the well-kept family resort of **Filey**✦, Filey Brigg makes a natural fishing pier of rocks and pools. North of Scarborough, the National Park extends to the coast, where the cliffs are of great geological interest: alum, iron ore, jet and potash. The picturesque, red-tiled fishing villages of **Robin Hood's Bay**✦✦ and **Staithes**✦ are popular tourist destinations.

Accommodation and food on or near the Heritage Coast

Manor House £ *Tower Street, Flamborough; tel/fax: 01262 850943; gm@flamboroughmanor.co.uk; www.flamboroughmanor.co.uk.* Lovely Georgian house near spectacular stretch of coast. Excellent cooking.

Seabirds £ *Tower Street, Flamborough; tel: 01262 850242.* Quaint old pub in charming village; lots of fresh fish.

Suggested tour

Eden Camp ££
*Malton; tel: 01653
697777;
www.edencamp.co.uk. Open
daily 1000–1700.*

Mount Grace Priory ££
*On A19 near Osmotherley;
tel: 01609 883494. Open
Apr–Sept daily 1000–1800,
Oct 1000–1700, Nov–Mar
Wed–Sun 1000–1600; EH.*

Nunnington Hall ££
*Nunnington; tel: 01439
748283. Open Apr–Oct
Wed–Sun 1330–1630
(Tue–Sun June–Aug, closes
1700); NT.*

**Ryedale Folk Museum
££** *Hutton-le-Hole; tel:
01751 417367. Open
Mar–Oct daily 1000–1730.
Open-air collection of
reconstructed period
houses; rural crafts and
industries.*

**World of James
Herriott ££** *23 Kirkgate,
Thirsk; tel: 01845 524234;
www.worldofjamesherriott.
org.uk. Open Apr–Oct
1000–1800, Nov–Mar
1000–1700.*

Shandy Hall ££ *Coxwold;
tel: 01347 868465; shandy-
hall.org.uk. Open May–Sept
Wed 1400–1630, Sun
1430– 1630; gardens
May–Sept Sun–Fri
1100–1630.*

Byland Abbey £ *2 miles S
of A170 near Coxwold; tel:
01347 868614. Open
Apr–Sept daily 1000–1800,
Oct 1000–1700 (closed
lunchtime); EH.*

Opposite
Robin Hood's Bay

Total distance: 130 miles (209km) for Moors route; 140 miles (225km) for Wolds and coast route. Add 16 miles (26km) for the Dalby Forest drive or the alternative route from Osmotherley.

Time: 5 hours. Make time also for a walk.

Links: Best connections for the Yorkshire Dales (*see page 90*) are from York to Harrogate (via A59), or Thirsk to Ripon (A61). From the A19, the A684 gives easy access to the A1 and the North Pennines (*see page 50*) from Scotch Corner.

Moors route: From **YORK ❶**, take the A64 north, skirting the Howardian Hills and following signs for **CASTLE HOWARD ❷** off to the left. Continue towards **Malton***, liveliest on market days (Tues, Fri for livestock; Sat for general produce). The **Eden Camp*** on its northeast side is a wartime experience attraction based in a former prisoner-of-war camp. Follow the A169 for **PICKERING ❸**, where a tantalising choice of moorland routes lies before you.

Detour: Two miles east of Pickering, go north from **Thornton Dale***, to a fine **forest drive**** (toll road), which leads through the Dalby Forest towards Scarborough. Intriguing natural features include the Bridestones (eroded sandstone outcrops) and the Forge Valley (a glacial gorge). Information point at Low Dalby.

From Pickering, head west along the A170 towards Helmsley and Thirsk, turning right at Wrelton, and following signs through **Lastingham*** to **Hutton-le-Hole****, where **Ryedale Folk Museum**** is a popular draw. In spring, **Farndale**** displays a mass of wild daffodils. Return towards **Rosedale**** through Church Houses, and continue through the heart of **THE CENTRAL MOORS ❹** towards **Danby**** (Moors Centre). Head west through minor roads signed Commondale. This scenic road leads over the heather-clad sandstone Cleveland Hills, where many prehistoric burial chambers and tumuli have been found. From **Great Ayton***, where James (Captain) Cook spent much of his boyhood, pick up the main A172 and head south to join the A19 near the well-preserved 14th-century ruins of **Mount Grace Priory**** (strict Carthusian order). To see another segment of the National Park, turn left at Osmotherley and take the pretty Ryedale road via Hawnby to **RIEVAULX ABBEY ❺**. From **Helmsley***, one of the main centres for the National Park, follow signs southeast via Harome to **Nunnington Hall****, a charming 16th- and 17th-century house. Continue south across the rolling Howardian Hills via the attractive historic villages of **Hovingham*** and **Sheriff Hutton*** back to York.

Detour: Continue south from Osmotherley along the A19 to the coaching town of **Thirsk***, which has close associations with the author James Herriott (real name Alf Wight). The house where the

country vet was born is open to visitors. Take the A170 east. After 5 miles, a 1-in-4 gradient at a sharp bend in the road will take you to **Sutton Bank***, a panoramic view-point with a white horse carved near by. A short distance south of the road lies pretty **Coxwold***. The village's rambling old **Shandy Hall*** was once the home of Coxwold's curate Laurence Sterne (1713–68), better known as the author of *Tristram Shandy*. A mile northeast stands **Byland Abbey***, a Cistercian foundation dating from 1177.

Wolds and coast route: Take the A166 east of York past the battleground of Stamford Bridge, crossing the **Yorkshire Wolds** and picking up the **HERITAGE COAST** ❻ near Bridlington. Head north on the A165 via Filey and **SCARBOROUGH** ❼, then follow the minor coastal route via Ravenscar and **Robin Hood's Bay** to **WHITBY** ❽. Continue on the A174 to **Runswick*** and **Staithes****. Return to York across the heart of the Moors, via Wheeldale or Rosedale (make for Egton Bridge or Danby).

North Yorkshire Moors Railway £££
Pickering Station; tel: 01751 472508;
www.nymr.demon.co.uk.
Daily services Apr–Oct (weekends only Nov–Dec) and additional special events.

Above
Harbour at Scarborough

Getting out of the car: One of the best non-car excursions in this area is a trip on the **North Yorkshire Moors Railway****. Steam trains clamber through 18 miles of toughly engineered but visually glorious moorland track from Pickering to Grosmont. Intermediate stations make excellent starting points for walks.

Accommodation and food on the route

Lastingham Grange £ *Lastingham; tel: 01751 417345; fax: 01751 417358; www.lastinghamgrange.com.* Peaceful, traditional country house hotel in showcase village.

Manor House Farm £ *Ingleby Greenhow, Great Ayton; tel: 01642 722384; mbloom@globalnet.co.uk.* Tranquil setting for a friendly guesthouse overlooking Captain Cook's monument. Good home cooking.

Chapters £ *27 High Street, Stokesley; tel: 01642 711888; fax: 01642 713387.* Chic but friendly bistro-with-rooms in bustling market town.

Ryedale Country Lodge £ *Nunnington; tel: 01439 748246; fax: 01439 748346; info@ryedalecountrylodge.com.* Warm colours and antiques create a cosy atmosphere in this stylish but informal country home. Enjoyable dinner menus.

Ranger's House £ *Sheriff Hutton; tel/fax: 01347 878397.* Charming, slightly idiosyncratic country house in a quiet parkland setting. Excellent home cooking.

Fauconberg Arms £ *Main Street, Coxwold; tel: 01347 868214; info@fauconbergarms.co.uk; www.fauconbergarms.co.uk.* Fine old inn in picturesque village. Imaginative food and comfortable rooms.

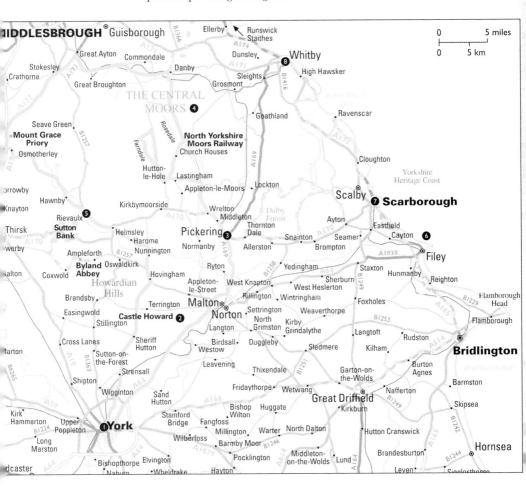

Yorkshire Dales

Ratings

Churches and abbeys	●●●●●
Landscape	●●●●●
Walking	●●●●●
Castles	●●●●○
Country markets	●●●●○
Geology	●●●●○
Towns and villages	●●●●○
Eating out	●●●○○

The beautiful limestone uplands of the Yorkshire Dales, within easy reach of Manchester and Leeds, feel surprisingly peaceful, even lonely in places. There are over twenty identifiable 'dales', some very familiar and well publicised, others obscure and remote. Three hundred million years ago, this land-locked region lay submerged under a tropical sea. Glaciers carved its steep-sided gorges and valleys; forests flourished and died. Today, the Dales consist of placid sheep-farming country, interspersed with patches of barren moorland, limestone pavement, and brooding hills – the Three Peaks (Ingleborough, Pen-y-Ghent and Whernside) rise to 2 300ft. Other elemental highlights are limestone caves, waterfalls and the extraordinary geological phenomena of Malhamdale. The ultra-civilised spa of Harrogate has elegant shops, stately architecture and gardens, while historic Ripon and Richmond have castles and cathedrals to explore. There are grand monastic ruins at Bolton, Jervaulx and Fountains, and many Dales towns hold traditional open-air country markets.

FOUNTAINS ABBEY✦✦✦

Fountains Abbey and Studley Royal Water Gardens ££ *Off B6265; tel: 01765 608888; www.fountainsabbey.org.uk. Open daily 1000–1800 (1600 or dusk Oct–Mar); abbey and garden tours in summer; visitor centre; NT.*

One of England's most romantic ruins, this ruined Cistercian monastery enjoys a wonderful setting in the wooded valley of the River Skell. Founded in 1132 by a dissident group of Benedictines, it grew to be the wealthiest abbey in the country. The church is well preserved, particularly the ornate Chapel of the Nine Altars at the east end. The undercroft was used to store fleeces, which the monks sold to Italian merchants. Surrounding the abbey are the 17th-century **Fountains Hall✦**, and the intricate 18th-century water gardens of **Studley Royal✦✦**. This combination of Elizabethan mansion and Georgian water garden simply enhances the magic of the abbey, with lakes, temples and cascades drawing the eye, and a herd of over 500 deer. The parkland approach provides a beautiful walk to the abbey, floodlit in summer. The complex is now a World Heritage Site.

Opposite
Fountains Abbey

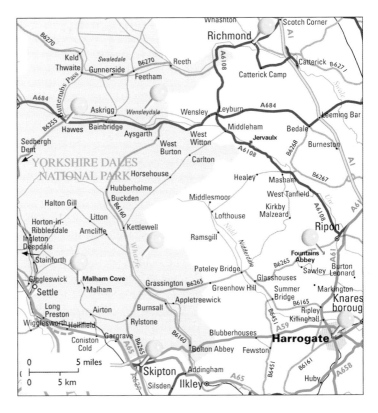

HARROGATE✦✦✦ AND KNARESBOROUGH✦✦

ⓘ Tourist Information *Royal Baths Assembly Rooms, Crescent Road, Harrogate; tel: 01423 537300; or 9 Castle Court, Market Place, Knaresborough; tel: 01423 866886.*

ⓗ Royal Pump Room Museum £ *Crown Place, Harrogate; tel: 01423 556188; www. harrogate.gov.uk/museums. Open Mon–Sat 1000–1700, Sun 1400–1700 (closes 1600 in winter).*

Harlow Carr Botanical Gardens ££ *Crag Lane, off B6162; tel: 01423 565418; open daily 0930–1800 (1700 or dusk in winter); RHS.*

Harrogate became a popular spa in the late 19th century; its palatial formal Royal Assembly Rooms, Opera House, Royal Hall and grand hotels date mainly from this period. A **museum**✦ records the history of the spa and its repulsive medicinal waters. Well-heeled Harrogate is strong on tearooms and toffee, and renowned for its specialist shops and beautiful gardens. **Harlow Carr Botanical Gardens**✦✦✦ to the southwest, are the Northern Horticultural Society's superbly planted headquarters. Just 3 miles east of Harrogate, the historic town of Knaresborough has a dramatic setting over the Nidd gorge, its battered Norman castle poised on the cliff edge. Mother Shipton's Cave and the Petrifying Well, to the south of town, are popular tourist attractions.

Accommodation and food in Harrogate

Balmoral £££ *Franklin Mount; tel: 01423 508208; fax: 01423 530652; info@balmoralhotel.co.uk; www.balmoralhotel.com.* Pleasingly eccentric mock-Tudor hotel near conference centre. Imaginative cooking.

Drum & Monkey ££ *5 Montpellier Gardens; tel: 01423 502650.* Acclaimed central restaurant offering accomplished seafood cooking.

Bettys £ *1 Parliament Street; tel: 01423 502746; www. bettysandtaylors.co.uk.* This scrumptious cake shop is the original of a small chain (also in York) founded by a Swiss confectioner in 1919. Light meals too.

Below
Harrogate gardens

HAWES**

Wensleydale Cheese Visitor Centre £ *Gayle Lane; tel: 01969 667664. Open Apr–Oct Mon–Sat 0930–1700, Sun 1000–1630; cheese-making between 1030 and 1530; shop, visitor centre and café.*

Dales Countryside Museum ££ *Station Yard; tel: 01969 667450. Open daily 1000–1700.*

Simonstone Hall ££ *Tel: 01969 667255; fax: 01969 667741; simonstonehall@demon.co.uk; www.simonstonehall.co.uk. Lavishly furnished country-house hotel offering hearty English cooking.*

This attractive Dales market town at the head of Wensleydale has a **cheese-making factory*** open to visitors, and a **countryside museum****, which acts as a National Park information centre. On Tuesdays, an animated livestock market takes place. Hawes is an excellent touring base, with superb drives and walks on its doorsteps, including the dramatic **Butter Tubs Pass**** to the north, and a wild route to Langstrothdale. **Hardraw Force***, just outside the town, is England's tallest single-drop waterfall (best after rain). You can walk right behind the cascade on a rock ledge.

Right
Hawes steam railway station

MALHAM***

Tourist Information *National Park Centre; tel: 01729 830363.*

A bus route runs along the road near Malham Tarn, so if you time your walk carefully, you needn't retrace your steps.

Few keen walkers, geologists, botanists and birdwatchers will not have heard of Malham, and the *karst* or limestone valley named after it. A well-beaten track from the village leads northwards to **Malham Cove****, where a 300-ft curtain of curved limestone greets onlookers. The black gash running vertically down the rockface marks the site of an ancient waterfall, once higher than Niagara. Above the cove lies an expanse of limestone pavement known as **Malham Lings****, where rare plants grow in the crevices. Further north is **Malham Tarn***, a mountain lake formed over a glacial moraine. **Gordale Scar**** lies northeast of Malham, a deep glacier-cut gorge where a stream leaps from the rock.

RICHMOND✧✧

ℹ **Tourist Information** Friary Gardens, Victoria Road; tel: 01748 850252; richmond@ytbtic.co.uk.

🏰 **Richmond Castle**
££ Tel: 01748 822493. Open Apr–Sept 1000–1800, July–Aug 0930–1900, Oct, Feb 1000–1700, Nov–Mar 1000–1600; EH.

Theatre Royal £ Victoria Road; tel: 01748 823021; www.georgiantheatre.com. Open Easter–Nov. Under restoration – closed for tours until May 2003.

Agreeable Richmond deserves an extra few miles of driving. Its striking **castle✧✧** is perched on a precarious-looking site above the River Swale. It was built soon after the Norman Conquest and has been little altered since. In Richmond's historic centre, many period buildings line the market place, including the unusual church of Holy Trinity (1135), with shops built into it, and the Georgian **Theatre Royal✧**, which dates from 1788.

Right
Richmond covered market

SKIPTON✧✧

ℹ **Tourist Information** 35 Coach Street; tel: 01756 792809.

🚂 **Embsay & Bolton Abbey Steam Railway ££** Embsay station, East Lane; tel: 01756 710614. Ring for timetable.

Skipton means 'sheeptown', an allusion to its farming traditions – its **market✧** (held most days) is one of the best in the Dales. The romantic-looking **castle✧✧** has well-preserved medieval, Tudor and Stuart sections. Conduit Court and its commemorative yew tree are particularly handsome. The church of **Holy Trinity✧** has a bossed 15th-century roof and a fine rood screen. The **Craven Museum✧** is a quirky free assortment of local history. Steam trains run to Bolton Abbey from the nearby station of Embsay.

Skipton Castle ££
Tel: 01756 792442.
Open Mon–Sat 1000–1800,
Sun 1200–1800 (1600 in
winter).

Craven Museum Town
Hall, High Street; tel: 01756
706407. Open Apr–Sept
Mon, Wed, Thur, Fri
1000–1700, Sat
1000–1700, Sun
1400–1700 (restricted hours
in winter).

The Wakeman blows...

Every night at 9pm, Ripon's resident red-coated bugler blows a buffalo horn
in the Market Square. The custom dates from the Middle Ages, when the
Wakeman, or nightwatch, charged an annual toll of 2p per household to
protect local citizens. Elsewhere in the Dales, in Bainbridge, a similar
evening horn was blown to guide travellers through the thick woods in
darkness or bad weather.

WENSLEYDALE***

**Theakston Brewery
££** Masham; tel: 01765
684333. Open for tours
Mar–Oct Mon–Fri am,
weekends and school
holidays in winter; book
ahead.

**Black Sheep Brewery
££** Masham; tel: 01765
689227; visitorcentre@
blacksheep.co.uk;
www.blacksheep.co.uk.
Visitor centre Mar–Dec
Wed–Sat 1100–2300,
Sun–Tue 1100–1700; rest
of year Wed–Sat 1100–
2300, Sun 1100–1700;
'shepherded' tours from
1100 (best to book); shop,
bar and bistro.

Brymor High Jervaulx
Farm, Masham; tel:
01677 460377; open daily
1000–1800. Real dairy ice-
cream parlour.

This broad, pastoral valley, with well-wooded slopes and classic
Pennine villages, is one of the richest of the Dales. Several waterfalls
punctuate the course of the River Ure, particularly at **Aysgarth Falls****.

This area of 'Richmondshire' has castles, Roman remains and abbey
ruins, but the main attraction for many is the TV location Georgian
village of **Askrigg***, which provided a backdrop to *All Creatures Great
and Small*. The village of Wensley has a fine church with a box pew
and rood screen.

Wensleydale sheep, with their long, curly fleeces, are an economic
mainstay. Besides its famous cheese, Wensleydale produces other
consumables – downstream at Masham, Theakstons and the rival
Black Sheep Brewery offer tours with tastings. For some proper dairy
ice cream, visit **Brymor** at High Jervaulx Farm.

Accommodation and food around Wensleydale

Floodlite ££ *7 Silver Street, Masham; tel: 01765 689000.* Simple
surroundings, candlelight and excellent cooking using top-quality
ingredients. Lunch is a bargain.

Wensleydale Heifer ££ *West Witton, Wensleydale; tel: 01969 622322,
fax: 01969 624183; heifer@dael.net.co.uk; www.wensleydaleheifer.co.uk.*
Solid Yorkshire pub in the heart of a popular village. Good food.

Helm ££ *Askrigg; tel/fax: 01969 650443; holiday@helmyorkshire.com;
www.helmyorkshire.com.* Quiet stone-built guesthouse; wonderful views
and interesting food.

Waterford House ££ *Kirkgate, Middleham; tel: 01969 622090; fax:
01969 624020.* Friendly restaurant-with-rooms near village square.
Super cooking in unpretentious French style.

WHARFEDALE✧✧

① Tourist Information
Yorkshire Dales National Park, Hebden Road, Grassington; tel: 01756 752774; grassington@ytbtic.co.uk.

ⓗ Upper Wharfedale Museum £ *The Square, Grassington; no tel available; open Easter–Oct daily 1400–1630; weekends in winter.*

Beautiful **Wharfedale✧✧** is the most accessible dale from industrial Yorkshire. The upper reaches wind through a mix of pasture and evergreen woodlands, past stone barns and sheltered villages. One of the prettiest is **Kettlewell✧**, a popular walking and climbing base. **Hubberholme** lies in the moorland headwaters of Langstrothdale, where the infant Wharfe babbles over limestone ledges beneath 2000-ft summits. Writer J B Priestley is buried in the churchyard. In Lower Wharfedale, **Grassington✧** is a market town with a quaint Georgian centre and a folk museum, and at **Bolton Abbey✧✧** a 12th-century priory makes a tranquil scene amid riverside meadows and waterfalls.

Accommodation and food around Wharfedale

Ashfield House £ *Summers Fold, Grassington; tel/fax: 01756 752584; info@ashfield-house.co.uk; www.ashfieldhouse.co.uk.* Friendly, family-run 17th-century hotel with good home cooking.

The Devonshire Arms £££ *Bolton Abbey; tel: 01756 710441; fax: 01756 710564; www.devonshirehotels.co.uk.* An elegant country-house hotel, with excellent restaurant. Dignified. More affordable meals in the Brasserie.

Below
Bolton Abbey

Suggested tour

Tourist Information *Town Hall, Cheapside, Settle; tel: 01729 825192; or Pen-y-Ghent Café, Horton-in-Ribblesdale; tel: 01729 860333.*

Settle–Carlisle Railway £££ *Settle Station; tel: 08457 484950; www.settle-carlisle-railway.org.uk for times and fares.*

Total distance: 160 miles (256km). The Bolton Abbey detour saves about 27 miles (43km). Add 12 miles (19km) for the Settle detour.

Time: 6 hours.

Links: From Hawes, the A684 through Garsdale leads through to Kendal and Lakeland (*see page 58*). From Harrogate or Ripon, straightforward routes lead to the North York Moors (*see page 80*). A minor road takes you from Swaledale to Barnard Castle, where you can pick up the North Pennines route (*see page 50*).

Route: From **HARROGATE ❶**, take the A59 west via Blubberhouses to the celebrated beauty spot of **Bolton Abbey✦✦**. See the priory ruins (the nave is still used as a parish church), and refuel at The Devonshire Arms.

Detour: A brief drive or walk along the Dales Way footpath north from Bolton Abbey up the B6160 takes you to the spectacular stretch of limestone gorge known as **The Strid✦✦**, where the Wharfe boils through a 12-ft cleft in the rock. Ruined Barden Tower, further north, dates from the 12th century. If you are short of time, continue through Wharfedale via Grassington, picking up the main route again near Kettlewell. The classic village of **Burnsall** is worth a stop. Beyond Grassington, this route takes you past Grass Wood (remains of an ancient forest) and Kilnsey Crag, a dramatic rock overhang.

Continue along the A59 to **SKIPTON ❷**, then take the A65 as far as Coniston Cold before turning right on unclassified roads to **MALHAM ❸**. The full walk taking in all the limestone scenery can take around four hours, but a bus can shorten the return leg. From Malham, head northeast following signs to **Arncliffe✦**, a delightful village in the **Littondale✦✦** valley, once a medieval hunting forest with striking limestone scenery; the River Skirfare vanishes in dry weather. Turn right to meet the B6160 near **Kettlewell✦**. Head upstream through Upper Wharfedale via Buckden to join the A684 near **Aysgarth✦✦**. Take the minor road from the **Falls** west via **Askrigg✦✦** through **WENSLEYDALE ❹**, as far as **HAWES ❺**.

Detour: To explore the quieter western Dales, continue along the A65 from Skipton to the pleasant market town of **Settle✦** (busy on Tuesday). Besides being the gateway to Ribblesdale, Settle is the starting point for the **Settle–Carlisle Railway✦✦✦**, a superb way to see the Western Dales. Turn up the B6479 through Stainforth. **Ribblesdale✦✦** attracts serious hikers, for the challenging Three Peaks Walk, and cavers. The scenery is grand but austere. **Deepdale✦✦** (approached from Ingleton) is even more remote and scenic, with just a few farms dotted about on the awesome whalebacks of Whernside, Gragareth and Baugh Fell. Upstream from Stainforth, Horton-in-

Swaledale Folk Museum £ The Green, Reeth; tel: 01748 884373. Open Easter–Oct daily 1030–1700.

The Violin-making Workshop £ Leyburn Business Park, Harmby Road, Leyburn; tel: 01969 624416. Open Apr–Sept Sun–Fri (daily in Aug; no demonstrations at weekends).

Middleham Castle £ Middleham; tel: 01969 623899. Open Apr–Sept daily 1000–1800, Oct 1000–1700, Nov–Dec 1000–1300, 1400–1600; Jan–Mar Wed–Sun; EH.

Jervaulx Abbey £ Jervaulx; tel: 01677 460226; ruins accessible all year.

Ribblesdale is a walking, climbing and caving base. A mile beyond Selside, turn right on the B6255, then left after 2.5 miles to explore **Dentdale❖❖**, where the Dee races through a fern-lined dell. **Dent❖❖** is a charming village, stone-built with a single cobbled street, set in high, lonely moorland. Rejoin the A684 at Sedbergh and head east again via **Garsdale❖**. Continue via Garsdale to meet up with the main route again at **Hawes**.

Take the **Buttertubs Pass❖❖** road north to **Thwaite**, stopping at **Hardraw Force❖❖** and the mysterious Buttertubs (naturally eroded limestone pits allegedly used by farmers to cool butter on the way to market). Detour briefly to Keld before returning on the B6270 through **Swaledale❖❖**, which presents a fine range of valley scenery, from rugged and steep to smiling and verdant around Reeth. The fast-flowing Swale begins its course on wild, high moorland west of **Keld❖**, a typical stone village on the Pennine Way. Populated mainly by hardy Swaledale sheep, with dark faces and curly horns, the ancient pastureland supports many unusual plants. Traditional stone hay barns, called *laithes*, are a classic feature of the carefully restored landscape. Thwaite and Muker are old Norse settlements, starting point of many good walks. Grinton's church is known as the Cathedral of the Dales. Further downstream, **Reeth❖** is a large, sophisticated village, with grey cottages around a green, and a folk museum. Arkengarthdale burrows into the hills to the north. From the A6108, make a short side trip to **RICHMOND ❻**. Return via the smartly attractive market town of **Leyburn❖** (visit the violin-maker's studio), past imposing castle ruins at **Middleham❖**, abbey ruins at **Jervaulx❖**, and ice cream and breweries at **Masham❖** (see **Wensleydale**). Stop off at **Ripon ❼** and FOUNTAINS ABBEY ❽ before heading back to Harrogate on the A61.

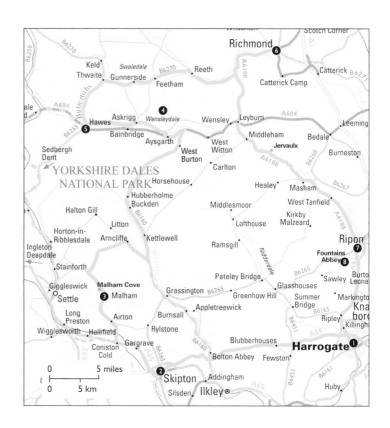

Tourist Information *18 High Street, Pateley Bridge; tel: 01423 711147.*

Stump Cross Caverns £ *On B6265 near Greenhow; tel: 01756 752780. Open Mar–Oct daily 1000–1800 (weekends and school holidays 1000–1600 in winter).*

Also worth exploring: Nidderdale once attracted attention for its deposits of lead and iron (now its main product is water, stored in half a dozen reservoirs). The Dales are mostly blanketed in heather moor, but breaking through in occasional bare, dramatic outcrops such as the weirdly shaped **Brimham Rocks✝** near Pateley Bridge. The intricate **Stump Cross Caverns✝** at Greenhow are classic limestone formations.

Accommodation and food on the route

Amerdale House £££ *Arncliffe, Littondale; tel: 01756 770250; fax: 01756 770266; www.amerdalehouse.co.uk.* Peaceful, beautifully located small hotel, serving ambitious cooking using local ingredients.

Arkleside £ *Reeth; tel/fax: 01748 884200; info@arklesidehotel.co.uk; www.arklesidehotel.co.uk.* Friendly family-run hotel with fine views and traditional cooking. Good value.

Stone Close £ *Main Street, Dent; tel: 01539 625231; fax: 01539 726567; accommodation@stoneclose.com; www.stoneclose.co.uk.* Delightful teashop-cum-guesthouse on the edge of the Dales. Well worth the trek.

Peak District

Ratings

Caves	●●●●●
Scenery	●●●●●
Stately homes	●●●●●
Walking/adventure sports	●●●●●
Children	●●●●○
Wildlife	●●●●○
Churches	●●●○○
Industrial heritage	●●●○○

From earliest times, when the ancient sundial stones of Arbor Low were assembled, people have worked and lived in the Peak District area, mining and quarrying, farming and weaving. The revived customs of well-dressing ceremonies and sheep-dog trials now draw large crowds. Buxton and Bakewell are both attractive destinations. Elsewhere, classic grey-stone villages cluster beside babbling rivers spanned by packhorse bridges. Grimmer farming hamlets brace themselves on windswept hillsides. The region's best sights include the great country houses of Chatsworth, Haddon and Lyme, and an assortment of colourful limestone caverns around Castleton. The Wirksworth area is packed with industrial heritage sites. Walkers and nature lovers are provided with easy trails and tougher long-distance paths. Roads are very busy in summer, and some may be impassable in winter, after snowfall; the narrower valleys or wilder moors are accessible only on foot.

ASHBOURNE*

Tourist Information
13 Market Place; tel: 01335 343666.

Ashbourne Gingerbread Shop
(and café) 26 St John's Street; tel: 01335 346753. This local speciality is made to a recipe allegedly passed on by Napoleonic prisoners of war.

This grey-stone market town at the foot of the White Peak is a National Park gateway access point. Its main landmark is the 212-ft pencil-slender spire of the parish church. Near by, the **Tissington Trail*** (one of four Peak District waymarked footpaths along disused railway tracks), leads from Ashbourne to Parsley Hay on the A515.

BAKEWELL✢✢

Tourist Information *The Old Market Hall, Bridge Street; tel: 01629 813227; or Peak District National Park HQ, Aldern House, Baslow Road, Bakewell; tel: 01629 816200.*

Above
Bakewell in winter

The main centre within the National Park draws crowds for its historic Monday livestock market (the charter dates from 1254), its famous pudding (*see page 108*), its warm brownstone buildings, and its photogenic composition of an ancient multi-arched **bridge** across the River Wye. A small **folk museum** occupies a Tudor house in Cunningham's Place (*tel: 01629 813165; open Apr–Oct daily 1430–1600, from 1100 July–Aug*). A mile west of Bakewell (best reached from the idyllic village of Ashford-in-the-Water, with its sheepwash bridge) is the **Magpie Mine**, the engine house of a 19th-century lead mine.

Rambling for victory

In 1932, the hills around Edale witnessed the 'mass trespass', the famous confrontation between landowners and walkers over public rights of access to open countryside. Dozens of hikers walked on to the privately owned grouse moors of Kinder Scout; five were imprisoned. Soon afterwards, the Ramblers' Association was formed. The story is told in Edale's National Park visitor centre. The row continues...

BUXTON***

ⓘ Tourist Information The Crescent; tel: 01298 25106.

ⓘ Buxton Museum and Art Gallery £ Terrace Road; tel: 01298 24658; www.derbyshire.gov.uk. Open Tue–Fri 0930–1730, Sat 0930–1700 (Sun 1030–1700 in summer).

Poole's Cavern ££ Buxton Country Park, Green Lane; tel: 01298 26978; www.poolescavern.co.uk. Open Mar–Oct daily 1000–1700.

Buxton's warm waters gush from subterranean springs at a rate of 1500 gallons an hour, and it has been a spa since Roman times. Take the waters free of charge at St Ann's Well. The town's finer buildings – including the Crescent (inspired by its namesake in Bath), Pump Room and Opera House – date from its Georgian heyday. Buxton makes an ideal base for exploring the western sections of the National Park, and glows particularly brightly during its annual summer music festival. **Poole's Cavern****, a show cave on the northern edge of town, rivals the stalagmite chambers of Castleton.

Accommodation and food in Buxton

Buxton's Victorian Guesthouse £ *3A Broad Walk; tel: 01298 78759; fax: 01298 74732; buxvic@tiscali.co.uk.* Charming B&B overlooking the Pavilion Gardens, dashingly decorated with Gilbert & Sullivan themes.

Columbine ££ *7 Hall Bank; tel: 01298 78752.* Simple, attractive restaurant with good wine list. Vegetarian options.

CASTLETON**

ⓘ Tourist Information Castle Street, Castleton; tel: 01433 620679; or Edale Information Centre; tel: 01433 670207.

ⓘ Peveril Castle £ Market Place; tel: 01433 620613. Open Apr–Sept 1000–1800, Oct 1000–1700, Nov–Mar Wed–Sun 1000–1600; EH.

Speedwell Cavern £££ Winnats Pass; tel: 01433 620512. Open Easter–Oct daily 0930–1730 (1000–1700 in winter); last boat trip 1600.

Treak Cliff Cavern ££ Off A6187 W; tel: 01433 620571. Open Mar–Oct daily 0930–1730, Nov–Feb 1000–1600; last tour 40 mins before closing.

This dramatically located dark-stone village makes a good base for exploring the central Peaks, where the limestone merges into millstone grit. The ruins of 11th-century **Peveril Castle*** command panoramic views. Impressive heights on the skyline suggest alluring walks and climbs around the Hope Valley and steep-sided Winnats Pass. **Mam Tor** (the Shivering Mountain, prone to shaly landslips) and **Kinder Scout** (highest peak in the Park, at 2088ft) overshadow nearby **Edale****. The Pennine Way starts in these hills.

Castleton's main interest lies underground in a group of limestone caverns, and the semi-precious mineral extracted from them, known as Blue John. Of the show caves, the best are the **Speedwell Cavern****, and the **Treak Cliff Cavern****, the last working Blue John mine. Be warned, though, that a trip underground is not for the claustrophobic! Speedwell Cavern involves travelling in a boat along a flooded tunnel scarcely big enough for the boat.

Accommodation and food in or near Castleton

Rose Cottage £ *Cross Street, Castleton; tel: 01433 620472.* Pretty cottage serving lunches, snacks and cream teas.

Waltzing Weasel Inn ££ *New Mills Road, Birch Vale; tel/fax: 01663 743402; w-weasel@zen.co.uk; www.w-weasel.co.uk.* Plain but friendly stone pub overlooking Kinder Scout. Appetising menus.

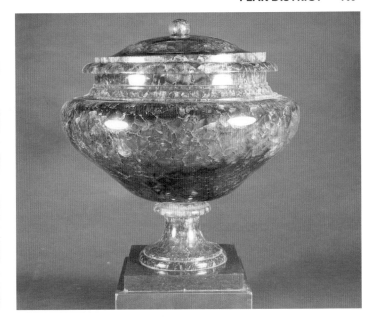

Blue John

A rare type of translucent fluorspar, beautifully banded and coloured in shades of purplish blue and yellow (the name actually comes from the French *bleue-jaune*). Most of the deposits around Castleton have been worked out now, but limited amounts of the brittle rock are still made into jewellery and ornaments sold in the village craft shops.

CHATSWORTH✦✦✦

ⓘ Chatsworth House and gardens £££ *Off B6012 near Baslow; tel: 01246 582204. Open late Mar–Dec 1100–1730 (1030 June–Aug; gardens until 1800), free access to park all year; adventure playground; excellent farm shop near Pilsley; estate village (Edensor).*

🍴 Fischer's Baslow Hall £££ *Calver Road, Baslow; tel: 01246 583259; fax: 01246 583818. Elegant Edwardian restaurant-with-rooms in peaceful setting. Acclaimed cooking.*

Above
Blue John vase, the Devonshire Collection, Chatsworth

Right
Chatsworth House

Chatsworth House, seat of the Dukes of Devonshire, is the Peak District's grandest stately home. The present Classical mansion was built during the 1690s in a vast estate of farmland, wooded park and spectacular **gardens✦✦** on the banks of the River Derwent. Inside, twenty-six sumptuous rooms are open to the public. Notable items include two magnificent vases made from Blue John. During the 18th century, Chatsworth's gardens and parkland were remodelled by Capability Brown, with ambitious water features, including the 620-ft cascade. Sadly, few of the elegant Crystal Palace glasshouses designed by Sir Joseph Paxton have survived, but a splendid modern hothouse encapsulates three separate microclimates.

DOVEDALE***

White-chested **dippers** can often be seen in and around the shallow rivers of the White Peak, feeding on small fish and aquatic insects.

The Peak's best-loved dale, where Izaak Walton (*The Compleat Angler*) fished for trout, has all the makings of a grand day out. The main access point for motorists is near Ilam, where you park and walk to the riverbank. Dramatised by steep-sided gorge scenery, caves and strangely shaped crags, prominent features of the valley include Lover's Leap, Reynard's Cave and Jacob's Ladder. A walk upstream to Milldale takes you away from some of the crowds. Famous stepping stones connect the counties of Derbyshire and Staffordshire in twenty precarious stages.

Right
Dovedale

EYAM**

Eyam Hall ££ *Tel: 01433 631976; www.eyamhall.co.uk. Open Tue–Thu, Sun 1100–1600 June–Aug (craft centre and café open Tue–Sun 1030–1700; Apr–May Sun only); timed tickets.*

In the mid-17th century, the inhabitants of this moorland village heroically isolated themselves after an outbreak of bubonic plague, to prevent spreading the infection to outlying communities. Over two-thirds of the villagers died, including the rector's wife, who became the 200th victim. The poignant story is told in the church. Many historic buildings survive from the time of the Great Plague, including **Eyam Hall***.

HADDON HALL***

Haddon Hall £££ *2 miles SE of Bakewell on A6; tel: 01629 812855. Open Apr–Sept daily 1030–1700, Oct Thu–Sun 1030–1630.*

Home of the Dukes of Rutland, mellow, rambling Haddon Hall is one of the most perfectly preserved medieval manor houses in England, surrounded by beautiful gardens. Inside, wall paintings were uncovered during early 20th-century restoration work.

MATLOCK GORGE❖❖

ℹ Tourist Information *Crown Square, Matlock; tel: 01629 583388; or The Pavilion, Matlock Bath; tel: 01629 55082.*

⛰ Heights of Abraham Cable Cars, Caverns and Hilltop Park £££ *Matlock Bath; tel: 01629 582365; www.heights-of-abraham.co.uk. Open Apr–Oct daily 1000–1700 (later in summer; weekends in Mar).*

Peak District Mining Museum ££ *The Pavilion, Matlock Bath; tel: 01629 583834; www.peakmines.co.uk. Open Apr–Oct daily 1000–1700, Nov–Mar daily 1100–1500.*

Arkwright's Cromford Mill £ *Mill Lane, Cromford; tel: 01629 824297. Open daily 0900–1700; free access to site, charge for tours.*

Crich Tramway Village ££ *Crich; tel: 01773 852565. Open Apr–Oct daily 1000–1730; rest of year Sun–Mon only 1030–1600; unlimited rides.*

Wirksworth Heritage Centre £ *Crown Yard, Market Place, Wirksworth; tel: 01629 825225. Open Feb–Nov Wed–Sat 1100–1600; Sun 1400–1700 (extended hours June–Sept, closed some days off season).*

National Stone Centre £ *Porter Lane, Middleton; tel: 01629 824833. Open daily 1000–1700 (1600 in winter).*

Right
Matlock Bath

Matlock Bath❖❖, the resort extension of Matlock town, developed as a spa during the 1780s. The **Heights of Abraham**❖❖, the cliffs on the west side of Matlock Gorge, can be reached by cable car. The **Peak District Mining Museum**❖❖ provides a tour of the old Temple Mine workings. Southeast of Matlock, **Cromford Mill**❖❖ has a reasonable claim to be the cradle of the Industrial Revolution since this is the place where, in 1771, Richard Arkwright developed his water-powered cotton-spinning machine.

The much-loved **Crich Tramway Village**❖❖ attracts transport fans from far and wide. **Wirksworth**❖❖ lies at the heart of a former lead-mining and stone-quarrying area. Handsome buildings grace the town, and a heritage centre occupies an old silk mill. Just outside the town, the **National Stone Centre**❖❖ is a lively and informative exhibition on the uses of stone.

Accommodation in and around Matlock

Riber Hall £££ *Matlock; tel: 01629 582795; www.riber-hall.co.uk.* A luxurious stay is assured at this lavish Elizabethan manor house.

Hodgkinson's Hotel ££ *150 South Parade, Matlock Bath; tel: 01629 582170; fax: 01629 584891; www.hodgkinsons-hotel.co.uk.* Charming, slightly eccentric hotel in town centre with gorge views. Good home cooking.

PEAK DISTRICT NATIONAL PARK✦✦✦

ℹ️ Tourist Information *The Gatehouse, Victoria Street, Glossop; tel: 01457 855920; or 49–51 Huddersfield Road, Holmfirth; tel: 01484 222444.*

Below
Hathersage

The wild scenic uplands of the southernmost vertebrae of the Pennine Chain were the first to be protected by National Park status in 1951. The Peak District National Park covers an area of 555 square miles, and two distinct types of landscape shape its appearance. The southern half is known as the **White Peak**. This is limestone country, a hilly plateau of grassland rising to about 1000ft, intersected by thousands of stone walls and craggy wooded dales. The soil supports a rich variety of rare plants. Settlements have developed mainly in the more fertile, sheltered valleys where water supplies were more reliable.

The High, or **Dark Peak**, is the wild stretch of almost empty moorland north of Castleton, where the pale limestone rocks give way to austere millstone grit. The acid soils of the rolling acres of heather, bracken and squelching peat bog support a completely different flora. Huge areas are consigned to grouse moors with no rights of public access. Few roads cross the moors, and they are often closed in wintry weather.

Opposite
Lose Hill

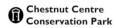

🐾 Chestnut Centre Conservation Park
££ Castleton Road, Chapel-en-le-Frith; tel: 01298 814099; www.ottersandowls.co.uk. Open daily 1030–1730 (weekends only Jan).

Suggested tour

Total distance: 117 miles (188km). Add 33 miles (53km) for the Holmfirth tour. The Winster route from Bakewell saves about 6 miles (10km).

Time: 5 hours.

Links: None very convenient.

Route: Leave **BUXTON** ❶ east on the A6 towards Bakewell and Matlock, turning left after 2 miles on the B6049 through **Miller's Dale**✦✦, one of the prettiest and most typical of the Derbyshire Dales.

Getting out of the car: The **Monsal Trail**✦✦, the best of the Peak's disused rail-track walks, crosses the road near Miller's Dale. The section to the west, through Chee Dale, passes spectacular cliffs.

Bakewell pudding

Local lore declares that this dish originated from a fortuitous mistake made by a flustered cook in about 1860, who accidentally put the egg-and-almond mixture intended for the pastry on top of the jam. The result became a regular fixture on the menu of the Rutland Arms Hotel. Incidentally, it is *always* called 'pudding' in Bakewell, never 'tart'!

Well dressing

This local tradition takes place in many White Peak villages during the summer. The practice of decorating local wells with biblical tableaux made from flower petals, leaves and seeds has been carried out for many centuries, and may even originate from Roman or pagan times. It is believed to be a thanksgiving ceremony for fresh water supplies, or in the case of Tissington, for escaping outbreaks of the Plague. Tourist Information Centres can provide a well-dressing calendar.

Just beyond Miller's Dale, the little town of **Tideswell**✦ is exceptionally attractive. Its handsome church is known as the 'Cathedral of the Peak'. Continue on the B6049 across the A623, turning left towards **CASTLETON** ❷. Backtrack slightly to the village of Hope and turn north on an unclassified road signed for **Edale**✦✦. This scenic loop takes you between the stately tabletop of **Kinder Scout**✦✦, the highest point in the Peak District, and the green shoulders of **Mam Tor**✦. Detour through delightful Edale to see its National Park visitor centre, and to set off for many popular walks, including the Pennine Way. From Edale, return to the main road and turn right for Chapel-en-le-Frith. Leave Chapel-en-le-Frith on the A624, heading north for **Glossop**, a sober cotton town.

Detour: North of Glossop, take the A628 heading northeast, between the reservoirs. Turn left on the A6024 over Holme Moss to picturesque **Holmfirth**✦, familiar as the location for TV's *Last of the Summer Wine*. Turn left from the town on the A635 across the dramatic and lonely Saddleworth Moor. Return to Glossop via Mossley and Stalybridge.

Right
Arbor Low stone circle

The Old Cheese Shop *Market Place, Hartington; tel: 01298 84935; www.hartingtoncheese.co.uk. Open daily 0930–1730 (0900–1630 in winter); closed lunchtime.*

Turn right on to the A57 and drive along Telford's **Snake Pass**❖❖, which ripples sinuously over a dome of wooded moorland. After 14 miles, turn left to see a trio of huge, interconnected **reservoirs**❖❖ (Ladybower, Derwent and Howden). (The northern section of this road is closed to traffic at weekends and bank holidays.) From Ladybower, turn south on the A6013 and left towards Hathersage. From here, turn south again, following signs for EYAM ❸, then continue on the A623 and A619 via **Baslow**❖ and CHATSWORTH ❹ (look out for the Chatsworth Farm Shop near Pilsley and the estate village of **Edensor**❖) to BAKEWELL ❺.

Detour: A pretty and less busy route cuts across country from Bakewell to Ashbourne, leaving out Matlock Gorge. Take the B5056 just after Haddon Hall towards **Winster**❖. Just west of the road, **Youlgreave**❖ has an exceptional church with Arts and Crafts features.

Take the A6 down the Wye and Derwent valleys past HADDON HALL ❻ to MATLOCK GORGE ❼, calling at **Cromford** and **Crich** before turning right on the B5035. **Carsington Water**❖, a reservoir a mile beyond **Wirksworth**❖, is a popular outdoor leisure area. From ASHBOURNE ❽, head north briefly on the A515, turning off at the pretty well-dressing village of **Tissington**❖❖ for DOVE-DALE ❾ (best avoided on sunny Sundays). Follow a maze of lanes via **Ilam**, a distinctive estate village at the lower end of the gorgeous **Manifold Valley**❖❖ (best seen on foot or by bike from the disused railway track). Beyond Alstonefield lies **Hartington**❖❖, with stone buildings around a green and a duckpond. Its **Hall**❖ is a fine 17th-century manor house (now a youth hostel, like Ilam Hall). The **Cheese Shop** at Hartington sells locally produced Stilton. Head northeast on the B5054, turning left on the A515. Within a mile or so, look out for signs to **Arbor Low Stone Circle**❖ on the right-hand side. This small, recumbent henge of about fifty stones dates from about 2000 BC. Three miles further on, the fields around Chelmorton are still divided by dry-stone walls into their medieval strip-farming system. Buxton is just a couple of miles up the road.

Accommodation and food on the route

Peacock Hotel ££ *Rowsley; tel: 01629 733518; fax: 01629 732671; www.jarvis.co.uk.* Handsome gritstone building in pretty village. Cosy, intimate interior with many period features. Hearty cooking.

Highlow Hall £ *Hathersage; tel/fax: 01433 650393.* Solid stone house offering comfortable accommodation in a wild part of the moors. Brontë associations.

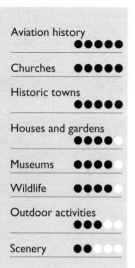

Wolds and Fens

Ratings

Aviation history	●●●●●
Churches	●●●●●
Historic towns	●●●●●
Houses and gardens	●●●●○
Museums	●●●●○
Wildlife	●●●●○
Outdoor activities	●●●○○
Scenery	●●○○○

The swathes of treeless farmland in Lincolnshire and Cambridgeshire are often dismissed as dull. Even the coastline north of The Wash is largely uneventful, although it provides plenty of room for donkey rides. The wetlands, windmills and wide skies of this little-known region deserve closer observation, however. Two distinctive features characterise it: the chalk escarpment of the Lincolnshire Wolds provides welcome contours east of Lincoln; in contrast, the Fens between Boston and Cambridge are relentlessly flat. A few patches of undrained fen support a unique ecosystem. The splendid cathedral cities of Cambridge and Lincoln are unmissable, while Boston and Stamford are smaller architectural gems. Many ancient villages have vanished over the centuries as a result of plague or economic decline. The flat, depopulated countryside is full of military airfields dating from the Second World War.

BOSTON✦

ⓘ Tourist Information *The Market Place; tel: 01205 356656; tourism@bostongb.freeserve. com.uk.*

🏛 Guildhall Museum *£ South St; tel: 01205 365954. Open all year Mon–Sat 1000–1700, Apr–Sept Sun 1330–1700.*

Right
The Boston 'Stump'

Boston was famously re-created on the other side of the Atlantic by the Pilgrim Fathers who left here in the 17th century. Once England's second-largest seaport, with a booming wool export trade with Flanders, it declined when the Witham silted up. The **Boston Stump✦** is the graceful tower of St Botolph's Church; also interesting are the **Maud Foster Mill✦** and the **Guildhall Museum✦**.

CAMBRIDGE✦✦✦

ℹ Tourist Information *Wheeler Street; tel: 01223 322640.*

🚌 Cambridge is best accessed by public transport (the railway station is some way from the centre, but there are plenty of buses – Park and Ride scheme). The centre is compact and easy to explore on foot, by bike or even by punt.

🏛 King's College Chapel *££ Tel: 01223 331212. Open Mon–Fri 0930–1630, Sun 1000–1700 (reduced hours term-time); evensong at 1730.*

Fitzwilliam Museum *Trumpington Street; tel: 01223 332900; www.fitzwilliam.cam.ac.uk. Open Tue, Thu, Fri 1000–1700, Wed 1000–1900, Sat–Sun 1200–1700.*

Kettle's Yard *Castle Street; tel: 01223 352124. Open house Tue–Sun 1400–1600, gallery 1130–1700.*

Wimpole Hall and Home Farm *£££ Tel: 01223 207257; Hall open Mar–Oct Tue–Thu and weekends 1300–1700; farm and park open all year; NT.*

Imperial War Museum *£££ Duxford; tel: 01223 835000; www.iwm.org.uk. Open daily 1000–1800 (1600 off season).*

Cambridge American War Cemetery *Coton; tel: 01954 210350. Open daily 0800–1800 (1700 off season).*

Right The Bridge of Sighs

Cambridge offers a mix of attractions: handsome college buildings, medieval churches, a romantic riverside setting, superb museums (several are free) and a civilised, scholarly atmosphere. Some of the most venerable **colleges**✦✦✦ line a grassy stretch of the River Cam (known as The Backs). Picturesque bridges (including the **Mathematical Bridge**✦ and the **Bridge of Sighs**✦) provide vantage points above a flotilla of punts and rowboats. Most famous of all the university buildings is **King's College Chapel**✦✦✦, named after its founding monarch, Henry VI. The excellent and important **Fitzwilliam Museum**✦✦✦ was built in 1816. **Kettle's Yard**✦✦ is an imaginative modern art gallery.

The pleasures of Cambridge also run to shopping (try Heffers bookshops), sitting in pubs (for example, the atmospheric Free Press), walking on the towpath alongside the willow-fringed Cam, or punting in the flat-keeled river boats. Try to catch the traditional 'Bumps' rowing races, in February, June and July.

The surroundings of Cambridge are full of interest: Ickleton, Fulbourn and the Shelfords are attractive villages of thatch and timber; the Gog Magog Hills have the remains of an Iron Age fort. At Arrington, **Wimpole Hall**✦✦ (southwest) is an 18th-century house, with a rare breeds centre. **Duxford** Airfield is the location of one of Britain's leading aviation museums✦✦. East of the city is Coton's poignant **Cambridge American War Cemetery**✦.

ELY❖❖

ℹ **Oliver Cromwell's House/Tourist Information ££** *29 St Mary's Street; tel: 01353 662062. Open Mon–Sat 1000–1700 (daily until 1730 in summer), Sun 1100–1500.*

ℹ **Ely Cathedral ££** *Tel: 01353 667735. Open Apr–Oct daily 0700–1900; rest of year 0730–1800.*

Stained Glass Museum ££ *Tel: 01353 660347; www.stainedglassmuseum.org. Open Mon–Fri 1030–1700, Sat 1030–1730, Sun 1200–1800 (closes earlier in winter).*

Right
Ely Cathedral's Octagon

The octagonal lantern tower of **Ely Cathedral❖❖❖** makes a dramatic landmark across the fenlands. In the Middle Ages Ely was an island surrounded by marshes, an Anglo-Saxon stronghold. When the Normans eventually defeated Hereward the Wake, they built a glorious church. In the south triforium, the **Stained Glass Museum❖❖** displays over a hundred panels. Oliver Cromwell is known to have lived near the cathedral green.

THE FENS❖❖

ℹ **Tourist Information** *2–3 Bridge Street, Wisbech; tel: 01945 583263; wisbech@eetb.info.*

ℹ **Wicken Fen ££** *Lode Lane, Wicken; tel: 01353 720274; www.wicken.org.uk. Open all year Tue–Sun 1000–1700 except Christmas Day; NT.*

Peckover House ££ *North Brink, Wisbech; tel: 01945 583463. Open Apr–Oct Wed and weekends 1230–1700; gardens also open Sat–Thu; NT.*

Wisbech and Fenland Museum *Museum Square, Wisbech; tel: 01945 583817. Open Tue–Sat 1000–1700 (1600 in winter).*

A few small patches of these ancient marshes remain in their natural undrained state, notably **Wicken Fen❖❖**, a 600-acre wetland site that is the UK's oldest nature reserve. **Wisbech** is one of the main fenland towns, with tranquil Georgian houses. **Peckover House❖** is an 18th-century building in rococo style. The **Wisbech and Fenland Museum❖❖** gives a good introduction to the area's history, while **Elgood's Brewery❖** offers tastings. Spalding's **Ayscoughfee Hall Museum❖** acts as a regional tourist office. Just north of Spalding, the **Pinchbeck Pumping Engine** is a fascinating survival of Victorian engineering, designed to drain the fens.

Right
Historic Lincoln

LINCOLN✧✧✧

Lincoln's setting makes an indelible first impression. Crowned by a spectacular three-towered cathedral, this fine Roman city stands on a sudden cliff above the River Witham. Fascinating Steep Hill links the historic 'uphill' and the commercial 'downhill' sectors of the city.

Medieval Lincoln was an important cloth-making centre, and the city has some grand well-preserved domestic buildings. Today, Lincoln presides over rich agricultural terrain, and manufactures farm machinery. Explore the upper town on foot: look out for the 12th-century **Jew's House**✧, bits of Roman wall still standing and Norman **Lincoln Castle**✧✧. The **Usher Gallery**✧✧✧ has a fine collection of clocks and watches, and the **Museum of Lincolnshire Life**✧✧ is the region's largest museum of social history. Children of all ages may enjoy the **Incredibly Fantastic Old Toy Show**✧✧.

The **cathedral**✧✧✧, on its hilltop, is impressive from a distance. The original church dates from 1092, but modifications continued into the 13th century. Inside, notable features include the dazzling rose windows in the transept, and the Gothic Angel Choir with its demonic 'Lincoln Imp'. The suggested donation is hard to refuse.

Accommodation and food in and around Lincoln

D'Isney Place ££ Eastgate, Lincoln; tel: 01522 538881; fax: 01522 511231; www.disneyplacehotel.co.uk. Characterful, friendly B&B in a Georgian house in the heart of historic Lincoln. Limited parking.

Jew's House ££ 15 The Strait, Lincoln; tel: 01522 524851. Built around 1190 and one of Britain's oldest inhabited houses. Now a smart restaurant with accomplished Anglo-French cooking.

PETERBOROUGH✧

ℹ **Tourist Information** 3–5 Minster Precincts; tel: 01733 452336; tic@peterborough.gov.uk.

Peterborough has many modern office blocks, but the city's origins stretch back over a millennium. The Norman **cathedral**✧✧✧ (*tel: 01733 343342; open daily*) is one of the finest in the country, even after being damaged by Cromwellian troops. Just east of the city centre, **Flag Fen**✧✧ is a working archaeological site of a Bronze Age settlement (*Fourth Drove, Fengate, tel: 01733 313414; open daily*).

STAMFORD✧✧

ℹ **Tourist Information** The Arts Centre, 27 St Mary's Street; tel: 01780 755611; stamfordtic@skdc.com.

🏛 **Stamford Museum** Broad Street; tel: 01780 766317. Open Mon–Sat 1000–1700 (also Sun pm in summer).

Burghley House £££ Tel: 01780 752451; burghley@burghley.co.uk; www.stamford.co.uk/burghley. Open Apr–Oct daily 1100–1630, Sculpture Garden 1100–1600.

A regular star of period costume dramas, Stamford has over 500 listed buildings. It has Roman and Viking roots, but grew wealthy on the medieval cloth trade, which left it with several handsome churches and one of Britain's best historic inns, The George. A small **museum**✧ tells its history. Just outside the town is **Burghley House**✧✧✧, a splendid Tudor palace. The grounds (landscaped by Capability Brown) are the setting for the annual Burghley Horse Trials.

Accommodation and food in or near Stamford

The George of Stamford ££ *71 St Martins, Stamford; tel: 01780 750750; fax: 01780 750701; www.georgehotelofstamford.com.* One of England's finest coaching inns, with a pedigree dating back centuries – a comfortable, welcoming place to stop for coffee, a bar snack or lunch. Courtyard gardens.

Hambleton Hall £££ *Upper Hambleton, Oakham; tel: 01572 756991; fax: 01572 724721; www.hambletonhall.com.* Luxury country-house hotel with magnificent views of Rutland Water and a serious restaurant.

Right
Stamford

Suggested tour

ⓘ Tourist Information New Market Hall, Louth; tel: 01507 609289.

ⓜ Lincolnshire Aviation Heritage Centre ££ The Airfield, East Kirkby; tel: 01790 763207; www.lincsaviation.co.uk. Open Mon–Sat 1000–1700 (1600 in winter).

Bolingbroke Castle Old Bolingbroke; www.lincsheritage.org. Open daily 0900–2100 (dusk in winter).

Trader Windmill £ Frithville Road, Sibsey; tel: 01205 750036. Open erratically, weekends, summer only; EH.

Battle of Britain Visitor Centre ££ RAF Coningsby; tel 01526 344041. Open Mon–Fri 1000–1700.

Tattershall Castle ££ Tattershall; tel: 01526 342543. Open Apr–Sept Sat–Wed 1100–1730 (1600 in Oct, some weekends in winter); closed for functions – ring to check; NT.

Denny Abbey ££ Waterbeach (off A10); tel: 01223 860489. Open Apr–Oct 1200–1700; EH.

Anglesey Abbey, Gardens and Lode Mill £££ Quy Road, Lode; tel: 01223 811200. Open Apr–Oct Wed–Sun 1300–1700; gardens 1030–1730 (daily in summer; until dusk in winter); NT.

Total distance: 230 miles (37km). The Louth detour is about the same distance. Add about 7 miles (11km) for the Stretham detour.

Time: 6–7 hours (the roads are quite fast). If you're short of time, stick to the main roads and concentrate on Lincoln, Ely and Cambridge.

Links: From Wisbech, it's easy to join the Norfolk tour at King's Lynn (*see page 146*). From Cambridge or Ely, you can pick up the Suffolk/Essex tour at Newmarket or Saffron Walden (*see page 156*).

Route: Leave **LINCOLN ❶** via the A46 heading northeast for **Market Rasen**, a bustling agricultural centre with a racecourse. Continue eastwards through the Lincolnshire Wolds on the A631 to **Louth***, a perfect Georgian market town with the tallest parish church spire in England. From here, the simplest route to **BOSTON ❷** is down the A16 (optional stops include East Kirkby's **Lincolnshire Aviation Heritage Centre*** and the remains of **Bolingbroke Castle***, birthplace of Henry IV, near the A155 turning beyond East Keal). Just west of Sibsey, **Trader Windmill***, on the right-hand side of the road, is a fine six-sailed windmill.

Detour: From Louth, take the A153 via **Horncastle*** and **Coningsby**, where the main attraction is the **Battle of Britain Visitor Centre****. **Tattershall Castle**** on the A153 (southwest) is one of England's finest moated towers. Rejoin the A16 at Boston, via the B1192.

From Boston, continue south on the A16 to **Spalding**, then east via Holbeach and Long Sutton, then south to **Wisbech** and **ELY ❸**. To see more of the fenland landscape, vary this route on minor roads across the Bedford Levels – use a good map! **Welney Reserve***, just over the Norfolk border, is a noted birdwatching site. From Ely, the quick way to **CAMBRIDGE ❹** is via the A10 (southwest), passing **Denny Abbey***.

Detour: A brief circuit eastwards off the A10 via the A1123 (east) from Stretham passes several interesting places, including the nature reserve of **Wicken Fen****, **Soham*** (noted for its windmills), **Burwell** (a magnificent Perpendicular church) and the grand Tudor mansion of **Anglesey Abbey**** at Lode.

From Cambridge, the southern exit routes give speedy access to Wandlebury Country Park and its Iron Age fort (A1307), **Duxford Imperial War Museum**** (M11) and **Wimpole Hall**** (A603). The return leg is a fast, straightforward route via the A14 to **Huntingdon**, then to **PETERBOROUGH ❺**, **STAMFORD ❻** and **Grantham ❼** (A1), returning to Lincoln on the A607.

The Welsh Marches

Ratings

Architecture	●●●●●
Castles and historic houses	●●●●●
Industrial archaeology	●●●●●
Canals	●●●●○
Countryside	●●●●○
Food and drink	●●●●○
Shopping	●●●●○
Walking/adventure sports	●●●●○

Rural Cheshire and Shropshire are two of England's least spoilt counties. Well-kept towns and villages contain many examples of the local 'magpie' architecture – ornate black-and-white box-framed timbering. The historic county towns of Chester and Shrewsbury make excellent bases, while smaller Ludlow is also enticing. The landscapes around here are surprisingly varied. Shropshire's rocks date from ten of the twelve officially designated geological eras, the smallest area in the world known to contain such a range. Dominant natural features are the windy ridges of the Long Mynd and Wenlock Edge, and the serpentine Severn and Dee rivers. In the 18th century these waterways were linked by the Shropshire Union Canal; a branch strays over the Welsh border to Llangollen, via a breathtaking aqueduct. This placid countryside was for a while an area right at the heart of the Industrial Revolution, fired by the blast furnaces of Ironbridge Gorge, and by the imaginative genius of Thomas Telford.

CHESTER✢✢✢

ⓘ Tourist Information *Town Hall, Northgate Street or Chester Visitor Centre, Vicars Lane; tel: 01244 402111 or 351609; www.chestertourism.com.*

Visitors stub their toes on fragments of history every few paces in this splendid little city, which dates back almost 2000 years. Chester is refreshingly down to earth, but quietly upmarket with excellent shops, hotels and restaurants. The city has a Roman **amphitheatre✢**, a Norman castle, superbly preserved **medieval walls✢✢**, an eclectic **cathedral✢** and a dazzling assembly of half-timbered buildings. It is best explored on foot (do walk the walls), but there are also sightseeing tours on an open-top bus or cruiseboats along the Dee. **The Rows✢✢✢**, at the central crossroads of the city, is a mixture of genuine Tudor and Victorian pastiche architecture. The **Roodee** is England's oldest racecourse, on a riverside site where the Roman docks once stood. **Chester's Visitor and Heritage Centres✢✢**, the **Deva Roman**

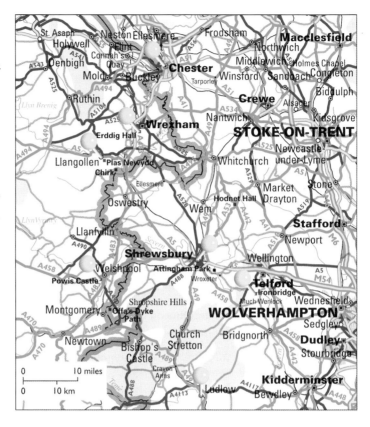

The Chester Tour ££ c/o Chester City Transport, Station Road; tel: 01244 347457; www.guidefriday.com/chester. Open Mar–Oct daily every 15–30 mins. Guided open-top bus sightseeing tours; tickets valid all day – get on and off where you like; check discount system with other city attractions.

Bithell Boats ££ Souters Lane; tel: 01244 325394; www.showboatsofchester.co.uk. Apr–Oct 1000–1730 (weekends only in winter); Sun evening cruises in high season.

Chester Heritage Centre Bridge Street Row; tel: 01244 322008. Open daily 1100–1700, Sun 1400–1700.

Deva Roman Experience ££ Pierpoint Lane; tel: 01244 343407. Open daily 0900–1700 (1600 Dec–Jan).

Grosvenor Museum 27 Grosvenor Street; tel: 01244 402012. Open Mon–Sat 1030–1700, Sun 1400–1700; donation welcome.

Chester Zoo £££ 2 miles N, off A41; tel: 01244 380280; www.chesterzoo.org.uk. Open daily from 1000.

Experience* and the **Grosvenor Museum**** give an overview of the city's rich past. The lozenge brickwork on many buildings denotes the hand of its local benefactors, the Dukes of Westminster. On the northern outskirts, **Chester Zoo**** is outstanding.

Accommodation and food in Chester

Grosvenor Hotel £££ *Eastgate Street; tel: 01244 324024; fax: 01244 313246; chesgrov@chestergrosvenor.co.uk.* The region's only five-star hotel, famed for its palatial historic architecture and its splendid restaurant (The Arkle), in the heart of the city centre.

Castle House £ *23 Castle Street; tel/fax: 01244 350354.* Central, pretty B&B dating from Elizabethan times.

Redland Hotel ££ *64 Hough Green; tel: 01244 671024, fax: 01244 681309.* Belying its humdrum Victorian exterior, this eccentric B&B is full of fascinating objects and lots of period interest.

ERDIGG✧✧

Erdigg £££ *Well signed S of Wrexham; tel: 01978 355314. Open Mar–Oct Sat–Wed 1200–1700 (1600 in Oct), gardens 1100–1800 (from 1000 July–Aug, until 1700 Oct); NT.*

This much-loved property just outside Wrexham dates from the late 17th century, and is particularly renowned for its exhibitions illustrating the 'upstairs, downstairs' relationship between master and servants. The opulent state rooms display many original features, while restored outbuildings reveal life below stairs. The walled gardens are in 18th-century style and the surrounding parkland has attractive woodland walks.

IRONBRIDGE✧✧✧

Tourist Information *The Wharfage; tel: 01952 432166; info@ironbridge.org.uk.*

Ironbridge Gorge Museum £££ *Tel: 01952 433522; www.ironbridge.org.uk. Most sights open daily 1000–1700.*

Severn Lodge £ *New Road; tel: 01952 432148; fax: 01952 432062; enquiries@ severnlodge.com. Stylish Georgian B&B.*

The bridge over the River Severn that gives this steep town its name is an apt monument for one of the most significant centres of the Industrial Revolution, now classed as a World Heritage Site. The 1779 casting in iron of this bridge revolutionised building methods, and transformed Ironbridge Gorge into a leading iron-smelting region. Today the industrial monuments that made the region's fortunes have been restored as heritage attractions along the riverbanks. A design and technology centre called **Enginuity** has recently joined the longer-established sights of the **Ironbridge Gorge Museum**: Blists Hill (a reconstructed Victorian town), the Museum of Iron (showing Abraham Darby's momentous coke-smelting process), and the Museum of the Gorge. The best way to see the sights is to buy an inclusive Passport Ticket, valid until you have seen everything. This is one of Britain's most rewarding industrial archaeology destinations.

Right
Ironbridge Gorge

LLANGOLLEN**

Tourist Information *Town Hall; tel: 01978 860828; llangollen.tic@virgin.net.*

Llangollen Railway *£££ Abbey Road; tel: 01978 860951; www.llangollen-railway.co.uk. Phone for timetable.*

Horse-drawn boat trips *££ Llangollen Wharf; tel: 01978 860702; www.horsedrawnboats.co.uk. Apr–Oct.* A silent trip through Dee scenery. The Wharf Centre is a good place for a Welsh cream tea afterwards.

Plas Newydd *££ Tel: 01978 861314. Open Apr–Oct daily 1000–1700.*

Gales *££ 18 Bridge Street; tel: 01978 860089; fax: 01978 861313; richard@ galesofllangollen.co.uk; www.galesofllangollen.co.uk.* This townhouse wine-bar-with-rooms has an enthusiastic following. The food and wines are splendid, in a setting of special charm.

On one of the main routes into North Wales, this lively market town is regularly invaded by visitors. In July it erupts, when the International Music Eisteddfod is held. Telford's 1000ft-long **Pontcysyllte Aqueduct**** is astonishing, poised on 126ft stilts above the River Dee. Walk along the hair-raising towpath, or take a narrowboat in summer. Intriguing **Plas Newydd**** was the home of an unconventional couple of 18th-century Anglo-Irish ladies, who became local celebrities.

Right
Plas Newydd

LUDLOW***

Tourist Information *Castle Street; tel: 01584 875053.*

Ludlow Castle ££ *Tel: 01584 873355. Open Apr–Sept daily 1000–1700 (1900 in Aug, 1600 off season, weekends only in Jan).*

Ludlow Museum £ *Castle Street; tel: 01584 875384. Open Apr–Oct Mon–Sat 1030–1300, 1400–1700 (Sun Jun–Aug).*

One of the prettiest and most interesting of English market towns, Ludlow has around 500 listed buildings, from an early Norman **castle*** to handsome Tudor and Georgian houses. Its attractions have brought prosperity, reflected in smart shops and a highbrow cultural programme, and its top-notch restaurants have made it a favourite place for foodies. One of its most famous buildings is the ornately timbered **Feathers Hotel** on the Bull Ring. The 13th-century Broadgate survives from the old walls, and the fine parish church of St Laurence dominates the town centre behind the historic buttermarket.

Gardens

There are some excellent gardens near the attractive old salt-mining centre of **Nantwich***. **Stapeley Water Gardens ££** claims to be the world's largest water-garden specialist: 1 mile S on A51; tel: 01270 623868. Open daily from 0900 (1000 on Sun). **Bridgemere Garden World** ** sells a mind-boggling selection of garden plants grown to very high standards, has award-winning show gardens, and a restaurant: Bridgemere, 8 miles S of Nantwich; tel: 01270 520381. Open Apr–Sept 0900–1900, Oct–Mar 0900–1700. Near Bridgemere, the **Dorothy Clive Garden** ** is a specialist plantsman's garden in a lovely setting (££): on A51 at Willoughbridge; tel: 01630 647237. Open Apr–Oct 1000–1730.

Accommodation and food in Ludlow

Dinham Hall ££ *By the Castle; tel: 01584 876464; fax: 01584 876019; www.dinhamhall.fsnet.co.uk.* Georgian hotel near the castle walls, slightly impersonal but with some historic interest plus good service and food.

Courtyard ££ *2 Quality Square; tel: 01584 878080.* Good-value restaurant serving simple, accomplished food with fresh ingredients and friendly service.

Merchant House £££ *Lower Corve Street; tel: 01584 875438, fax: 01584 876927.* If you feel like pushing the boat out in Ludlow, this is one place to do it. Ambitious, carefully prepared dishes, in pleasantly modest, low-key surroundings.

Mr Underhill's £££ *Dinham Weir; tel: 01584 874431; www.mr-underhills.co.uk.* Another place to empty your wallet! Attractively set above the River Teme, this classy, deceptively simple restaurant-with-rooms offers the last word in serious cooking. Professional service and excellent wines.

POWIS CASTLE**

Powis Castle £££
Welshpool (1 mile S off A483); tel: 01938 551920. Open Apr–Oct Wed–Sun (Tue July–Aug) 1300–1700, gardens 1100–1800; NT.

The battlements on the present building are purely for show, but Powis Castle was originally an early 13th-century fortress built by Welsh princes. The gateway is a rare survival of a medieval defence system, and the castle has a grand interior. Its **hanging gardens**** are remarkable: formal Italianate terraces cascading down a steep hillside.

SHREWSBURY***

Tourist Information *The Music Hall, The Square; tel: 01743 281200; tic@shrewsburytourism.co.uk.*

Shrewsbury Museum and Art Gallery *Barker Street; tel: 01743 361196; www.shrewsburymuseums. com. Open Tue–Sat 1000–1700 (1600 in winter; daily in summer).*

Wroxeter Roman City Museum £££ *Wroxeter; tel: 01743 761330. Open Apr–Sept daily 1000–1800, Oct 1000–1700, Nov–Mar 1000–1300, 1400–1600; EH.*

Shropshire's county town stands on a defensive loop of the River Severn, guarded by an ancient sandstone castle. Many of its historic timber-framed buildings date from the 16th century, when the wool trade made the town prosperous. Finds from a Roman garrison town are displayed in Wroxeter's **Roman City Museum**. Extensive remains of Viroconium, once the fourth-largest Roman settlement in Britain, are laid out in a grid pattern on the banks of the Severn.

Accommodation and food in Shrewsbury

Albright Hussey ££ *Ellesmere Road; tel: 01939 290571; fax: 01939 291143; abhhotel@aol.com; www.albrighthussey.co.uk.* Charming Italian-owned hotel in a mix of architectural styles, furnished with antiques.

Sol ££ *82 Wyle Cop; tel: 01743 340560, fax: 01743 340552.* Acclaimed, colourfully decorated venture in the centre of town, serving sophisticated Anglo-French cuisine.

Opposite
The Feathers Hotel

Right
Shrewsbury

Suggested tour

Old Fire Station Chocolate Shop 57 High Street, Tarporley; tel: 01829 733736; www.firestationchocolateshop.co.uk. Open Mon–Sat 0900–1800, Sun 1000–1700. Demonstrations of chocolate-making, with a chance to make and eat your own.

Cheshire Herbs Forest Road, 3 miles NE of Tarporley on A49; tel: 01829 760578. Open daily 1000–1700. Specialist herb nursery selling plants and herbal products. Display garden.

Attingham Park ££ Atcham, 3 miles E of Shrewsbury; tel: 01743 708123; www.nationaltrust.org.uk. Open Apr–Oct Fri–Tue 1300–1630, grounds daily all year; NT.

Stokesay Castle ££ Craven Arms; tel: 01588 672544. Open Apr–Oct daily 1000–1800, Oct 1000–1700, Nov–Mar Wed–Sun 1000–1600; EH.

Chirk Castle ££ Just W of Chirk; tel: 01691 777701; chirkcastle@ntrust.org.uk. Open Apr–Sept Wed–Sun 1200–1700 (1600 in Oct), gardens same days 1100–1800; NT.

Total distance: 160 miles (256km). Add 9 miles (14km) for the Market Drayton detour; 8 miles (13km) for the Bridgnorth one.

Time: 5–6 hours. Allow at least a day to see the Ironbridge museums.

Links: From Chester, the fast A55 takes you to Snowdonia (*see page 166*) in no time. From Ludlow, take the A49 southwards to join up with the Brecon Beacons route at Hereford (*see page 184*).

Route: From **CHESTER ❶**, take the A51 east via **Tarporley✦✦**, a classic Cheshire village of great character. Following the course of the Shropshire Union Canal southeast, you reach **Nantwich✦** in 10 miles. Take the A530 southwest to Whitchurch, followed by the A41 and then the A49 south to **SHREWSBURY ❷**.

Take the B4380 east from Shrewsbury, passing **Attingham Park✦** on the left, an elegant 18th-century mansion. A couple of miles further on lies **Wroxeter✦**, where the important Roman settlement of *Viroconium* has been excavated. Continue on the same road, to **IRONBRIDGE ❸**, then take the Broseley road to **Much Wenlock✦**, an old market town with many pretty magpie cottages. Head southwest on the B4378 to **LUDLOW ❹**. The breezy escarpment of **Wenlock Edge✦** is visible to the right of this picturesque road.

Detour: The well-preserved town of **Bridgnorth✦✦** (8 miles southeast of Much Wenlock) stands on a ridge of red sandstone. The castle keep was blown up by the Parliamentarians during the Civil War. The High and Low Towns are connected by a quaint cliff railway. The B4364 southwest is a pleasant route to Ludlow through the Clee Hills.

From Ludlow, head northwest on the A49 through the charming village of **Craven Arms✦**, best known for evocative 13th-century **Stokesay Castle✦✦**, a magnificent example of a fortified medieval manor. A mile beyond the village, take a left turn on to the A489.

Getting out of the car: To the northeast is the 10-mile ridge of bleak moorland called the **Long Mynd✦✦**, which offers some fine walks. Prehistoric earthworks and barrows litter this natural defensive site.

Detour on the B4385 through the former tiny county town of **Montgomery✦**, which has some pleasant half-timbering and red-brick houses. The ruined castle, a typical example of the border fortresses scattered all over the Marches, guarded the Severn Valley as it entered Wales. Just outside the Georgian market town of **Welshpool✦** is **POWIS CASTLE ❺**. Head north on the A483 via **Oswestry✦**, another attractive market town, then take the A5 north through **Chirk✦**, which has an elegantly furnished 700-year-old Marcher **castle✦**, and another of Telford's daring canal aqueducts. A well-preserved section of the Offa's Dyke earthwork can be seen near Chirk. Continue to

Boat Museum £££
South Pier Road, Ellesmere Port; tel: 0151 355 5017. Open daily 1000–1700 (Sat–Wed 1100–1600 in winter).

Blue Planet Aquarium £££ *Ellesmere Port, off A5117 near J10 on M53; tel: 0151 357 8800; www.blueplanetaquarium.com. Open Apr–Oct daily 1000–1800 (reduced hours in winter).*

Port Sunlight Village Trust £ *95 Greendale Road, Port Sunlight, Wirral; tel: 0151 644 4803; fax: 0151 645 8973; www.portsunlightvillage.com. Open daily 1000–1600 (Sat–Sun 1100–1600 in winter).*

Lady Lever Art Gallery ££ *Port Sunlight; tel: 0151 478 4136; www.ladyleverartgallery.org.uk. Open Mon–Sat 1000–1700, Sun 1200–1700; discount scheme with other Liverpool museums.*

LLANGOLLEN ❻, where Telford's **Pontcysyllte Aqueduct** is best approached from Froncysyllte on the A5 east of the town. Return to the A483 via the A539 on the north side of the valley, seeing **ERDDIG ❼** just south of Wrexham. Return to Chester to complete the tour.

Also worth exploring: The Wirral Peninsula is easily reached from Chester. Main sights are at **Ellesmere Port**❖❖, where there is a boat museum and a new aquarium as well as a huge factory outlet shopping village. **Port Sunlight**❖❖ is a model mock-Tudor garden village built by Lord Leverhulme for the workers at his soap factory. The **Lady Lever Art Gallery**❖ is a splendid collection of 18th- and 19th-century works of art.

Accommodation and food on the route

The Swan ££ *50 High Street, Tarporley; tel: 01829 733838; fax: 01829 732932.* Handsome red-brick coaching inn with well-kept interior and good food, in the centre of one of Cheshire's most enticing villages.

Wenlock Edge Inn £ *Hilltop, Wenlock Edge, Much Wenlock; tel: 01746 785678; fax: 01746 785285.* A popular walking base with views over the Welsh border. Hearty pub fare and comfortable bedrooms.

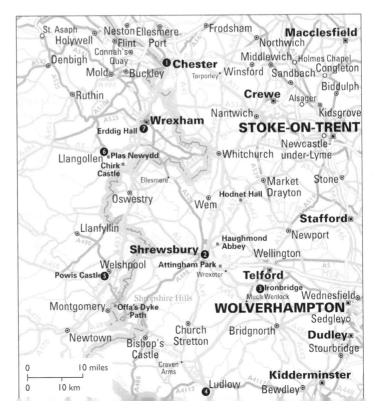

The Cotswolds

Ratings

Heritage	●●●●●
Villages	●●●●●
Architecture	●●●●
Children	●●●●
Churches	●●●●
Houses and gardens	●●●●
Scenery	●●●●
Walking	●●●

The area of the Cotswolds evokes a timeless English idyll of teashops and roses round the door, honey-coloured stone cottages and green-and-gold fields patched with woodland. It is compact but subtly varied, and very pretty. On the western edge of this oolitic limestone escarpment, gradients are steep, gradually levelling out further east towards the Vale of Evesham. The uplands are sprinkled with cairns, hillforts and barrows, and afford spectacular views. Scraps of primeval woodland and unimproved meadow remain, but mostly this is a carefully managed landscape of mixed farmland separated by hedgerows and traditional dry-stone walls. Cirencester has the best claim as a regional centre. Cheltenham and Gloucester are large and rather atypical, but definitely worth a visit for sightseeing or shopping. Stratford, slightly north of the true Cotswolds, is included here as a magnet for theatre lovers.

CHELTENHAM✤✤

ℹ Tourist Information 77 The Promenade; tel: 01242 522878.

♨ Pittville Pump Room £ Pittville Park; tel: 01242 523852. Open Wed–Mon 1000–1630 (1000–1600 in winter). Special exhibitions from time to time.

This large spa town is renowned for its gentility, but has a livelier side, with expensive shops and restaurants, and crowd-pulling annual arts festivals. Its racecourse (Prestbury Park) hosts the prestigious Gold Cup each March. Elegant Regency architecture and ornamental gardens surround The Promenade and the domed **Pittville Pump Room✤**, a 19th-century Greek Revival building where naturally alkaline spa water is dispensed. A fascinating **Art Gallery and Museum✤✤** contains a collection of Arts and Crafts furniture. The **Holst Birthplace Museum✤** is a carefully restored Regency house on Clarence Road, where visitors may see the composer's own piano.

Below
Arlington Row, Bibury

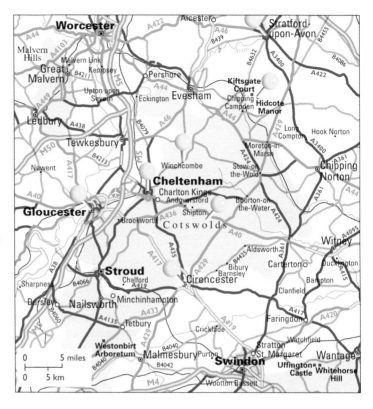

Cheltenham Art Gallery and Museum *Clarence Street; tel: 01242 237431; artgallery@cheltenham.gov.uk; www.cheltenhammuseum.org. uk. Open Mon–Sat 1000–1720, Sun 1400–1620; donations welcome.*

Holst Birthplace Museum £ *4 Clarence Road; tel: 01242 524846; www.holstmuseum.org.uk. Open Jan–Nov Tue–Sat 1000–1600.*

CHIPPING CAMPDEN❖❖❖

P Parking is a problem in the town centre; park on the edge of town and enjoy it on foot.

This honey-coloured town provides the perfect Cotswold scene. All its central buildings are beautiful; of special note are the 15th-century wool **church**❖❖ of St James, full of elaborate brasses and monuments; **Grevel House**❖, dating from 1380; and the Jacobean **market hall**❖ (1627) and the ruined **Campden Manor**❖ (1613), with its surviving almshouses.

The Cotswold Way

The 100-mile corkscrew journey of this long-distance footpath is best walked south–north with the prevailing wind at your back. Any reasonably fit walker should be able to tackle it within about ten days. The final 10-mile section links two of the most beautiful Cotswold settlements: Stanton and Chipping Campden.

Accommodation and food in or near Chipping Campden

Cotswold House £££ *The Square, Chipping Campden; tel: 01386 840330; fax: 01386 840310; reception@cotswold-house.com; www.cotswoldhouse.com.* Quiet, charming 17th-century town house hotel with magnificent period interior. Superb cooking in the Garden Restaurant or Hicks' Brasserie – a good place for lunch.

Malt House ££ *Broad Campden; tel: 01386 840295; fax: 01386 841334; nick@the-malt-house.freeserve.co.uk; www.malt-house.co.uk.* Exquisite cottage with imaginatively decorated interior in a gorgeous village. Excellent cooking.

Old Bakery £££ *High Street, Blockley; tel/fax: 01386 700408.* Archetypal Cotswold guesthouse with stylish décor and ambitious cooking.

CIRENCESTER❖❖

ℹ Tourist Information *Market Place; tel: 01285 654180; cirencestertic@cotswold.gov.uk.*

🏛 Corinium Museum ££ *Park Street; tel: 01285 655611. Closed for restoration until autumn 2003.*

🍴 Swan Yard Café £ *6 Swan Yard; tel: 01285 641300. Small, family-run café offering good-value home cooking.*

Right
Cirencester parish church

The former Roman settlement of *Corinium* developed at the intersection of three major routes – the Foss Way, Ermin Street and Akeman Street – and was second only to *Londinium* in size. The **Corinium Museum**❖❖ contains finds from the Roman era, including some splendid mosaics. Today this lively and attractive market town is still an important hub, and is often called 'capital of the Cotswolds'. The **church of St John the Baptist**❖ is one of the Cotswolds' finest 'wool churches'. **Cirencester Park** on the west side of town is an 18th-century estate surrounded by the tallest yew hedge in Europe.

GLOUCESTER✢✢

ℹ️ **Tourist Information**
28 Southgate Street; tel: 01452 396572; tourism@gloucester.gov.uk.

Below
Batsford Arboretum

Gloucester's heyday was in Norman times, and it rose to great heights as a medieval religious centre. As the Severn silted, it declined as a trading centre, but a canal, opened in 1827, made it a viable inland port. The city was badly damaged in wartime, but its superb **cathedral**✢✢✢, with the second-largest medieval east window in England, was miraculously spared.

In Gloucester Docks, the **National Waterways Museum**✢✢ (*Llanthony Warehouse, Gloucester Docks; tel: 01452 318054; www.nwm.org.uk. Open daily*) traces the history of Britain's inland waterways network, with lots of interactive displays, including a miniature lock chamber.

Cotswold gardens✢✢

There are dozens of lovely gardens in the Cotswolds, from the stately municipal parks of Cheltenham to a host of small cottage plots opened occasionally to the public through the National Gardens Scheme. **Hidcote Manor**✢✢ is a series of elegant garden 'rooms', with lots of rare shrubs and old roses. **Snowshill Manor**✢✢ has a delightful organic cottagey garden with superb views. The manor's eccentric museum is an eclectic assembly of curios. Privately owned **Kiftsgate Court**✢✢ is famous for its roses. **Batsford Arboretum**✢ contains over 1500 trees from all over the world, including many magnolias, and has lovely spring bulbs and autumn colour. **Painswick Rococo Garden**✢ is a unique 18th-century garden in a hidden valley. Gorgeous views and quaint Gothic follies add to its charms.

Hidcote Manor Garden £££ *Hidcote Bartrim, 4 miles NE of Chipping Campden; tel: 01386 438333; hidcote@ntrust.org.uk. Open Apr–Oct Sat–Wed 1030–1730 (Thu June–July); NT.*

Snowshill Manor and Garden £££ *Snowshill, 3 miles SW of Broadway; tel: 01386 852410; snowshillmanor@ntrust.org.uk. Open Apr–Oct Wed–Sun 1200–1700 (Mon July–Aug); timed ticket system; NT.*

Kiftsgate Court ££ *Off B4081 3 miles NE of Chipping Campden; tel: 01386 438777; info@kiftsgate.co.uk; www.kiftsgate.co.uk. Open Apr–Sept Wed, Thu and Sun 1400–1800 (1200–1800 June–July including Sat).*

Batsford Arboretum ££ *Batsford, 1 mile W of Moreton-in-Marsh on A44; tel: 01386 701441: batsarb@batsfound. freeserve.co.uk. Open Mar–Nov daily 1000–1700 (weekends only in winter).*

Painswick Rococo Garden ££ *Painswick, on B4073; tel: 01452 813204; info@rococogarden.co.uk; www.rococogarden. co.uk. Open Wed–Sun 1100–1700 (May–Sept daily, closed Dec).*

NORTHLEACH✦✦

Cotswold Heritage Centre ££ *Fosseway; tel: 01451 860715; www.cotswold.gov.uk. Open Apr–Oct Mon–Sat 1000–1700, Sun 1400–1700; seasonal TIC.*

Keith Harding's World of Mechanical Music ££ *High Street; tel: 01451 860181. Open daily 1000–1800.*

Chedworth Roman Villa ££ *Off A429 near Yanworth; tel: 01242 890256. Open Mar–Oct Tue–Sun 1000–1700 (1100–1600 off season); NT.*

This enticing town on the Fosse Way has a wonderful **church✦**, famed for its memorial brasses to local wool merchants. Other sights are the **Cotswold Heritage Centre✦**, in the old House of Correction, and a **World of Mechanical Music✦** in an old wool merchant's house. Four miles southwest, down leafy lanes, is 2nd-century AD **Chedworth Roman villa✦✦**, with its well-preserved baths, mosaics and a shrine.

STRATFORD-UPON-AVON✦✦✦

Tourist Information *Bridgefoot; tel: 01789 293127.*

An inclusive ticket (valid for a year) admits visitors to the following six properties, though separate admissions are available. Tel: 01789 204016; www.shakespeare.org.uk.

Shakespeare's Birthplace ££ *Henley Street. Open Mon–Sat 0900–1700 (1000–1600 in winter), Sun 0930–1700 (1030–1600 in winter).*

Hall's Croft ££ *Old Town; open Mon–Sat 0930–1700 (1100–1600 in winter), Sun 1000–1700 (1100–1600 in winter). Will's daughter Susanna lived here. Walled garden and a restaurant.*

Right
Shakespeare's birthplace

Stratford has become a world-famous literary shrine, besieged by visitors on the Shakespeare trail. The best aspects of the town are its picturesque riverside setting, its theatres, where the Royal Shakespeare Company stages some of the world's finest productions, and the quaint Tudor properties owned by the **Shakespeare Birthplace Trust**, including the half-timbered house in which William Shakespeare was allegedly born on 23 April 1564. The **Royal Shakespeare Theatre** and the adjacent Swan Theatre offer backstage tours. Boat trips on the Avon are a popular diversion in summer.

Nash's House and New Place ££ *Chapel Street. Open Mon–Sat 0930–1700 (1100–1600 in winter), Sun 1000–1700 (1200–1600 in winter).* Shakespeare died in New Place in 1616. The house next door was the home of his grand-daughter's husband, Thomas Nash.

Anne Hathaway's Cottage ££ *Shottery, 1 mile NW of centre. Open Mon–Sat 0900–1700 (1000–1600 in winter), Sun 0930–1700 (1030–1600 in winter).* The family home of Shakespeare's wife.

Mary Arden's House and Shakespeare Countryside Museum ££ *Wilmcote, 3 miles N. Open Mon–Sat 0930–1700 (1000–1600 in winter), Sun 1000–1700 (1030–1600 in winter).* Shakespeare's mother was instantly courted by his father once she inherited her legacy of this fine house. Rare breeds, working forge, falconry displays.

Harvard House and Museum of British Pewter *High Street. Open May–Oct Fri–Sun 1130–1630 (Thu July–Aug).* Dating from 1596, this ornate building was the home of Katherine Rogers, whose son founded Harvard University.

Royal Shakespeare Company *Waterside; tel: 0870 6091110 (box office bookings); 01789 403405 (theatre tours); www.rsc.org.uk.*

Right
The Garrick Inn and Harvard House

🌙 Be selective – Stratford has loads of guesthouses and some decent pubs, but eating places are often expensive and indifferent.

Victoria Spa Lodge £
Bishopton Lane, Bishopton, Stratford-upon-Avon; tel: 01789 267985; fax: 01789 204728; ptozer@ victoriaspalodge. demon.co.uk. Canalside B&B in an elegant Victorian house.

Right
Rooftops, Nash's House

WINCHCOMBE✢✢

🏛 **Hailes Abbey ££**
Hailes, off B4632; tel: 01242 602398; customers@english-heritage.org.uk. Open Apr–Sept daily 1000–1800, Oct 1000–1700; NT/EH.

Sudeley Castle £££ *Off B4632; tel: 01242 602308; www.sudeleycastle.co.uk. Open Apr–Oct daily 1100–1700, gardens Mar–Oct 1030–1730.*

The grandeur of Winchcombe's impressively gargoyled **church**✢✢ indicates something of the town's medieval stature. It was once the most important town in the Cotswolds. **Hailes Abbey**✢, 2 miles northeast, was one of England's greatest Cistercian monasteries. **Sudeley Castle**✢, former home of Katherine Parr (Henry VIII's last wife), reconstructed as a domestic residence in the 19th century, has fine Tudor-style gardens. **Belas Knap**✢, to the south of the town, is a fine example of a ridge-top neolithic long barrow dating from about 3000 BC.

Right
Stanway House

Suggested tour

Tourist Information The Brewery, Sheep Street, Burford; tel: 01993 823558; or 33 Church Street, Tetbury; tel: 01666 503552; or Hollis House, The Square, Stow-on-the-Wold; tel: 01451 831082; stowtic@cotswold.gov.uk.

Prinknash Abbey and Pottery £ Prinknash; tel: 01452 812066; www.prinknashabbey.org.uk. Open daily 0900–1730 (1630 in winter).

Owlpen Manor ££ Uley 2 miles E of Dursley; tel: 01453 860261; sales@owlpen.com; www.owlpen.com. Open Apr–Sept Tue–Sun 1400–1700 (restaurant from 1200; tel: 01453 860816).

Westonbirt Arboretum ££ Westonbirt; tel: 01666 880220; www.westonbirtarboretum.com. Open 1000–dusk.

Cotswold Water Park On A419 near South Cerney; tel: 01285 861459; www.waterpark.org. Parking charge.

Total distance: 110 miles (177km). Ad 34 miles (55km) for the Stroud detour.

Time: 4–5 hours.

Links: From Gloucester, a 16-mile drive along the A40 takes you to Ross-on-Wye for the Wye Valley (*see page 184*), or join the M5 for southwest England. Cirencester's good road connections give easy access to Wiltshire and North Somerset (*see page 222*).

Route: From **STRATFORD** ❶, take the B439 southwest signed Bidford-on-Avon, turning south on the A46 through **Evesham**. Leave on the A44 across the fertile plains of the **Vale of Evesham**◦, calling at the pretty village of **Broadway**◦◦ (enjoyable out of season). A teddy-bear museum attracts children of all ages and an 18th-century tower is the second-highest point in the Cotswolds. Take the B4632 southwest, signed for Winchcombe. Just off to the left of this road are **Buckland**◦, **Stanton**◦◦ and **Stanway**◦◦, all thatch and mellow stone, with superbly kept gardens. Stanway House is beautiful, with deep golden walls and mullioned windows. **Snowshill Manor**◦◦ (*see page 129*) lies a short distance to the east (jiggle round a few lanes to reach it). From **WINCHCOMBE** ❷, take the Charlton Abbots lane south past Belas Knap (climb to the long barrow for breathtaking views). Turn left at Andoversford on to the A40 and head for **NORTHLEACH** ❸. After seeing **Chedworth Roman villa**◦◦, head south on the Fosse Way (A429) to **CIRENCESTER** ❹.

Detour: Take the A40 right from Andoversford into **CHELTENHAM** ❺ and **GLOUCESTER** ❻, exiting via the A417 to pick up the A46, heading south past **Prinknash Abbey**◦ a modern building housing a Benedictine community whose distinctive pottery is now exported all over the world. Just south lies **Painswick**◦◦, famed for its churchyard of 99 ancient yew trees, and its **Rococo Garden**◦ (*see page 129*). At the workaday mill town of **Stroud**, the contours plunge through deep wooded combes. A scenic route along a valley ridge leads south (B4066) towards Dursley via **Uley**◦, which is crowned with a huge hillfort. **Owlpen Manor**◦ is a romantic Cotswold house with a lovely garden and a medieval tithe barn restaurant. Pick up the A4135 east and head for the pleasant stone country town of **Tetbury**◦◦. On the A433 south of Tetbury just beyond Highgrove, home of the Prince of Wales, is the **Westonbirt Arboretum**◦◦, one of the largest temperate tree collections in the world. Return to Cirencester on the A433.

Getting out of the car: The River Thames begins its course near Kemble, a couple of miles southwest of Cirencester. The source is marked with a fenced monument (a statue of Father Thames). From here you can follow the **Thames Path**◦◦ all the way downstream, past the 132 lakes of the **Cotswold Water Park**◦ near South Cerney.

ⓘ **Cotswold Wildlife Park £££** Bradwell Grove, on A361 2 miles S of A40; tel: 01993 823006; www.cotswoldwildlifepark.co.uk. Open daily 1000–1700 or dusk.

Cotswold Farm Park ££ Guiting Power; tel: 01451 850307; www.cotswoldfarmpark.co.uk. Open Apr–Sept daily 1030–1700.

Sezincote ££ Moreton-in-Marsh off A424 1 mile S of Bourton-on-the-Hill; tel: 01386 700444. Open May–July and Sept Thu–Fri 1430–1800; gardens Jan–Nov Thu–Fri 1400–1800 or dusk.

Kelmscott Manor £££ Tel: 01367 252486; www.kelmscottmanor.co.uk. Open Apr–Sept Wed only 1100–1700 and some Sats 1400–1700.

From Cirencester, take the B4425 northeast to **Bibury**✦✦, described by William Morris as the most beautiful village in England. Just across the River Coln is a line of weavers' cottages that date back some 300 years. Haunted Arlington Mill is now a folk museum, next door to a trout farm. **Burford**✦✦ is full of pleasant old pubs and tearooms and enticing shops; its nearby **Cotswold Wildlife Park**✦✦ is a popular family attraction. From Burford, take minor roads northwest signed through the **Barringtons**✦ in the Windrush valley, then head north via the **Rissingtons**✦ to picturesque **Bourton-on-the-Water**✦✦. The **Slaughters**✦ (Upper and Lower) are worth another brief detour before you get to **Stow-on-the-Wold**✦, a well-kept regional centre and the highest town in the Cotswolds. Three miles west is the popular **Cotswold Farm Park**✦, which looks after rare breeds. From Stow, head north to pleasantly bustling **Moreton-in-Marsh**✦. Head west on the A44, where the main sights are the **Batsford Arboretum**✦✦ (see page 129) and **Sezincote**✦✦ (an exotically domed mansion, said to have inspired the Brighton Pavilion), near Bourton-on-the-Hill. Head north on the B4479, through the classic stone villages of **Blockley**✦, **Broad Campden**✦, CHIPPING CAMPDEN ❼ and **Mickleton**, calling at **Hidcote Manor**✦✦ and **Kiftsgate**✦✦ (see page 129) before returning on the B4632 to Stratford.

Also worth exploring: East of Cirencester, the A417 leads to the attractive riverside town of **Lechlade**, the last navigable point on the Thames (a busy boating centre). There are handsome churches nearby, at Fairford and Inglesham. Just beyond Lechlade, a left-hand turn takes you to **Kelmscott Manor**✦✦, William Morris's house, a fascinating repository of Arts and Crafts and Pre-Raphaelite style.

Accommodation and food on the route

Evesham Hotel ££ Coopers Lane, off Waterside, Evesham; tel: 01386 765566; fax: 01386 765443; reception@eveshamhotel.com; www.eveshamhotel.com. Idiosyncratically managed but disarming manor-house hotel by the banks of the Avon. Excellent cooking.

Dial House ££ The Chestnuts, High Street, Bourton-on-the-Water; tel: 01451 822244; fax: 01451 810126; info@dialhousehotel.com. Friendly, relaxed small hotel in centre of a popular Cotswold village. Antiques in the main house; modern pine in the Coach House annexe.

Burford House ££ 99 High Street, Burford; tel: 01993 823151; fax: 01993 823240; stay@burfordhouse.co.uk; www.burford-house.co.uk. Upmarket B&B accommodation in the middle of this charming historic town; beautifully decorated, cosy rooms with teddy bears and sloping ceilings.

Lamb Inn ££ Sheep Street, Burford; tel: 01993 823155; fax: 01993 822228. Lovely rambling 17th-century inn on a quiet side street.

Barn House £ *152 High Street, Broadway; tel/fax: 01386 858633;* *barnhouse@btinternet.com.* Charming 17th-century property in extensive grounds, offering B&B with a sense of style and character.

Lygon Arms £££ *Broadway; tel: 01386 852255; fax: 01386 858611;* *info@the-lygon-arms.co.uk; www.savoy-group.co.uk.* Famous old coaching inn with fascinating period features; very pricy, but very comfortable. The Brasserie makes a good lunch stop.

Cardynham House £ *The Cross, Painswick; tel: 01452 814006; fax: 01452 812321; info@cardynham.co.uk.* Lovely stone cottage hotel with sumptuous décor, owned by an artistic Californian.

Lords of the Manor £££ *Upper Slaughter; tel: 01451 820243; fax: 01451 820596; lordsofthemanor@btinternet.com; www.lordsofthemanor.com.* Glorious Cotswold manor house hotel, skilfully modernised and with attractive gardens. Ideal for a cossetted, tranquil stay.

Marsh Goose ££ *Moreton-in-Marsh; tel: 01608 653500.* Inventive cooking in pleasing stone house decorated with local artists' work.

Thames Valley and Chilterns

Ratings

Heritage	●●●●●
Pubs/restaurants	●●●●○
Scenery	●●●●○
Towns and villages	●●●●○
Walking	●●●●○
Archaeology	●●●○○
Boating	●●●○○
Children	●●●○○

The outstanding sightseeing attractions on this route are the dreaming spires of England's oldest university city, Oxford. At the other end of the tour, Windsor and Eton provide another dose of English heritage. These are immensely rewarding places to visit, but a complete nightmare for motorists. Inevitably, the alluring countryside between Oxford and London suffers from overcrowding. The area's dominant geographical features are the River Thames and the band of chalk hills known as the Chilterns, which stretch between Dunstable and Reading. The breezy downs southeast of Oxford also make wonderful walking or touring territory, and are generally less crowded. The ancient 85-mile Ridgeway path, believed to be 5000 years old, can be walked or cycled. There are several dozen well-groomed villages along its route, all of which provide a good excuse to stop – usually at a splendid pub.

ETON ❖❖

Eton College ££ *Tel: 01753 671177; www.etoncollege.com. Open Apr–Sept 1030–1630 (closed am in term time); guided tours; residential summer courses.*

Right
Fourth of June celebrations at Eton

Opposite
Oxford's Radcliffe Camera

Eton College, Britain's most exclusive public school, was founded in 1440 by Henry VI. Parts of the existing buildings date from this time, notably the superb frescoed late-Gothic Chapel in Perpendicular style. Official tours and a small museum explain the arcane origins of Etonian traditions.

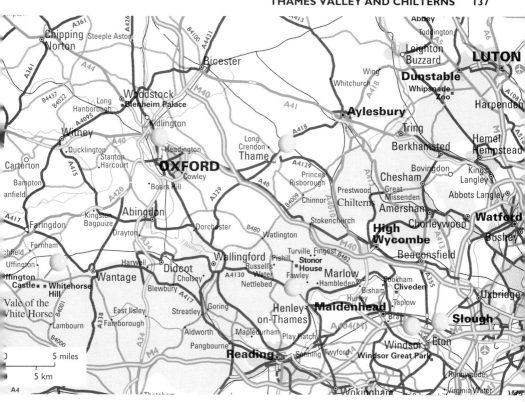

OXFORD***

ℹ Tourist Information The Old School, Gloucester Green; tel: 01865 726871.

🏛 Ashmolean Museum Beaumont Street; tel: 01865 278000; www.ashmol.ox.ac.uk. Open Tue–Sat 1000–1700, Sun 1400–1700 (June–Aug Thu 1000–1900); free.

Pitt Rivers Museum Parks Road; tel: 01865 270927; www.prm.ox.ac.uk. Open Mon–Sat 1200–1630; Sun 1400–1630.

University Botanic Gardens £ High Street; tel: 01865 286690; www.botanic-garden.ox.ac.uk. Open daily from 0900.

Oxford Story £££ 6 Broad Street; tel: 01865 728822; www.oxfordstory.co.uk. Open daily all year; July–Aug 0930–1700 (reduced hours off season).

Oxford's venerable university claims origins some 50 years older than Cambridge's. In 1167, a number of English scholars expelled from the Parisian Sorbonne settled here. There are now 39 colleges in total, each largely self-governing, with romantic buildings and mysterious ancient academic traditions. Most of the historic parts of the city lie within easy walking distance of the **Carfax** central crossroads. The surviving tower of a 14th-century church marks the spot. To see some of the best college quads (courtyards), join one of the walking tours from the Tourist Information Centre. At **Christ Church***, founded by Cardinal Wolsey, the bell (Great Tom) in the main gate rings 101 times every evening at 9pm, originally to summon students back to their rooms. Across Tom Quad stands the college **chapel**, which doubles as Oxford's cathedral (England's smallest). **Magdalen**, perhaps the most beautiful college, has a medieval gargoyled tower and a deerpark. After that, track down Queen's, Merton, All Souls, Corpus Christi, Trinity, St John's and New College, and perhaps Hertford, with its Bridge of Sighs. Oxford's great university library, the **Bodleian**, houses over 5.5 million volumes (guided tours show you a tiny fraction of these). One of its reading rooms, the Baroque domed **Radcliffe Camera**, and the classical **Sheldonian Theatre** (used for academic ceremonies) are two of central Oxford's most striking architectural landmarks. The biggest and most famous of Oxford's museums is the **Ashmolean***, the oldest in England and one of its best. The **Pitt Rivers** is a fascinating assembly of ethnographic curios in a splendid cast-iron building.

There are plenty of ways to relax in Oxford. The city has many gardens and green spaces – from the riverside Christ Church Meadow, walk to the **Botanic Gardens*** and Magdalen bridge, and try punting on the River Cherwell. Further afield lie the University Parks and **Port Meadow***, beyond the Oxford canal. If you have children with you, head for the **Oxford Story***, an entertaining trip through 800 years of university history.

Accommodation and food in Oxford

Brown's £ 5–11 Woodstock Road; tel: 01865 511995. Ever-popular informal restaurant serving tempting meals and snacks on bentwood furnishings in jungly greenery. Live piano music.

Café Varvara £ Modern Art Oxford, 30 Pembroke Street; tel: 01865 722733. A good reason to visit this attractive art gallery; a stylish, light café with friendly staff. Good cakes and vegetarian options.

Turf Tavern ££ 4 Bath Place, off Holywell Street; tel: 01865 243235. Atmospheric 17th-century pub serving good food in a quaint alleyway. An Oxford institution with students and residents.

The Perch ££ *Binsey Lane; tel: 01865 240386.* Worth the walk across Portmeadow for this bustling thatched inn; lovely setting and good food.

Le Petit Blanc ££ *71–72 Walton Street; tel: 01865 510999; oxford@lepetitblanc.co.uk.* Stylish brasserie in Oxford's Jericho area, serving breakfast and tea as well as imaginative set-price meals.

Cherwell Boathouse ££ *50 Bardwell Road; tel: 01865 552746; www.cherwellboathouse.co.uk.* One of the nicest ways to enjoy a typically Oxford scene, beside the punt-hire slipway. Charming, deceptively simple ambience; short, sophisticated menus and excellent wines.

Old Parsonage Hotel ££ *1 Banbury Road; tel: 01865 310210; fax: 01865 311262; www.oldparsonage-hotel.co.uk.* Conveniently central, but with some parking, this 17th-century townhouse offers charmingly relaxing accommodation and outstanding food (reserve a table).

Below
The Bodleian Library

THAME❖❖

Tourist Information Tel: 01844 212834.

The unspoilt centre of this ancient market town has well-preserved brick and half-timbered houses spanning five centuries on its wide mile-long main street, and several fine inns (especially the 15th-century Birdcage).

Accommodation and food in or near Thame

Sir Charles Napier ££ *Sprigg's Alley, nr Chinnor; tel: 01494 483011.* Stylish, characterful country pub with informal atmosphere, serving terrific food and wines.

Old Trout ££ *29–30 Lower High Street, Thame; tel: 01844 212146; fax: 01844 212614; mj4trout@aol.com.* Olde worlde charm (thatched and buckled timberwork) enhances this restaurant-with-rooms. Fishy menus.

THAMES VALLEY❖❖❖

South of Oxford the Thames cuts a bold, sinuous course between the chalky uplands of the Chilterns and the Lambourn Downs. Along the leafy watercourse are attractive historic towns, a host of pleasure craft, and bridges, locks, weirs and islands. The best way to see it is by boat; all the main centres offer cabin cruiser hire, moorings or river trips. The 180-mile Thames Path also follows the river, served by efficient public transport routes.

Accommodation and food in the Thames Valley

George Hotel ££ *25 High Street, Dorchester-on-Thames; tel: 01865 340404; fax: 01865 341620.* Attractive timbered hotel on High Street, comfortably modernised but with some antiques.

Beetle & Wedge ££ *Ferry Lane, Moulsford-on-Thames; tel: 01491 651381; fax: 01491 651376.* This classily converted boatyard is set on one of the best bits of the Thames.

Ye Olde Bell £££ *High Street, Hurley; tel: 01628 825881; fax: 01628 825939; sales@ramadajarvis.co.uk.* Supremely comfortable and very ancient inn (allegedly the oldest in England), now an impressive chain hotel with a good restaurant.

VALE OF THE WHITE HORSE✧✧

ⓘ Tourist Information/Vale and Downland Museum
£ *19 Church Street, Wantage; tel: 01235 760176. Open Tue–Sun.*

ⓘ Lambourn Trainers Association ££
Windsor House, Lambourn; tel: 01488 71347. Open Mon–Sat 1000–1200; tours by appointment only; wear suitable shoes.

ⓒ The Craven £
Fernham Road, Uffington; tel: 01367 820449; carol@thecraven.co.uk. Prettily thatched B&B in country setting near the White Horse. Dinners available.

This chalk downland area on the Oxfordshire–Berkshire borders is rich in archaeological remains. On the popular walking route of the ancient Ridgeway path, which runs along the uplands, **Uffington Castle** is an Iron Age camp, and **Wayland's Smithy** is a neolithic burial mound. In the smooth green hillside above Uffington a stylised **horse**✧ is thought to be Britain's oldest chalk carving, possibly as early as 3000 BC. Real-live thoroughbreds can be seen exercising all around this area, where many trainers have stables. Guided tours round the racehorse training centre can be arranged. The quiet market town of Wantage is the area's main centre; its **Vale and Downland Museum**✧ in the Tourist Information Centre gives a good regional overview.

Right
View from Uffington White Horse

WINDSOR✦✦✦

ℹ Tourist Information 24 High Street; tel: 01753 743900; www.windsor.gov.uk.

ℙ Parking in central Windsor can be very difficult, especially in summer. The best option is the vast Park and Ride car park at Legoland (free); regular shuttle buses operate to the centre of town every half-hour (£).

ℚ It is easy to reach central Windsor by public transport. Tour buses follow a circular route, including Eton and Datchet.

🏰 Windsor Castle £££ Saxon Tower; tel: 01753 869898; www.the-royal-collection.org.uk. Open daily 0945–1715 (1615 in winter); St George's Chapel closed for sightseeing on Sun; official engagements may mean some sections are inaccessible (admission reduced); Changing of the Guard Apr–June Mon–Sat at 1100 (alternate days off season excluding Sun).

Savill Garden ££ Wick Lane, Englefield Green; tel: 01753 874518. Open daily 1000–1800 (1600 in winter); admission charges vary seasonally (highest Apr–May).

Valley Gardens Englefield Green; no tel; parking charge (automatic barrier).

Legoland £££ Winkfield Road; tel: 08705 040404; www.legoland.co.uk. Open Mar–Oct 1000–1700 (later in school holidays).

Windsor Castle✦✦✦ dominates the skyline of this riverside town in truly regal style. The oldest continuously inhabited royal residence in the country, the castle was originally built in 1070 to defend the western approaches to London. In 1917, George V changed his family's surname (Saxe-Coburg) to Windsor, after his favourite home. After a serious fire in 1992, Windsor Castle has risen like a phoenix from its ashes in renewed splendour. Principal features include **St George's Chapel✦✦✦**, an outstanding example of late-Gothic architecture; the Round Tower built by Henry II, housing the Royal Archives; and the **State Apartments✦✦✦**, which house treasures dating from the time of Edward III. **Queen Mary's Dolls' House✦✦** is an exquisite 1:12-scale model. The Queen's Golden Jubilee in 2002 was marked by a contemporary garden by the entrance.

The town is mainly Victorian. Its immediate surroundings encompass **Windsor Great Park✦**, a tranche of well-kept parkland covering 4800 acres. **Savill Garden✦✦**, within the Park, is a stunning collection of rare trees, shrubs and roses. A mile away, the **Valley Gardens✦** contain an enormous planting of rhododendrons. **Legoland✦✦** is an immensely popular attraction for families with young children. Allow a full day to see this imaginative and ever-expanding universe of plastic building bricks.

Accommodation and food in or near Windsor

Sir Christopher Wren's House £££ Thames Street, Windsor; tel: 01753 861354; fax: 01753 860172. Smart luxury complex in elegant, historic buildings near Windsor Castle. Expensive, but very comfortable.

Waterside £££ Ferry Road, Bray; tel: 01628 620691; fax: 01628 78710; www.waterside-inn.co.uk. A top-flight gastronomic establishment. Very French food in very English surroundings, right on the riverside. Book ahead, and take a full wallet.

Alfonso's ££ 19–21 Station Hill Parade, Cookham; tel: 01628 525775. Long-established family restaurant serving pricey but accomplished menus (some with a Spanish tang).

Above
An Oxfordshire cottage

🛈 **Tourist Information** 25 Bridge Street, Abingdon; tel: 01235 522711; or Town Hall, Market Place, Wallingford; tel: 01491 826972; or King's Arms Barn, King's Road, Henley-on-Thames; tel: 01491 578034; or Central Library, St Ives Road, Maidenhead; tel: 01628 796502.

🏛 **Stonor House ££** Stonor; tel: 01491 638587; www.stonor.co.uk. Open Apr–Sept Sun 1400–1730 (July–Aug Wed).

Suggested tour

Total distance: 114 miles (183km). Add 14 miles (22km) for the Goring detour.

Time: 4–5 hours.

Links: It's an easy step from Oxford to Burford, or from Wantage to Faringdon, for the Cotswolds (*see page 126*). South of Wantage, the A338 picks up the Wiltshire and North Somerset route at Hungerford (*see page 222*).

Route: Leave **OXFORD** ❶ on the London road (A40 east) turning off left for **THAME** ❷ via the A418. Take a brief detour northeast to the historic village of **Long Crendon❖**. Returning to Thame, take the B4445 southeast to **Chinnor**, then turn right across the Bledlow Ridge (good views and walks) on the B4009, crossing the A40 and M40 motorway. Continue southwest to **Watlington**, an appealing Georgian settlement on the Icknield Way. Take the B480 southeast to Russell's Water and Pishill, where **Stonor House❖** is an ancient house in a deerpark. Several local villages near by (Nettlebed, Turville,

River and Rowing Museum ££ *Mill Meadows, Henley-on-Thames; tel: 01491 415600; www.rrm.co.uk. Open May–Aug daily 1000–1730 (1700 off season).*

Stanley Spencer Gallery £ *King's Hall, Cookham; tel: 01628 471885; diana.benson@ntworld.com; www.stanleyspencer.org. Open Easter–Oct daily 1030–1730, weekends only in winter 1100–1700.*

Cliveden £££ *Taplow, Maidenhead; tel: 01628 605069; cliveden@ntrust.org.uk. Open Apr–Oct Thu and Sun 1500–1730, gardens Mar–Oct daily 1100–1800 (1600 in Nov–Dec); NT.*

Salter's Steamers ££ *Thames Side, Windsor; tel: 01753 865832. Boat trips May–Sept.*

Hobbs of Henley ££ *Station Road, Henley-on-Thames; tel: 01491 572035; www.hobbs-of-henley.com. Boat trips and self-drive hire Apr–Sept.*

Fawley, Fingest, Hambleden) have good pubs. Christmas Common makes a super start for walks. Follow signs for **Henley-on-Thames****, a historic **THAMES VALLEY ❸** town of brick and timbered architecture. An award-winning **River and Rowing Museum*** documents its main obsession. From Henley, the widening river flows past private moorings and manicured lawns.

Downstream, tree-lined **Hurley** and **Bisham** make good picnic spots, with well-preserved cottages, locks and islands south of the attractive waterfront town of **Marlow***. The imposing Compleat Angler hotel dominates the river here; fishing is still a favourite pastime, and boat cruises operate in summer. Downstream, at **Cookham****, the **Stanley Spencer Gallery**** contains a good range of his strange visionary paintings, inspired by this idyllic stretch of willow-shaded riverside. An unusual ceremony called 'swan upping' takes place during July, when cygnets are caught and marked to signify royal ownership. Follow the Thames south on its east bank via **Cliveden****, a palatial 19th-century house with racy political associations. The pretty village of **Bray*** gives a final fling of cottagey charm before the Thames enters Greater London.

To follow the river by road, turn left after Taplow on the A4, then right on the B3026 to **ETON** ❹** and **WINDSOR*** ❺**. Circle the Great Park clockwise. At **Runnymede***, memorials commemorate the Magna Carta, sealed here by King John in 1215. The A328, A30 and A329 take you past the **Savill Garden****, **Valley Gardens*** and **Virginia Water***. Take the B383 and the A330 to White Waltham. Turn left to join the B3024 via Twyford, continue west through Sonning, turn left at Playhatch (A4155), right on the A4074, detouring left for the remote little hamlet of **Mapledurham***, with its watermill and a mullioned Elizabethan mansion clustered in watermeadows. Take the next left turn off the A4074; **Pangbourne** is reached by a Victorian toll bridge where the Thames tumbles over a weir. A few handsome buildings survive from Georgian and Edwardian times. Head north through the **Goring Gap***, a gorge-like channel carved during the Ice Age. **Goring**** presides over one of the river's most scenic and accessible reaches. At picturesque **Streatley*** beyond the lock on the opposite bank, Georgian houses mingle with knapped flint.

Detour: From Goring, head west on the B4009, turning right at Aldworth on unclassified roads running parallel to the Ridgeway via **East Ilsley** and Farnborough. Turn right on the B4494 to **Wantage***, then west on the B4507 along the **VALE OF THE WHITE HORSE ❻**. The White Horse, Uffington Castle and Wayland's Smithy lie to the left of the road after 6 miles. Turn right via Uffington village, and join the A420 via Fernham. The old town of **Faringdon*** is worth a brief detour. Return to Oxford northeast on the A420, detouring via Abingdon (right on the A415 after 9 miles) if you prefer.

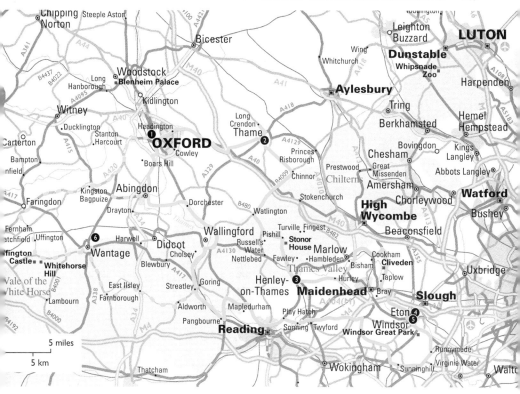

Wallingford Museum £ *Flint House, High Street; tel: 01491 835065; museum@ galatham.demon.co.uk. Open Mar–Nov Tue–Fri 1400–1700, Sat 1030–1700 (July–Aug Sun 1400–1700).*

Blenheim Palace £££
Woodstock; tel: 01993 811325; www.blenheimpalace.com. Open Mar–Oct daily 1030–1730, park open all year daily 0900–1700.

From Goring, head north on the west bank via Moulsford (A329), crossing the river south of the pretty riverside town of **Wallingford**◆◆ to join the A4074. Detour left through charming **Dorchester**◆◆, where a late Norman abbey stands in stately ruins, and brick or half-timbered houses and antique shops line the streets. Turn left when you reach the A415. The Benedictine Abbey at the water's edge at **Abingdon**◆ was founded in the 7th century in one of Britain's oldest settlements. Today, the tranquil watermeadows around the town offer marvellous walks. Return to Oxford on the A34.

Also worth exploring: Any exit point from Oxford's ring road takes you through pleasant scenery and interesting villages. The route northwest on the A44 leads to the enjoyable and civilised little town of **Woodstock**◆◆; **Blenheim Palace**◆◆ (Vanbrugh's palatial stately home) is near by. Winston Churchill is buried at Bladon churchyard.

Accommodation and food near the route

Royal Oak ££ *The Square, Yattendon; tel: 01635 201325; fax: 01635 201926; theroyaloakhotel@hotmail.com; www.regalhotels.co.uk.* Slightly off the tour route, but well worth a side trip, this superbly comfortable country inn has wonderful food and lovely furnishings.

Norfolk: the Broads and the Samphire Coast

Ratings

Outdoor activities	●●●●●
Stately homes and gardens	●●●●●
Wildlife	●●●●●
Beaches	●●●●○
Historic sites	●●●●○
Museums	●●●●○
Shopping	●●●●○
Scenery	●●○○○

'Very flat, Norfolk,' remarks a character in Noël Coward's *Private Lives*, yet every year thousands head eastwards for boating or birdwatching holidays. The county is still largely unspoilt, with traditional market towns and rural villages built in brick-and-flint, stately homes, gardens, interesting archaeological sites and museums, and nostalgia railways. Aside from the watery wildernesses of The Broads, and the cathedral city of Norwich, Norfolk's main interest lies on its Heritage Coast, particularly between Hunstanton and Sheringham. Stiffkey blues (cockles), Cromer crab and pickled samphire are widely available along here. In the interior – a mix of rich cereal-growing land interspersed with woodland – quiet lanes and long-distance footpaths make good walking and cycling country. Britain's oldest trading route, the Icknield Way, crosses Norfolk near Thetford. Norfolk's present-day main roads mostly radiate from Norwich, while a maze of tiny lanes trickles past hidden villages and ancient churches.

BLICKLING HALL✢✢

🏛 **Blickling Hall £££**
Blickling; tel: 01263 738030. Open Apr–Sept Wed–Sun 1300–1700 (1600 in Oct); gardens open 1015–1715, Tue in Aug and weekends in winter; NT.

🍴 **Ark ££** *The Street, Erpingham; tel: 01263 761535.* Serious French provincial cooking using home-grown produce in an old flint house with a stone-flagged floor. Good-value wines.

Blickling, with its memorable symmetrical Jacobean façade, was the childhood home of Anne Boleyn. It was extensively remodelled in 1628. Inside, prize features include the ornate plasterwork ceiling of the Long Gallery. The grounds contain miles of footpaths.

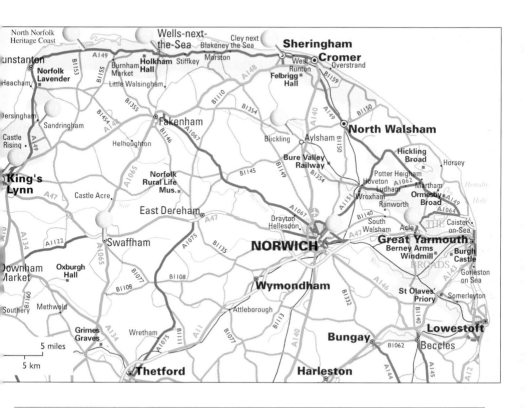

THE BROADS✵✵

ⓘ Tourist Information Station Road, Hoveton; tel: 01603 782281. Seasonal opening.

🏛 NWT Broads Wildlife Centre Ranworth; tel: 01603 270479; admin@ norfolkwildlifefund.org.uk. Open Apr–Oct daily 1000–1700.

Fairhaven Woodland and Water Garden ££ School Road, South Walsham; tel: 01603 270449; fairhavengardens@ norfolkbroads.com; www.norfolkbroads.com/ fairhaven. Open daily 1000–1700 (2100 May–Aug Wed–Thu).

Ⓒ Ivy House Farm ££ Ivy Lane, Oulton Broad, Lowestoft, Suffolk; tel: 01502 501353; fax: 01502 501539; admin@ivyhousefarm.co.uk. A little way off the main route, this excellent farmhouse conversion is within reach of the southern Broads. Faultless rooms, and brilliant cooking in the timbered Crooked Barn restaurant. Walks through the gardens lead to the water's edge.

About thirty shallow man-made lakes were formed east of Norwich in medieval times, when peat-diggings became flooded. The best way to see this area is by boat, and dozens of companies now offer holidays afloat on the interconnected waterways, of which about 125 miles are navigable. The main boating centres are Wroxham, Hickling, Horning and Potter Heigham. The Broads' low-lying reed-beds and woodland are now carefully protected. The distinctive ecology is described in Norfolk Wildlife Trust's **Broads Wildlife Centre✵✵** at Ranworth, a thatched waterfront village. Visitors can climb the flint tower of 900-year-old **St Helen's Church✵**, sometimes dubbed the Cathedral of the Broads. Near Ranworth, the **Fairhaven Garden Trust✵✵** is particularly spectacular in May and June.

Previous page Cromer's fishermen

Right The Broads at Ludham

HOLKHAM HALL✧✧

Holkham Hall £££
Wells-next-the-Sea; tel: 01328 710806; www.holkham.co.uk. Open bank holidays and June–Sept Sun–Thur 1300–1700.

This sallow Palladian mansion built for Sir Thomas Coke in the mid-18th century provides a good day out. The grounds contain the model farms and tree-planting schemes pioneered by a later Thomas Coke, whose agricultural experiments revolutionised farming methods in the 18th and 19th centuries. Inside, the house is sumptuously furnished.

Accommodation and food near Holkham Hall

Hoste Arms £££ *The Green, Burnham Market; tel: 01328 738777; fax: 01328 730103; reception@hostearms.co.uk; www.hostearms.co.uk.* A lively hostelry, one of the well-kept period buildings on the village green, offering charming accommodation and excellent cooking in a cosy interior. Informal bistro meals available.

Lord Nelson £ *Walsingham Road, Burnham Thorpe; tel: 01328 738241; enquiries@nelsonslocal.co.uk; www.nelsonslocal.co.uk.* The naval hero gave his 'going to sea' party here in 1793, in the village of his birth. Good blackboard fare, and cask beers brought straight to your table. Try the rum-based house special (Nelson's Blood) – if you dare.

KING'S LYNN✧✧

Tourist Information *The Custom House, Purfleet Quay; tel: 01553 763044; kings-lynn.tic@west-norfolk.gov.uk.*

True's Yard Heritage Centre £
3–5 North Street; tel: 01553 770479; trues-yard@virgin.net; welcome-to/truesyard. Open daily 0930–1545.

England's fourth-largest town in medieval times, King's Lynn was once an important port with links to Germany and Scandinavia, but it has always been subject to flooding. It still has some fine historic buildings, including two splendid **guildhalls**✧✧ (Trinity and St George's). **True's Yard Heritage Centre**✧✧, in a couple of restored fishermen's cottages, shows the reality of 19th-century life.

Right
The Custom House, King's Lynn

NORTH NORFOLK HERITAGE COAST❖❖❖

ℹ️ **Tourist Information** *Staithe Street, Wells-next-the-Sea;* tel: 01328 710885. *Seasonal opening.*

🏠 **Holme Bird Observatory Reserve** *Holme-next-the-Sea;* tel: 01485 525406. *Open Tue–Sun 1000–1700.*

Titchwell Marsh *Titchwell;* tel: 01485 210779. *Visitor centre open Mar–Nov daily 1000–1700 (1600 in winter); reserve open at all times; RSPB (parking charge for non-members).*

Cley Marshes ££ *Cley-next-the-Sea;* tel: 01263 740008. *Visitor centre open Apr–Oct daily 1000–1700; Nov–Dec Wed–Sun 1000–1600; reserve daily 1000–1700.*

East of Hunstanton, fast-moving tides and longshore drift create an ever-shifting patchwork of mudflats, saltmarsh, shingle and shining pale sand. It is a potentially hazardous seascape. Its many nature reserves provide important breeding grounds and stopovers for migrant birds, and habitats for seals and unusual plants. The environment is particularly fragile at Holme-next-the-Sea, where the recent discovery of a mysterious 'sea henge' of Iron Age tree stumps (now relocated) attracted a sudden influx of visitors.

Accommodation and food on or near the North Norfolk Heritage Coast

Cley Mill £ *Cley-next-the-Sea; tel/fax: 01263 740209.* Charming guesthouse accommodation in an 18th-century windmill. Characterful rooms (some round) with marvellous views – bring your binoculars. Good home cooking.

White Horse £ *4 High Street, Blakeney; tel: 01263 740574; fax: 01263 741303.* Friendly pub-with-rooms in a prime quayside location in one of Norfolk's most popular villages, yet prices are still reasonable. Good food and comfortable rooms.

Old Bakehouse £ *33 High Street, Little Walsingham; tel/fax: 01328 820454; chris.padley@btopenworld.com.* Three simple guest rooms add to the attractions of this restaurant in a historic building. Plain but accomplished Anglo-French cooking.

Below
Wells-next-the-Sea

NORWICH✧✧✧

ⓘ Tourist Information *The Forum, Millennium Plain; tel: 01603 727927.*

ⓕ Dragon Hall £ *115–123 King Street; tel: 01603 663922. Open Mon–Sat 1000–1600 (not Sat in winter).*

Norwich Castle ££ *Castle Hill; tel: 01603 493625; www.norfolk.gov.uk. Open Mon–Sat 1030–1700, Sun 1400–1700; later in school holidays.*

Sainsbury Centre for Visual Arts £ *University of East Anglia; tel: 01603 593199. Open Tue–Sun 1100–1700.*

The historic core of the East Anglian capital seems miraculously unscathed, even after wartime raids. The bobbled spire of the cathedral presides over thirty lesser flint churches, dozens of colourful streets, and chunks of medieval wall. In Norman times, this cloth-producing centre was one of the richest cities in the country. Although it lost ground during the Industrial Revolution, it has recently attracted many high-tech businesses.

The chequerboarded 15th-century **Guildhall**✧✧ and the **Dragon Hall**✧ have outstanding medieval timbering. Two medieval **gateways**✧, Ethelbert and Erpingham, lead from the cathedral close into Tombland, the old Saxon market place. Quaint **Elm Hill**✧ and the art-nouveau **Royal Arcade**✧ are full of attractive shops. On a central mound stands the blind-arcaded **castle keep**✧✧ containing the city's impressively refurbished museum. On the western outskirts are the modern University of East Anglia, and the innovative **Sainsbury Centre for Visual Arts**✧✧, designed by Norman Foster.

Built of pale Caen limestone, Norwich's flamboyant **cathedral**✧✧✧ is easy to spot: its 315-ft spire is the second-highest in England. Its cloisters are the largest in the country, decorated with over 400 carved roof bosses.

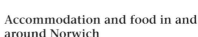

Accommodation and food in and around Norwich

Old Rectory ££ *103 Yarmouth Road, Thorpe St Andrew, Norwich; tel: 01603 700772; fax: 01603 300772; www. oldrectorynorwich.com.* Tranquil, elegant Georgian house in immaculate gardens on the eastern outskirts of Norwich (handy for the Broads). Smart, thoughtfully converted guest rooms and good dinner menus.

By Appointment ££ *25–29 St George's Street, Norwich; tel/fax: 01603 630730.* Memorably flamboyant restaurant-with-rooms in the city centre. Charming 16th-century building, fine cooking and welcoming hosts. Private car park.

SANDRINGHAM❖❖

Sandringham £££
*Sandringham; tel:
01553 612908. Open
Easter–Oct except during
Royal visits; free access to
country park.*

The Queen's intimate country retreat is a favourite venue for the Royal Family, especially at Christmas and New Year. It was originally bought by Queen Victoria for the Prince of Wales in 1862, and extensively remodelled. The interior is a mix of neo-Jacobean and Edwardian styles. The extensive gardens and country park are beautifully kept.

SHERINGHAM❖

**Tourist
Information** *Station
Approach; tel: 01263
824329; in@north-
norfolk.gov.uk. Seasonal
opening.*

This traditional seaside resort has an excellent Blue Flag beach, elaborate sea defences, and a working fishing harbour. Quaint shops and cottages line its main street. The **North Norfolk Railway**❖ (Poppy Line) runs steam excursions to Holt (*tel: 01263 820800; enquiries@nnr.co.uk; www.nnrailway.co.uk; services daily in summer, weekends only off season*).

SWAFFHAM❖

**Iceni Village and
Museums ££** *Cockley
Cley; tel: 01760 724588.
Open Apr–Oct daily
1100–1730.*

**Castle Acre Castle and
Priory ££** *Stocks Green; tel:
01760 755394 or 755161.
Priory open Apr–Sept daily
1000–1800; Oct
1000–1700, Wed–Sun
1000–1600 in winter; castle
ruins open at any time; EH.*

This well-kept Georgian town presides over a large domain of well-to-do farming country, and holds a lively market on Saturdays. Its church has an exceptionally fine 'angel' ceiling. Not far from the town lies the reconstructed village of **Cockley Cley**❖, on the site of an ancient Iceni settlement. Northwards is **Castle Acre**, a charming little place dominated by the imposing ruins of a Norman castle and a Cluniac **priory**❖❖ founded in about 1090.

Suggested tour

**Roots of Norfolk at
Gressenhall ££**
*Beech House, Gressenhall;
tel: 01362 860563. Open
Apr–Oct daily 1000–1700.*

Peter Beales Roses
*London Road, Attleborough;
tel: 01953 454707. Open
Mon–Fri 0900–1700, Sat
0900–1630, Sun
1000–1600.*

Total distance: 136 miles (219km). Add 17 miles (27km) for the Thetford detour; 29 miles (47km) for the Broads.

Time: 5 hours.

Links: At King's Lynn or Downham Market, it's easy to join the Wolds and Fens route (*see page 110*), while any of the main routes leading south (A12, A140, A134) will take you into Suffolk (*see page 156*).

Route: From **NORWICH ❶**, head west on the A47. A couple of miles north of East Dereham is Gressenhall's **Roots of Norfolk**❖❖. Returning to the A47, carry on via **SWAFFHAM ❷** to **KING'S LYNN ❸**, through prosperous farming country.

Right
Burnham Overy windmill

Ancient House Museum £ *White Hart Street, Thetford; tel: 01842 752599; www.norfolk.gov.uk.tourism. Open Mon–Sat 1000–1700, Sun pm in summer; closed lunchtime.*

East Wretham Heath Nature Reserve
Wretham; tel: 01603 625540. Open daily 0800–dusk.

Grimes Graves £ *The Exhibition Building, Lynford; tel: 01842 810656. Open Apr–Sept daily 1000–1800, Oct 1000–1700, Wed–Sun 1000–1600 in winter; closed lunchtime; EH.*

Detour: Take the A11 southwest of Norwich, pausing to see one of East Anglia's finest abbey churches, at **Wymondham**❖❖. Gardeners might like to visit **Peter Beales Rose Nursery** at Attleborough, to the south. Continue towards **Thetford**❖, through changing landscape. Thetford's **Ancient House Museum**❖❖ is an early Tudor timbered structure, housing a magnificent late Roman horde of gold and silver. Waymarked walks lead through the **East Wretham Heath Nature Reserve**❖. Don't miss the extraordinary neolithic flint pits known as **Grimes Graves**❖❖. Head up the A134, calling at moated **Oxburgh Hall**❖❖, which dates from 1482. The present structure of **Denver Sluice**❖❖, just south of Downham Market, is a modern incarnation of the impressive scheme designed by Dutch water engineer Cornelius Vermuyden in 1651.

Just north of King's Lynn is the Norman keep of **Castle Rising**❖, a setting for mock jousts in summer. Heading up the A149, **SANDRINGHAM ❹** is signed on the right-hand side, and further north, **Norfolk Lavender**❖❖ near Heacham is a startling blaze of purple. From the old-fashioned resort of **Hunstanton**❖, with its stripy cliffs, follow the coastal route through the evocative shingle banks and saltings along the **NORTH NORFOLK HERITAGE COAST ❺**.

Oxburgh Hall £££
Oxborough; tel: 01366
328258;
oxburghhall@ntrust.org.uk.
Open Apr–Oct Sat–Wed
1300–1630; garden
1100–1730 (1600 in
winter); NT.

Castle Rising Castle ££
Castle Rising; tel: 01553
631330;
www.castelrising.com. Open
Apr–Sept daily 1000–1800;
Oct 1000–1700; Wed–Sun
1000–1600 in winter.

Felbrigg Hall £££
Felbrigg; tel: 01263 837444;
felbrigg@ntrust.org.uk. Open
Apr–Oct Sat–Wed
1300–1700; gardens
1100–1730; NT.

**Norfolk Shire Horse
Centre ££** West Runton
Stables; tel: 01263 837339;
bakewell@norfolkshirehorse.
fsnet.co.uk; www.norfolk-
shirehorse-centre.co.uk. Open
Apr–Oct Sun–Fri
1000–1700 (daily Aug).

The Burnham* villages are particularly attractive. Burnham Overy Staithe has quaint fishermen's cottages; Burnham Thorpe was Nelson's birthplace; Burnham Deepdale has a charming church with a round tower and Norman font. Soon afterwards, **HOLKHAM HALL ❻** is on the right-hand side of the road. Two of the best and most accessible beaches are at Holkham Gap, and **Wells-next-the-Sea**✶✶ (now about a mile inland). Beware the dangerous currents off its vast, tempting beach.

Further east, near Stiffkey and Morston, the shore is pink with sea lavender. **Blakeney**✶✶ is one of the prettiest of the coastal villages, now a smart sailing centre. Banks of shingle increase in height towards **Cley**✶.

Getting out of the car: Make time for at least one walk along the Norfolk Coast Path, but do check the tide-tables. Bring binoculars – the nature reserves at Titchwell and Cley Marshes chalk up recently spotted rare birds on blackboards. At **Wells-next-the-Sea**, an interesting inland detour is possible on the Wells and Walsingham Light Railway to the pilgrim shrine of **Little Walsingham**. Boat trips from **Blakeney** are a good way to see the birds and seals around Blakeney Point or Scolt Head.

Cromer✶ is a popular Victorian seaside resort, famed for its crabs. Standing in impressive grounds, 17th-century **Felbrigg Hall**✶ is a short drive southwest. At nearby West Runton, the **Norfolk Shire Horse Centre**✶✶ is popular with children. From Cromer, duck inland down the A140 towards Aylsham (a pretty market town with Dutch-gabled buildings) and **BLICKLING HALL ❼**. From here you can return swiftly to Norwich on the A140, or take an extended route via **THE BROADS ❽**. Make sure you have a detailed map or you may end up in a reed-bed.

Detour: In northeast Norfolk, a waymarked walk called the Paston Way links sixteen local churches on and near the coast. At **Horsey**✶ (thatched church and a fine windpump), detour inland via Martham and Rollesby. The countryside around **Ormesby Broad**✶ gives some of the most open Broadland views accessible by road. **Caister-on-Sea**✶ has a long pedigree as capital of the *Iceni* tribe, and has a Roman fort and a moated castle.

Take the B1354 from Aylsham towards Hoveton and Wroxham, then the A1062 via **Ludham** (a footpath leads to the strange ruins of **St Benet's Abbey**✶, enclosing the stump of an old windmill) towards **Potter Heigham**✶ (see its medieval bridge, and the Museum of the Broads). **Hickling Broad**✶, up the road, is the largest stretch of water in the area, and a nature reserve. Head south to Acle (unusual thatched church), then up the B1140. See the **Fairhaven Gardens**✶✶ at South Walsham, then turn on to tiny lanes to **Ranworth**✶✶, where you can get a good overview of the Broads from the Wildlife Centre and

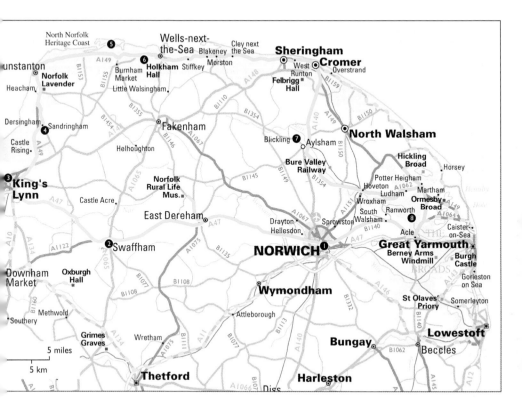

Bure Valley Railway ££ *Norwich Road, Aylsham; tel: 01263 733858; info@bvrw.co.uk; www.bvrw.co.uk. Open Apr–Oct (ring for timetable).*

Lowestoft and East Suffolk Maritime Museum £ *Sparrows Nest Park, Whaplode Road; tel: 01502 561963. Open Easter–Oct 1000–1630.*

Somerleyton Hall ££ *Somerleyton; tel: 01502 730224; www.somerleyton.co.uk. Open Apr–Oct Thu, Sun 1200–1730, (July–Aug also Tue–Wed).*

from the tower of St Helen's Church. Return to the B1140 and head back to Norwich.

Getting out of the car: Sample something of the Broads by taking a combined boat and train excursion and a steam railway trip on the 15in-gauge **Bure Valley Railway**✦✦, which runs for 9 miles between Aylsham and Wroxham.

Also worth exploring: To see the southerly Broads (partly in Suffolk), take the A146 southeast from Norwich. **Lowestoft**, Britain's easternmost town, has a well-kept seafront. Boating enthusiasts should head for Lowestoft's **Maritime Museum**✦✦, a collection of working boats from around the world. Take the B1074 past Jacobean **Somerleyton Hall**✦, the eyecatching smock mill at Herringfleet✦ and a ruined priory at **St Olaves**✦. Detour off the A143 to **Burgh Castle**✦ (a Roman coastal fortress) on the banks of the Yare, a lovely peaceful spot from where you can see the seven-storey **Berney Arms Windmill**✦, tallest on the Broads, formerly used to drain the marshes. (There's a good pub here, reachable only by boat or footpath.)

Suffolk and North Essex

Ratings

Heritage	●●●●●
Arts and crafts	●●●●○
Churches	●●●●○
Coastal interest	●●●●○
Eating out	●●●○○
Scenery	●●●○○
Walking	●●●○○
Wildlife	●●●○○

Few regions boast as many beautifully kept towns and villages as Suffolk and Essex. Architectural glory is seen not only in the churches that date from the heyday of the wool trade that brought prosperity to the area, but also in hundreds of ordinary houses and cottages. Dick Turpin and Constable would still recognise many of the places. The countryside is picturesque, but never spectacular. There are some striking vistas, especially in the Vale of Dedham and the upper Stour, but no significant hills, and parts of the coast can be quite mournful. As an enjoyable base for motorists, Bury St Edmunds is central and especially appealing, and Woodbridge, Saffron Walden, Long Melford and Southwold have great charm too. Dedham has an exceptional choice of good places to stay and eat. To see the best of these predominantly rural counties, you need to stray well off the beaten track.

BURY ST EDMUNDS✦✦✦

ⓘ Tourist Information 6 Angel Hill; tel: 01284 764667.

ⓗ Moyse's Hall £ Cornhill; tel: 01284 706183. Open Mon–Fri 1030–1630; Sat–Sun 1100–1600. Social history museum.

Manor House Museum £££ 5 Honey Hill; tel: 01284 757072. Open Wed–Sun 1100–1600; closed Jan.

Ickworth House £££ Horringer; tel: 01284 735270. Open Apr–Oct pm (not Mon or Thu); NT.

A core of historic buildings radiates from Angel Hill, in front of the recently completed **Cathedral of St Edmundsbury✦✦**, dedicated to the memory of the saintly Edmund, last king of the East Angles. King Canute's earlier abbey lies in romantic ruins behind the 14th-century Abbey Gate. **Moyse's Hall✦✦** is one of the town's oldest buildings. The Georgian **Manor House Museum✦✦** contains a splendid array of historic timepieces. On the outskirts of town are the fuming sugar factory that processes the local beet, and **Ickworth House✦✦**, a late 18th-century building with an eyecatching centrepiece rotunda.

Accommodation and food in Bury St Edmunds

Ounce House ££ Northgate Street; tel: 01284 761779; fax: 01284 768315; enquiries@ouncehouse.co.uk; www.ouncehouse.co.uk. A smart, central B&B, friendly and family run, with well-furnished, comfortable rooms.

The Angel £££ *Angel Hill; tel:
01284 714000; fax: 01284 714001;
reception@theangel.co.uk; www.
theangel.co.uk.* A fine old coaching
inn with refurbished rooms in
smart upbeat colours. Dickens
wrote part of *The Pickwick Papers*
while staying here.

COLCHESTER✦✦✦

ⓘ Tourist Information / Queen Street; tel: 01206 282920.

ⓗ Colchester Castle Museum ££ Castle Park; tel: 01206 282939; www.colchestermuseums.org. uk. Open Mon–Sat 1000–1700, Sun 1100–1700.

Tymperley's Clock Museum Trinity Street; tel: 01206 282931. Open Mon–Sat 1000–1700; Sun 1100–1700.

Colchester Zoo £££ Maldon Road, Stanway; tel: 01206 331292; www.colchester-zoo.co.uk. Open daily 0930–1830 (sunset in winter).

Beth Chatto Gardens ££ Elmstead Market (east of Colchester); tel: 01206 822007; www.bethchatto. co.uk. Open Mon–Sat 0900–1700 (Mon–Fri 0900–1600 in winter).

ⓧ Warehouse Brasserie ££ 12 Chapel Street North; tel/fax: 01206 765656. Cheerful, effervescent atmosphere draws lively young crowd. Good-value fixed-price menus and lots of organic produce.

Famed for its Roman heritage and its associations with the tribal queen Boadicea, Colchester lays claim to being Britain's oldest recorded town. Its Norman **castle✦✦** contains a museum of Roman Britain; the Dutch quarter all around was founded by Flemish weavers who settled here in the 16th century. There are several interesting central museums, including **Tymperley's Clock Museum✦✦**. On the outskirts lie the ruins of **St Botolph's Priory✦**, England's oldest Augustinian monastery. **Colchester Zoo✦** is 2 miles southwest. Keen gardeners should make a beeline for the **Beth Chatto Gardens✦✦**, which were painstakingly reclaimed from wilderness by the renowned garden writer.

ESSEX VILLAGES❖❖

The Dunmow flitch

Every four years, the Essex town of Great Dunmow is the scene of a curious mock trial, unique in England. Originally a Breton custom, it was revived in the mid-19th century. A flitch (or side) of bacon is presented to any married couple who can swear before witnesses and a bewigged judge and counsel that they have had no rows or regretted their marriage in the preceding year and a day.

Many of this much-maligned county's villages have both charm and a civilised character. South and west of Saffron Walden, a cluster of picturesque settlements have vernacular domestic architecture in brick and clapboard, thatch and timber-framing, as well as lovely churches, historic inns and moated manors. In **Thaxted**❖❖, there are colourwashed period houses, a superb church and a guildhall of drunken timbering. **Great Bardfield**❖ on the River Pant has a well-kept High Street and many medieval and Georgian buildings. **Finchingfield**❖❖ is a classic scene of houses around a village green with a duckpond and a stream. If you have time, head further south to the Dunmows (Great and Little) and the eight Rodings.

Pargeting

The ornamental plasterwork seen on many houses in Suffolk was first used in Elizabethan times, and lasted until the 17th century. It was often applied to the upper storeys and jettied gables of timbered buildings. Today, less elaborate patterns are often stamped in low relief in damp plaster on renovated houses.

LAVENHAM❖❖

ℹ️ **Tourist Information** Lady Street; tel: 01787 248207; lavenhamtic@babergh.gov.uk.

🏠 **Little Hall £** Market Place; tel: 01787 247179; www.suffolksociety.com. Open Apr–Oct Wed–Thu, Sat–Sun 1400–1730, Bank Hol Mon 1030–1730.

Lavenham Guildhall of Corpus Christi ££ Market Place; tel: 01787 247646. Open June–Sept daily 1100–1700, Apr–May, Oct Wed–Sun, weekends until 1600.

One of the most delightful East Anglian wool towns, Lavenham has a dazzling heritage of timber-framed buildings, notably **Little Hall**❖❖ and the **Guildhall**❖❖ on the market place. The Swan and the Angel are beautiful inns. The gorgeous church has rich woodcarving, which commemorates the Tudor victory in 1485 over Richard III at the Battle of Bosworth Field.

LONG MELFORD**

Kentwell Hall £££
Tel: 01787 310207.
Open variably Mar–Oct;
check for special events.

Melford Hall ££ Tel:
01787 880286. Open
May–Sept Wed–Sun, Bank
Hol Mon 1400–1730,
weekends Apr and Oct.

Long Melford's 2-mile High Street gave this village its name. Lined with historic pubs, antique shops and period houses, the street opens into a wide 'village green' by magnificent 15th-century **Holy Trinity***, possibly the best of all Suffolk's churches. Just off the green, the Tudor mansions of **Kentwell Hall** and **Melford Hall** * are both lovely.

SAFFRON WALDEN***

**Tourist
Information**
1 Market Place, Market
Square; tel: 01799 510444;
tourism@uttlesford.gov.uk.

**Saffron Walden
Museum £** Museum
Street; tel: 01799 510333;
museum@uttlesford.gov.uk.
Open Mon–Sat 1000–1700
(1630 in winter), Sun
1400–1700 (1630 in
winter).

Audley End £££ Audley
End; tel: 01799 522399.
Open Apr–Sept Wed–Sun
and bank hols; house
1200–1600; grounds
1100–1800 (1500 in Oct –
guided tours only); EH.

The saffron industry flourished here in medieval times, and the town is a gem, with a superb array of half-timbered and pargeted buildings, a ruined castle and a delightful little **museum**, one of the oldest in England. Nearby **Audley End*** is one of the most splendid and costly of all England's Jacobean houses, built in 1614 for Thomas Howard, Lord Treasurer and 1st Earl of Suffolk. Part of the house was demolished in the early 18th century to make it more manageable. There is an ornamental lake, in Capability Brown grounds. Inside, about 30 sumptuous rooms can be visited.

Right
Audley End

STOUR VALLEY❖❖

Tourist Information *Town Hall, Market Hill, Sudbury; tel: 01787 881320.*

Gainsborough's House ££ *46 Gainsborough Street, Sudbury; tel: 01787 372958. Open Apr– Oct Tue–Sat 1000–1700, Sun and Bank Hol Mon 1400– 1700 (closes 1600 in winter).*

Bridge Cottage *Flatford; tel: 01206 298260. Open Apr–Oct 1100–1730, closed Mon–Tue in winter (weekends only in Jan); NT.*

Sir Alfred Munnings Art Museum ££ *Castle House, Dedham; tel: 01206 322127; open Apr–Oct Wed, Sun 1400–1700 (Bank Hol Mons and Thu, Sat in Aug).*

The Stour forms the boundary between Suffolk and Essex. Its upper reaches run through deep green, well-wooded farmland, past the pretty towns of Clare, Cavendish and Long Melford, famed for their antique shops. Several artists are associated with this picturesque river. Thomas Gainsborough was born at **Sudbury**❖ in 1727. John Constable was born downstream in East Bergholt in 1776. One of his best-known paintings depicts the mill at **Flatford**. **Dedham**❖❖, the village where Constable went to school, has a number of historic buildings. The 20th-century artist Alfred Munnings lived here, at **Castle House**❖ (now a museum). The Stour meets the open sea at Harwich, a salty working ferry port with a good fish restaurant and several small maritime and military museums.

Right
Flatford Mill

SUFFOLK COAST❖❖❖

Tourist Information *152 High Street, Aldeburgh; tel: 01728 453637; atic@suffolkcoastal.gov.uk; or 69 High Street, Southwold; tel: 01502 724729; southwoldtic@waveney.gov.uk. Both seasonal.*

Suffolk's coast between Lowestoft and Felixstowe is all designated as Heritage Coast. It has exceptional scenic and environmental interest, although it is badly affected by erosion. **Orford**❖❖ is a remote, evocative place of charming mellow brick cottages and rare shingle plants, dominated by a 12th-century Norman castle keep. Boat trips take visitors to the RSPB reserve on Havergate Island in the estuary, where avocets breed. **Aldeburgh** is inextricably associated with the Suffolk-born composer Benjamin Britten, who lies buried in its church and whose works are regularly performed at the annual Aldeburgh Festival held in **Snape Maltings** on the River Alde. The town itself has great character and some interesting buildings, including the Tudor **Moot Hall**❖❖ (small museum). In medieval times, **Dunwich**❖❖ to the north was a large, thriving port. It was hit by a terrible storm in 1326 and gradually succumbed to the waves over succeeding centuries. To the southwest, the **Minsmere Reserve**❖❖ (RSPB) is another important breeding site for avocets. **Southwold** is a delightful, civilised seaside

Snape Maltings *Snape, Saxmundham; tel: 01728 688303; www.snapemaltings.co.uk. Open daily 1000–1700. Centre with shops, restaurants and entertainments.*

Dunwich Museum *St James's Street, Dunwich; tel: 01728 648796. Open Apr–Sept daily 1130–1630, Mar and Oct 1200–1600.*

Minsmere Reserve ££ *Westleton; tel: 01728 648281. Open Wed–Mon 0900–2100 or dusk; visitor centre 0900–1700 (1600 in winter); RSPB members free.*

town of whitewashed houses dominated by a lighthouse tower. Its fine Saxon church has a jaunty 15th-century sword-wielding figure called Southwold Jack, who strikes the hours. A number of good pubs serve Southwold's excellent beer, Adnams. A little ferry connects the town with the charming village of **Walberswick***, south of the creek.

Accommodation and food on or near the Suffolk Coast

Crown and Castle ££ *Orford; tel: 01394 450205; fax: 01394 450176; info@crownandcastlehotel.co.uk; www.crownandcastlehotel.co.uk.* Stylish bistro-with-rooms serving local oysters on its inventive menus. Good-sized rooms, some with views to Orford Ness.

Plough & Sail £ *The Maltings, Snape; tel: 01728 688413.* Relaxed, friendly pub with bustling restaurant and real ales.

Flora Tearooms £ *Dunwich; tel: 01728 648433. Closed Dec–Feb.* Excellent, no-frills fish and chips, right on the beach in a former fisherman's hut. Good cakes and snacks too.

WOODBRIDGE**

Tourist Information *Station Buildings; tel: 01394 382240.*

Woodbridge Tidemill *Tidemill Quay; tel: 01473 626618. Open May–Sept daily 1100–1700, Apr and Oct weekends 1100–1700; machinery subject to tides.*

Woodbridge Museum £ *5a Market Hill; tel: 01394 380502. Open Apr–Oct Thur–Sat 1000–1600, Sun 1430–1630, daily except Wed in summer school holidays.*

Sutton Hoo ££ *Tel: 01394 389700. Open Apr–Oct Wed–Sun 1000–1700 (June–Sept daily), Nov–Mar weekends 1000–1600. Guided tours; NT.*

It is hard to imagine today's genteel Woodbridge as the bustling Tudor ship-building centre which it once was. Now, the watercraft are rarely more than dinghies, but it is a delightful town. Its most interesting building is a working 18th-century **Tidemill****, handsomely weatherboarded. An ambitious visitor centre focuses on the Anglo-Saxon archaeological sites at nearby Sutton Hoo (a royal ship burial 2 miles southeast) and Burrow Hill.

Right
Woodbridge

Suggested tour

National Stud ££
Tel: 01638 663464;
www.nationalstud.co.uk.
Open Mar–Sept by
appointment and racedays;
conducted tours at 1115 and
1430.

National Horse-racing
Museum ££ *99 High*
Street, Newmarket; tel:
01638 667333;
www.nhrm.co.uk. Open
Easter–Oct Tue–Sun
1100–1700 (daily July–Aug).

Total distance: 178 miles (286km). The Newmarket variant is about the same distance; add 100 miles (160km) for all the Colchester detours.

Time: 7 hours.

Links: Use Saffron Walden or Newmarket as a springboard for Cambridge and the Wolds and Fens (*see page 110*), or strike northwards via the A12, A140 from Diss or A134 from Bury St Edmunds to connect with the Norfolk route (*see page 146*).

Route: Leave **BURY ST EDMUNDS ❶** on the A134 (south), turning left at Cross Green on the A1141 to **LAVENHAM ❷**, then rejoin the A134 on minor roads signed **LONG MELFORD ❸**. Head west on the A1092 along the upper reaches of the wooded Stour valley, through Cavendish and Clare. Take the B1054 near Baythorne End through Hempstead (where Dick Turpin was born) towards **SAFFRON WALDEN ❹**.

Detour: Horse-racing enthusiasts may prefer to take the fast A14 west from Bury St Edwards towards prosperous, bustling **Newmarket***, to see the **National Stud** and the **National Horse-racing Museum****, then head south over the breezy turf on the B1052 via Linton (there's a good little zoo here) to rejoin the tour at Saffron Walden.

See **Audley End*****on the west side of Saffron Walden, then take the B184 to **Thaxted****. Turn left here on minor roads for the three **Bardfield** villages, then left again at Great Bardfield, taking the B1057 for classically pretty **Finchingfield****. Turn right here on the B1053, then left at Wethersfield, through Castle Hedingham to **Sudbury***, another well-preserved wool town. Gainsborough's house is near the market place. Take the A134 east from Sudbury, turning off at Nayland on the B1087. Both Nayland and Stoke-by-Nayland have splendid churches. The Vale of Dedham, bright with fruit blossom in spring, and softened by the feathery plumage of willows and poplars, offers pretty views. Follow Constable's footsteps to the tree-lined watercourses of **Flatford Mill****and **Dedham****.

Getting out of the car: Footpaths link the scenes Constable painted along the banks of the Stour (*guided walks from the National Trust Bridge Cottage Information Centre at Flatford Mill, May–Sept; ££*). There is a parking charge.

Detour: From the A12 near Dedham, you can reach the heart of **COLCHESTER ❺** fairly easily from the north (follow 'City centre' signs). Colchester makes a good starting point for several mini tours. West of the city, **Coggeshall****is easily accessible along the A120. There are two interesting National Trust buildings in the centre:

Park in one of Colchester's NCP car parks near the castle to explore the central sights.

Paycocke's £ West Street, Coggeshall; tel: 01376 561305. Open Apr–Oct Tue, Thu, Sun, Bank Hol Mon 1400–1730; NT.

Grange Barn £ Grange Hill; tel: 01376 562226. Open Apr–Oct Tue, Thu, Sun, Bank Hol Mon 1400–1700; NT.

Layer Marney Tower ££ Layer Marney; tel: 01206 330784; www.layermarneytower.co.uk. Open Apr–Oct 1200–1700 (not Sat).

Tiptree Tearoom, Museum and Shop Tiptree; tel: 01621 814524; tiptree@tiptree.com; www.tiptree.co.uk. Open all year Mon–Sat 1000–1700, June–Aug Sun also 1200–1700.

Tourist Information Coach Lane, Maldon; tel: 01621 856503; tic@maldon.gov.uk.

Maeldune Heritage Centre £ Market Hill, Maldon; tel: 01621 851628. Open Apr–Sept Mon–Sat 1330–1630, Thu–Sat 1200–1500 in winter.

Bressingham Steam Experience and Gardens ££ Bressingham; tel: 01379 687386; www.bressingham.co.uk. Open Apr–Oct daily 1030–1730.

Paycocke's**, a half-timbered merchant's house dating from around 1500, with rich carving and panelling in exceptional condition, and the **Grange Barn** at the east end of town, a superb example of 12th-century timber-framing, which originally belonged to a Cistercian monastery. South of Colchester, take the B1022 past Colchester Zoo, which emphasises conservation. Four miles further on, the extraordinary Elizabethan gatehouse of **Layer Marney**** is worth a brief detour (signposted from the B1022). The region between Maldon and Colchester is famed for soft fruit, and **Tiptree** is a renowned jam-making centre. Wilkin, which makes some of Britain's poshest preserves, has a little visitor centre in the town. The lowest bridging point on the Blackwater is the charming old town of **Maldon****, the scene of a great battle against Viking invaders in 991. The **Maldon Embroidery***, on display in the Maeldune Centre, was created by local residents to mark the battle's millennium. Bradwell-on-Sea, on the remote and eerie reclaimed marshes south of the river, has an ancient church, St Peter on the Wall, dating from AD 654.

Return to the A12 and head for **Ipswich****, which has two excellent free museums and one of the region's best examples of pargeting (see box, page 159), on the **Ancient House**** in the Buttermarket. Continue north to **WOODBRIDGE ❻**, then take the B1084 via Butley to Orford, then the minor road via Sudbourne signed Snape, which takes you past The Maltings at the head of the Alde estuary. Turn right on the A1094 to **Aldeburgh**. Take the coast road via Thorpeness (good walks and birdwatching), and the extraordinary House in the Clouds (a water tower converted into holiday accommodation). Follow the minor coastal roads past Sizewell's nuclear power station (visitor centre). Sandy heath and woodland characterises the terrain around the Minsmere Nature Reserve and **Dunwich**. Detour briefly to **Walberswick**. Backtrack west again via **Blythburgh** (the **church**** has a glorious angel ceiling), and take the A1095 for **Southwold**. Complete the tour on the B1123 via Halesworth and stray briefly into Norfolk to rejoin the main A143 at Diss. A brief detour west along the A1066 takes you to plantsman Adrian Bloom's magnificent **Bressingham Steam Experience and Gardens****. Return to the A143, to complete the circuit at Bury St Edmunds.

Accommodation and food on the route

Dedham Hall ££ Brook Street, Dedham; tel: 01206 323027; fax: 01206 323293; jimsarton@dedhamhall.demon.co.uk; www.dedhamhall. demon.co.uk. Relaxed, charming country accommodation offering residential art courses and excellent home cooking.

Maison Talbooth £££ Stratford Road, Dedham; tel: 01206 322367; fax: 01206 323689; maison@talbooth.co.uk; www.talbooth.com. Luxury accommodation to go with acclaimed sister restaurant **Le Talbooth** just up the road.

Angel Inn ££ *Stoke-by-Nayland; tel: 01206 263245; fax: 01206 263373.* Informal but sophisticated country pub with wonderful cooking and lots of period character.

Mortimers ££ *Wherry Quay, Ipswich; tel: 01473 230225.* Deceptively simple but accomplished fish restaurant with good wines and relaxed service.

Hintlesham Hall £££ *George Street, Hintlesham; tel: 01473 652334; fax: 01473 652463; reservations@hintleshamhall.com.* Grand country-house hotel and celebrated restaurant close to Ipswich. Lavish facilities and furnishings.

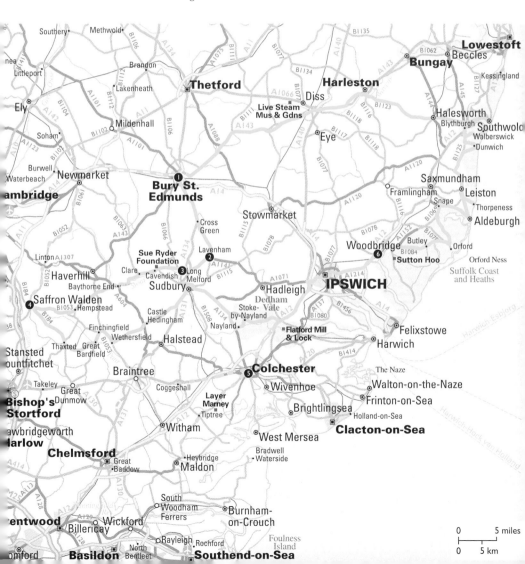

Snowdonia

Ratings

Castles	●●●●●
Nostalgia railways	●●●●●
Outdoor activities	●●●●●
Scenery	●●●●●
Beaches	●●●●○
Industrial archaeology	●●●●○
Wildlife	●●●●○
Children	●●●○○

At 3 560ft, Snowdon is higher than any other summit in England or Wales, a sensational ensemble of knife-edged peaks, cliffs and waterfalls. The Snowdonia National Park is a paradise for adventure sports fans, but others can reach the high ground either in one of Wales's 'Great Little Trains', or by cablecar and tramway. During medieval times, this often impassable terrain was the scene of fierce clashes between Welsh princes and Anglo-Norman kings. The English fortified the coastal gateways with massive castles, but the interior remained a stronghold of Celtic nationalist fervour. This part of northwest Wales is still predominantly Welsh-speaking. The coastline around Snowdonia is magnificent. While tourism is now essential to the economy, this rural conservation zone is also an industrial region. Slate quarries and mine-workings scar many hillsides; today, reservoirs and power stations provide employment, and have even become tourist attractions.

ANGLESEY✧✧

ⓘ Tourist Information *Town Hall, Deiniol Road, Bangor; tel: 01248 352786; bangor.tic@gwynedd.gov.uk.*

🏰 Beaumaris Castle *££ Beaumaris; tel: 01248 810361; www.beaumaris.com. Open Apr–Oct 0930–1700 (1800 in high season), Nov–Mar Mon–Sat 0930–1600, Sun 1100–1600; CADW.*

This low-lying island is anchored to the British mainland by a couple of superbly engineered 19th-century bridges across the Menai Straits. Much of its coastline is designated as being of Outstanding Natural Beauty, with a number of magnificent Blue Flag **beaches✧✧**. **Beaumaris✧✧** is a handsome little town where the last and most sophisticated of Edward I's great 'Iron Ring' fortresses was built in the 1290s. The **Sea Zoo✧** near the Menai Straits is a popular undercover attraction. **Llanfair PG** is the mercifully short form of Britain's longest place name (the full version is to be found on the railway station – whisper it not in the village, but the whole name is a 19th-century fabrication, dreamt up to put Llanfair PG on the tourist map, and it certainly seems to have succeeded). The main local sight is the elegant 18th-century mansion of **Plas Newydd✧**, with superb views to the Snowdonia mountains.

Anglesey Sea Zoo
££ Brynsiencyn; tel:
01248 430411;
www.angleseyseazoo.co.uk.
Open Apr–Oct daily
1000–1800. Touch pools,
walk-through shipwreck,
etc.

Plas Newydd £££ *On*
A4080 2 miles S of
Llanfairpwll, Anglesey; tel:
01248 714795. Open
Apr–Oct Sat–Wed, house
1200–1700, garden
1100–1730; NT.

Olde Bull's Head
££ Castle Street,
Beaumaris; tel: 01248
810329; fax: 01248
811294. Comfortable
15th-century coaching inn
full of olde-worlde charm.

Edward's 'Iron Ring'

The awesome castles
that scatter the Welsh
landscape date from the
13th century, marking
the epic struggle
between Edward I of
England and his
formidable Welsh
adversary, Llywelyn the
Last. Edward ordered
the construction of a
chain of fortresses, a
day's march apart. Some
of the earlier ones are
now in ruins, but the
second batch drew on
the genius of Edward's
military engineer,
Master James of St
George, and survived
many succeeding
conflicts. Incomplete
Beaumaris Castle on
Anglesey, begun in the
1290s, represents the
most advanced
experiment in this
military technology.

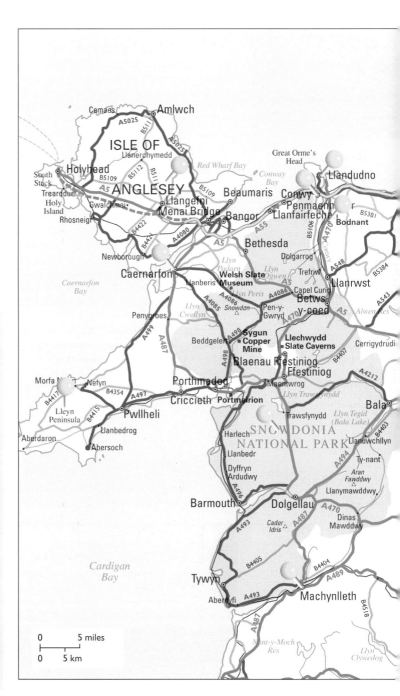

Bodnant Garden✧✧✧

Bodnant Garden ££
Tal y Cafn; tel: 01492 650460; office@ bodnantgarden.co.uk; www.bodnantgarden.co.uk. Open Mar–Oct 1000–1700; NT and RHS.

This superb garden in the Conwy Valley is enhanced by its spectacular setting overlooking Snowdonia. Dating from 1875, it is the creation of four generations of the Aberconway family (two were former presidents of the Royal Horticultural Society). It is a wonderful sight all through the season: in the Dell, rhododendrons, camellias and magnolias provide spring interest; the Laburnum Arch is a magical sight in May; herbaceous borders and roses bloom all summer and autumn sees a wonderful show of colours.

Caernarfon✧✧

Tourist Information *Oriel Pendeitch, Castle Street; tel: 01286 672232; caernarfontic@gwynedd.gov. uk.*

Caernarfon Castle ££ *Tel: 01286 677617; www.caernarfon.com. Open Apr–Oct 0930–1700 (1800 in high season), Nov–Mar Mon–Sat 0930–1600, Sun 1100–1600; CADW.*

Segontium Roman Fort and Museum £ *Beddgelert Road; tel: 01286 675625. Open Mon–Sat 1000–1700, Sun 1400–1700.*

Ty'n Rhos ££ *Seion, Llanddeiniolen; tel: 01248 670489; fax: 01248 670079; enquiries@ tynrhos.co.uk; www.tynrhos.co.uk.* Hard to fault this unpretentious but immaculately kept farmhouse overlooking peaceful countryside near the Menai Straits. Excellent cooking.

One of Edward I's principal strongholds (*see box, page 167*), Caernarfon was conceived as a royal citadel, to consolidate English rule in Wales. The town is closely attached to the vast **fortress**✧✧ that once protected it, and became a thriving port in more peaceful times. The **castle** was the location for the investiture of the Prince of Wales in 1969. The excavated remains of a **Roman fort** (*Segontium*) crown the neighbouring hilltop.

CONWY❖❖

The **castle**❖❖, and a whole series of almost perfect **town walls**❖❖, still with towers and gateways, are all survivals from Norman times. The **suspension bridge**❖ was built by Telford in 1826. A minute fisherman's cottage only 10ft high claims to be Britain's **smallest house**. **Aberconwy House**❖ is a prosperous merchant's home dating from the 14th century, and **Plas Mawr**❖ is an ornate Tudor mansion with wonderful plasterwork.

LLANDUDNO❖❖

Between the limestone headlands of the Great and Little Orme, North Wales's most attractive resort has a well-preserved Victorian seafront, a crescent-shaped beach and a charming pier. A corniche toll road leads round the **Great Orme's Head**❖❖, and a cable car and funicular tramway lead up to the 680-ft summit, where there are Bronze Age copper mines, and other attractions.

Accommodation and food in Llandudno

Bodysgallen Hall £££ *Off A470 S of Llandudno; tel: 01492 584466; fax: 01492 582519; info@bodysgallen.com; www.bodysgallen.com.* An outstanding country-house hotel in a very fine stone house dating back to the 13th century amid 200-acre grounds. A health spa helps work off some of the excesses induced by the restaurant.

LLEYN PENINSULA✧✧

ⓘ Tourist Information Min y Don, Station Square, Pwllheli; tel: 01758 613000; pwllheli.tic@gwynedd.gov.uk.

ⓗ Portmeirion ££ 2 miles E of Porthmadog, off A487; tel: 01766 770000; enquiries@ portmeirion-village.com; www.portmeirion.wales.com. Open daily 0930–1730.

Cut off by mountains as well as by its remote geographical location, this 24-mile tongue of land has retained its staunch Welshness, and its wild, unspoilt beauty. On the north coast, the quartz grains of Porth Oer's Whistling Sands squeak underfoot. **Portmeirion**✧✧, in a steep wooded valley, is an Italianate holiday village designed by Sir Clough Williams Ellis, with pastel cottages, zigzag steps and follies in beautiful gardens. The Ship Shop sells the famous pottery. Nearby, Porthmadog is the terminus of the **Ffestiniog Railway**✧✧✧, perhaps the finest of all Wales's narrow-gauge lines. **Pwllheli**, Lleyn's largest resort, has shingle-backed belts of dunes. Charming **Abersoch**✧ still has something of the fishing village about it, on twin golden bays. **Aberdaron**, at the tip of the peninsula, was a busy spot in medieval times, with pilgrims making the perilous crossing to **Bardsey Island**.

Accommodation and food on the Lleyn Peninsula

Hotel Portmeirion £££ Portmeirion; tel: 01766 770000; fax: 01766 771331; hotel@portmeirion-village.com; www.portmeirion-village.com. A memorable stay is assured at this unique luxury hotel in this fairytale village. The ghosts of previous guests – Noël Coward, George Bernard Shaw, H G Wells and the cast of cult TV series The Prisoner, filmed here during the 1960s – will haunt you.

Porth Tocyn ££ Bwlch Tocyn, Abersoch; tel: 01758 713303; fax: 01758 713538; www.porth-tocyn-hotel.co.uk. Charmingly relaxed country house hotel in a lovely Lleyn Peninsula setting. Magnificent cooking.

Tir-a-Mor ££ 1–3 Mona Terrace, Criccieth; tel: 01766 523084; fax: 01766 523049. Townhouse restaurant with cheerful brasserie-style décor. Accomplished food.

MACHYNLLETH✧✧

ⓘ Tourist Information Canolfan Owain Glyndwr; tel: 01654 702401.

ⓗ Parliament House Tel: 01654 702827. Open Easter–Oct Mon–Sat.

Celtica ££ Y Plas; tel: 01654 702702; www.celticawales.com. Open daily 1000–1800.

At the southern tip of the National Park, this handsome, lively little town has many well-kept period buildings. Welsh leader Owain Glyndwr was crowned Prince of Wales here (the 16th-century **Parliament House** is now a museum). Plas Machynlleth houses **Celtica**✧, a presentation on the Celts. Nearby in an old slate quarry, the **Centre for Alternative Technology**✧ investigates and demonstrates green living.

Centre for Alternative Technology £££ *3 miles N on A487; tel: 01654 705950; www.cat.org.uk. Open daily 1000–1700 (1600 in winter).* Water-powered cliff railway; organic gardens; wind, wave and solar power.

Right
The Centre for Alternative Technology

SNOWDONIA NATIONAL PARK❖❖

Tourist Information *Royal Oak Stables, Betws-y-coed; tel: 01690 710426; or 41b High Street, Llanberis; tel: 01286 870765; or Pensarn Road, Bala; tel: 01678 521021.*

The Snowdonia National Park was established in 1951, the first in Wales, extending over 840 square miles between Conwy and Machynlleth. It encompasses coastline and moorland, forested valleys, lakes and waterfalls as well as the crags of the highest peaks. Its glaciated cirques (called *cwms* here) represent a classic 3D geology lesson. Walkers and climbers have flocked here since the 18th century. Even when clouds roll over the summits, or snow blocks the passes, there is always something to do.

Accommodation and food in Snowdonia National Park

Tan-y-Foel £££ *Capel Garmon, Betws-y-coed; tel: 01690 710507l; fax: 01690 710681; enquiries@ tyfhotel.co.uk.* Small, elegant country-house hotel with imaginative interior décor and excellent cooking.

The Ferns £ *Holyhead Road, Betws-y-coed; tel/fax: 01690 710587.* Simple, inexpensive but welcoming B&B in the centre of this popular touring base.

Y Bistro ££ *43–45 High Street, Llanberis; tel/fax: 01286 871278; ybistro@fsbdial.co.uk.* Welcoming bistro using good local produce. Welsh wines available.

Suggested tour

Total distance: 194 miles (312km). Add 85 miles (137km) for the Anglesey detour.

Time: 9 hours.

Links: It's a fast run eastwards along the A55 (mostly dual carriageway) from Conwy/Llandudno to Chester for the Welsh Marches (*see page 124*). The A487 south from Machynlleth is a straightforward route down Cardigan Bay to pick up the Pembrokeshire itinerary (*see page 181*) from Cardigan.

Route: This figure-of-eight tour goes through the heart of the National Park converging on Betws-y-coed; many variations are possible, including extensions around Anglesey and Lleyn. From **LLANDUDNO ❶**, take the scenic Marine Drive toll road round Great Orme's Head (an anticlockwise one-way system), following signs for **CONWY ❷** from the A546 beyond Deganwy. Take the old Telford bridge into the town, then pick up the A55 and head west along the coast. It doesn't take long to reach **Bangor**, a quiet university town (turn off right on the A5122). The main sights are the magnificent **bridges✦✦** built by Telford and Stephenson over the Menai Straits.

Detour: To explore **ANGLESEY ❸**, take the Menai Bridge route, turning immediately right along the A545 signed for **Beaumaris✦✦**. Then hug the coast roads past **Red Wharf Bay** to Amlwch, made prosperous by copper mining in the 19th century; the old workings scar the low hills inland. Wylfa Head's nuclear power station near **Cemaes** has nature trails and guided tours. Continue on the A5025 to the A5. The B4545 and a minor road via Trearddur Bay take you to the bird reserve and rugged scenery of **South Stack✦**. Return to the A5 and head southeast, turning right after 3 miles to follow the coast road (A4080) past the lovely beaches of Rhosneigr and **Newborough Warren** – take the toll road through the forestry plantations. Return to Bangor past the **Anglesey Sea Zoo✦** and **Plas Newydd✦**.

Head southwest on the A487 to **CAERNARFON ❹**, then turn left on the A4086 via the **Llanberis Pass✦✦** to the SNOWDONIA NATIONAL PARK ❺. **Llanberis✦✦** is one of Snowdonia's most popular centres. Several attractions include **Electric Mountain✦✦**, Europe's largest and fastest hydro-electric pumped storage generator. The **Welsh Slate Museum✦** is housed in a handsome stone building. The **Llanberis Lake Railway** trundles along the shores of Padarn Lake. Llanberis makes a good starting point for seeing **Snowdon** on the **mountain railway✦✦** (see 'Getting out of the car'). Continue through Pen-y-Gwyrd to Capel Curig, turning right on the A5 through **Betws-y-coed✦**, where the hectic **Swallow Falls✦** are best seen after rain. Telford's fine Waterloo Bridge triumphantly carries the A5 across the

Harlech Castle ££
*Harlech; tel: 01766
780552; www.harlech.com.
Open Apr–Oct 0930–1700
(1800 in high season),
Nov–Mar Mon–Sat
0930–1600, Sun
1100–1600; CADW.*

Sygun Copper Mine ££
*2 miles NE of Beddgelert on
A498; tel: 01766 510100;
www.syguncoppermine.co.uk.
Open daily, tours from 1000
(weekends only Nov–Feb).*

**Llechwedd Slate
Caverns £££** *Off A470,
1m north of Blaenau
Ffestiniog; tel: 01766
830306;
www.llechwedd.co.uk. Open
daily 1000–1715 (1615 off
season).*

Trefriw Woollen Mills
*On B5106 at Trefriw; tel:
01492 640462;
www.trefriw-woollen-
mills.co.uk. Mill open
Easter–Oct Mon–Fri
0930–1730, Sat
1000–1700; demonstrations
weekdays all year in turbine
house.*

**Snowdon Mountain
Railway £££**
*Llanberis, on A4086; tel:
01286 870223;
www.snowdonrailway.co.uk.
Trains Mar–Oct, weather
permitting (book ahead).*

Ffestiniog Railway £££
*Harbour Station,
Porthmadog; tel: 01766
516073;
www.ffestiniograilway.org.uk.
Open Apr–Oct; restricted
service in winter; phone for
timetable.*

fast-flowing River Conwy. Local **Ty Hyll**, 'the Ugly House', was thrown together with boulders in a single night to obtain freehold rights to the surrounding land. Continue along the A5 for 12 miles to Cerrigydrudion, then turn right on the B4501 to the Welsh-speaking chapel town of Bala. **Bala Lake***, on the quiet eastern fringes of the National Park, is Wales's largest natural lake. A narrow-gauge railway runs beside the eastern lake shore for 4 miles. Following the railway line along the B4403, take the unclassified road left from Llanuwchllyn via Ty-nant and Llanymawddwy to **Dinas-Mawddwy**. This is the highest road in Wales, a spectacular route past Aran Fawddwy (the highest mountain outside the Snowdon range at 2970ft) called the Pass of the Cross (not recommended in poor weather). Head south on the A470 to **MACHYNLLETH ❻**, returning on the A487 to the popular walking and fishing centre of **Dolgellau***, famous for its gold. To the left the majestic summit of **Cader Idris*** ('Arthur's Chair') looms to nearly 3000ft. From Dolgellau, head west via **Barmouth** along the Mawddach estuary on the A496, following the coast through **Harlech**, which has a splendid cragtop medieval castle**, built by Edward I in the 13th century, back to the A487 at Maentwrog. Turn left past **Portmeirion*** to **Porthmadog**.

Detour: To see **LLEYN ❼**, take the A497 through **Criccieth***, **Pwllheli** and **Abersoch***, then take the lanes skirting Porth Neigwl to **Aberdaron**. Return via the north coast lanes, detouring to Porth Oer, and the B4417 through Morfa Nefyn. Return to Porthmadog on the B4354, or pick up the A499 near Trefor and return via Caernarfon.

Take the A498 north through the picturesque Aberglaslyn Pass to **Beddgelert***, a pretty village much enhanced by the tall tale of Gelert's grave (*see page 174*). Just northeast, the **Sygun Copper Mine*** offers a tour through disused workings. Return on the A4085 and B4410 east back to Maentwrog before taking the A496 northeast to **Blaenau Ffestiniog****, terminal of the 14-mile narrow-gauge **Ffestiniog Railway*** from Porthmadog. The nearby **Llechwedd Slate Caverns*** offer exciting rides through old mining tunnels. Continue along the A470 through Betws-y-coed and the Gwydyr Forest, returning to Llandudno via the Vale of Conwy and **BODNANT GARDEN ❽**. The quieter B5106 is pretty, but sometimes floods after heavy rain. The water-powered **Trefriw Woollen Mill*** on this road gives free demonstrations of spinning and weaving.

Getting out of the car: Over half a dozen walking routes lead to the Snowdon massif, ranging from the gentle Llanberis Track to the spectacular Snowdon Horseshoe or the gruelling Watkin Path. An entertaining way to conquer the mountain is to take the narrow-gauge rack-and-pinion **Snowdon Mountain Railway***, which starts at Llanberis and clambers to the highest post box in Britain. The splendid **Ffestiniog Railway*** was built to transport slate from the

Gelert's grave

In Beddgelert is the alleged burial place of Llywelyn the Great's faithful hound, left behind on guard while he went hunting. When he returned, the dog was covered with blood, and Llywelyn slaughtered it, thinking it had attacked his infant son. When he discovered the carcass of a wolf near the unharmed baby's cradle, he realised Gelert had been unjustly accused.

quarries of Blaenau Ffestiniog to the quaysides of Porthmadog. It closed as a working route in 1946, but was reopened as a nostalgia railway by volunteers in 1955. The 14-mile track executes a tight loop-the-loop near Dduallt.

Accommodation and food on the route

George III Hotel ££ *Penmaenpool, Dolgellau; tel: 01341 422525; fax: 01341 423565; reception@george-3rd.co.uk; www.george-3rd.co.uk.* Lively whitewashed inn in attractive waterfront location.

Dylanwad Da ££ *2 Ffos-y-Felin, Dolgellau; tel: 01341 422870.* Cheery bistro offering robust, interesting cooking with local ingredients.

Castle Cottage £ *Penllech, Harlech; tel: 01766 780479; fax: 01766 781251; glyn@castlecottageharlech.co.uk; www.castlecottageharlech.co.uk.* Small central guesthouse offering good cooking and Snowdonian views. Pigs are an insistent motif.

Maes-y-Neuadd £££ *Talsarnau; tel: 01766 780200; fax: 01766 780211; maes@neuadd.com; www.neuadd.com.* Soothing stone-built manor in deeply rural location providing stylish comfort and astonishing food. Take a walk to work up an appetite.

Pen-y-Gwryd Hotel £ *Nantgwynant; tel: 01286 870211; www.pyg.co.uk.* Rugged climbing base amid bleak moorland and mountains. Everest expedition memorabilia sets the tone – not for softies.

Below
Cader Idris

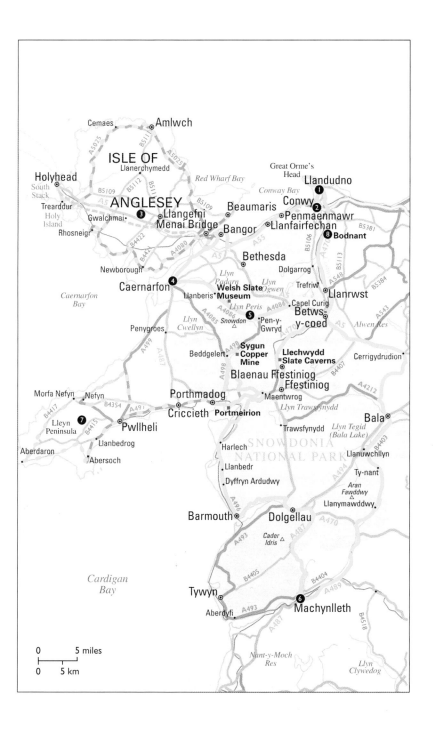

Pembrokeshire Coast

Ratings

Beaches	●●●●●
Outdoor activities	●●●●●
Scenery	●●●●●
Walking	●●●●●
Castles	●●●●○
Islands	●●●●○
Wildlife	●●●●○
Children	●●●○○

The southwest corner of Wales has had close ties with England since Norman days. Its castles were built to protect English settlers who arrived there in the Middle Ages, attracted by the mild climate and fertile soil. More recently, Tenby and Manorbier have been the scene of countless family seaside holidays. The interior of Pembrokeshire is mostly low lying. Its highest point (at 1760ft) lies in the Preseli Hills, a region of ancient settlement, thought to be the source of Stonehenge's bluestones. The coastline is magnificent enough to be designated as a National Park, and the vast majority of it is classed as Heritage Coast. Even Pembrokeshire's 'urban' zones are positive assets. Who could fail to warm to castle-crowned Pembroke or feisty Fishguard, while the alluring 'city-village' of St Davids wins almost universal acclaim.

CARDIGAN*

ℹ Tourist Information *Theatr Mwldan, Bath House Road; tel: 01239 613230; cardigantic@ceredigion.gov.uk.*

🏰 Cilgerran Castle £ *Cilgerran; tel: 01239 615007; www.castle.wales. com. Open daily 0930–1830 (1600 in winter); NT.*

Welsh Wildlife Centre ££ *Cilgerran; tel: 01239 621212; www. wildlifetrust.org.uk/wtsww. Open Easter–Oct 1030–1700 (parking charge).*

The National Park and the coastal path terminate just outside the modest county town of Cardigan. Once, this was a flourishing ship-building centre, and the last place seen by many emigrants. The old wharves and warehouses still have some character. There is a ruined Norman **castle** and a Victorian **Guildhall**, which houses a covered market. Just inland at **Cilgerran*** stands another romantic **castle**, immortalised by the artist Turner. The head of the estuary is an extensive wetland nature reserve, with an excellent **visitor centre****.

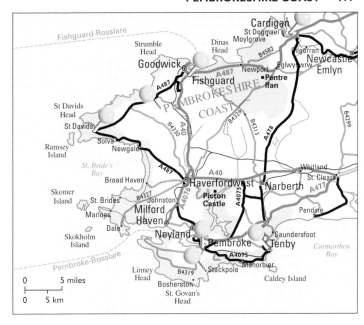

FISHGUARD❖❖

ⓘ **Tourist Information** *Town Hall, The Square; tel: 01348 873484.*

Opposite
Cilgerran Castle

Below
Fishguard Harbour

Gabled cottages cluster around a stone harbour in this picturesque town where the River Gwaun meets the sea. Upper Fishguard, with its attractive old buildings, extends along the hillside. Fishguard's finest hour came in 1797, when a determined band of local women dressed in red cloaks repelled the last foreign invasion of British soil. A party of Franco-Irish troops landed here, mistook the women for infantry – and meekly surrendered. See mementoes in The Royal Oak Inn. On the nearby headland of Strumble Head, the sea boils around the lighthouse and seals bask on the rocks.

Accommodation and food in Fishguard

Manor Town House £ *Main Street; tel/fax: 01348 873260; davies.themanor@amserve. net.* Gorgeous views and antiques grace this attractive house in the upper town. Imaginative home cooking.

Three Main Street ££ *3 Main Street; tel: 01348 874275; fax: 01348 874017.* Splendid restaurant-with-rooms in the heart of the upper town. Just three rooms in an elegant Georgian townhouse, but food to die for.

PEMBROKE⬦

ⓘ Tourist Information *Visitor Centre, Commons Road; tel: 01646 622388; or Ferry Terminal, Pembroke Dock; tel: 01646 622753.*

This small town has a very impressive Norman fortress, poised on a wooded bluff moated on three sides by the river. In 1457, Welshman Henry VII, first of the Tudors, was born within its walls. Battered into ruins by Cromwell's troops, it was extensively restored in late Victorian times. Attractive buildings grace the town centre. One is now the **Museum of the Home⬦⬦** (£) (*7 Westgate Hill; tel: 01646 681200. Open May–Sept Mon–Thu 1100–1700*), a delightful collection of domestic bygones.

ST DAVIDS⬦⬦⬦

ⓘ Tourist Information *The Grove; tel: 01437 720392; enquiries@stdavids. pembrokeshirecoast.org.uk.*

Thousand Island Expeditions *Ocean Base, Cross Square; tel: 01437 721686; 1000islands@stdavids.co.uk. Boat trips Easter–Oct. Whale-watching trips and coastal wildlife spotting.*

Cathedral and Bishop's Palace £ *Tel: 01437 720517. Open daily 0930–1700 (1800 June–Sept, Mon–Sat 1600 in winter); admission charged for palace; donation requested for cathedral; CADW.*

Adventure Days *1 High Street; tel: 01437 721611; www.tyf.com/advdays.htm. Supervised outdoor activities for the over-8s.*

Britain's smallest cathedral city, no larger than a village, has a charm quite disproportionate to its size. A Christian shrine founded here in about AD 550 became an important place of pilgrimage throughout the Middle Ages. The present **cathedral⬦⬦⬦**, the largest in Wales and built of local purplish sandstone, dates from the 12th century. The once-grand **Bishop's Palace⬦⬦** was added a century later. St Davids makes a good base for walking the coastal path, with its rugged coves, islands and sea stacks. Rock climbing and abseiling can also be arranged, as well as boat trips. The volcanic rocks at Caerfai Bay to the south are spectacularly mauve, green and silver. St Patrick was guided to convert Ireland to Christianity at Whitesands Bay, south of St Davids Head, and set sail from its splendid beach of pale sand.

Accommodation and food in St Davids

Warpool Court Hotel £££ *Tel: 01437 720300; fax: 01437 720676; warpool@enterprise.net.* Superbly located country-house hotel with sea views close to the coastal path. Lovely big gardens and good leisure facilities. Quality cooking.

Morgan's Brasserie ££ *20 Nun Street; tel/fax: 01437 720508; morgans@stdavids.co.uk.* A smart but relaxed little restaurant in the centre, with freshly caught fish and local Welsh cheese featuring on the blackboard menus.

Alandale £ *43 Nun Street; tel: 01327 720404; alandale@tinyworld.co.uk.* Welcoming accommodation in an old coastguard's house.

> **St David** habitually drenched himself in icy water in order to subdue the lusts of the flesh; the habit earned him the nickname 'David the Waterman'. Appropriately, he was also born during a violent thunderstorm. A nearby chapel by a well marks his birthplace, and is dedicated to his mother, St Non.

Opposite
St Davids Cathedral

STACKPOLE**

ℹ Stackpole Estate
Off B4319; tel: 01646 661359; tearoom, exhibition, information point; parking charge; NT.

🍴 Armstrong Arms £
Jason's Corner, Stackpole; tel: 01646 672324. Stone-built pub dating from 16th century on the Stackpole Estate. Plenty of sustaining fare to set you up for a coastal walk.

The southern tip of Pembrokeshire has some glorious and interesting coastal scenery, characterised by rock arches, cliffs, blowholes, stacks and islets. Most of it forms part of the well-kept 2000-acre **Stackpole Estate**. From Stackpole Quay car park, a half-mile footpath leads to magical **Barafundle Bay***, a superb stretch of sand in a breathtaking setting. **Stackpole Head** to the south is a wonderful vantage point. (Take great care near the precipitous drops.) Between here and St Govan's Head, at the bay of **Broadhaven South**, jagged rock pinnacles lie offshore. In late spring and summer, the three-fingered ornamental lake at **Bosherston** is carpeted with white waterlilies. The road through the village leads down to **St Govan's Chapel***, a tiny, ancient building wedged in a crack in the cliffs. A deep narrow ravine near by is known as **Huntsman's Leap***, allegedly jumped by a horseman, who died of shock when he realised the risk he had taken. Further west along the coastal path lie the limestone **Elegug Stacks*** and the **Green Bridge of Wales*** (a huge natural rock arch).

Above
St Govan's Chapel

TENBY**

ℹ Tourist Information *The Croft; tel: 01834 842402; tenby.tic@ pembrokeshire. gov.uk.*

🏛 Tenby Museum £
Castle Hill; tel: 01834 842809; www.tenbymuseum. free-online.co.uk. Open daily 1000–1700 in summer, Mon–Fri in winter.

Tudor Merchant's House £ *Quay Hill; tel: 01834 842279;* open Apr–Sept Thu–Tue 1000–1700, Sun 1300–1700; Oct 1000–1500 (closed Wed and Sat), Sun 1200–1500; NT.

This civilised family resort has elegant Georgian terraces, well-preserved walls and a fine arched gateway. From a pretty, partly medieval jumble of narrow streets, steep steps lead down to coves and clean and spacious beaches. The **museum*** contains works by Gwen and Augustus John. The **Tudor Merchant's House*** is a fine example of 15th-century architecture. The coastal path begins nearby, at Amroth (*see page 181*). Neighbouring resorts (Saundersfoot, Penally, Lydstep) offer an even greater choice of delightful beaches. Offshore lies **Caldey Island**, where a monastic community of Cistercians welcomes visitors.

Accommodation and food in or near Tenby

Penally Abbey ££ *Penally, Tenby; tel: 01834 843033; fax: 01834 844714; penally.abbey@btinternet.com.* Creeper-clad abbey just outside Tenby, with a grand interior and huge bedrooms offset by a homely welcome and down-to-earth cooking with fresh local produce.

Caldey Island £££
Tel: 01834 844453;
Boat trips Mon–Sat
Easter–Sept, weather
permitting. Information from
tourist office. Conducted
tours by the monks; crafts
and produce, including
cream, honey and
chocolate for sale. Gorse
perfume is the local
speciality.

Celtic Fare Tearooms £ *Vernon House, St Julian Street, Tenby; tel: 01834 845258*. Cosy café with open fires and an array of teapots and jugs on the beams.

Plantagenet House ££ *Quay Hill, Tenby; tel: 01834 842350*. Good cooking in stylish medieval surroundings.

Mermaid on the Strand £ *Saundersfoot; tel: 01834 811873*. Open-plan bar-restaurant overlooking the beach. Lots of fresh fish.

PEMBROKESHIRE COAST NATIONAL PARK✢✢✢

The Pembrokeshire Coast Path
(*www.pembrokeshirecoast. org.uk*) snakes round the National Park from Amroth (3 miles NE of Tenby) to Poppit Sands near Cardigan. Walking the whole 186-mile length of it is an exhilarating challenge, but short sections can also be enjoyed. Its dangers should not be underestimated – every year, there are a number of fatalities, as walkers fall off the cliffs.

This is the smallest but least compact of Britain's National Parks. All along its length, rugged sea cliffs and headlands jut into the Atlantic; the scene is especially memorable around the Stackpole Estate (*see page 180*), or the windswept peninsulas of Strumble and Dinas Head. The terrain in the south is mild, rather English-looking farmland, becoming wilder and stonier towards the north. Offshore islands provide a breeding ground for seals and seabirds. The Park is best seen from the long-distance Pembrokeshire Coast Path.

Suggested tour

Total distance: 130 miles (209km). Add 18 miles (29km) for the Dale detour.

Time: 5 hours.

Links: The A487 runs all the way up the west coast of Wales; from Cardigan, it's a 56-mile journey to Machynlleth, where you can pick up the Snowdonia route (*see page 166*).

Route: From **TENBY ❶**, follow the coast road A4139 and B4585 through the holiday village of **Manorbier✢✢**. King's Quoit, on the southeast headland, is an ancient burial chamber with a massive capstone. Head west again on the A4139, detouring left (B4584), following signs for **STACKPOLE ❷** and **Bosherston✢✢**. Take the B4319 to **PEMBROKE ❸**, then main roads (A477 and A4076) to **Haverfordwest ❹**. Continue northwest on the A487 towards **ST DAVIDS ❺**.

Detour: From Haverfordwest, take the B4327 to explore the Dale Peninsula**, where there is some lovely quiet coastal scenery and beaches. The flat golden sands of Marloes Sands** are reached after a 10-minute walk. From Dale village, or Martin's Haven**, on the north side of the peninsula, summer boat trips run to the nature reserves of Skomer, Skokholm or Grassholme Islands*. From Marloes, pick a route along the coast through Broad Haven and Nolton Haven.

Ten miles northwest of Haverfordwest, the 2-mile stretch of Newgale Sands** is popular with surfers. At very low tide, the remains of a fossilised forest can be seen offshore. A brief turn off the A487 3 miles further on takes you to the fishing village of Solva*, on a tidal inlet. Its safe moorings once made it a prosperous trading port; today, pleasure boats fill the harbour. From St Davids, take the A487 to FISHGUARD ❻, detouring for a look at the grand scenery of Strumble Head**. Further east is Dinas Head*; a walk around the headland takes about an hour, starting from the 12th-century church of Cwm-yr-Eglwys, wrecked in a great storm in 1859. Three miles further east is Newport, a small, attractive resort with fine beaches, and once a flourishing port full of schooners. Just inland, Carningli Common is believed to be the place where Stonehenge's blue dolerite blocks originated. Beyond Newport, the main road deviates inland. Take lanes northeast along the Heritage Coast via Moylgrove and St Dogmael's (ruined abbey) before you reach CARDIGAN ❼, to complete the coastal section of the tour.

On the return leg, take in some of Pembrokeshire's best inland scenery, through the Preseli Hills, which rise to about 1800ft. From Cardigan, take a detour south via the A478 to Cilgerran** to see its fine castle. Pick up the B4332 west to Eglwyswrw on the A487, then turn left almost immediately to take the B4329 southwest. A detour to the right from Crosswell takes you to the striking prehistoric burial chamber of Pentre Ifan*. Six miles southwest of Crosswell is a magnificent viewpoint called Foel Eryr. Descend to the crossroads and turn left by the New Inn (see Tafarn Newydd, Accommodation and food on the route) on to the B4313 through Rosebush. Continue through the eastern Cleddau valley. Narberth* straddles the landsker line, which separated the Anglicised parts of Pembrokeshire from the staunchly Welsh regions further north. Continue south on the A478, and follow signs via the quiet, attractive resort of Saundersfoot* before completing the tour at Tenby.

Also worth exploring: If you have children to amuse, head west from Narberth on the A4115 to Oakwood*. It is one of Wales's largest theme parks.

Accommodation and food on the route

Fernley Lodge £ Manorbier; tel: 01834 871226. Elegant country house

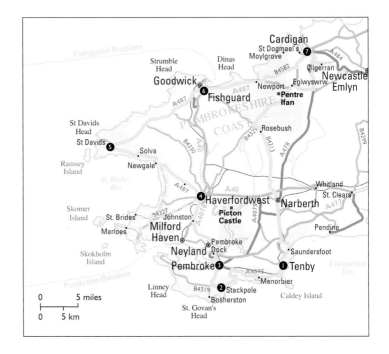

close to castle and beach; large gardens and cosy bedrooms.

Trefalen Farm £ *Bosherston; tel: 01646 661643; trefalen@aol.com.* Clifftop farm B&B with lots of animals and welcoming hosts.

Cambrian Inn £ *Main Street, Solva; tel: 01437 721210.* Good cooking with Italian touches at a friendly inn in this picturesque village.

Cnapan £ *East Street, Newport; tel: 01239 820575; cnapan@online-holiday.net; www.online-holidays.net/cnapen.* Relaxed little hotel in friendly seaside village with cheerful décor and a popular restaurant.

Trewarren £ *Newport; tel: 01239 820455.* Charming B&B with superb views.

The Druidstone ££ *Broad Haven; tel: 01437 781221; fax: 01437 781133; www.druidstone.co.uk.* Informal, relaxing coastal hideaway with rather bohemian 1970s atmosphere. Good wholefood cooking.

Tates at Tafarn Newydd ££ *Rosebush; tel: 01437 532542.* Otherwise known as the New Inn, this former drovers' tavern is on the coaching route through the Preseli Hills. A no-nonsense country pub offering above-average cooking and real ales, plus an extensive wine list. No bedrooms.

Wye Valley and the Brecon Beacons

Ratings

Outdoor activities	●●●●●
Churches	●●●●
Crafts and shopping	●●●●
Food and drink	●●●●
Heritage	●●●●
Scenery	●●●●
Wildlife	●●●
Children	●●

The border area around the Lower Wye is a pastoral idyll of lush, intimate countryside, delightful villages, country churches and good pubs. The Wye Valley, Offa's Dyke Path and the Brecon Beacons offer a tremendous range of walks. There are antiquarian bookshops, gardens, birdwatching and cider, as well as family attractions, especially in the Forest of Dean. The black-and-white villages north of Hereford are immaculate, while the Elgar trail winds through the contours of the Malvern Hills. Unpretentious country towns like Ledbury, Hay-on-Wye and Ross-on-Wye are full of smart little shops and galleries. The history of the area is bloody, though, and the Marches are scarred with many ancient battlegrounds. On the peaks of the Brecon Beacons, signal fires were often lit to warn of impending invasion.

BRECON BEACONS NATIONAL PARK**

ℹ Tourist Information *Cattle Market car park, Brecon; tel: 01874 622485.*

🏠 Dan-yr-Ogof Showcaves £££ *On A4067 N of Craig y Nos; tel: 01639 730284. Open daily Easter–Oct; tours 1030–1500.*

🚂 Brecon Mountain Railway £££ *Pant Station, Merthyr Tydfil; tel: 01685 722988. Services Easter–Oct and Dec.*

This rolling belt of mountains consists of four distinct ranges, only one of which is actually called the Brecon Beacons. Most of the rocks are old red sandstone, and glacial lakes in remote hollows are replenished by high rainfall. The uplands are clad in heather and bilberry, with rare alpine flora in places. Within the National Park are the limestone **Dan-yr-Ogof Caves*** and **Llanthony Priory****, an evocative ruin in the Black Mountains. The **Monmouthshire and Brecon Canal*** and the **Brecon Mountain Railway*** provide popular excursions. **Brecon***, the main centre, is a well-preserved Georgian market town.

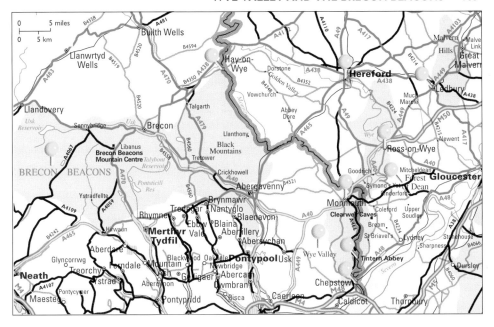

CHEPSTOW❖

Chepstow, guarding the Welsh end of the original Severn crossing at the mouth of the Wye, is the first gateway into south Wales. The historic centre of the handsome old port (once the largest in Wales) remains appealing. The substantial remains of its medieval **castle❖❖**, the very first Norman stone fortress in Britain, begun barely a year after the Conquest, stand dramatically on limestone cliffs.

FOREST OF DEAN*

ℹ️ **Tourist Information** *High Street, Coleford; tel: 01594 812388.*

🚂 **Perrygrove Railway** *££ Coleford; tel: 01594 834991; trains run Feb–Dec 1115–1615 (phone for timetable).*

The ancient forests between the Wye and the Severn Estuary have provided a livelihood since Roman times, from grazing, forestry and charcoal-making, and also from substantial coal and iron-ore deposits. Today, the region boasts over 2000 miles of footpaths and cycle routes, and a superb Sculpture Trail. Several attractions bring in families, particularly the **Clearwell Caves***, **Hopewell Colliery*** and the narrow-gauge steam **Perrygrove Railway***. The **Dean Heritage Centre**** gives a good introduction.

HAY-ON-WYE*

ℹ️ **Tourist Information** *Oxford Road; tel: 01497 820144; www.hay-on-wye.co.uk.*

Straddling the border in the Black Mountains, this little town has more than 20 miles of bookshelves, in over 25 separate shops. Each May, a famous festival fills the town. Offa's Dyke runs past the town, and beautiful countryside lies all around.

HEREFORD***

Tourist Information / King Street; tel: 01432 268430; tic-hereford@ herefordshire.gov.uk.

Mappa Mundi and Chained Library Exhibition ££ Hereford Cathedral; tel: 01432 374209; www.herefordcathedral.co.uk. Open summer Mon–Sat 1000–1615, Sun 1100–1515, winter Mon–Sat 1100–1515.

Hereford's **cathedral***** draws the crowds for its great treasure the **Mappa Mundi*****, a map of the world drawn in about 1300. The unmissable **Chained Library**** contains over 1500 volumes. Once capital of a Saxon kingdom, Hereford is now a regional administrative centre with a bustling mid-week market. The River Wye flows through it, under a handsome six-arched bridge. Beyond, rich pastureland and orchards produce beef cattle and cider apples.

Accommodation in or near Hereford

Castle House £££ *Castle Street, Hereford; tel: 01432 356321; fax: 01432 365909; info@castlehse.co.uk; www.castlehse.co.uk.* Luxury hotel in smartly restored 'mansion' premises in the centre of Hereford.

Ancient Camp Inn £ *Ruckhall, Eaton Bishop; tel: 01981 250449; fax: 01981 251581.* Excellent country inn deep amid the lanes west of Hereford with a splendid view overlooking the Wye Valley. Civilised food, pretty gardens, comfortable bedrooms.

Above
Forest of Dean

LEDBURY❖❖

ⓘ Tourist Information *3 The Homend; tel: 01531 636147.*

ⓘ Butcher Row Folk Museum *Church Lane; tel: 01531 632942. Open Apr–Oct daily 1100–1700 (1500 in Oct); donation welcome.*

Ledbury Heritage Centre *Old Grammar School, Church Lane; tel: 01531 635680. Open Easter–Oct daily 1030–1630; donation welcome.*

The High Street here has many eye-catching buildings, notably the 17th-century **Market Hall❖**, raised on wooden columns. Picturesque **Church Row❖❖** is a narrow alleyway lined with quaintly jettied Tudor and Stuart houses. Find out more about Ledbury's past at the **Butcher Row Folk Museum❖** or the **Ledbury Heritage Centre❖**. Even the council offices have medieval frescos in the **Painted Room** (*tel: 01531 632306; open summer Mon–Fri 1100–1500*).

Accommodation and food in Ledbury

Feathers Hotel ££ *High Street; tel: 01531 635266; fax: 01531 638955; mary@feathers-ledbury.co.uk.* Half-timbered coaching inn with smart bedrooms and serving an excellent range of bar and restaurant food.

Mrs Muffin's Tea Shop £ *Church Lane; tel: 01531 633579.* Attractive café in the pretty alleyway leading to the church.

MONMOUTH❖❖

ⓘ Tourist Information *Shire Hall, Agincourt Square; tel: 01600 713899; monmouth.tic@ monmouthshire.gov.uk.*

This ancient market town has many historical associations. A ruined castle stands near **Agincourt Square**, where there are statues of Henry V, born in Monmouth Castle in 1387, and of local boy Charles Rolls, of Rolls-Royce. A unique medieval **fortified bridge❖** has a 13th-century gateway.

ROSS-ON-WYE❖❖

ⓘ Tourist Information *Edde Cross Street; tel: 01989 562768.*

ⓘ Market House Heritage Centre *Market Place; tel: 01432 260673. Open Apr–Oct Mon–Sat 1000–1700, Sun 1030–1600; Nov–Mar Mon–Sat 1030–1600; donation welcome.*

This charming market town, which has many historic buildings, is perched on a sandstone cliff high above the Wye. In the main street stands the arcaded **Market House❖**. The public clifftop gardens of **The Prospect❖** provide good river views. The Wye Valley in either direction offers magnificent walks.

Accommodation and food in or near Ross-on-Wye

The Pheasant at Ross ££ *52 Edde Cross Street, Ross-on-Wye; tel: 01989 565751; fax: 01989 763069.* Traditional country cooking using local ingredients. Interesting, good-value wine list.

The Lough Pool Inn ££ *Sellack; tel: 01989 730236.* Worth tracking down for a hearty plateful in rustic surroundings near Ross-on-Wye.

Glewstone Court ££ *Glewstone, Ross-on-Wye; tel: 01989 770367; fax: 01989 770282; glewstone@aol.com.* Secluded country-house hotel in charming orchard setting, with informal atmosphere and plenty of good local cooking.

TINTERN ABBEY***

Tintern Abbey ££
Tel: 01291 689251.
Open Apr–Oct 0930–1700
(1800 in summer), Nov–Mar
Mon–Sat 0930–1600, Sun
1100–1600; CADW.

Abbey Mill £ *Main Road,
Tintern; tel: 01291 689228;
www.abbeymill.com. Open
Mon–Fri 1030–1700,
Sat–Sun 1030–1730.* Crafts
complex and coffee shop
in old mill buildings in the
village itself. Waterfront
setting.

Parva Farmhouse ££
*Tintern; tel: 01291
689411; fax: 01291
689557; parva_hoteltintern@
hotmail.com;
www.hoteltintern.co.uk.* This
upmarket guesthouse makes
an excellent base for
exploring Tintern Abbey and
the enticing countryside
around.

The evocative skeleton of Wales's richest and most impressive Cistercian monastery has attracted visitors since awestruck Romantics immortalised it in paint and poetry. Founded in 1131, Tintern was an immensely powerful centre of learning for over four centuries. The graceful **Gothic church** was constructed from about 1269. Many lovely walks are possible along this stretch of the river.

WYE VALLEY***

Goodrich Castle ££
Tel: 01600 890538.
Open Apr–Sept daily
1000–1800 (1700 in Oct,
Nov–Mar Wed–Sun
1000–1300, 1400–1600).

The long-distance Wye Valley Walk runs from the river's source high in the hills of central Wales (near Rhayader) to Chepstow. The river's lower reaches are picturesque, passing by steep cliffs of red sandstone. **Symond's Yat***** is a spectacular gorge, with a panoramic viewpoint from the Yat Rock. Birdwatchers come from far and wide to see peregrine falcons here. Just upstream, **Goodrich Castle**** dominates another looping bend.

Suggested tour

❶ Brecon Beacons Mountain Centre
Libanus, Brecon; tel: 01874 623366; www.brecon-beacons.com. Open daily from 0930 (parking charge).

❶ Hellens ££ Much Marcle; tel: 01531 660668. Open Easter–Sept Sat, Sun, Wed 1400–1600; guided tours.

Weston's Cider Farm ££ Much Marcle; tel: 01531 660233; www.westons-cider.co.uk. Tours by appointment Mon–Fri 0930–1630, Sat 1000–1300.

Abbey Dore Court Garden ££ Abbey Dore; tel: 01981 240419. Open Apr–Sept Thu–Sun, Tue 1100–1800.

Tretower Court and Castle ££ Tretower; tel: 01874 730279. Open Mar–Oct 1000–1700 (seasonal variations); CADW.

Total distance: 115 miles (185km). Add 51 miles (82km) for the Brecon detour.

Time: 4–5 hours.

Links: Join the Cotswolds route (*see page 126*) by taking the A48 or A40 to Gloucester. Hop over the Severn Bridge (M48) at Chepstow to join any of the West Country routes from the M4 or M5. No tolls are charged on either of the Severn crossings as you leave Wales, only as you enter it.

Route: From **ROSS-ON-WYE ❶**, take the A449 northeast for 6 miles, to the traditional village of **Much Marcle***. **Hellens*** is an ancient manor house dating back to Norman times. **Weston's Cider Farm*** does tours and tastings. From **LEDBURY ❷**, take the A438 west to **HEREFORD ❸**. Head southwest on the A465, turning right after 2 miles on the B4349/4348 through the placid scenery of the **Golden Valley****. Vowchurch, Peterchurch and **Abbey Dore*** are the best villages along this pretty drive in sight of the distant summits of the Black Mountains. Abbey Dore has an impressive Cistercian abbey church. **Abbey Dore Court Garden*** has a charming riverside setting. Bear left beyond Dorstone following signs to **HAY-ON-WYE ❹**.

Detour: Hay is a good starting point for a tour of the **BRECON BEACONS ❺**. Take the B4350 southwest via Three Cocks (a tangle of roads where the River Wye abruptly changes course), continuing on the A438/A470 signed for **Brecon***. Take the A470 southwest of town for 3 miles, turning briefly left at Libanus for the **Brecon Beacons Mountain Centre****. Turn right on the A4215 and head for Sennybridge. From here, a choice of routes takes you south across the heart of the Brecon Beacons. The A4067 takes you past the **Dan-yr-Ogof Caves*** (*see page 184*), but a wilder unclassified road leads through **Ystradfellte** and its waterfalls. Turn left when you reach the south edge of the National Park, skirting the colliery valleys of Rhondda and following signs to **Merthyr Tydfil**. Take the minor road left off the A465 along the course of the Brecon Mountain Railway past the reservoirs of Pen-Twyn and Talybont – a steep and spectacular route past Pen-y-Fan. Join the A40 and head right past **Tretower Court*** (a fortified manor house) and the pretty old coaching town of **Crickhowell***, then rejoin the main route at Abergavenny.

Take the unclassified road southeast past Hay Bluff to **Llanthony Priory****, a romantic Augustinian ruin. A useful car park here makes a base for walks. This Black Mountain drive is extremely beautiful, but steep and very narrow in places. Don't try it in bad weather. Turn right at the T-junction with the A465 (stop at the Skirrid Inn for lunch), following signs to the historic market town of **Abergavenny***.

Right
Ledbury

Big Pit Mining Museum *Blaenavon, off B4248; tel: 01495 790311; www.hmgw.ac.uk/bigpit. Open Mar–Nov 0930–1700; underground tours (no children under 1 metre tall) daily 1000–1530.*

Gwent Rural Life Museum £ *New Market Street, Usk; tel: 01291 673777. Open Apr–Oct Mon–Fri 1000–1700, Sat–Sun 1400–1700.*

The **Big Pit Mining Museum**✦✦✦ at Blaenavon 7 miles southeast is one of Britain's best industrial heritage attractions. From Abergavenny, take the B4598 southeast signed for the border town of **Usk**✦, where the **Gwent Rural Life Museum**✦✦ is housed in an old malthouse. The looping river here is famed for its salmon. Continue down the B4235 towards **CHEPSTOW ⑥**, then turn north up the A466 through the **WYE VALLEY ⑦** to **TINTERN ABBEY ⑧** and **MONMOUTH ⑨**, hugging the river through wooded scenery.

Detour: From Tintern, take lanes northeast via St Briavel's to **Coleford** in the **FOREST OF DEAN ⑩**, passing the **Clearwell Caves**✦ on the left. Turn right on the B4226 through the heart of the forest, past 17th-century Speech House Hotel. You can start the Sculpture Trail walk

🧀 Herefordshire Cheesemaking £
The Pleck, Monkland, Leominster; tel: 01568 720307; www.mousetrapcheese.co.uk. Open Easter–Oct daily 1000–1730 (Tue–Sat 1030–1700 in winter); cheesemaking Mon, Wed and Fri 1000–1400. Café and farm shop selling traditionally made cheeses and a wide range of other local produce.

Pembridge Terracotta
East Street, Pembridge; tel: 01544 388696; www.gardenpots.co.uk. Open May–Dec Mon–Fri 0900–1700, Sat–Sun 1000–1700. Working pottery producing an imaginative range of frost-proof garden pots (25-year guarantee).

from the Forestry Commission visitor centre (signposted). Follow signs right to Soudley and the excellent **Dean Heritage Centre**, then continue through Cinderford to the A40. Turn left to complete the tour at Ross.

From Monmouth, the obvious route back to Ross is along the A40, but staying on the east bank enables you to reach **Symond's Yat** more easily. Take the A4136 east towards Staunton. Turn left on the B4432, following through more wooded scenery to **Yat Rock**. Take the minor road across a narrow bridge past **Goodrich Castle**, and continue on the B4234 back to Ross-on-Wye

Also worth exploring: To see the rural countryside north of Hereford, head for Leominster, a perfect assembly of timbered houses, then pick a route through Eardisland, Pembridge and Weobley to see some classically picturesque English villages with black-and-white architecture.

Ledbury is a good starting point for a tour of the Malverns, a range of granite hills south of Worcester, associated with the composer Edward Elgar (1857–1934), who lived in Little Malvern. The spa water of Great Malvern, a popular watering-hole in the 19th century, still has avid fans, including the Queen.

Accommodation and food on the route

Red Gate £ *32 Avenue Road, Malvern; tel/fax: 01684 565013; enquiries@the-red-gate.co.uk.* Charming B&B in large Victorian house in quiet residential area.

Salutation Inn £ *Market Pitch, Weobley; tel: 01544 318443; fax: 01544 318216; info@salutationinn.com.* Weobley is one of the most fetching of the half-timbered villages near Hereford, and this traditional inn looks all of a piece with the historic buildings around. Friendly service and accomplished food add to its attractions, along with several pretty bedrooms.

Clytha Arms ££ *Clytha, Abergavenny; tel: 01873 840206; fax: 01873 840209; one.bev@lineone.net.* Charming dower-house inn with cosy Victorian-style bedrooms and tremendously imaginative food. The bars are traditional and civilised, with a pleasing lack of gibbering slot machines or piped muzak.

Penyclawdd Court ££ *Llanfihangel Crucorney; tel: 01873 890719; fax: 01873 890848; pyccourt@hotmail.com; www.1stmanorhouse.com.* For a genuinely memorable stay, try this extraordinary, painstakingly restored Tudor manor with a Norman motte-and-bailey in the garden.

Skirrid Mountain Inn £ *Llanfihangel Crucorney; tel: 01873 890258.* A friendly local with real character in a very ancient building. Lunch served in the garden with Black Mountain views. Some simple rooms.

Bear Hotel ££ *High Street, Crickhowell; tel: 01873 818408; fax: 01873 811696; bearhotel@aol.com; www.bearhotel.com.* Popular inn with good food and traditional interior attractively located in the National Park.

Gliffaes Country House ££ *Crickhowell; tel: 01874 730371; fax: 01874 730463; calls@gliffaeshotel.com; www.gliffaeshotel.com.* Superb gardens overlooking the National Park are one of the main assets of this grand Victorian house; public areas are slightly old-fashioned, but bedrooms are smartly traditional.

Nantiffin Cider Mill Inn ££ *Brecon Road, Crickhowell (on A40/A479 junction); tel/fax: 01873 810775; info@cidermill.co.uk.* Converted stone barn inn offering a great range of imaginative food and traditional ciders. New World wine list.

Crown at Whitebrook ££ *Whitebrook; tel: 01600 860254; fax: 01600 860607; crown@whitebrook.demon.co.uk; www.crown@whitebrook.co.uk.* A thriving restaurant-with-rooms in a lovely wooded part of the Wye Valley, serving ambitious food.

Walnut Tree Inn £££ *Llandewi Skirrid, on B4521; tel: 01873 852797; www.thewalnuttreeinn.com.* Despite a change of ownership, devotees of this justly famous establishment will not be disappointed. Superlative cooking in a simple, unpretentious whitewashed country pub. It's not cheap, but it is outstanding.

The Boat Inn £ *Penallt; tel: 01600 712615.* Park in England and cross the footbridge to reach this Welsh pub on the River Wye. Traditional pub grub and real ales in a cosy setting.

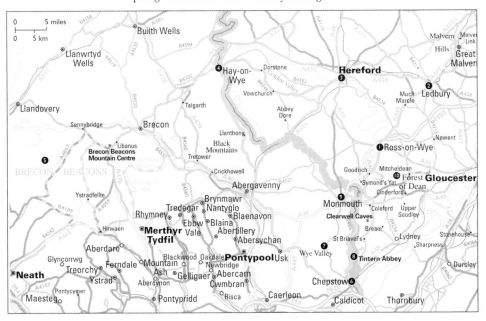

Rural Kent and the Cinque Ports

Ratings

Family attractions	●●●●●
Gardens, orchards and vineyards	●●●●●
Military and naval history	●●●●●
Towns and villages	●●●●●
Heritage	●●●●
Beaches	●●●
Scenery	●●●
Walking	●●●

England's southeast corner, pinned between Europe and London, is gradually becoming ever more crowded. The area's rural character may be in some jeopardy, but for the time being many of its villages could not be more traditionally English in their appearance and way of life. The countryside is never wild or dramatic, but it does have variety: eerie marshes around Romney, belts of shingle along the coast, rich orchards and vineyards in the Weald, and breezy heights along the North Downs. Kent and Sussex have some fascinating coastal towns (not the most popular seaside resorts, incidentally). The historic pilgrim city of Canterbury makes an interesting base, having more attractions than either the county town of Maidstone or the burgeoning centre of Ashford. If you prefer a smaller, more intimate place to stay, Rye, Sandwich or Battle make charming alternatives.

CANTERBURY✧✧✧

ℹ Tourist Information *12–13 Sun Street; tel: 01227 378100. Daily guided walks at 1400 (and 1130 in summer).*

🎫 Canterbury Cathedral ££ *Tel: 01227 762862; www.canterbury-cathedral.org. Open Mon–Sat 0900–1900 (1700 in winter), Sun 1230–1430, 1730–1830; obligatory admission charges for all sections.*

St Augustine's arrival in the year 597 turned this ancient settlement into the centre of Anglican Christendom. The **cathedral✧✧✧**, dramatically floodlit in summer, dates from around 1070. A century later, Thomas à Becket was murdered in the northwest transept – his shrine created a place of pilgrimage. The glories of the cathedral include its medieval stained glass, and a forest of late Perpendicular pinnacles and towers. Close by are the ruins of **St Augustine's Abbey✧** and some well-preserved stretches of city wall. The layout of medieval Canterbury can still be detected in the city's crooked alleys. **St Martin's Church✧** is England's oldest still in continual use. Two gateways survive from the original walls: ornate **Christ Church Gate✧✧** and the crenellated **West Gate✧✧**, which contains a small museum. Other museums display Canterbury's Roman heritage, and the city's history (the **Canterbury Heritage Museum✧✧**).

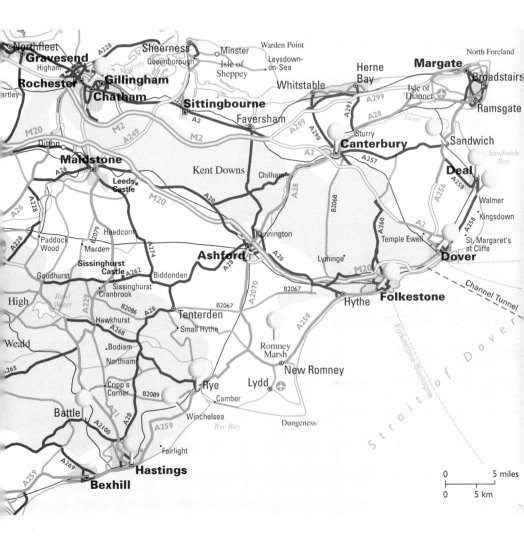

Museum of Canterbury ££ *Stour Street; tel: 01227 452747; www.canterbury-museum.co.uk. Open Mon–Sat 1030–1700.*

Roman Museum ££ *Longmarket, Butchery Lane; tel: 01227 785575. Open June–Oct Mon–Sat 1000–1700, Sun 1330–1700 (closed Sun off season).*

Accommodation and food in Canterbury

Falstaff Hotel ££ *8–10 St Dunstan's Street; tel: 01227 462138; fax: 01227 463525; www.comshotels.co.uk.* Fine historic inn with period architecture. Attractive interior and a good modern restaurant. Rooms at the rear are quieter.

Magnolia House ££ *36 St Dunstan's Terrace; tel/fax: 01227 765121; magnolia_house_canterbury@yahoo.com; http://freespace.virgin.net/ magnolia. canterbury.* Cheerful Georgian B&B in quiet central side street. Pretty little gardens.

DOVER✶✶ AND FOLKESTONE✶✶

ℹ Tourist Information
Townwall Street, Dover; tel: 01304 205108; or Harbour Street, Folkestone; tel: 01303 258594.

🏰 Dover Castle and Secret Wartime Tunnels £££ Dover Cliffs; tel: 01304 211067. Open Apr–Sept 1000–1800, Oct 1000–1700, Nov–Mar 1000–1600; EH.

Roman Painted House £ New Street; tel: 01304 203279. Open Apr–Sept Tue–Sat 1000–1700 (daily July–Aug).

Grand Shaft £ Snargate Street; tel: 01304 201066. Open July–Aug Tue–Sun 1400–1700.

🌙 Wallett's Court ££ Westcliffe, St Margaret's at Cliffe, Dover; tel: 01304 852424; fax: 01304 853430; www.wallettscourt.com. Long-established family-run hotel with plenty of historic interest. Good cooking and a swimming pool.

Dover's natural harbour, below the famous **White Cliffs✶✶**, serves the busiest shipping lanes in Europe. **Dover Castle✶✶**, occupied since prehistoric times, has always played a significant role in Britain's defences, especially during World War II. A few old buildings survive in Dover, including the **Roman Painted House✶**. The **Grand Shaft✶** is a triple spiral staircase allowing fast access up or down the cliffs.

Folkestone still has vestiges of charm around the church and old High Street, and along the clifftop promenade known as **The Leas✶**. A statue of a seated pilot gazing out over the Channel commemorates the Battle of Britain.

The Cinque Ports

From Saxon times, five Channel ports were granted special privileges and the right to levy taxes. Their duties were to defend the Channel, and to keep the royal fleet equipped with ships and men. The Cinque (pronounced 'sink') Ports still have some ceremonial status, and a Lord Warden (hitherto the Queen Mother). The original Ports were Hastings, Romney, Hythe, Sandwich and Dover. Others co-opted later included Deal, Walmer, Rye and Winchelsea. Some of these places are no longer on the coast, following the silting up of their harbours.

DEAL✧✧ AND WALMER✧✧

ⓘ **Tourist
Information** *Town
Hall, High Street, Deal; tel:
01304 369576.*

🏰 **Time Ball Tower £**
*Victoria Parade, Deal;
tel: 01304 360897. Open
July–Aug Tue–Sun
1000–1700.*

Shipping passes close inshore here, avoiding the treacherous Goodwin Sands 5 miles from the coast. Signals from the seafront **Time Ball Tower**✧ have aided mariners for centuries. Deal has a well-preserved Georgian quarter and a long pier. Deal was Julius Caesar's landing point in 55 BC. To defend against further invasions, both Deal and Walmer built **castles**✧. Deal's (*Victoria Road; tel: 01304 372762. Open Apr–Sept 1000–1800, Oct 1000–1700, Nov–Mar Wed–Sun 1000–1600; EH*) has a particularly striking Tudor rose shape; Walmer's is the traditional residence of the Lord Warden of the Cinque Ports (*Kingsdown Road, Walmer; tel: 01304 364288. Open Apr–Oct 1000–1800, Nov 1000–1700, Dec Wed–Sun 1000–1600, Jan–Feb weekends only 1000–1600; closed when Lord Warden is in residence; EH*).

Shingle-loving plants colonise the pebble storm ridges at the back of the quiet beaches at Walmer and Kingsdown, including sea kale and horned poppies.

HASTINGS✧✧ AND BATTLE✧✧

ⓘ **Tourist
Information** *The
Slade, Old Town, Hastings,
or Queens Square, Hastings;
tel: 01424 781111; or 88
High Street, Battle; tel:
01424 773721;
battletic@rother.gov.uk.*

🏰 **Battle Abbey and
Battlefield ££** *High
Street, Battle; tel: 01424
773792. Open Apr–Sept
daily 1000–1800, Oct
1000–1700, Nov–Mar
1000–1600; EH.*

Weatherboarded **net shops**✧ stand on the shingle beach behind the pretty fishing harbour of Hastings Old Town. The Norman ruins beside one of them are the remains of William the Conqueror's first motte-and-bailey castle, constructed after his landmark victory just up the road at **Battle**✧✧. Here, a waymarked trail with an audio tour explains the event that changed England's history. **Battle Abbey**✧ was constructed by William in thanksgiving.

Accommodation and food in Hastings and Battle

Harris ££ *58 High Street, Hastings; tel: 01424 437221.* Casual, friendly atmosphere and fair prices at this pleasant Spanish *tapas* bar in the Old Town.

Fox Hole Farm £ *Kane Hythe Road, Battle; tel: 01424 772053; fax: 01424 773771.* Tranquil B&B in an old woodcutter's cottage in rural surroundings.

MEDWAY TOWNS✦✦

ℹ Tourist Information 95 High Street, Rochester; tel: 01634 843666; visitor.centre@ medway.gov.uk.

🏰 Rochester Castle ££ The Keep; tel: 01634 402276; kay.hill@medway.gov.uk; www.medway.gov.uk. Open Apr–Sept daily 1000–1800, Oct–Mar 1000–1600.

Charles Dickens Centre ££ High Street, Rochester; tel: 01634 844176. Open Apr–Sept daily 1000–1730 (1600 in winter).

Historic Dockyard £££ Chatham; tel: 01634 823800; www.chdt.org.uk. Open Apr–Oct daily 1000–1800, Feb, Mar and Nov Wed, Sat–Sun 1000–1600, closed Dec–Jan.

Fort Amherst ££ Dock Road, Chatham; tel: 01634 847747; www.fortamherst.co.uk. Open daily 1030–1700 (Easter–Oct Sat–Sun 1030–1630 in winter).

Royal Engineers Museum ££ Brompton Barracks, Prince Arthur Road, Gillingham; tel: 01634 406397; www.royalengineers.org.uk. Open Mon–Thu 1000–1700, Sat–Sun 1130–1700.

Of the three Medway Towns, **Rochester✦✦** is the oldest, an attractively preserved Roman settlement on the London–Dover road. The city walls follow the lines of the original Roman fortifications. The square-towered 100-ft keep of the sturdy-looking Norman **castle✦✦** commands the Medway's lowest bridging point. Charles Dickens, who spent his last years at Gad's Hill near by, is remembered in the **Charles Dickens Centre✦**, and an annual Dickens Festival. **Chatham✦✦** was established as a naval base by Henry VIII. The former **Royal Naval Dockyard✦✦** is now a major tourist attraction. **Fort Amherst✦**, nearby, is probably the finest example of an 18th-century fort in Britain. **Gillingham**, third of the Medway towns, has less appeal for visitors, although its **Royal Engineers Museum** may interest military history enthusiasts.

Right
Rochester

ROMNEY MARSH✣

Tourist Information Red Lion Square, Hythe; tel: 01303 267799; or Magpies, Church Approach, New Romney; tel: 01797 364044.

Romney, Hythe & Dymchurch Railway ££ Tel: 01797 362353; www.rhdr.demon.co.uk. Services Apr–Sept daily, weekends Oct and Mar.

St Leonard's Church Crypt £ Church Road, Hythe; tel: 01303 262370; www.stleonardschurchhythe. co.uk. Open May–Sept Mon–Sat 1030–1200 and daily 1430–1600.

Dungeness Visitor Centre Dungeness Power Stations; tel: 01797 321815; www.bnfl.com. Open Mar–Oct daily 1000–1600; no children under 5; book ahead.

Romney Bay House ££ Coast Road, Littlestone-on-Sea, New Romney; tel: 01797 364747; fax: 01797 367156. Pleasantly secluded seafront hotel with stylish décor and good food. Plenty of character about the house – designed by Clough Williams Ellis of Portmeirion fame.

Once a malarial marsh, this mysterious low-lying corner of Britain lies well below sea level. St Leonard's **crypt✣** in the church at **Hythe✣**, at its northeast edge, is full of stacked skulls. The **Romney, Hythe & Dymchurch Light Railway✣✣** is a popular public service, running nearly 14 miles on 15-in track. The desolate promontory of **Dungeness** is dominated by two nuclear power stations, but provides a fascinating habitat for wildlife.

In the spring, large **marsh frogs** croak in Romney Marsh, descendants of a dozen specimens that escaped from a zoologist's garden pond in 1935. This species, the largest in Europe at about 5in long, is found nowhere else in Britain.

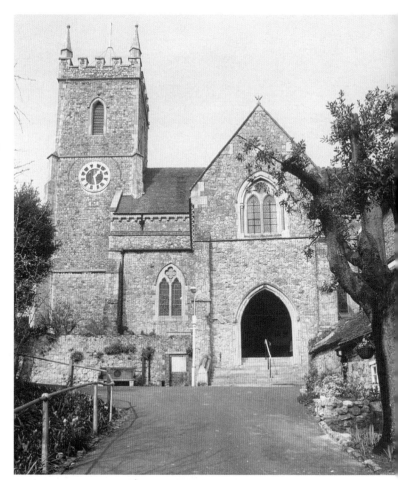

Right
St Leonard's church, Hythe

RYE✦✦✦ AND WINCHELSEA✦✦

ⓘ Tourist Information £ *The Heritage Centre, Strand Quay, Rye; tel: 01797 226696; www.visitrye.co.uk. The Story of Rye (sound and light show) Mar–Oct daily 0900–1730, Nov–Feb daily 1000–1600.*

ⓘ Rye Castle Museum *££ 3 East Street and Ypres Tower; tel: 01797 226728. Open summer Thu–Mon 1030–1300, 1400–1700, weekends only Nov–Mar 1030–1530.*

The enchanting historic town of **Rye✦✦✦** is perched above the waterline near the mouth of the Rother. In 1287 a storm diverted the river, making Rye a prime Channel port, but silting eventually stranded the town over 2 miles away from its harbour. Today, **Mermaid Street✦✦**, with its picturesque cobbles and lopsided, clay-tiled buildings, is one of Rye's prettiest corners. Other streets in the old town boast fine Georgian houses, or medieval relics such as the 14th-century **Land Gate** and the **Ypres Tower✦**.

Winchelsea✦✦ is less well known than Rye, but just as interesting in its way, with an unchanged medieval street grid. The **church of St Thomas à Becket✦✦** and three surviving gates are its main landmarks; below it lie the sheep meadows of the Winchelsea Levels.

Accommodation and food in Rye

Jeake's House £ *Mermaid Street; tel: 01797 222828; fax: 01797 222623; jeakeshouse@btinternet.com; www.jeakeshouse.com.* A charming B&B in one of the prettiest streets in England. Lots of character.

Little Orchard House ££ *West Street; tel/fax: 01797 223831; www.littleorchardhouse.com.* Interesting period B&B with a lovely garden. Lots of personal touches and some antiques.

Old Vicarage £ *66 Church Square; tel: 01797 222119; fax: 01797 227466; www.oldvicaragerye.co.uk.* This B&B is another winner, in a charming quiet cottage near the church.

Below
Rye's Land Gate

SANDWICH**

ⓘ Tourist Information
Guildhall; tel: 01304 613565; www.sandwich-kent-uk.net; tours of building Mar–Dec.

Ⓠ Sandwich River Bus ££ Sandwich Quay, Old Toll Bridge; tel: 0795 8376183. Mini cruises around Sandwich daily in summer.

Ⓗ Gazen Salts Nature Reserve
Tel: 01304 611925 (eves). Wildfowl colonise a man-made lake; Sandwich terns search for food on sandy flats below the shingle.

Richborough Roman fort ££ Tel: 01304 612013. Open Apr–Sept 1000–1800, Oct 1000–1700, Nov–Feb weekends only 1000–1600; EH.

Right
Sandwich parish church

Ⓗ Bodiam Castle ££
Bodiam; tel: 01580 830436. Open Feb–Oct daily 1000–1800 or dusk, weekends in winter 1000–1600; NT.

Great Dixter House and Gardens ££
Northiam; tel: 01797 252878; www.greatdixter.co.uk. Open Apr–Oct Tue–Sun 1400–1700. Spectacular gardens created by gardening writer Christopher Lloyd in the grounds of a wonderful 15th-century manor restored by Sir Edwin Lutyens.

Oldest and quaintest of the Cinque Ports, Sandwich now stands well inland on the silted River Stour, a charming knot of medieval buildings including three fine churches, a Barbican and a Guildhall, and some old town walls. Its quiet nature reserve beach lies behind the prestigious Royal St George Golf Course. This stretch of the Saxon Shore Way is especially peaceful, and good for birdwatching. **Richborough Roman fort***, 2 miles northwest, is an impressive ruin from which the Romans launched their invasion of Britain.

Suggested tour

Total distance: 156 miles (250km). Add 22 miles (35km) for the Thanet variant and 64 miles (102km) for the Medway towns.

Time: 6 hours.

Links: The Sussex tour (*see page 204*) can easily be joined from Hastings (A21 to Tunbridge Wells or A529 to Eastbourne).

Route: From **CANTERBURY ❶**, head east on the A257, leaving the old pilgrim route on the North Downs ridgeway over a belt of rich, flat farmland. At **SANDWICH ❷**, turn southeast on the A258 to **DEAL** and **WALMER ❸**. Follow the coast route (A258, A20, A259) clockwise via **DOVER ❹**, **FOLKESTONE ❺** and **Hythe**, past **ROMNEY MARSH ❻**. During Napoleonic times, a chain of 74 small forts was built between Folkestone and Seaford in Sussex – just 15 remain. At the Pilot Inn near **Dungeness** headland, take the minor road northwest

Tenterden Vineyard *Small Hythe; tel: 01580 763033; www.newwavewines.com. Open daily 1000–1700; guided tours by arrangement (charge). Herb garden and winery.*

Stocks Mill £ *Wittersham; tel: 01797 270295. Open Easter–Sept Sun 1400–1700.*

Sissinghurst Castle garden £££ *Sissinghurst; tel: 01580 710700. Open Apr–Oct Fri–Tue 1100–1830, Sat–Sun 1000–1830; NT. Outstanding garden created by Vita Sackville-West. Timed ticket system at peak periods.*

Union Mill *The Hill, Cranbrook; tel: 01580 712256. Open Easter–Sept Sat 1400–1700; donation welcome. Seven-floored smockmill, largest in England, in full working order.*

Finchcocks £££ *Goudhurst; tel: 01580 211702; www.finchcocks.co.uk. Open Easter–Sept Sun (Wed–Thu in Aug) 1400–1800. Working keyboard instruments in an early Georgian house – played whenever the house is open.*

Leeds Castle £££ *Leeds, off M20 3 miles E of Maidstone; tel: 01622 765400; www.leeds-castle.co.uk. Open Mar–Oct daily 1000–1700, Nov–Feb 1000–1500.*

past an RSPB reserve. Turn left on the B2075 over the Sussex border via **Camber Sands***. Head for **RYE** ❼, then **WINCHELSEA** ❽ and **HASTINGS** ❾ on the A259. Turn inland on the A2100 to **BATTLE** ❿ .

Some of Kent's prettiest villages lie between Maidstone and Rye, west of the M20 on the eastern fringes of the sandstone Weald. This fertile rural area is called the Garden of England. Oasthouses still stud the landscape, and the orchards glow with blossom in spring. Returning to the A21, follow signs via Cripp's Corner to **Bodiam****, which has perhaps the most perfect moated **castle** in England, and **Northiam****, to see the garden of **Great Dixter****. On the A28, head north for **Tenterden****, once a ship-building centre. Several vineyards and a herb garden can be visited near here. Nearby **Small Hythe*** (2 miles southeast) on the Isle of Oxney above the low-lying Rother Levels (flooded after rain) has a tall postmill. Continue on the A262 to **Biddenden***, another lovely old village of weavers' cottages with a medieval cloth hall and a fine church (1 mile south). Take the A262 west to **Sissinghurst*****, one of the best of the southeast's gardens. At **Cranbrook****, see the restored **Union Mill***. **Goudhurst****, 7 miles further west on the A262, is another gorgeous village of golden stone and antique shops. **Finchcocks****, just west of the village, is worth visiting. Head north on the B2079 through **Marden**, which has a good ragstone church with a weatherboarded tower, then turn right across country through Staplehurst to **Headcorn**. Join the main A274 north, turning right in 3 miles for moated **Leeds Castle*****, converted into a royal residence by Henry VIII, and now a major attraction. From here, take the A20 across the M20, and follow the North Downs Way back to Canterbury along the A252. **Chilham***, at the junction of the A28, is one of Kent's prettiest villages.

Detours: From Canterbury, head northeast on the A290 to the appealing old oyster port of **Whitstable***, then follow the A299 east to the **Isle of Thanet** (for Margate, **Broadstairs*** and Ramsgate). Pick up the main route at Sandwich.

Head west on the M2 to the **MEDWAY TOWNS** ⓫ . Return on the old Roman road (A2, Watling Street) via Sittingbourne and Faversham, which have attractive old centres.

Accommodation and food on the route

Sissinghurst Castle Farm £ *Sissinghurst; tel: 01580 712885; fax: 01580 712601; sissinghurstcastlefarm@farmersweekly.net.* Smart welcoming B&B handily placed for garden visiting in the grounds of the castle, with grand architecture but an informal, family atmosphere.

Kennel Holt Hotel £££ *Goudhurst Road, Cranbrook; tel: 01580 712032; fax: 01580 715495; hotel@kennelholt.demon.co.uk.* Smart country-house accommodation with accomplished cooking. Some splendid antiques.

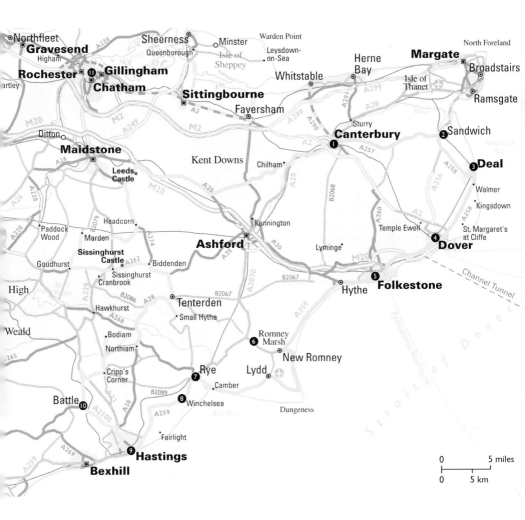

Whitstable Oyster and Fishery Exhibition £ *East Quay, The Harbour; tel: 01227 262003. Open May–Aug daily 1000–1600, weekends Sept–Apr. Oysters on sale.*

Old Cloth Hall Oast ££ *Cranbrook; tel/fax: 01580 712220.* Glorious 15th-century secluded manor furnished with antiques. Dinners using local produce. Dream gardens and a swimming pool.

Ringlestone Inn ££ *Ringlestone, nr Harrietsham; tel: 01622 859900; fax: 01622 859966; bookings@ringlestone.com; www.ringlestone.com.* Well-kept historic inn serving excellent traditional English fare; comfortable well-equipped accommodation available. Just ten minutes' drive on tiny lanes from Leeds Castle.

Whitstable Oyster Fishery Co ££ *Royal Native Oyster Stores, The Horsebridge, Whitstable; tel: 01227 276856; fax: 01227 770666.* Six weatherboarded huts, with pine furnishings and bright décor, majoring on fishy stuff.

Sussex and the Weald

Ratings

Gardens	●●●●●
Heritage	●●●●●
Stately homes	●●●●●
Children	●●●●○
Countryside	●●●○
Eating out	●●●●○
Walking	●●●○○
Beaches	●●○○○

Stately home and garden fans will have a field day in this region. Other attractions include the coastline – the section between Brighton and Eastbourne is one of Britain's most memorable stretches of Heritage Coast. Here, the sheer chalk walls of the Seven Sisters culminate in awesome Beachy Head. Inland, the rolling chalk continues over the expansive uplands of the South Downs, carved by deep river valleys from the rich farmland of the Weald. Walks along the South Downs Way are a wonderful way to enjoy this scenery. The historic towns of Lewes, Arundel and Tunbridge Wells are interesting, as are numerous smaller places (Cuckfield, Steyning, Fletching and Alfriston, among others). Poohsticks Bridge appeals to visitors of all ages, as they wander through the Ashdown Forest in search of the innocent world of Christopher Robin and his friends.

ARUNDEL✥✥

ⓘ Tourist Information 61 High Street; 01903 882268.

🏰 Arundel Castle £££ Tel: 01903 883136; www.arundelcastle.org. Open Apr–Oct Sun–Fri 1200–1700.

Arundel Wildfowl and Wetland's Centre ££ Mill Road; tel: 01903 883355; www.wnt.org.uk. Open Apr–Sept daily 0930–1730 (1630 in winter).

Right Arundel Castle

The fairytale **castle✥✥** on a wooded mound overlooking the Arun valley, seat of the Dukes of Norfolk for over 700 years, dates from Norman times. Its keep is the oldest part. Arundel's other charms are its unspoilt brick, flint and timbered buildings lining hilly narrow streets. To the north the Arun flows through a nature reserve belonging to **Arundel Wildfowl and Wetland's Centre✥**.

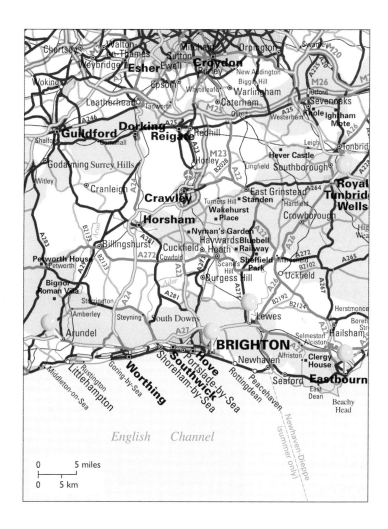

BRIGHTON✦✦✦

ℹ️ **Tourist Information**
Bartholomew Square; tel: 0906 711 2255; brighton-tourism@brighton-hove.gov.uk.

The flamboyant **Royal Pavilion**✦✦✦ was constructed for the Prince Regent in the 1770s by John Nash. **Brighton Pier**✦✦ overlooks the mainly stony beach, while elegant Regency squares and terraces grace other parts of the town. **The Lanes**✦✦ is a maze of narrow alleys in what was once the original fishing village. The **Sea Life Centre**✦ is a popular family attraction. Brighton, with a youthful dynamism and conspicuous gay scene, has an avant-garde cultural programme, as well as an excellent range of restaurants, shops and nightspots.

Brighton does its best to discourage motorists, with an expensive voucher scheme in central streets. Madeira Drive car park (between the Pier and the Marina) might have spaces, but one of the Park and Ride schemes would be a better option.

Royal Pavilion ££ *Pavilion Parade; tel: 01273 290900; visitor.services@brighton-hove.gov.uk; www.royalpavilion.org.uk. Open Apr–Sept daily 0930–1745 (1000–1715 in winter).*

Brighton Pier *Madeira Drive; tel: 01273 609361; info@brightonpier.co.uk; www.brightonpier.co.uk. Open summer 0900–0200; winter 1000–2400.*

Sea Life Centre £££ *Marine Parade; tel: 01273 604234; www.sealife.co.uk. Open daily from 1000.*

Accommodation and food in Brighton

Hotel Pelirocco ££ *10 Regency Square; tel: 01273 327055; fax: 01273 733845; info@hotelpelirocco.co.uk; www.hotelpelirocco.co.uk.* Behind this seemly Regency façade lies a funky scene of cool kitsch and pop art. The hippest place to stay in fashionable Brighton.

Black Chapati ££ *12 Circus Parade, New England Road; tel: 01273 699011.* Well-established restaurant serving carefully prepared oriental cooking from several traditions.

Terre à Terre ££ *71 East Street; tel: 01273 729051; fax: 01273 327561.* Inventive vegetarian cookery drawing on cuisines from all around the world.

Mock Turtle £ *4 Pool Valley; tel: 01273 327380.* Charming, traditional English teashop in The Lanes with home-made cakes. Light lunches (local fish and sausages).

Right
Brighton Royal Pavilion

EASTBOURNE✦✦

Tourist Information
Cornfield Road; tel: 01323 411400; eastbournetic@btclick.com.

Rising as a seaside resort from the 1840s, Eastbourne has taken good care of its architecture and its delightful Victorian pier. Its greatest asset, however, is its location, near the Seven Sisters white cliffs, which culminate at 575ft **Beachy Head✦✦✦**, just south of the town.

LEWES✤✤

ℹ **Tourist Information** 187 High Street; tel: 01273 483448.

🏛 **Lewes Castle and Barbican House Museum ££** 169 High Street; tel: 01273 486290. Open Mon–Sat 1000–1730, Sun 1100–1730 (closed Mon in Jan).

Anne of Cleves House ££ 52 Southover High Street; tel: 01273 474610; www.sussexpast.co.uk. Open Mar–Oct Mon–Sat 1000–1700, Sun 1200–1700; Nov–Feb Tue–Sat 1000–1700.

Southover Grange Gardens Southover High Street; tel: 01273 472555. Open in daylight hours.

The location of this ancient settlement, on a hilltop above the floodplain of the Ouse, made it a defensible site from Saxon times (the **castle**✤ is a Norman addition). Narrow lanes (called 'twittens' locally) of tile-hung or timbered buildings huddle around it, but the town's buildings are mainly Georgian. The Tudor **Anne of Cleves House**✤ formed part of a divorce settlement for Henry VIII's fourth wife. The ruined Cluniac **Priory**✤ was once one of the largest in the country; the lovely gardens of **Southover Grange**✤ offer a pleasant stroll. The South Downs run past Lewes in swathes of inviting chalk upland. Nearby Rodmell and the Charleston Farmhouse (5 miles east) attract those on the trail of the Bloomsbury Group.

Accommodation and food in Lewes

Millers £ 134 High Street; tel: 01273 475631; fax: 01273 486226; millers134@aol.com; http://hometown.aol.com/millers134. Friendly B&B in an intriguing cottagey townhouse with lots of character.

Shelleys Hotel £££ High Street; tel: 01273 472361; fax: 01273 483152; www.shelleys-hotel-lewes.com. Elegant Georgian townhouse furnished in classic style. Ambitious cooking and smart country-house bedrooms.

ROYAL TUNBRIDGE WELLS❖❖

ⓘ Tourist Information *The Old Fish Market, The Pantiles; tel: 01892 515675; touristinformation@ tunbridgewells.gov.uk.*

🏛 A Day at the Wells *££ The Pantiles; tel: 01892 546545; www.heritageattractions.co.uk. Open Apr–Oct daily 1000–1700, Nov–Mar 1000–1600.*

☾ Hotel du Vin and Bistro *££ Crescent Road; tel: 01892 526455; fax: 01892 512044; info@tunbridgewells. hotelduvin.com; www.hotelduvin.com.* Bustling operation in a fine listed building. Elegant décor and stylish bedrooms enhanced by unpretentious but masterly cooking.

Right
The Pantiles, Royal Tunbridge Wells

Tunbridge Wells was given its 'Royal' prefix by Edward VII in 1909. The town's spa architecture and well-kept open spaces evoke the gentility of another age. **The Pantiles**❖❖, an elegantly colonnaded street, is now full of shops and pavement cafés. Its name refers to the clay 1700s paving stones. Health-giving iron-rich waters – 25p a glass – still emerge from the Chalybeate Spring. **A Day at the Wells**❖❖ recreates Tunbridge's Georgian heyday.

Houses and gardens

Sussex and the Weald offer stately homes, castles, historic houses and gardens. Here are some of the best:

Bateman's ££ *Off A265 near Burwash; tel: 01435 882302. Open Apr–Sept Sat–Wed 1100–1730; NT.* Rudyard Kipling's mellow 17th-century home, a former iron-master's house. Watermill and lovely gardens.

Groombridge Place Gardens £££ *Groombridge, on B2110; tel: 01892 863999; www.groombridge.co.uk (events hotline: 01892 861444). Open Apr–Oct daily 0900–1800 or dusk.* Spectacular walled gardens around a 17th-century moated mansion. Enjoyable family day out.

Herstmonceux Castle Gardens ££ *SE of Herstmonceux; tel: 01323 834457; c_dennett@isc.queensn.ac.uk; www.herstmonceux-castle.com. Open Apr–Oct 1000–1800 (1700 in Oct); separate admission charge for Science Centre.* Extensive parkland and gardens around a handsome fairytale moated castle. Interactive science and astronomy displays in the former premises of the Greenwich Royal Observatory.

Hever Castle and Gardens £££ *Hever, nr Edenbridge; tel: 01732 865224; www.hevercastle.co.uk. Open Mar–Nov daily 1200–1800 (1100–1600 in winter), gardens from 1100.* Romantic 13th-century double-moated castle associated with Henry VIII's wives. 30 acres of award-winning gardens, and a water maze.

Ightham Mote ££ *Off A227 nr Ivy Hatch; tel: 01732 810378; ighthammote@ntrust.org.uk. Open Apr–Oct Mon, Wed–Fri, Sun 1000–1730; NT.* Unique medieval moated manor with restored interior and lovely gardens.

Knole £££ *E of Sevenoaks; tel: 01732 450608; knole@ntrust.org.uk. Open Apr–Oct Wed–Sun 1100–1600; NT.* Vast medieval palace in picturesque deer park, one of the grandest private residences in the country, filled with precious collections. Lots of walks in the grounds (free to pedestrians, but a parking charge).

Leonardslee Gardens ££–£££ *Lower Beeding; tel: 01403 891212; www.leonardslee.co.uk. Open Apr–Oct 0930–1800; variable admission charges (most expensive May weekends).* Considered the most beautiful of Sussex's gardens, this 240-acre lake-valley site is ablaze with rhododendrons in May.

Nymans Garden ££ *Off B2114 nr Handcross; tel: 01444 400321; nymans@ntrust.org.uk. Open Mar–Oct Wed–Sun 1100–1800 or dusk, weekends in winter 1100–1600; NT and RHS members free.* Family garden with impressive collection of rare trees and shrubs.

Parham House ££ *Pulborough; tel: 01903 744888; www.parhaminsussex.co.uk. Open Apr–Oct Wed, Thu, Sun 1200–1800 (1700 in Oct).* Elizabethan house with beautiful furnishings and lovely grounds (deer park).

Penshurst Place and Gardens £££ *Penshurst; tel: 01892 870307; enquiries@penshurstplace.com; www.penshurstplace.com. Open Apr–Oct daily 1030–1800, weekends in Mar.* Tudor gardens and parkland surround this lovely 14th-century manor overlooking the Weald. Birthplace of Sir Philip Sidney.

Petworth House and Park £££ *Petworth; tel: 01798 342207; petworth@ntrust.org.uk. Open Apr–Oct Sat–Wed 1100–1730, gardens 1100–1800, park daily 0800–sunset; NT.* Impressive art collection and Grinling Gibbons carving in 17th-century house. Capability Brown deer park.

Sheffield Park Garden ££ *Nr Uckfield; tel: 01825 790231; sheffieldpark@ntrust.org.uk. Open Mar–Oct Tue–Sun 1030–1800 (1600 in Mar and Nov–Dec, weekends only Jan–Feb); NT and RHS members free.* Capability Brown gardens around interlinked lakes, magnificently planted.

Standen ££ *Off B2110 S of East Grinstead; tel: 01342 323029. Open Mar–Oct Wed–Sun 1100–1700; NT.* Arts and Crafts house designed by Philip Webb, furnished and wallpapered in William Morris style. Lovely gardens.

Wakehurst Place ££ *Selsfield Road, Ardingly; tel: 01444 894066; wakehurst@kew.org.uk; www.kew.org.uk. Open daily 1000–dusk; NT members and Friends of Kew free.* The Royal Botanic Gardens' second home is a magnificent 180-acre site of woodland and ornamental gardens around an Elizabethan mansion. **The Millennium Seed Bank**, one of the largest conservation projects ever undertaken, aspires to safeguard thousands of plant species from extinction.

Suggested tour

Total distance: 173 miles (278km). You save about 9 miles (14km) on the garden tours variant from East Grinstead.

Time: 6 hours.

Links: Pick up the Kent itinerary (*see page 194*) from Eastbourne (A259) or Tunbridge Wells (A21). The Solent route (*see page 214*) is easily reached from Arundel (A27) or Petworth (A272).

Route: Several sights lie just off the A27 near **LEWES ❶**. Virginia Woolf's home, **Monk's House⁕**, at Rodmell is a small weatherboarded building furnished with literary memorabilia. Virginia ended her life just across the fields, in the River Ouse. **Charleston Farmhouse⁕**, near Selmeston off the A27 east, was the home of Virginia Woolf's sister Vanessa Bell and her lover Duncan Grant. This charming old house became a regular haunt for the Bloomsbury Groupies. **Glynde Place⁕** is a 16th-century building containing fine displays of needlework and china; **Firle Place⁕**, south of the A27, is an ancestral home with notable paintings and furniture. A mile beyond Alciston lies **Drusillas Park⁕⁕**, a reputable zoo specialising in smaller creatures. Turn right down the Cuckmere valley through the gorgeous ancient village of **Alfriston⁕⁕**. Among its thatched and timbered houses is the 14th-century **Clergy House⁕⁕**, the first property acquired by the National Trust. Cross the bridge to the east bank of the River Cuckmere. On the chalky South Downs to the east is a primitive carving known as the **Long Man of Wilmington⁕**. Follow the minor road south to West Dean, and the entertaining **Sheep Centre⁕**. **Exceat Farm** (on the A259) is a fine old barn housing a visitor centre for the **Seven Sisters Country Park⁕⁕⁕**.

Getting out of the car: An enjoyable level mile-long walk or cycle ride (bikes for hire from beside the visitor centre) leads from Exceat Farm (all that remains of a village hit by the Black Death) to **Cuckmere Haven**, following the River Cuckmere's meanders over saltmarsh and meadowland. Coastal views include the seven spectacular chalk cliffs of the Sussex Heritage Coast. If you're feeling energetic, walk over the South Downs cliff path southeast past Birling Gap to **Beachy Head**, returning inland via East and West Dean. Take great care near the unstable cliff edges.

Beachy Head⁕⁕⁕ can be reached by road (take the loop road from East Dean via Birling Gap); park near the Beachy Head pub, a popular family pitstop. Next to it cliffs, the **Beachy Head Countryside Centre⁕** contains a good exhibition and lots of suggestions for walks. Well-made paths lead to the spectacular cliffs. Northeast of **EASTBOURNE ❷**, quiet coastal roads lead to the shingly shores of **Pevensey**, where William's forces are thought to have landed in 1066.

ⓘ Tourist Information Boship Roundabout, Lower Dicker, Hailsham; tel: 01323 442667.

ⓗ Monk's House ££ Rodmell, Lewes; tel: 01892 890651. Open Apr–Oct Wed and Sat 1400–1730; NT.

Charleston £££ Off A27 between Firle and Selmeston; tel: 01323 811265. Open Apr–Oct Wed–Sun 1400–1700 (Wed–Sat 1130–1700, Sun 1400–1700 July–Aug).

Glynde Place ££ Glynde; tel: 01273 858224. Open June–Sept Wed and Sun 1400–1700 (Thu July–Aug).

Firle Place ££ Off A27 at Firle; tel: 01273 858335. Open Easter holidays and May–Sept Wed, Thu, Sun 1345–1615.

Above
Beachy Head

Opposite
Penshurst

Drusillas Park £££ *Off A27 north of Alfriston; tel: 01323 874100. Open daily 1000–1800 (1700 in winter).*

Clergy House ££ *The Tye, Alfriston; tel: 01323 870001. Open Apr–Oct Sun–Mon, Wed–Thu, Sat 1000–1700; Nov–Dec Wed–Sun 1100–1600; NT.*

Seven Sisters Sheep Centre ££ *Gilberts Drive, East Dean; tel: 01323 423302. Open Mar–Sept Mon–Fri 1400–1700, Sat–Sun and school holidays 1100–1700. World's largest collection of sheep breeds, with lambing, shearing, spinning and milking demonstrations.*

Head north to Boreham Street, then west on the A271 past **Herstmonceux Castle gardens**** (*see box, page 209*).Take the A22 from the market town of Hailsham via **Uckfield**, a cluster of tile-hung and weatherboarded houses with sweeping views over the South Downs. Fork right on the B2026 northwest of Uckfield, heading north through the **Ashdown Forest****, last remnant of a vast primeval woodland that once covered most of the Sussex Weald. It was felled in Elizabethan times to provide fuel and timber. This is the land of Winnie the Pooh (A A Milne's stories were set here). Just southeast of **Hartfield**, look for Poohsticks Bridge, deep in the forest. (*Warning:* the car parks here are regular targets for thieves.) From Hartfield, take the B2110 past **Groombridge Place**** (*see box, page 209*) and the A264 east to **ROYAL TUNBRIDGE WELLS ❸**. Continue north on the A26, taking the A227 north of Tonbridge and following signs for **Ightham Mote**** (*see box, page 209*) on the left after 6 miles near Ivy Hatch. Continue through Stone Street northwest to Sevenoaks, following signs for **Knole***** (*see box, page 209*) west of the town. Return to the A21, head south for 3 miles, then turn right on the B2027 via the picturesque villages of Leigh and Chiddingstone to **Hever Castle***** (a brief detour on the B2188 takes in **Penshurst Place**** and its pretty village). Take the B2026 south and A264 west to **East Grinstead**.

Beachy Head Countryside Centre *Beachy Head; tel: 01323 737273. Open Easter–Sept daily 1000–1730, Oct–Feb 1000–1600, weekends Nov–Dec; guided walks (parking charge).*

Roman Villa ££ *Bignor; tel: 01798 869259; www.pyrrha.demon.co.uk. Open Mar–Oct Tue–Sun 1000–1700, May 1000–1730 (June–Sept daily 1000–1800).*

Amberley Working Museum £££ *Houghton Bridge; tel: 01798 831370; www.amberleymuseum.co.uk. Open Apr–Oct Wed–Sun 1000–1800, daily in school holidays. 36-acre site in chalk quarry with crafts, workshops, etc.*

Cuckmere Cycle Co *Granary Barn, Seven Sisters County Park; tel: 01323 870310; www.cuckmere-cycle.co.uk.*

Bluebell Line £££ *Sheffield Park Station, on A275; tel: 01825 722370; www.bluebell-railway.co.uk. Trains May–Sept daily, weekends and school holidays all year.*

Detour: From East Grinstead, take the B2110 southwest, turning left for **Standen**** (*see box, page 209*) 2 miles south. At Turner's Hill, turn left on the B2028 past **Wakehurst Place**** (*see box, page 209*). Cut west across country from Ardingly via Balcombe, and left on the B2110 for **Nyman's Garden**** and **Leonardslee Gardens****** (*see box, page 209*). Rejoin the A272 from the A281 at Cowfold.

Take the A22 southeast of East Grinstead via Forest Row, forking right on the A275 past **Sheffield Park**** and the vintage steam railway, the **Bluebell Line****. At the North Common crossroads, turn right on the A272 through Haywards Heath and the pretty village of **Cuckfield***. Follow the A272 west via Billingshurst to **Petworth House**** (*see box, page 209*), then take the A283 and B2138 south. Look out for signs to the Roman villa at **Bignor*** on the right, then continue (A29 and A284) to **ARUNDEL** ❹. Backtrack 3 miles, then turn right on the B2139 over the Arun valley via charming **Amberley***, with its open-air museum; **Parham House**** (*see box, page 209*) lies 2 miles east near Rackham. Join the A283 at Storrington and continue east along the South Downs. The prehistoric hillforts of **Chanctonbury Ring*** and **Cissbury Ring*** give wonderful views south of the road near **Steyning**** (lots of Tudor houses). From here, head southeast on the A283 and A27 to **BRIGHTON** ❺ before completing the tour at Lewes.

Accommodation and food on the route

Grand £££ *King Edward's Parade, Eastbourne; tel: 01323 412345; fax: 01323 412233; www.grandeastbourne.com.* This dignified institution keeps up the high standards of food, service and accommodation it had when it opened over 100 years ago.

Hooke Hall ££ *250 High Street, Uckfield; tel: 01825 761578; fax: 01825 768025; www.hookehall.co.uk.* Rather grand B&B in a fine Queen Anne townhouse. Interesting furnishings from around the world.

Griffin Inn £ *Fletching, Uckfield; tel: 01825 722890; fax: 01825 722810; www.thegriffininn.co.uk.* Smart, imaginative food in a popular, deceptively sophisticated pub in a very pretty village. Some hit-and-miss bedrooms.

Hungry Monk £££ *Jevington, off A22; tel/fax: 01323 482178; www.hungrymonk.co.uk.* A regular fixture in most gourmet guides, this well-established place has 35 years of practice, yet the menus remain fresh and inventive. Try the classic banoffi pie, which originated here.

Bolebrook Mill ££ *Edenbridge Road, Hartfield; tel/fax: 01892 770425; bolebrokemill@btinternet.com; www.bolebrokemillhotel.co.uk.* Delightful Domesday Book watermill skilfully converted into guest accommodation. Award-winning breakfasts.

Old Wharf £ *Newbridge, Wisborough Green, Billingshurst; tel/fax: 01403 784096.* This tranquil waterside house was a warehouse in the 19th century, the heyday of the canal era. Three cottagey bedrooms with plenty of character offer charming B&B accommodation.

Old Forge ££ *6 Church Street, Storrington; tel: 01903 743402; fax: 01903 742540; enquiry@oldforge.co.uk.* Carefully prepared food in 15th-century beamed restaurant.

Jeremy's at Borde Hill ££ *Balcombe Road, Haywards Heath; tel: 01444 441102; fax: 01444 443936; jeremys.bordehill@btinternet.com; www.homeofgoodfood.co.uk.* Inspired cooking in a colourful, airy setting. Good wine list.

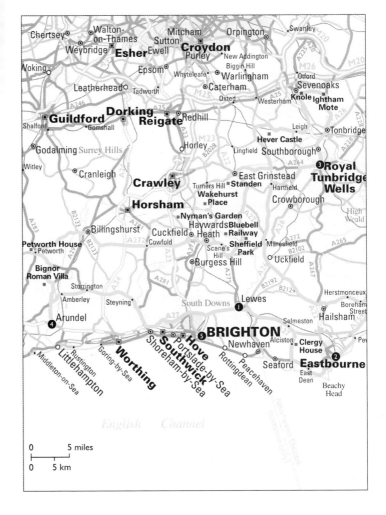

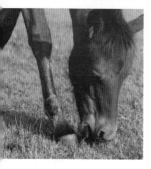

Around the Solent

Ratings

Cathedrals and abbeys	●●●●●
Ships and sails	●●●●●
Children	●●●●
Houses and gardens	●●●●
Scenery	●●●●
Walking	●●●●
Wildlife	●●●●
Beaches	●●

The Solent coastline is only patchily sandy, but several magnificent harbours have made this area not only the keystone of Britain's naval defences, but a paradise for peacetime sailors too. Portsmouth and Southampton have an important maritime heritage. The cathedral cities of Chichester and Winchester make enjoyable touring bases, with good shops and restaurants and well-kept historic centres. Hampshire is often considered to be a deeply rural area of ancient villages, trout streams and dappled woodland, but traffic jams are not uncommon, especially around Lyndhurst in the New Forest. There is great pleasure to be had in pottering on quieter roads around the South Downs or Meon Valley villages near Petersfield. As a family holiday or day-trip excursion destination, the Isle of Wight is hard to beat, with plenty to see and do, good beaches and varied scenery.

CHICHESTER✦✦✦

ⓘ Tourist Information 29A South Street; tel: 01243 775888.

ⓗ Chichester Cathedral West Street; tel: 01243 782595. Open daily 0715–1900 (1800 in winter); donation requested.

Goodwood House £££ Goodwood; tel: 01243 755040; www.goodwood.co. uk. Open Easter–Sept Sun–Mon 1300–1700 (Aug Sun–Thu 1300–1700).

The handsome market town of Chichester dates from Roman times, but is now substantially Georgian; large parts of its medieval **walls✦** still stand around the ancient cruciform street grid. The pale limestone **cathedral✦✦✦**, England's only one visible from the sea, is a mix of Norman and Gothic styles. 'Glorious Goodwood' racecourse, 5 miles north, lies on the estate of **Goodwood House✦✦**. **Fishbourne Palace✦✦✦**, west of Chichester, is Britain's largest Roman villa, with several remarkable mosaics. West of the city, the splendid natural **Chichester harbour✦✦** is a placid scene of tidal creeks, saltflats and bobbing sailboats.

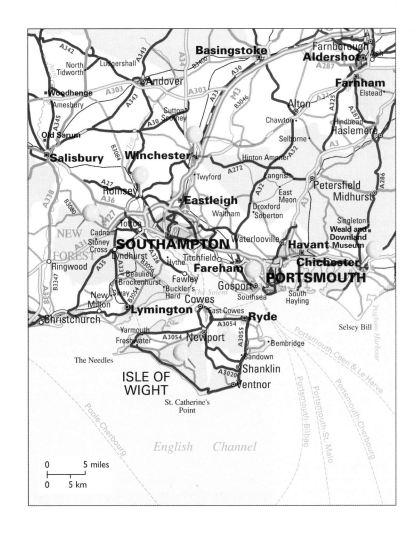

Accommodation and food in or near Chichester

Fishbourne Roman Palace ££ *Salthill Road, Fishbourne; tel: 01243 785859; www.sussexpast.co.uk. Open Feb–Dec daily 1000–1700 (1800 in Aug) or dusk, Sat–Sun only in Jan; EH.*

Crouchers Bottom ££ *Birdham Road, Apuldram, Chichester; tel: 01243 784995; fax: 01243 539797; info@crouchersbottom.com.* Friendly, family hotel with fresh, streamlined restaurant. Clean, soothing bedrooms with pine furnishings.

The Millstream ££ *Bosham Lane, Bosham, Chichester; tel: 01243 573234; fax: 01243 573459; www.millstream-hotel.co.uk.* Idyllic waterfront location in pretty village on Chichester Harbour; pretty bedrooms and spacious public rooms. Very popular, sometimes swamped by private functions.

ISLE OF WIGHT✦✦

You can easily explore 'The Island', as locals call it, within a day by car. This diamond-shaped land mass is a mecca for keen sailors, who converge in early August for prestigious Cowes Week. **Yarmouth** and **Bembridge** are also sailing centres. Italianate **Osborne House✦✦** near East Cowes was Queen Victoria's favourite home. **Carisbrooke Castle✦✦** provided less comfort for another monarch, Charles I, imprisoned here in 1647. The best beaches lie on the eastern side of the island. **Ventnor**, zigzagging down steep hillsides, is the most characterful resort. Breezy downland fringed by cliffs and chasm-like 'chines' characterises the southwest coast. The chalk stacks known as **The Needles✦** punctuate the island's western extremity.

Accommodation and food on the Isle of Wight

Seaview Hotel ££ *High Street, Seaview; tel: 01983 612711; fax: 01983 613729; reception@seaviewhotel.co.uk; www.seaviewhotel.co.uk.* Friendly service and excellent, unpretentious food make this hotel one of the best, despite its modest setting in a quiet Victorian resort.

George Hotel ££ *Quay Street, Yarmouth; tel: 01983 760331; fax: 01983 760425; res@thegeorge.co.uk; www.thegeorge.co.uk.* Smartly renovated period townhouse in a charming setting close to the island's most appealing ferry terminal.

NEW FOREST**

i Tourist
Information *Main
Car Park, Lyndhurst; tel: 023
8028 2269;
information@nfdc.gov.uk.*

**New Forest
Museum and
Visitor Centre ££** *High
Street, Lyndhurst; tel: 023
8028 3914;
nfmuseum@lineone.net.
Open summer daily
1000–1800; winter
1000–1700 (closed for
refurbishment until July
2003).*

Beaulieu £££
*Tel: 01590 612345;
www.beaulieu.co.uk. Open
May–Sept daily 1000–1800,
Oct–Apr daily 1000–1700.
Combined site entrance
includes abbey, Palace
House and Motor
Museum.*

Buckler's Hard ££ *Tel:
01590 614645;
www.bucklershard.co.uk.
Open Easter–Sept daily
1030–1700, 1100–1600 in
winter. Admission charge
includes entry to village,
maritime museum and
other exhibitions.
Riverside walks to
Beaulieu; summer boat
trips.*

Exbury Gardens ££
*Exbury; tel: 023 8089 1203;
www.exbury.co.uk. Open
Mar–Oct daily 1000–1730;
Nov weekends only
1000–1600.*

The oldest of England's forests, now protected by the National Parks Authority, covers about 145 square miles, an expanse of sand heath, mixed woodland, rough grazing and marsh freely enjoyed by over seven million visitors a year. The inhabitants or 'commoners' of the New Forest enjoy a unique set of jealously upheld privileges, and their ponies roam and graze freely alongside deer, pigs, donkeys and other live-stock. The Forest also supports a complex ecosystem of less familiar wildlife, and exotic imports that grow alongside native trees. A **museum*** in Lyndhurst explains the history and traditions of the Forest.

Some of the most popular spots in the Forest lie on the Beaulieu River, to the southeast. Close to the village of **Beaulieu**** (pronounced 'Bewley'), Lord Montagu's estate includes a Cistercian **abbey*** founded by King John, the **Palace House**** (the Montagu family mansion) and the **National Motor Museum*****. Further downstream is the waterside hamlet of **Buckler's Hard****, where huge men o'war, built of New Forest timber, were once launched for Nelson's fleet. A **maritime museum**** relates the local ship-building story. On the opposite bank of the estuary, **Exbury Gardens**** has a superb woodland collection of rhododendrons and azaleas. The ancient coastal town of **Lymington***, just outside the Forest, is a charming, lively sailing centre.

Accommodation and food in or near the New Forest

Nurse's Cottage ££ *Station Road, Sway; tel/fax: 01590 683402; nursescottage@lineone.net.* Friendly, cottagey hotel deep in the Forest. Small but comfortable bedrooms. Imaginative cooking.

Le Poussin at Parkhill £££ *Beaulieu Road, Lyndhurst; tel: 023 8029 2944; fax: 023 8028 3268; www.lepoussin.co.uk.* Smart country-house restaurant-with-rooms in peaceful Forest setting. Traditional interior; lovely views. Acclaimed cooking.

Stanwell House ££ *13–15 High Street, Lymington; tel: 01590 677123; fax: 01590 677756; www.stanwellhousehotel.co.uk.* Fine coaching inn at the heart of a very attractive little town. Cosy bar and bistro.

Above
Beaulieu

PORTSMOUTH✦✦✦

ℹ Tourist Information
The Hard, Portsmouth; or Clarence Esplanade, Southsea; tel: 023 9282 6722; or Bus Station Complex, South Street, Gosport; tel: 023 9252 2944.

🏛 Portsmouth Historic Dockyard
£££ The Hard, 1–7 College Road, HM Naval Base, tel: 023 9286 1533; www.historicdockyard.co.uk. Open Apr–Oct daily 1000–1730; rest of year daily 1000–1700.

D-Day Museum and Overlord Embroidery
££ Clarence Esplanade, Southsea; tel: 023 9282 7261. Open Apr–Oct daily 1000–1730, Nov–Mar 1000–1700. The 272ft Overlord Embroidery depicts the Allied invasion of Normandy in 1944.

Royal Marines Museum
££ Southsea; tel: 023 9281 9385; www. royalmarinesmuseum.co.uk. Open June–Aug daily 1000–1700 (1630 in winter).

Blue Reef Aquarium
££ Clarence Esplanade, Southsea; tel: 023 9287 5222; www.bluereefaquarium.co.uk. Open Apr–Dec daily from 1000.

Southsea Castle £
Clarence Esplanade, Southsea; tel: 023 9282 7261. Open Apr–Oct daily 1000–1730.

Royal Navy Submarine Museum
££ Haslar Jetty Road, Gosport; tel: 023 9252 9217; www.rnsubmus.co.uk. Open Apr–Oct daily 1000–1730, Nov–Mar 1000–1630.

This sprawling port's visitor attractions centre around its maritime heritage in the renovated **Historic Dockyard✦✦✦**. The complex is worth a full day. Centre stage are Nelson's flagship HMS *Victory*, the Tudor warship *Mary Rose*, and the 19th-century iron-clad HMS *Warrior*. The **Royal Naval Museum✦✦✦** and **Action Stations✦✦** bring you up to speed on current methods of defending the realm. A **D-Day Museum✦✦**, **Royal Marines Museum✦✦** and **Blue Reef Aquarium✦✦** extend the repertoire. The harbour fortifications are well worth seeing – **Southsea Castle✦✦** and its museum is the best place to start. Gosport on the harbour's west bank is dusting off **Fort Brockhurst✦** and the **Royal Navy Submarine Museum✦✦**. **Explosion!✦✦** tells the story of naval firepower from gunpowder to the Exocet missile.

ROMSEY❖❖

ℹ️ **Tourist Information**
13 Church Street; tel: 01794 512987.

🏛️ **Broadlands ££** S of Romsey off A3090, tel: 01794 505010. Open June–Aug daily 1200–1730.

The **abbey church**❖❖ of SS Mary and Ethelfleda is one of the finest examples of Norman architecture in England, with dog-tooth chevrons decorating its rounded arches, and Saxon carvings. The handsome Palladian mansion of **Broadlands**❖❖ nearby is best known as the former home of Lord Mountbatten.

WINCHESTER❖❖❖

ℹ️ **Tourist Information**
Guildhall, Broadway; tel: 01962 840500.

🏛️ **Winchester Cathedral** 10a The Close; tel: 01962 857224. Open daily 0830–1800, except during services.

Hospital of St Cross £
St Cross Road; tel: 01962 851375. Open Apr–Oct daily 0930–1700, Nov–Mar Mon–Sat 1030–1530.

Left
HMS *Victory*

Below
Winchester Cathedral

The capital of Wessex, headquarters of Anglo-Saxon England until Norman times, Winchester was also an ecclesiastical centre and a place of learning. The **cathedral**❖❖❖ is one of the finest in England, with a lengthy Gothic nave and fascinating interior monuments. The **library**❖ contains over 4000 precious medieval tomes. Before the Dissolution, the appealing **Cathedral Close**❖❖ contained the monks' domestic quarters. **Winchester College**❖ is England's oldest public school (originally founded in 1382 for 'poor scholars' by William of Wykeham). The **Great Hall**❖❖ is the only surviving section of Winchester's Norman castle. Its most memorable feature is a 13th-century Round Table, claimed to have belonged to King Arthur. A pleasant wander through the River Itchen's watermeadows to the south of the town leads to the **Hospital of St Cross**❖❖, an ancient almshouse built in 1446.

Accommodation and food in Winchester

Wykeham Arms ££ *75 Kingsgate Street; tel: 01962 853834, fax: 01962 854411; doreen@wykehamarms.fsnet.co.uk*. A place of enormous character and convivial charm. Terrific food; delightful bedrooms. Book ahead for a table.

Cathedral Refectory £ *Visitors' Centre, Inner Close, Winchester Cathedral; tel: 01962 857258*. Award-winning home cooking in a light, modern conservatory setting. Light lunches, afternoon teas, children's menus. Informal and friendly. Fresh local produce.

Suggested tour

Needles Old Battery ££ *West Highdown, Totland, Isle of Wight; tel: 01983 754772. Open Apr–Oct Sun–Thu 1030–1700 (July–Aug daily); NT.*

Weald and Downland Open Air Museum ££ *Singleton; tel: 01243 811348; www.wealddown. co.uk. Open Mar–Oct daily 1030–1800, Nov–Feb Wed, Sat–Sun 1030–1600.* Historic buildings rescued and reconstructed on a 50-acre site. Traditional farm animals; rural craft demonstrations.

Total distance: 124 miles (200km). Add 60 miles (96km) for the Isle of Wight route.

Time: 5 hours. Allow a full day extra if you want to do the Isle of Wight.

Links: Join the Sussex route (*see page 204*) at Midhurst (A272) or Chichester (A27); the A31 from the New Forest takes you to coastal Dorset (*see page 232*); the A36 from Southampton (J2 from the M27) leads to Salisbury (*see page 222*).

Route: Take the A3090 southwest from **WINCHESTER ❶** to **ROMSEY ❷**, continuing in the same direction to Cadnam in the **NEW FOREST ❸**. Turn left on the A337 through **Lyndhurst** and **Brockenhurst** to **Lymington❖**, where you can take a ferry to the **ISLE OF WIGHT ❹**.

Detour: Most points of interest on the Isle of Wight lie near the coast. From the sailing port of **Yarmouth❖**, head east to Newport (**Carisbrooke Castle❖❖**). Follow the east bank of the Medina to East Cowes and **Osborne House❖❖**, then continue round the island clockwise via **Ryde❖** (information centre). Detour off the main road via pretty **Bembridge❖❖**, then through the seaside resorts of Sandown, **Shanklin** and **Ventnor❖**. Continue west on the A3055, past some excellent beaches. The **Needles❖❖** near Freshwater are a popular spot; the access point of Alum Bay ruthlessly exploits the multi-coloured sands found in its stripy cliffs. There's a good view from the **Old Battery❖**, a coastal fortress. Head back to Yarmouth for a return ferry.

At Lymington, follow the coastal roads east to **Buckler's Hard❖❖**, then head upstream to **Beaulieu❖❖**. Take the B3054 (**Exbury Gardens❖❖** lies 3 miles off to the right). At the A326, turn left and head up to **Southampton❖**, Britain's foremost passenger port, and the location for the country's largest commercial dry dock. Continue to **PORTSMOUTH ❺**, following signs for the **Historic Dockyard** off the M275. Retrace steps to the A27, heading east to **CHICHESTER ❻**. Head north on the A286 via Singleton, and the **Weald and Downland Museum❖❖**. Continue to **Midhurst**, then head west through Petersfield, following the A272 back to Winchester.

Getting out of the car: To see the best of the New Forest, park the car and walk, ride or picnic away from the traffic. **Brockenhurst❖** is a popular starting point.

Also worth exploring: The delightful valley of the River Meon, once famed for its watercress beds, was a favourite haunt of 'compleat angler' Izaak Walton. Turn left off the A272 at Langrish (3 miles west of Petersfield) following minor roads through East Meon, past Old Winchester Hill, to Soberton, Droxford and Hinton Ampner. North of

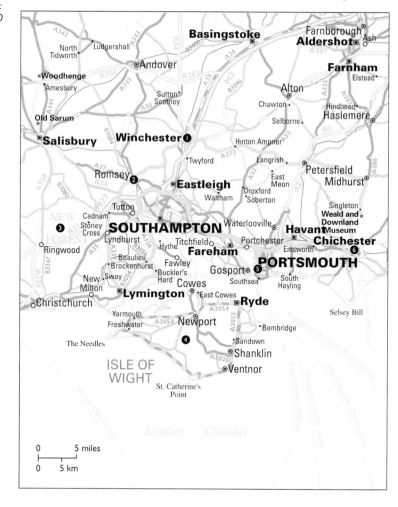

Jane Austen's House *££ Chawton; tel: 01420 83262. Open Mar–Nov daily, weekends only Dec–Feb 1100–1600.*

Gilbert White's House and Garden/Oates Museum *££ The Wakes, High Street, Selborne; tel: 01420 511275. Open daily 1100–1700. A neighbouring exhibition is devoted to the Antarctic explorer.*

Mizzards Farm *£ Rogate, Petersfield; tel: 01730 821656; fax: 01730 821655. Rural B&B with lots of antique character and charm.*

the A272, the Alton area is famously associated with two very English writers. **Chawton** is a place of pilgrimage for Jane Austen fans (she lived here from 1809 to 1817). **Selborne** is forever linked with the great natural historian Gilbert White, whose charming house is also a museum.

Accommodation and food on the route

Park House *££ Bepton, Midhurst; tel: 01730 812880; fax: 01730 815643; reservations@parkhouse.com.* Serene country house in lovely quiet location; traditional style. Exceptional gardens.

Chewton Glen *£££ New Milton; tel: 01425 275341; fax: 01425 272310; reservations@chewtonglen.com.* Unashamed luxury and lavish leisure facilities at this outstanding New Forest hotel. Exceptional cooking.

Wiltshire and North Somerset

Ratings

Archaeology	●●●●●
Architecture	●●●●●
Churches, abbeys and cathedrals	●●●●●
Food and drink	●●●●
Heritage	●●●●
Scenery	●●●●
Walking	●●●○○
Children	●●○○○

Anyone with an interest in archaeology and architecture should make a beeline for this chalk and cheese region, with its mysterious prehistoric structures, like Stonehenge and Silbury Hill. Visit elegant, sophisticated Bath, which combines Roman ruins with England's most complete Georgian architecture. Seek out abbey churches at Bath and Glastonbury, cathedrals at Salisbury, Wells and Bristol, magnificent houses and gardens at Wilton, Longleat, Stourhead and Great Chalfield, and spectacular limestone features like Cheddar Gorge or Wookey Hole. The countryside varies greatly, from open chalk downs to willow-fringed wetlands. Picturesque towns and villages of gold-tinged stone – Corsham, Lacock, Bradford-on-Avon, Mells, Pilton and Stourton – make these parts of Wiltshire and Somerset enormously enjoyable for pottering. In complete contrast, the lively historic trading port of Bristol, which once grew rich on sugar, wine and slavery, is one of Britain's most attractive industrialised cities.

AVEBURY✦✦✦

ⓘ **Tourist Information** *Avebury Chapel Centre, Green Street; tel: 01672 539425.*

🔁 **Access** to the prehistoric sites of Avebury (run jointly by the NT and EH) is free of charge (*except for parking*). Climbing on the stones or on Silbury Hill is prohibited.

There is much to see in this enjoyable area, which is as important archaeologically as Stonehenge. The **Avebury Stone Circle✦✦✦** is a massive henge (the largest in Europe) of about 100 'sarsen' standing stones, some weighing over 40 tons. The wide **West Kennet Avenue✦** of another 100 stones stretches a mile beyond the henge, and earthworks and inner circles add to its complexity. The charming village of Avebury has a partly Saxon church, an Elizabethan manor and a fine thatched tithe barn. The **Alexander Keiller Museum✦** introduces the archaeology of the area. Just south of Avebury is **Silbury Hill✦✦**, the largest man-made mound in Europe. Nobody knows quite why it was built, and excavations have yielded no information, but it remains an impressive hillock in this magical landscape. South of the A4 lies the **West Kennet Long Barrow✦✦** (a 5000-year-old chambered tomb), largest and most impressive of many similar neolithic burial sites in this area.

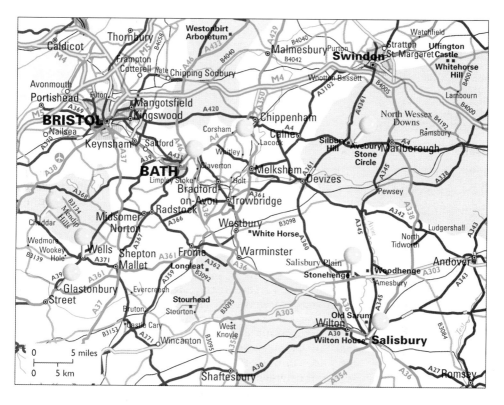

Alexander Keiller Museum £
Tel: 01672 539250;
avebury@ntrust.org.uk.
Open daily 1000–1800
(1600 in winter); NT and
EH.

The Circle £
Tel: 01672 539514.
Superb National Trust café
near the prehistoric circle
serving vegetarian and
organic soups, cakes,
country wines.

Right
Avebury

BATH***

ⓘ **Tourist Information** Abbey Chambers, Abbey Church Yard; tel: 01225 477101; tourism@bathres.gov.uk; ask about guided walking or open-top bus tours.

Ⓟ Bath's traffic wardens are ubiquitous and merciless – don't think of parking on central streets. Try the Park and Ride services on main approach roads (on the A367 S, the A4 W, or at the A46/A420 junction S of the M4), or head for one of the official central car parks.

🏛 **Roman Baths £££** Pump Room, Abbey Church Yard; tel: 01225 477785; www.romanbaths. co.uk. Open Mar–Oct daily 0900–1700 (2100 in July–Aug), rest of year daily 0930–1630.

Museum of Costume ££ Assembly Rooms, Bennett Street; tel: 01225 477785; open daily 1000–1700.

Holburne Museum ££ Great Pulteney Street; tel: 01225 466669. Open Feb–Dec Tue–Sat 1000–1700, Sun 1430–1730 (free parking).

🍴 **Sally Lunn's House** 4 North Parade; tel: 01225 461634; www.sallylunns.co.uk. Museum and café open Mon–Sat 1000–1800, Sun 1200–1800; restaurant open 1800–2200.

Over a quarter of a million gallons of warm water per day gush from Britain's only hot springs. The Romans named the place *Aquae Sulis* after a Celtic goddess, and Bath became England's first spa resort in the first century AD. The steaming jade-green waters of the **Roman Baths***, with their associated hypocausts, statuary and temple, are the main attraction today. Under royal patronage from Elizabethan times, Bath once again became fashionable, and in the 18th century Beau Nash, Jane Austen, Gainsborough and many others flocked to take the waters in the **Pump Room**, where teas and lunches are now served. Meanwhile, the grand geometrical designs (**Queen Square**, **The Circus** and **The Royal Crescent***) of the John Wood team (Elder and Younger) were being built in golden stone. **Bath Abbey** is renowned for its charming west front, where carved angels climb and fall. Edgar, first King of England, was crowned here in 973.

There are hours of enjoyment to be had from wandering around the hilly streets of unspoilt period architecture, or by the River Avon over **Pulteney Bridge**. The **Museum of Costume and Assembly Rooms** has a spectacular collection of clothes through the centuries; the **Holburne Museum** houses an impressive array of decorative arts; **No 1, Royal Crescent*** has been meticulously restored in Georgian style; **Sally Lunn's*** is a charming medieval house in which the legendary Huguenot refugee baked her *brioches* (Bath buns) in the 1680s. In addition, Bath has at least ten other museums, as well as galleries, gardens, fine shops and great places to eat or stay.

Accommodation and food in Bath

Royal Crescent £££ *16 Royal Crescent; tel: 01225 823333; fax: 01225 339401.* Unbridled elegance slap in the middle of this beautiful terrace. A very sophisticated, very discreet, very expensive hotel.

Paradise House ££ *86–88 Holloway; tel: 01225 317723; fax: 01225 482005; info@paradise-house.co.uk; www.paradise-house.co.uk.* Good views and period furnishings at this attractive Georgian B&B.

Holly Lodge ££ *8 Upper Oldfield Park; tel: 01225 424042; fax: 01225 481138; stay@hollylodge.co.uk; www.hollylodge.co.uk.* Outstanding B&B overlooking the city, immaculate inside and out.

Lettonie ££ *35 Kelston Road; tel: 01225 446676; fax: 01225 447541; www.lettonie.co.uk.* Georgian restaurant-with-rooms. Splendid cooking, attractive bedrooms with lots of extras.

Right
Pulteney Bridge, Bath

CHEDDAR✤✤✤

Cheddar
**Cheddar
Showcaves £££**
*Cheddar Gorge; tel:
01934 742343;
www.cheddarcaves.co.uk.
Open daily 1000–1700
(1630 off season); guided
tours.*

Pretty Cheddar village has a fine market cross, tearooms, cheese and cider shops and roadside strawberry stalls, but visitors come here principally for the breathtaking **limestone gorge✤✤✤**. Formed by fast-flowing streams cutting through the porous Mendip plateau during the Ice Age, the ravine twists below towering sheer cliffs. Jacob's Ladder is a staircase (274 steps) up to a panoramic viewpoint on the plateau above. The nearby **Showcaves✤✤** are two cathedral-like caverns with spectacular limestone pillar formations.

GLASTONBURY✦

ⓘ Tourist Information/Lake Village Museum £ *The Tribunal, 9 High Street; tel: 01458 832954; glastonbury.tic@ ukonline.co.uk; www.glastonburytic.co.uk. Open daily 1000–1700 (reduced hours off season); EH.*

ⓕ Glastonbury Abbey £ *Abbey Gatehouse, Magdalene Street; tel: 01458 832267; glastonbury.abbey@ dial.pipex.com; www.glastonburyabbey.com. Open daily 0930–1800, June–Aug 0900–1800, Dec–Feb 1000–1800.*

Somerset Rural Life Museum ££ *Abbey Farm, Chilkwell Street; tel: 01458 831197; county-museums@ somerset.gov.uk; www.somerset. gov.uk/museums. Open Apr–Oct Tue–Fri 1000–1900, Sat–Sun 1400–1800; rest of year Tue–Sat 1000–1500.*

Right
Glastonbury Abbey

The Vale of Avalon, where this pleasant town lies, has been a place of Arthurian legend for centuries. These days, its annual rock festival attracts hordes of New Age visitors. Its evocative ruined **Abbey✦✦**, once one of the richest in the country, is closely associated with Joseph of Arimathea, who is said to have brought the Holy Grail here. The **Somerset Rural Life Museum✦** has displays of traditional crafts. A mile away is the famous conical hill known as **Glastonbury Tor✦✦**, topped by a ruined 14th-century church tower. Below the Tor lies a prehistoric lake village. Finds from the site are displayed in **The Tribunal✦**, a fine 15th-century courthouse, which houses the Tourist Information Centre.

LACOCK✦✦

ⓕ Lacock Abbey and Fox Talbot Museum £££ *Tel: 01249 730227 (abbey) or 730459 (museum); museum, cloisters and grounds open Mar–Oct daily 1100–1730 (and winter weekends); abbey Apr–Oct Wed–Mon 1300–1730; NT.*

This extraordinarily photogenic village holds a significant place in the history of photography. One of the windows in **Lacock Abbey✦✦** (a domestic residence since the Dissolution) was the subject of the world's first photographic negative, made in 1835. A barn in the grounds now houses a **museum✦✦** dedicated to pioneering photographer William Henry Fox Talbot. **St Cyriac Church✦** is a lovely Perpendicular 'wool church'. The entire village is now owned by the National Trust.

SALISBURY✦✦✦

ⓘ Tourist Information *Fish Row; tel: 01722 334956.*

🏛 Salisbury Cathedral *The Close; tel: 01722 555120. Open daily 0715–1815 (2015 in summer); donation requested.*

Mompesson House ££ *The Close; tel: 01722 335659; open Apr–Oct Sat–Wed 1200–1730; NT.*

Salisbury and South Wiltshire Museum ££ *King's House, The Close; tel: 01722 332151; open Mon–Sat 1000–1700 (July–Aug Sun 1400–1700).*

The graceful spire of Salisbury's **cathedral**✦✦✦ is, at 404ft, the tallest in England, dominating the surrounding watermeadows of the Avon and Nadder. The cathedral's other glories are its ornate **West Front**✦✦, an ancient **clock**✦ dating from 1386, and a wonderfully airy **nave**✦✦. Salisbury grew to prominence in the 13th century, and is now a pleasant commercial and agricultural centre. The **Cathedral Close**✦✦ is the largest and most impressive of its kind. Among its seemly Queen Anne and Georgian façades are **Mompesson House**✦✦ and the **King's House**✦ (both museums), and **Malmesbury House**✦. The main part of the old town, with narrow alleys full of old medieval houses and quaint inns, is accessed via the **North Gate**✦. The **Poultry Cross**✦ stands on stilts near the market square.

Food and accommodation in Salisbury

Old Mill ££ *Town Path, Harnham, Salisbury; tel: 01722 327517.* Views of the cathedral from a quiet waterside pub in a former papermill. Good country cooking; rustic furnishings; pleasing bedrooms.

STONEHENGE✦✦✦

🏛 Stonehenge ££ *Off A344/A303 3 miles W of Amesbury; tel: 01980 624715; www.stonehenge.co.uk. Open daily 0930–dusk (0900 June–Aug); EH and NT. Excellent audio tour included with ticket. No access to the stones except on special organised tours.*

Stonehenge is a most impressive prehistoric antiquity – but what was its purpose? Possibly much depleted, the henge now consists of several incomplete concentric rings of massive dolerite and sandstone blocks (some weighing as much as 40 tons). One mystery is that the nearest source of some of its giant bluestones is the Preseli Hills in Wales. Were they deposited here by an Ice-Age glacier, or transported hundreds of miles by prehistoric peoples? The alignment of the stones indicates some connection with the movements of the sun – maybe it was a calendar or observatory. Stonehenge seems to have been constructed between about 3000 and 1600 BC. Controversial plans are afoot to improve access and facilities at the site via the much-used A303 (which itself is also due for widening).

Right
Stonehenge

WELLS**

Tourist Information *Town Hall, Market Place; tel: 01749 672552.*

Bishop's Palace ££ *The Close; tel: 01749 678691. Open Apr–Oct Tue–Fri 1030–1800 and Sun 1400–1800 (daily in Aug).*

Wells Cathedral *Chain Gate, Cathedral Green; tel: 01749 674483. Open daily summer 0700–1900, rest of year 0700–1815; donation requested.*

Wookey Hole Caves and Papermill £££ *Wookey Hole; tel: 01749 672243; www.wookey.co.uk. Open daily 1000–1700 (reduced hours in winter).*

England's smallest city on the Somerset Levels is full of historic buildings. The **Vicars Close**** is one of the most authentic 14th-century streets in the country, and the **Bishop's Palace**** clearly evokes the Middle Ages. The **cathedral*****, dating from the late 1100s, has an elaborate **West Front*****, crowded with saints and kings. Inside, is an intriguing astronomical **clock****, which bursts into life every quarter-hour. Northeast of Wells are the limestone caves of **Wookey Hole****, a popular if touristy attraction.

Accommodation and food in Wells

Swan Hotel ££ *11 Sadler Street; tel: 01749 836300; fax: 01749 836301; swan@bhere.co.uk.* Traditional old coaching inn with varied bedrooms, some overlooking the cathedral's West Front.

Ritchers ££ *5A Sadler Street; tel: 01749 679085; ritchers@btinternet.co.uk.* Bistro-style restaurant in the heart of the old town, with friendly service and moderate wines.

Suggested tour

American Museum in Britain ££
Claverton Manor, SE of Bath; tel: 01225 460503. Open Apr–Oct Tue–Sun 1400–1700 (gardens 1300–1800).

Great Chalfield Manor ££ *2 miles NE of Bradford-on-Avon; tel: 01225 782239. Open Apr–Oct Tue–Thu; guided tours only at 1215, 1415, 1500, 1545 and 1630; NT.*

Corsham Court ££ *Corsham; tel: 01249 701610. Open Apr–Sept Tue–Sun 1400–1730, Oct–Mar weekends 1400–1630; closed Dec.*

Bowood House £££ *Bowood, Calne; tel: 01249 812102. Open Apr–Oct daily 1100–1730 (grounds 1800).*

Wilton Carpet Factory ££ *King Street, Wilton; tel: 01722 742733. Open Mon–Sat 0930–1730, Sun 1100–1700; hourly tours.*

Wilton House £££ *Wilton; tel: 01722 746729. Open Apr–Oct daily 1030–1700.*

Longleat £££ *Warminster; tel: 01985 844400. Open Apr–Dec daily 1000–1730; Jan–Mar (safari park and other attractions Apr–Oct weekends only 1000–1600).*

Stourhead £££ *Stourton, Warminster; tel: 01747 841152; garden open daily 0900–1900, or sunset if earlier, house April–Oct Sat–Wed 1200–1730 or dusk; NT.*

Opposite
Wells Cathedral

Total distance: 157 miles (251km). Add 6 miles (10km) for the Wilton detour.

Time: 6 hours.

Links: Salisbury is the easiest springboard for the Solent route (*see page 214*): take the A36 southeast. Cheddar or Glastonbury lie within easy reach of the M5 for the rest of the West Country or the Wye Valley (*see page 184*). You can also pick up coastal Dorset (*see page 232*) from the A350 (Warminster–Shaftesbury) or A37 (Shepton Mallet–Yeovil).

Route: From BATH ❶, follow signs southeast to **Claverton** to see the **American Museum in Britain✶✶**, a fascinating slice of US life and history. Turn right at the A36, heading south through a steep wooded combe for a mile before turning left over the river at Limpley Stoke towards the charming old wool town of **Bradford-on-Avon✶✶**. Look out for the Saxon church of **St Lawrence✶** and the medieval **tithe barn✶** at Barton Farm. Follow signs east via **Great Chalfield Manor✶✶**, dating from about 1470. Head north via Whitley to **Corsham✶✶**, a handsome little weaving village with Cotswold-looking architecture and an Elizabethan mansion called **Corsham Court✶** (1582). Head towards **LACOCK ❷**. Continue east, turning left briefly on the A342, then right on the A4. **Bowood House✶✶**, on the right, is a magnificent Robert Adam house in superb grounds. Drive through Calne to **AVEBURY ❸**. **Marlborough✶**, 7 miles east, is a Georgian coaching stop with period houses, and a Victorian public school. Turn right down the A345 (southwest) across the chalky uplands of **Salisbury Plain✶✶**, extensively used by the Ministry of Defence. **Pewsey✶** (6 miles southwest of Marlborough) is one of the most charming of the villages that cling to the chalky streams. A mile north of Amesbury, look for signs to **Woodhenge✶**, a Bronze Age site where concrete pillars mark the postholes of a timber circular structure. Two miles southwest off the A303 is **STONEHENGE ❹**.

Return towards Amesbury and head south via depopulated **Old Sarum✶**, an ancient fortified settlement on a bleak hilltop, formerly home to communities of Celts, Romans, Saxons and Normans. Take the A36 west from **SALISBURY ❺** to **Wilton**, a famous carpet-making centre. **Wilton House✶✶** is a fine Tudor mansion remodelled by Inigo Jones. Follow the A36 to Warminster, turning west on the A362. **Longleat✶✶**, signed left of the road, was one of Britain's earliest stately homes opened to the public; its safari park is famous. Take the A361 to the historic mill town of **Shepton Mallet✶**.

Detour: Two miles west of Wilton, take the B3089, turning left on the A303 near West Knoyle. Turn right after 5 miles to **Stourhead✶✶✶**, one of Britain's most splendid landscaped gardens, and the village of

ℹ️ Tourist Information
Cromwell House, Market Place, Devizes; tel: 01380 729408.

Sally Boats The Marina, Trowbridge Road, Bradford-on-Avon; tel: 01225 864923; www.sallyboats.ltd.uk. Narrow-boat hire.

🚤 Kennet & Avon Canal Museum £
Canal Centre, Couch Lane, Devizes; tel: 01380 721279. Open Feb–Dec daily 1000–1600.

Above
Royal Crescent, Bath

Stourton*. Take signs from Kilmington Common (1 mile northwest) west through Hardway, turning right on the B3081 to Shepton Mallet.

Head west on the A361 for 10 miles to **GLASTONBURY ❻** and right on the A39 to **WELLS ❼**, then northwest past **Wookey Hole****, returning to the A371 to **CHEDDAR ❽**. Take the Gorge road across the **Mendip Hills*** on the B3135 and B3371, following signs via Midsomer Norton and Radstock back to Bath.

Getting out of the car: Seven miles east of Melksham, at **Devizes***, the **Caen Hill**** flight of 29 locks over the restored **Kennet & Avon Canal**** is an amazing sight. Boat trips and towpath walks are possible from Bradford-on-Avon.

Also worth exploring: The bustling city of **Bristol***** makes a great day trip. The main areas worth exploring are the elegant Regency suburbs of **Clifton**** (where Isambard Kingdom Brunel's **suspension bridge**** spans the Avon Gorge) and the waterfront areas around the revitalised **docklands****, where the **Arnolfini**** contemporary arts complex and the **SS** *Great Britain*** (the world's first iron-built ocean-going ship, also by Brunel) are located.

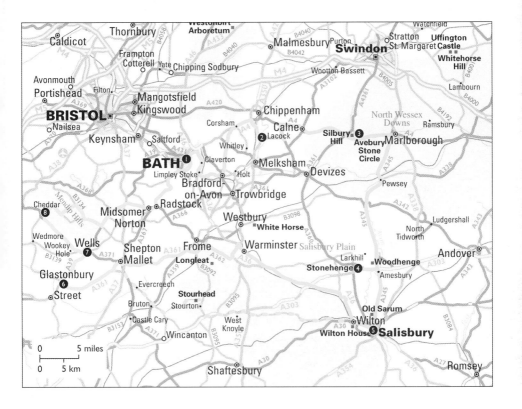

Accommodation and food on the route

Bridge Tearooms £ *24a Bridge Street, Bradford-on-Avon; tel: 01225
865537.* Quaint 17th-century café with mob-capped waitresses;
excellent cakes.

Shurnhold House ££ *Shurnhold, Melksham; tel: 01225 790555; fax:
01225 793147.* Elegant B&B in charming Jacobean manor, tastefully
but unpretentiously furnished.

Chilvester Hill House ££ *Calne; tel: 01249 813981; fax: 01249 814217;
www.chilvesterhillhouse.co.uk.* Long-established, welcoming hospitality
in a fine Victorian house in substantial grounds. Guests dine around a
single table in unstuffy house-party style.

Bowlish House £ *Wells Road, Shepton Mallet; tel/fax: 01749 342022.*
Splendid, good-value set-price menus in a handsome period property.
Several inexpensive, comfortable bedrooms too.

Dorset and East Devon

Ratings

Geology	●●●●●
Scenery	●●●●●
Seaside resorts	●●●●●
Archaeology	●●●●○
Beaches	●●●●○
Family attractions	●●●●○
Literature	●●●●○
Villages	●●●●○

The works of poet and novelist Thomas Hardy have created something of a mini industry for Dorset. 'Hardy Country' centres around Dorchester, his 'Casterbridge'; he was born, and buried, within 5 miles of the town. This cheering region has gold-stoned towns and villages in a subtle patchwork of rolling farmland, barren heath and forested hills. The coast presents a combination of grand harbours and spectacular geological formations, such as the limestone arch of Durdle Door, the fossil-filled cliffs of Lyme Regis, and the impressively huge blue-clay shingle bank known as Chesil Beach. The best stretches of sand lie well away from this hazardous reef; the largest of the popular holiday resorts are Bournemouth and Weymouth. Archaeological remains also rate highly here; the huge earthworks of Maiden Castle and the Cerne Abbas Giant are the most memorable of many ancient monuments.

DORCHESTER✤✤

❶ Tourist Information
Antelope Walk; tel: 01305 267992.

🏛 Dorset County Museum ££ *High West Street; tel: 01305 262735. Open Mon–Sat 1000–1700 (and Sun May–Oct).*

Athelhampton House and Gardens £££
Tel: 01305 848363; www.athelhampton.co.uk. Open Mar–Oct Sun–Fri 1030–1700, Sun only off season.

Hardy's birthplace is a busy country town, with a main street of 17th-century and Georgian buildings. The **Dorset County Museum✤** gives a good overview of local life. Just outside the town are **Hardy's Cottage✤** (the writer's 1840 birthplace) and **Max Gate** (the house Hardy designed and lived in until his death in 1928). His heart lies buried at Stinsford, about a mile outside the town. **Maiden Castle✤✤** is a massive Iron Age fort of concentric grassy ramparts (freely accessible). **Athelhampton House✤**, to the west, is a splendid 15th-century house with topiary gardens.

Accommodation in Dorchester

Casterbridge Hotel ££ *49 High East Street; tel: 01305 264043; fax: 01305 260884; reception@casterbridgehotel.co.uk; www.casterbridgehotel. co.uk.* Elegant, unpretentious townhouse B&B in town centre.

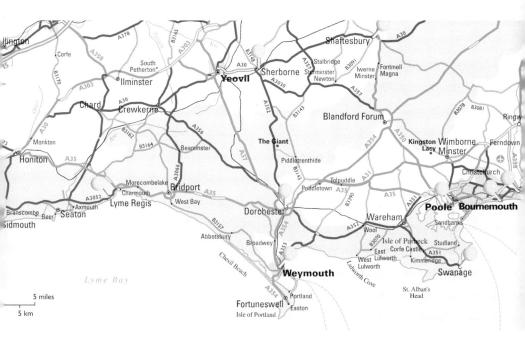

ISLE OF PURBECK✧✧

ℹ Tourist Information *Holy Trinity Church, South Street, Wareham; tel: 01929 552740; or Shore Road, Swanage; tel: 01929 423636.*

A chain ferry across the narrow neck of Poole Harbour at Sandbanks links this peninsula with the rest of Dorset; there may be long queues in summer.

Corfe Castle ££ *Corfe; tel: 01929 481294. Open Apr–Oct daily 1000–1800, reduced hours off season; NT.*

Clouds Hill ££ *Bovington Camp; tel: 01929 405616. Open Apr–Oct Thu–Sun 1200–1700; NT.*

Beautiful beaches fringe the eastern bays of this peninsula, around **Studland**✧✧ and **Swanage**✧, the port from which Purbeck's famous 'marble' (a dark grey oolitic limestone) was once shipped. The ruins of **Corfe Castle**✧✧, which has Civil War associations, crown a hill beside the village. **Wareham**✧✧, an attractive little waterside town of Saxon origins surrounded by ancient earthen ramparts, is the alternative access point for Purbeck. Lawrence of Arabia spent his last years in Dorset, and was killed near by in a motorcycle accident. His cottage, **Clouds Hill**✧, is 7 miles northwest. Near Furzepot is the **Blue Pool**✧ – suspended clay particles give the water its intense turquoise colour. The South West Coast Path leads past Kimmeridge Bay to oyster-shaped **Lulworth Cove**✧✧, where a **Heritage Centre**✧✧ explains the history, geology and wildlife of the area. A mile west stands the celebrated limestone rock arch of **Durdle Door**✧✧.

Accommodation and food on the Isle of Purbeck

Priory Hotel £££ *Church Green, Wareham; tel: 01929 551666; fax: 01929 554519; www.theprioryhotel.co.uk.* Tranquil retreat in romantic old priory with private moorings and gorgeous gardens. Very good restaurant in atmospheric vaulted cellar.

Heritage Centre *Main car park, Lulworth Cove; tel: 01929 400587; www.lulworth.com. Open daily 1000–1800 (1600 in winter).*

Shell Bay *££. Ferry Road, Studland; tel: 01929 450363, fax: 01929 450570.* Fishy menus in relaxed, simple surroundings with superb views of Poole Harbour.

Lobster Pot *£ Portland Bill; tel: 01305 820242.* Unpretentious café overlooking the sea serving probably the best crab sandwiches in the world. Sometimes overrun with coach parties.

Worth Café and Craft Centre *£ Worth Matravers; tel: 01929 439360.* Home-cooked cakes, light lunches, etc, with a vegetarian slant, on the Isle of Purbeck.

Below
Durdle Door

LYME REGIS**

Tourist Information *Church Street; tel: 01297 442138.*

Marine Aquarium and Cobb History *£ The Cobb; tel: 01297 444230. Open Easter–Oct 1000–1700 (later July–Aug).*

The steep streets of pretty Georgian architecture in this enticing wool port rise sharply from the seafront, where the curved stone breakwater known as **The Cobb** extends a protective arm. The rocks and cliffs here have generated intense interest since 1811, when 12-year-old Mary Anning discovered a complete icthyosaurus skeleton. Giant ammonite fossils can be seen in some walls and pavements. Gorse-clad Golden Cap is the highest cliff on the south coast (617ft).

Hotel Alexandra
££ *Pound Street; tel:*
01297 442010; fax: 01297
443229; enquiries@
hotelalexandra.co.uk;
www.hotelalexandra.co.uk.
Comfortable, traditional,
family-run hotel in
Georgian dower house
with lovely gardens
overlooking Lyme Bay.

Right
The Cobb, Lyme Regis

Tourist
Information *Chesil*
Beach Centre, Ferrybridge,
Portland; tel: 01305
760579.

Fleet Observer
Ferrybridge, Weymouth;
tel: 01305 773396. Glass-
bottomed boat trips on
The Fleet.

Abbotsbury
Subtropical
Gardens ££ *Abbotsbury;*
tel: 01305 871387;
www.abbotsbury-
tourism.co.uk. Open daily
1000–1800 or dusk.

Chesil Beach***

This remarkable shingle bank extends west of Portland for over 10 miles on
beds of blue clay, in places 200 yards wide and over 40ft high. It forms a
formidable natural sea defence; without it, Dorset's coastline would be
many miles inland. The main section traps a huge tidal lagoon called **The
Fleet**, now a nature reserve colonised by a fascinating range of birds and
plants. The brown stones of Chesil gradually decrease in size from baking
potatoes near Portland to peas somewhere near Bridport, graded by the
powerful currents. The stones absorb the sun's heat and slowly release it;
the resultant microclimate allows subtropical plants to flourish at the
Abbotsbury Gardens. Many terrible shipwrecks have occurred on
these shores. Chesil is not a swimming beach; steep shelving causes perilous
undertows.

POOLE✣✣, CHRISTCHURCH✣✣ AND BOURNEMOUTH✣

ℹ Tourist Information
Westover Road, Bournemouth; tel: 0906 802 0234, or 4 High Street, Poole; tel: 01202 253253.

Brownsea Island £££
Poole Harbour; tel: 01202 707744. Open daily 1000–1700 (1800 July–Aug); boat trips Apr–Oct; NT. This 500-acre island, site of Lord Baden-Powell's first scout camp, in 1907, makes a marvellous excursion for picnics, walks and wildlife spotting. Look out for red squirrels.

Waterfront and Scaplen's Court Museums £££ High Street, Poole; tel: 01202 262600. Open daily 1000–1700 (Sun 1200–1700); Scaplen's Court open Aug only.

Compton Acres ££
Canford Cliffs, Poole; tel: 01202 700778; www.comptonacres.co.uk. Open Mar–Oct 1000–1800.

⬤ Poole Pottery ££
The Quay, Poole; tel: 01202 668681. Open Mon–Sat 0900–1730, Sun 1030–1630; some summer evenings.

◖ Mansion House £££ Thames Street, Poole; tel: 01202 685666; fax: 01202 665709; www.themansionhouse.co.uk. Dignified Georgian dining club with luxurious country-house-style bedrooms, rather masculine décor and rich menus.

Bournemouth✣ has long and lovely sandy beaches sheltered by attractive cliffs, and numerous green open spaces. Its mild climate and beautiful setting first began to attract holiday development in the early 1800s. Its neighbours, **Christchurch✣✣** and **Poole✣✣**, are much older and historically more interesting. In Christchurch, a number of old buildings survive on the town's main street and near the quaysides. Its shallow harbour is almost completely enclosed by the beautiful rural promontory of **Hengistbury Head✣✣**.

Poole's main feature is its huge, land-locked **harbour**, scattered with islands, sailboats and wooded inlets. Its historic quaysides contain many handsome old buildings, including the Tudor **Scaplen's Court**, the 18th-century **Customs House** and the **Guildhall**. **Poole Pottery** is a popular craft centre, and the **Waterfront Museum✣** covers local history. On the cliffs of Poole Bay, the spectacular gardens of **Compton Acres✣✣** make an interesting visit.

SHAFTESBURY✢✢

ℹ️ Tourist Information *8 Bell Street; tel: 01747 853514.*

🏛️ Shaftesbury Abbey Museum and Garden £ *Park Walk; tel: 01747 852910. Open Apr–Oct daily 1000–1700.*

Shaftesbury is perched on a spur of greensand with steep drops on three sides. Views extend to the Blackmoor Vale over the rooftops of the picturesque brick and thatched cottages lining **Gold Hill✢**. A few scraps of the ancient **abbey church**, founded by King Alfred in 888, survive; a small museum and an Anglo-Saxon herb garden stand on the site.

Left
Poole Quay

Right
Shaftesbury's Gold Hill

SHERBORNE✢✢

ℹ️ Tourist Information *Digby Road; tel: 01935 815341; sherborne.tic@ westdorset-dc.gov.uk.*

Once the capital of Wessex, this lovely town retains many medieval buildings. Its magnificent honey-coloured **Abbey Church✢✢** dates from Saxon times; Norman features and fan vaulting adorn its stonework. Within the original monastic complex are a rare medieval **almshouse✢** and **Sherborne School**, founded in 1550 by Edward VI. The town's two **castles✢** both belonged to Sir Walter Raleigh in Elizabethan times.

SIDMOUTH✢✢

ℹ️ Tourist Information *Ham Lane; tel: 01395 516441.*

Striking red cliffs of warm sandstone add character to this handsome and well-kept Georgian resort. Fashionable during Regency times, the town's best architecture dates from this period (over 500 buildings are listed as being of special interest). Cliff walks lead along the cliffs to some enticing beaches.

WEYMOUTH❖❖

ℹ Tourist Information The King's Statue, The Esplanade; tel: 01305 785747; tourism@ weymouth.gov.uk.

🏛 Sea Life Park £££ Lodmoor Country Park; tel: 01305 761070; www. sealife.co.uk. Open daily.

Civilised but lively Weymouth is one of England's most appealing family resorts, on a wide, gently shelving bay of safe clean sand. A colourful old fishing harbour forms the nucleus of the mostly Victorian and Georgian town. Attractions include an excellent **Sea Life Park❖** and a **Timewalk❖**, re-creating scenes from the town's history. **Lodmoor Country Park** and **Radipole Lake** are wetland nature reserves, good for birdwatching. South of Weymouth, **Portland Castle❖** is one of Henry VIII's best-preserved coastal fortresses.

ℹ Tourist Information / Greyhound Yard, Blandford Forum; tel: 01258 454770; or 47 South Street, Bridport; tel: 01308 424901; bridport.tic@westdorset-dc.gov.uk.

🅿 For Lulworth Cove, park in the main car park, (steep charges in high season), otherwise you will have a long walk. The quickest access to **Durdle Door** is through a caravan park (toll for parking), then it's a steep climb down the cliff paths.

🏛 Abbotsbury Swannery ££ New Barn Road, Abbotsbury; tel: 01305 871858; www. abbotsbury-tourism.co.uk. Open Apr–Oct 1000–1800; cygnet season May–June; feeding times 1200 and 1600.

Bridport Museum ££ South Street, Bridport; tel: 01308 422116. Open Apr–Oct Mon–Sat 1000–1700.

Suggested tour

Total distance: 206 miles (330km). Add 32 miles (51km) for the Cerne Abbas detour.

Time: 7–8 hours.

Links: Christchurch makes a convenient start for the Solent route (*see page 214*). From Honiton it's easy to reach the M5 on the A373 for other West Country tours.

Route: From DORCHESTER ❶ take the A354 south to WEYMOUTH ❷ and the **Isle of Portland❖**, then head northwest on the B3157. The charming village of **Abbotsbury❖❖** is a good road access point to see **Chesil Beach** (*see page 235*). Pause here to visit the **Subtropical Gardens❖❖** and the **Abbotsbury Swannery❖❖**. Continue west through the old rope-making town of **Bridport❖** and its lively little harbour at West Bay. Join the A35 and head for LYME REGIS ❸, calling at the roadside **bakery❖** at Morecombelake to stock up on biscuits and cheese. From the little resort of Charmouth, see the **Golden Cap❖** sandstone cliff. Follow the coast road (A3052), turning left on the B3172 through Axmouth, Seaton, and **Beer❖**, a pretty huddle of fishing cottages beneath tall white cliffs. **Branscombe❖❖**, one of Devon's prettiest cob-and-thatch villages, has a lovely rural stream-washed beach of brown pebbles. East of Branscombe Mouth lie the jumbled Hooken Cliffs, where a huge landslip occurred in 1890. From SIDMOUTH ❹, take the A375 north to **Honiton❖**, a pottery and lace-making centre with handsome Georgian buildings and interesting shops. Take the A30 northeast through Chard and Crewkerne. Continue through Yeovil, a busy agricultural and glove-making centre (good local museum), to SHERBORNE ❺ and SHAFTESBURY ❻. Turn right on the A350 south past the hunting forest of Cranborne Chase and a number of pretty villages (Fontmell Magna, Iwerne Courtney) to **Blandford Forum❖**, a fine example of a Georgian market town, rebuilt after a disastrous fire in 1731. Take the B3082 past the

Moore's Biscuits,
Morecombelake Bakery;
tel: 01297 489253;
enquiries@moores-
biscuits.co.uk; www.moores-
biscuits.co.uk. Open Mon–Fri
0900–1700. Excellent
range of home-made
biscuits, Blue Vinney
cheese and other local
products.

**Charmouth
Heritage Coast
Centre** *Lower Sea Lane;*
tel: 01297 560772. Open
Easter, May–Sept
1030–1700.

Kingston Lacy House
£££ On B3082 northwest of
Wimborne; tel: 01202
883402;
kingstonlacy@ntrust.org.uk.
Open Apr–Oct Wed–Sun
1200–1730, gardens and
park Apr–Oct daily
1100–1800; weekends in
winter; NT.

Mapperton Gardens £££
Mapperton; tel: 01308
862645. Open Mar–Oct
daily 1400–1800; HHA.

Montacute House £££
Montacute; tel: 01935
823289. Open Apr–Oct
Wed–Mon 1100–1700,
garden and park
1100–1730 (Wed–Sun
1130–1600 in winter); NT.

Iron Age hillfort of **Badbury Rings** where three Roman routes once met. Close by on the right-hand side of the road is **Kingston Lacy**, a beautiful 17th-century house in fine parkland with Red Devon cattle. Georgian buildings cluster around **Wimborne Minster**, a handsome, solid-looking Norman church in red and grey masonry. From here you will soon reach **BOURNEMOUTH ❼**. Take the A341 and A3060 to **CHRISTCHURCH ❽** and work west round the bay towards **POOLE ❾**. Take the chain ferry from **Sandbanks** to the ISLE OF PURBECK **❿**. **Studland Bay** is a gorgeous beach of icing sugar sand backed by nature reserves containing all six British reptiles. Notice the Old Harry chalk stacks at Foreland Point. From **Swanage**, head inland to **Corfe** and **Wareham**, then southwest on the B3070 to **Lulworth Cove** and **Durdle Door**. Return to **Wool** on the B3071, seeing **Bindon Abbey**. Take the A352 back to Dorchester.

Detour: From Wool, head northwest on unclassified roads to **Clouds Hill**. Turn west on the A35 through **Tolpuddle**, where the story of six agricultural workers, who formed a 'friendly society' to prevent their families from starving, is told in a little museum. A mile further west is **Athelhampton House** near Puddletown. Turn northwest on the B3142 to Piddletrenthide, then left to **Cerne Abbas**, whose priapic **Giant** (a chalk carving in the hillside) attracts much attention. Turn left on the A352 to complete the tour at Dorchester.

Getting out of the car: The South West Coast Path runs all the way along the coast west of Poole. **Tyneham**, east of Lulworth, is a particularly interesting place for a walk. This village was deserted in 1943 when the Ministry of Defence took over the countryside. The inhabitants never regained their homes, even after the war. Ironically, these 'no-go' firing ranges have one of the richest floral ecosystems anywhere in Britain. They are open during holidays and most weekends – check the red flags and warnings carefully. A small exhibition in the former church tells the poignant story of the village.

Also worth exploring: Beaminster, on the A3066 6 miles north of Bridport, is a pleasant little place. It is the home of John Makepeace, one of Britain's leading modern furniture-makers. Visit his studio at *The Farrs, Whitcombe Road (tel: 01308 862204; info@johnmakepeacefurniture. com; www.johnmakepeacefurniture.com).* Nearby **Mapperton Gardens** are also worth visiting (2 miles southeast). Two miles northwest of Yeovil is **Montacute House**, another gorgeous stone mansion in a lovely village. The house contains part of the national collection of Tudor and Jacobean portraits.

Left
Corfe Castle

Accommodation and food on the route

Riverside Restaurant ££ *West Bay; tel: 01308 422011; www.riverside-restaurant.co.uk.* Acclaimed seafood restaurant on harbourside. Busy and bustling, with informal but sprightly service. Good value.

Manor Hotel ££ *West Bexington; tel: 01308 897616; fax: 01308 897035; www.themanorhotel.com.* One of the best places for a bite to eat on the Dorset coast. An attractive stone house with a good range of restaurant or cellar-bar meals and simple, pleasant bedrooms. Lawns and play areas for children.

Bridge House Hotel ££ *3 Prout Bridge, Beaminster; tel: 01308 862200; fax: 01308 863700; enquiries@bridge-house.co.uk; www.bridge-house.co.uk.* Interesting old house near town centre with lots of period features; pretty walled gardens and excellent cooking.

Masons Arms ££ *Branscombe; tel: 01297 680300; fax: 01297 680500; www.masonsarms.co.uk.* Cheerful English pub-with-rooms in idyllic Devon seaside village. Good bar and restaurant food.

The Sea Shanty £ *Branscombe Mouth; tel: 01297 680577.* Imaginative range of snacks and hot dishes in an ornately thatched beach café. Tables outside.

Beechleas ££ *17 Poole Road, Wimborne Minster; tel: 01202 841684; fax: 01202 849344; www.beechleas.com.* Well-kept red-brick Georgian hotel close to the centre. Conservatory restaurant with good home cooking using organic ingredients.

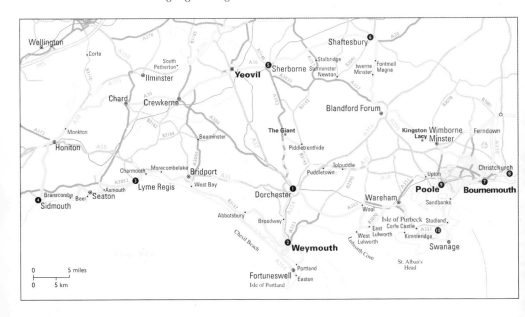

Exmoor and Hartland

Ratings

Scenery	●●●●●
Walking	●●●●●
Wildlife	●●●●●
Country markets	●●●●○
Family attractions	●●●●○
Outdoor pursuits	●●●●○
Villages	●●●●○
Beaches	●●●○○

The Exmoor National Park is roamed by red deer, ponies and literary ghosts. Overlooking the Bristol Channel, with distant glimpses of Welsh hills, North Devon compares favourably with any of the West Country's spectacular coastal scenery. Contrasting with mostly rocky or pebbly shores, wonderful sand-and-surf beaches fringe the Taw estuary, especially around Morte Bay. Coastal drama reaches a crescendo at the jutting capes of Hartland and Foreland Point. Off the National Park (although a geological extension of it) stretch the enticing, lesser-known sandstone uplands of the Quantocks. Taunton is a convenient regional springboard with good places to stay and eat, but there's a strong case for choosing a more rural or coastal retreat as a base. Dunster, Dulverton, Mortehoe, Lynton, Lynmouth and Porlock top the list.

BARNSTAPLE✧✧

ⓘ Tourist Information
36 Boutport Street;
tel: 01271 375000;
barnstapletic@visit.org.uk;
or The Bake House,
Caen Street, Braunton;
tel: 01271 816400;
braunstontic@visit.org.uk.

North Devon's agreeable main town presides over the Taw estuary. The ancient **Long Bridge✧** guards the lowest crossing point, providing several convenient fishing piers at low tide. **Queen Anne's Walk✧** is a handsome colonnade on the site of the old merchant exchange dating from Barnstaple's more active days as a port. Not far from here is the 19th-century glass-and-iron **Pannier Market✧**, the focus of activity on Tuesdays and Fridays, when farm stalls appear. **St Peter's Church** is memorable mainly for its twisted spire, the result of a lightning bolt in 1810. A **Heritage Centre✧** fills in more regional background.

West of Barnstaple is **Braunton Burrows✧✧**, an extensive sand-dune habitat remarkable for rare plants, birds, and marine life; watch out for red flags during Ministry of Defence training exercises. Currents make swimming dangerous anywhere near the Taw estuary.

Right
Barnstaple bridge

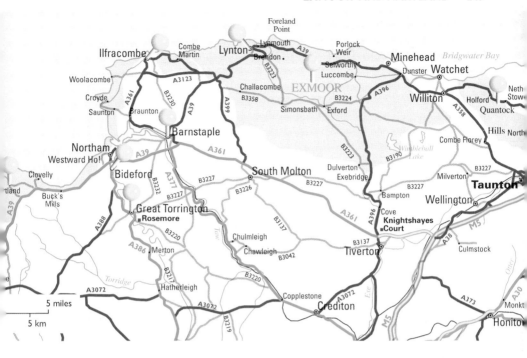

Accommodation and food in or near Barnstaple

Brannam Pottery ££ *Roundswell Industrial Estate, A39 W; tel: 01271 343035; brannam@brannam.com; factory shop open daily in summer (Mon–Sat winter); tours on weekdays.*

Barnstaple Heritage Centre ££ *Queen Anne's Walk; tel: 01271 373003; www.devonmuseums.net/ barnstapleheritage. Open Apr–Oct Mon–Sat 1000–1700, Nov–Mar Tue–Fri 1000–1630, Sat 1000–1530.*

Lynwood House ££ *Bishop's Tawton Road, Barnstaple; tel: 01271 343695; fax: 01271 379340; info@lynwoodhouse.co.uk.* Family-run restaurant-with-rooms on outskirts of town, with smart, fish-based menus.

Squires £ *Exeter Road, Braunton; tel: 01271 815533.* Excellent fish and chips in attractive premises – take-away and eat in.

BIDEFORD* AND GREAT TORRINGTON**

**ⓘ Tourist
Information** *Victoria
Road, Bideford; tel: 01237
477676; or Castle Hill,
South Street, Great
Torrington; tel: 01805
626140.*

ⓟ *Boat trips go from
Appledore harbour up
the Torridge estuary.*

ⓣ The Big Sheep ££
*Abbotsham, A39, 2
miles W of Bideford; tel:
01237 472366. Open
1000–1800 (weekends only
in winter); shows and events
all day.*

Dartington Crystal ££
*Linden Close, Torrington; tel:
01805 626242. Open
Mon–Fri 0930–1700 for
tours; shop Mon–Sat
0930–1700, Sun
1030–1630.*

Rosemoor Garden ££
*Off B3220 just S of
Torrington; tel: 01805
624067; www.rhs.org. Open
all year daily 1000–1700
(1800 in summer); RHS
members free.*

An estuary town, **Bideford** prospered during Elizabethan times from
the tobacco trade. Its most striking feature is the long medieval
bridge* (666ft with 24 arches) spanning the River Torridge. Just west
of Bideford, the woolly incumbents of **The Big Sheep*** are
accompanied by performing ducks and sheepdogs. In the peaceful
market town of **Great Torrington** are the well-known glassworks of
Dartington Crystal*, and the outstanding **Rosemoor Garden****,
belonging to the Royal Horticultural Society.

Above
Bideford's Egyptian House

EXMOOR NATIONAL PARK***

**ⓘ Tourist
Information** *Exmoor
House, Dulverton; tel: 01398
323841; dulverton@
exmoor-nationalpark.gov.uk;
or Dunster Steep; tel: 01643
821835.*

Exmoor is one of Britain's smallest national parks (265 square miles),
but still has great diversity and grandeur. This high plateau of
sandstones, grits and slates once lay under the sea, but it now rises to
a maximum altitude of 1706ft, at Dunkery Beacon. Fast-flowing
streams and rivers incise deep valleys sculpted with smooth green
spurs. The coastline, followed by the South West Coast Path, is
especially dramatic. The open moorland provides the classic bracken-
and heather-clad panoramas. Prized red deer roam its deciduous
woodlands, as well as Exmoor ponies (a distinct native breed), Exmoor
Horn sheep and Devon Red cattle. There is an extensive network of
footpaths and bridleways, and motorists can cross the entire park in
several directions. Good bases for walks are Dulverton, Simonsbath,
Exford and Winsford.

Accommodation in or near Exmoor National Park

Ashwick House ££ *Dulverton; tel/fax: 01398 323868; www.ashwickhouse.co.uk.* A rather grand Edwardian house in the heart of Exmoor makes a peacefully remote base. Traditional dinners.

Savery's at Karslake House £ *Halse Lane, Winsford; tel/fax: 01643 851242; karslakehotel@aol.com.* Simple but characterful accommodation in a charming Exmoor location, with accomplished cooking.

Oaks Hotel ££ *Porlock; tel: 01643 862265; fax: 01643 863131; www.oakshotel.co.uk.* Small, cosy hotel high over the pretty village of Porlock. Smart bedrooms and good-value menus.

Bales Mead £ *West Porlock; tel: 01643 862565; fax: 01643 862544; balesmead@btinternet.com.* Delightful B&B in Edwardian house offering excellent value. Overlooks Porlock Bay. Very good breakfasts.

Heddon's Gate ££ *Heddon's Mouth, Parracombe; tel: 01598 763313; fax: 01598 763363; info@hgate.co.uk; www.hgate.co.uk.* Imposing late-Victorian house in extensive and beautiful grounds. Old-fashioned style but smart and well kept.

Marsh Hall ££ *South Molton; tel: 01769 572666; fax: 01769 574230.* Friendly Victorian country house in extensive, secluded grounds.

HARTLAND❖❖

🅗 **Hartland Abbey and Gardens ££**
Hartland; tel: 01237 441264;
www.hartlandabbey.com.
Open Apr–Sept Wed, Thu, Sun 1400–1730 (Tue in July–Aug); gardens Apr–Oct Sun–Fri 1400–1730.

🌙 **Docton Mill £**
Lymebridge, Hartland;
tel/fax: 01237 441369;
www.doctonmill.co.uk.
Charming B&B in an ancient mill surrounded by showpiece gardens.

Salt-laden Atlantic gales back-comb the trees and hedgerows into strange shapes on this extremity of the North Devon coast. **Hartland Point❖❖❖** is a spectacular headland of jagged black reefs stretching out to sea below precipitous cliffs and waterfalls. St Nectan's church tower, the tallest in Devon, does its best to warn shipping off the perilous rocks from the village of Stoke. The ruins of **Hartland Abbey❖** were given by Henry VIII to the Keeper of the Wine Cellar. All that remains of **Hartland Quay❖❖** (once a thriving port) is a smattering of buildings; a 19th-century storm swept away the harbour.

ILFRACOMBE✧

ⓘ Tourist Information *The Landmark, Sea Front; tel: 01271 863001; ilfracombetic@aol.com; or The Esplanade, Woolacombe; tel: 01271 870553; woolacombetic@visit.org.uk.*

The mainly Victorian and Edwardian resort of Ilfracombe stands sheltered by high wooded cliffs. Its chapel of St Nicholas acts as a seamark on Lantern Hill. A few miles west of the town lie North Devon's best beaches, below the slate headland of Morte Point – a mecca for surfers. **Woolacombe Bay✧✧✧** is a magnificent 3-mile sweep of golden sands below gorse-covered downs and dunes. Croyde Bay and Saunton, further south, have more good sand.

LYNTON AND LYNMOUTH✧✧

ⓘ Tourist Information *The Town Hall, Lynton; tel: 01598 752225.*

Extravagantly nicknamed 'Little Switzerland' in Victorian times, these picturesque twin resorts stand in the steep, thickly wooded valley of the Lyn Gorge. A 600ft water-powered **cliff railway✧** connects hillside Lynton with Lynmouth, at sea level, where, in 1952, a flash flood caused devastation. The villages have lattice-paned teashops and thatched pubs, while the rollercoaster cliffs provide exhilarating walks. **Watersmeet✧**, **Woody Bay✧** and **Heddon's Mouth✧** are classic local beauty spots of woods and water. Feral horned goats graze through the strange, shattered crags in the **Valley of the Rocks✧**.

Right
The Valley of the Rocks

Accommodation and food in Lynton and Lynmouth

Victoria Lodge £ *Lee Road, Lynton; tel/fax: 01598 753203; enquiries@victorialodge.co.uk; www.victorialodge.co.uk.* Period style is the watchword at this trim guesthouse, crammed with Victoriana and 19th-century furnishings.

Rising Sun Hotel £££ *Harbourside, Lynmouth; tel: 01598 753223; fax: 01598 753480; risingsunlynmouth@easynet.co.uk.* Thatched inn in harbourside setting; fine sea views. Literary associations. Cosy restaurant with ambitious menus; elegant bedrooms.

QUANTOCK HILLS

ⓘ Tourist Information
Quantock Hills Visitor Centre, Castle Street, Nether Stowey; tel: 01278 732741.

ⓘ Coleridge Cottage
££ 35 Lime Street, Nether Stowey; tel: 01278 732662. Open Apr–Sept Tue–Thu and Sun 1400–1700; NT.

ⓒ Three Horseshoes
£ Langley Marsh; tel: 01984 623763. Straightforward Quantock pub serving imaginative range of food and real ales. Traditional pub games.

The uplands west of Taunton and Bridgwater are gently contoured and stream-washed. The summits, scattered with cairns and burial mounds, give fine views over the Bristol Channel. The village of **Nether Stowey**✦ has close associations with the Romantic poet Samuel Taylor Coleridge, who composed some of his most famous works in the cottage that is now a small museum.

Suggested tour

Total distance: 197 miles (315km). Add 15 miles (24km) for the coastal route west of Lynmouth.

Time: 8 hours.

Links: Connections can be made to other West Country tours via the M5 from Taunton or Bridgwater, or on the A39 from Hartland.

Route: From the busy, well-heeled market town of **Taunton**✦, take the B3227 west to Bampton, then follow signs northwest to cheerful and sophisticated **Dulverton**✦✦, a regional centre for Exmoor. Continue northwest on the B3223 up Winsford Hill, turning right through the pretty village of **Exford**, then northeast to **Luccombe**, leaving Dunkery Beacon on your right hand. Follow signs right to **Dunster**✦✦, with its castle-crowned main street of beautifully kept medieval and Georgian houses, and National Park information centre. Turn left on the coastal A39 past **Minehead** (a popular seaside resort with a charming older quarter) and picturesque **Selworthy**. Go down the steep gradient into **Porlock**✦. To avoid the ascent out of the village, follow a coastal detour through **Porlock Weir**✦, an old fishing port on a pretty bay of mauve pebbles, then take one of the longer toll roads through wooded hills back to the A39. Continue along the coastal route past Brendon and the grand hills of Countisbury to **LYNTON**

To visit Clovelly, you must park in a horribly commercialised visitor centre (tel: 01237 431781; www.clovelly.co.uk), and pay a toll to enter the village. (It's very steep down to the harbour, but a Land Rover can bring you back in summer.)

Grand Western Horseboat Co ££
The Wharf, Canal Hill, Tiverton; tel: 01884 253345; www.horseboat.co.uk; canal trips Easter–Oct.

Arlington Court £££ Off A39 near Arlington; tel: 01271 850296; Open Apr–Oct Wed–Mon 1100–1730; June–Sept daily; gardens 1030–1630; park open all year until dusk; NT.

Quince Honey Farm ££ North Road, South Molton; tel: 01769 572401. Open Easter–Oct daily 0900–1800 (1700 in Oct).

Knightshayes Court £££ Bolham, 1 mile NE of Tiverton; tel: 01884 254665. Open Apr–Sept Sat–Thu 1100–1730, Oct Sat–Wed 1100–1600; garden Apr–Oct daily 1100–1730; NT.

Bideford Bicycle and Canoe Hire Torrington Street, Bideford; tel: 01237 424123.

The Bike Shed The Square, Barnstaple; tel: 01271 328628. Cycle hire.

Tarka Line Barnstaple station; tel: 08457 484950 for train times.

and **LYNMOUTH ❶**. Take the A39 inland via charming Parracombe to **BARNSTAPLE ❷**.

Detours: Carry on from Lynton along intricate coastal lanes past Woody Bay west to Combe Martin, then take the A399 to **ILFRACOMBE ❸**. Follow signs to **Woolacombe Bay✦✦✦** on the northwest coast. Follow the lanes round Croyde Bay and Saunton Sands to **Braunton Burrows✦✦** (sand dunes and nature reserve). Return to Barnstaple to pick up the main route. Alternatively, strike inland from Lynton to see some more of Exmoor. Head down the B3223 to **Simonsbath**, then turn right on the B3358 to Challacombe. Follow signs left to Barnstaple.

Continue west on the A39 through **BIDEFORD ❹**, past the attractive village of **Buck's Mills**, and picturesque and expensive **Clovelly✦**. After Clovelly, the wild grandeur of **HARTLAND ❺** will seem a breath of fresh air. This area is best seen from the coastal path, but motorists can thread through a web of tiny lanes from the main A39. Follow signs for Hartland Point, Stoke and Hartland Quay.

Retrace your steps, turning off south at Bideford to **GREAT TORRINGTON ❻**, then northeast on the B3227 to South Molton, and the **Quince Honey Farm✦** (all about bee-keeping). Take the A361 to **Tiverton✦**, a pleasant old wool town with an interesting castle, St Peter's Church, Jacobean council offices and a craft centre. Just north of the town is **Knightshayes Court✦✦**, an exotic Gothic Revival house with a wonderful garden. Return to Taunton to complete the tour.

Getting out of the car: The 180-mile figure-of-eight **Tarka Trail** is based on Henry Williamson's *Tarka the Otter*, set in the Taw and Torridge valleys. Leaflets are available from tourist offices. Barnstaple and Bideford are good starting points, and many stretches are ideal for cycling (bike hire in the town centres or at Barnstaple station). The **Tarka Line** (Exeter–Barnstaple railway) runs through glorious Taw Valley scenery.

From Bideford, regular boats visit **Lundy Island** in the Bristol Channel, a quiet hideaway of puffins and seals 11 miles offshore. The crossing can be very choppy.

Also worth exploring: Pick a route along some literary trails through the intricate lanes of the Quantock Hills to the north: the warm sandstone village of **Combe Florey** (Evelyn, and now Auberon Waugh), **Nether Stowey** (Coleridge), and **Holford**, where William and Dorothy Wordsworth lived, until they were suspected of being foreign spies and given notice to quit!

Bude, south of Hartland, just over the Cornish border, is a popular surfing centre with huge beaches of crashing Atlantic breakers. The town has an attractively restored waterfront area.

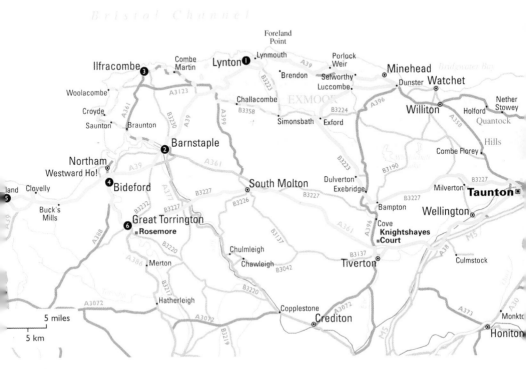

Accommodation and food in Taunton

Castle Hotel £££ *Castle Green; tel: 01823 272671; fax: 01823 336066; reception@the-castle-hotel.com; www.the-castle-hotel.com.* A pricy but comfortable, family-run hotel in the town's creeper-covered Norman fortress. Traditional, accomplished restaurant, modernised bedrooms.

Brazz ££ *Castle Bow; tel: 01823 252000.* Under the same management as the Castle Hotel, this urbane café-brasserie-bar in the heart of the old town brings in a sophisticated, youthful crowd.

ⓘ Lundy Island £££
The Quay, Bideford; tel: 01271 863636; regular sailings all year (weather permitting); summer only from Ilfracombe or Clovelly. Simple but delightful holiday accommodation available from the Landmark Trust (www.landmarktrust.co.uk).

Dartmoor and South Hams

Ratings

Beaches	●●●●●
Family attractions	●●●●●
Outdoor pursuits	●●●●●
Scenery	●●●●●
Seaside resorts	●●●●●
Eating out	●●●●○
Towns and villages	●●●●○

Dartmoor dominates Devon's heartland – the largest open space in southwest England. Its harsh granite uplands seem inhospitable in grim weather, but there are also softer landscapes of wooded streams and grazing ponies, ancient stannary towns and villages of cob and thatch. When the sun shines, South Devon is idyllic, serving cream teas to ravenous walkers, caravanners, and bucket-and-spaders. Gateway to the southwest is Devon's capital, large and lively Exeter. Despite heavy wartime bombing, it is a surprisingly rewarding city. Further south is the giant holiday complex of Torbay, offering families a ready-made selection of resort attractions and beaches. Presiding over the scenery of the South Hams, Dartmouth and Salcombe will appeal to those who enjoy messing about in boats, on the glorious Dart and Kingsbridge estuaries. Further west lies professionally maritime Plymouth, scene of Sir Francis Drake's adventures.

DARTMOOR NATIONAL PARK✦✦✦

ⓘ Tourist Information *St Leonards Road, Ivybridge; tel: 01752 897035.*

🏠 Castle Drogo ££ *Drewsteignton; tel: 01647 433306; castledrogo@ntrust.org.uk. Open Apr–Oct Sat–Thu 1100–1730, garden all year daily 1030–dusk; NT.*

Birds of prey wheel over tors of hardened magma that loom from the mists like stacks of plates, and the remains of prehistoric settlements. Much of Dartmoor's scenery is wild, but man-made influences emerge in the form of leats (mini canals), abandoned tin-mine workings, and grazing livestock. A National Park since 1951, Dartmoor is a roughly circular plateau rising to over 2000ft, encompassing 365 square miles of wooded valleys, farmland, bog and open moor. In its more inhabited eastern parts, Dartmoor is a scene of thatched cottages, quaint bridges, and reservoir lakes. Landmarks are mostly natural ones, except for the old stannary (tin-trade) towns, and **Castle Drogo✦✦**, a stunning Edwardian 'castle' designed in every detail by Edwin Lutyens and with a fine garden. The heart of the moor is crossed by just two intersecting roads; to see more you must walk or ride, but be very careful – wear sensible clothing and take a detailed map. Conditions can be hostile.

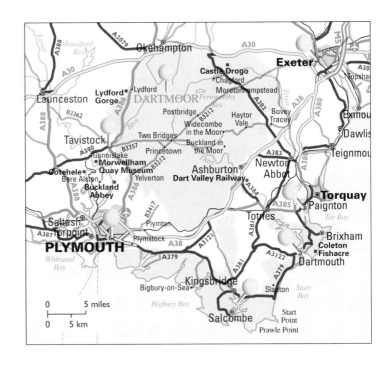

Accommodation and food on Dartmoor

Blackaller Hotel ££ *North Bovey; tel: 01647 440322; fax: 01647 441131; www.blackaller.co.uk.* Peaceful but sheltered Dartmoor retreat in a converted woollen mill. Excellent dinners; attractive bedrooms.

The Cider House £ *Buckland Abbey, Yelverton; tel: 01822 853285; sarah.stone@cider-house.co.uk.* Charming B&B in an imposing historic setting, with lovely gardens.

Lydgate House ££ *Postbridge; tel: 01822 880209; lydgatehouse@email.com; www.lydgate-house.fsnet.co. uk.* Peaceful hideaway in the heart of Dartmoor. Fresh, light bedrooms.

Prince Hall £££ *Two Bridges, Yelverton; tel: 01822 890403; fax: 01822 890676; info@princehall.co.uk; www.princehall.co.uk.* Comfortable, classy country-house style in a wild, central Dartmoor setting.

Gidleigh Park £££ *Chagford; tel: 01647 432367.* Expect to spend a small fortune here, for an exceptional Dartmoor location, luxurious country-house accommodation and superlative cooking.

DART ESTUARY✦✦✦

ℹ **Tourist Information** Mayors Avenue, Dartmouth; tel: 01803 834224; enquiries@dartmouth-information.fsnet.co.uk; or The Town Mill, Coronation Road, Totnes; tel: 01803 863168; ask about river trips.

🏰 **Dartmouth Castle ££** Off B3205 1 mile SE; tel: 01803 833588. Open Apr–Oct daily 1000–1800 (1700 in Oct), Nov–Mar Wed–Sun 1000–1600; EH.

Totnes Castle £ Totnes; tel: 01803 864406. Open Apr–Sept daily 1000–1800; Oct 1000–1700; EH.

Totnes Museum £ 70 Fore Street, Totnes; tel: 01803 863821; coletonfishacre@ntrust.org.uk. Open Apr–Oct Mon–Fri.

Coleton Fishacre ££ 3 miles E of Kingswear; tel: 01803 752466. Open Apr–Oct Wed–Sun 1100–1630; gardens 1030–1730 including weekends in Mar; NT.

Above
Dartmouth

The River Dart winds between deeply wooded banks, its creeks forming secretive havens. Historic and enjoyable **Dartmouth✦✦**, at the mouth of the estuary, preserves its salty character. The **Royal Naval College** is a prominent landmark on the hill; the inner harbour areas are a maze of cobbled streets and old buildings, with interesting shops, upmarket restaurants and cultural activities. **Dartmouth Castle✦✦** guards the entrance to this secluded, deep-water anchorage. Picturesque **Bayard's Cove✦✦** has another fortress; the *Mayflower* docked here in 1620. Upstream, photogenic **Totnes✦✦** stands at the highest navigable point on the river. Its Elizabethan quarter (The Narrows) is especially interesting. The **castle✦** and **Guildhall** are local landmarks. East of Kingswear, **Coleton Fishacre✦✦** is an Arts and Crafts house with a marvellous garden.

Accommodation and food around the Dart estuary

Ford House £ *44 Victoria Road, Dartmouth; tel/fax: 01803 834047; www.ford-house.co.uk.* Smart but streamlined B&B a short walk from the historic waterfront area, run by relaxed Australian owners. Closed Oct–Mar.

Carved Angel £££ *2 South Embankment, Dartmouth; tel: 01803 832465; www.thecarvedangel.com.* A culinary legend using excellent ingredients with accurate simplicity. Impressive wine list.

Nonsuch House ££ *Church Hill, Kingswear; tel: 01803 752829; www.nonsuch-house.co.uk.* Wonderful estuary views from this Edwardian house, flamboyantly decorated inside. Good home cooking and hospitable, enthusiastic owners.

EXETER✦✦

ℹ **Tourist Information** Paris Street; tel: 01392 265700.

🏰 **Quay House Visitor Centre** 46 The Quay; tel: 01392 265213. Open Apr–Oct daily 1000–1700; rest of year Sat–Sun only 1100–1600.

Devon's capital is a cathedral and university city, with an upbeat and civilised air. The old street plan set out by the Romans still prevails within the city walls. The **cathedral✦✦** is a wonderful example of Decorated Gothic with magnificent vaulting. Other historic buildings include the medieval **Guildhall✦** and a network of **tunnels✦** built in the 13th century to bring water into the cathedral district. For the city's history, visit the **Quay House Interpretation Centre✦**, in the revived waterfront area. The historic waterfront town of **Topsham✦** is also worth a visit.

PLYMOUTH✧✧

ℹ **Tourist Information** Island House, The Barbican; tel: 01752 304849.

Plymouth Dome ££ The Hoe; tel: 01752 603300. Open daily 0900–1730 (later in summer); joint ticket to Smeaton's Tower (lighthouse) available.

National Marine Aquarium £££ Rope Walk, Coxside; tel: 01752 600301; www.national-aquarium.co.uk. Open Apr–Oct daily 1000–1800 (rest of year 1000–1700).

Mount Edgcumbe ££ Cremyll, Torpoint; tel: 01752 822236. Open Apr–Oct Wed–Sun 1100–1630; park free of charge all year. Reachable by ferry from Plymouth Harbour.

Antony House and Garden ££ 2 miles NW of Torpoint; tel: 01752 812191; Open Apr–Oct Tue–Thu 1330–1730 (June–Aug Sun only). Fine woodland gardens; NT.

Saltram £££ Off A38 2 miles W of Plympton; tel: 01752 333500. Open Apr–Sept Sat–Thu 1200–1630, Oct 1130–1530 (garden 1100–1600); NT.

Plymouth Mayflower ££ 3–5 The Barbican; tel: 01752 306330; www.plymouth-mayflower.co.uk. Open daily 1000–1800 (1700 Nov–Mar).

🌑 **Athenaeum Lodge £** 4 Athenaeum Street; tel/fax: 01752 665005. Good-value B&B in the heart of historic Plymouth.

Plymouth Sound✧✧, formed from five separate river mouths, is one of Europe's finest anchorages. Sir Francis Drake, Sir Walter Raleigh, Captain Cook, the Pilgrim Fathers and Charles Darwin all set off from Plymouth on momentous voyages. Following wartime bombing, only the twisting alleys of the harbour area known as the **Barbican**✧ survived reasonably intact. The grassy platform of the **Hoe**✧, and its lighthouse, give marvellous views over the Sound. Near by is the **Royal Citadel**✧, built by Charles II in the 1660s. The **Plymouth Dome**✧✧ offers a high-tech presentation on the city's past and present, while the interactive **Plymouth Mayflower**✧✧ exhibition focuses on the Pilgrim Fathers (joint admission to the **Aquarium**✧✧). **Mount Edgcumbe**✧, **Antony House**✧✧ and **Saltram**✧✧ are fine historic mansions just outside the city.

SOUTH HAMS***

ℹ Tourist Information *The Quay, Kingsbridge; tel: 01548 853195; or Market Street, Salcombe; tel: 01548 843927.*

🚢 Kingsbridge–Salcombe Rivermaid Cruises ££ *The Quay; tel: 01548 853607.*

🏛 Overbecks Museum and Garden ££ *Sharpitor, Salcombe; tel: 01548 842893; overbecks@ntrust.org.uk. Open Apr–Sept Sun–Fri (daily in Aug), Oct Sun–Thu 1100–1730, garden all year daily 1000–2000 or dusk; NT.*

Cookworthy Museum £ *108 Fore Street, Kingsbridge; tel: 01548 853235; www.devonmuseums.net. Open Apr–Sept Mon–Sat 1000– 1700, Oct 1000–1600.* William Cookworthy, born in the town in 1705, discovered the secret of porcelain manufacture, using Cornish china clay.

The picturesque Kingsbridge estuary is familiar to countless keen sailors. A mosaic of green and gold fields divided by hedges, wooded combes and deep sunken lanes cloaks the hilly interior. The mild climate, with short winters and early springs, encourages flowers and subtropical vegetation. A varied coastline of cliffs, shingle banks, estuaries and sandy bays makes up the South Devon Heritage Coast. Best beaches east of Kingsbridge include **Blackpool Sands***** and the 6-mile stretch of Start Bay shingle known as **Slapton Sands****. More intimate sandy cove beaches lie around Salcombe and Bigbury Bay (**Thurlestone*** is one of the prettiest; **Bigbury*** is good for windsurfing). The best stretches for walks lie between Start Point and East Portlemouth, or between Bolt Head and Bolt Tail. **Salcombe**** is Devon's southernmost resort at the mouth of the estuary. The steep, pretty fishing village has cheerful teashops, pubs, chandlery stores and upmarket shops. Eccentric **Overbecks*** house, once owned by a scientist, has splendid sea views. **Kingsbridge***, at the head of the estuary, is a handsome market town with attractive slate-hung buildings. The refurbished **Cookworthy Museum*** depicts rural life through the ages.

Accommodation around South Hams

Burgh Island £££ *Bigbury-on-Sea; tel: 01548 810514; fax: 01548 810243; reception@burghisland.com; www.burghisland.com.* An experience straight out of Agatha Christie (who wrote two thrillers here), this art-deco hotel has an amazing period interior. It stands on a tidal island reached only by sea tractor at high water. The heart-stopping tariff includes an excellent dinner.

Soar Mill Cove Hotel £££ *Soar Mill Cove, Salcombe; tel: 01548 561566; fax: 01548 561223; www.makepeacehotels.co.uk.* A functional exterior disguises a comfortable well-run hotel in a magnificent setting on a peaceful isolated sandy cove. Good cooking.

South Sands ££ *South Sands, Salcombe; 01548 843741; fax: 01548 842112; enquire@southsands.com; www.southsands.com.* Family-friendly hotel in lovely location at the water's edge. Anyone can enjoy lunch in the Terrace Bar or an elegant dinner downstairs.

Sloop Inn £ *Bantham, Kingsbridge; tel: 01548 560489; fax: 01548 561940.* Unpretentious 16th-century smugglers' pub with good fishy bar menus and adequate bedrooms.

Above
Salcombe harbour

Opposite
Castle Drogo

TAVISTOCK❖

ⓘ Tourist Information *Town Hall, Bedford Square; tel: 01822 612938; tavistocktic@visit.org.uk.*

ⓘ Morwellham Quay *£££ Morwellham, 3 miles SW of Tavistock; tel: 01822 832766; info@ morwellham-quay.co.uk; www.morwellham-quay.co.uk. Open Mar–Oct daily 1000–1730. Costumed guides, train ride into the mines, craft demonstrations.*

Cotehele *££ St Dominick, Saltash, Cornwall; tel: 01579 351346; cotehele@ ntrust.org.uk. Open Apr–Oct Sat–Thu 1100–1700 or dusk; gardens daily all year 1030–dusk; NT. Splendid woodland gardens. Visitor numbers restricted at busy times; no electric light.*

ⓘ Horn of Plenty *£££ Gulworthy, Tavistock; tel/fax: 01822 832528; www.thehornofplenty.co.uk. Well-known gourmet restaurant-with-rooms in a secluded setting overlooking the Tamar Valley; the emphasis is firmly on the food.*

This pleasant old market town once claimed one of the most influential Benedictine abbeys in the region, remnants of which are incorporated into the Town Hall. In the 13th century, Tavistock was the largest of Dartmoor's four 'stannary towns', where tin was weighed and assayed. A statue commemorates local boy Sir Francis Drake, born in 1542. Nearby **Morwellham Quay**❖❖ is an open-air industrial heritage attraction re-creating the heyday of a copper-exporting port. Just over the Cornish border is **Cotehele**❖❖❖, one of the county's most fascinating houses.

Opposite
Torquay harbour

Right
Village shop, Morwellham Quay

TORBAY✦✦✦

ⓘ Tourist Information *Vaughan Parade, Torquay or The Esplanade, Paignton; paignton.tic@torbay.gov.uk or The Old Market House, The Quay, Brixham; all tel: 0906 680 1268.*

Ⓟ Parking can be tricky in high season all around Torbay.

ⓘ Torre Abbey ££ *King's Drive, Torquay; tel: 01803 293593. Open Apr–Oct daily 0930–1800.*

Kents Cavern ££ *Ilsham Road, Wellswood; tel: 01803 215136. Open daily 0930–1700 (Tue–Sun 1000–1600 in winter; some summer evenings). Many ancient animal bones were found in this prehistoric cave dwelling. Some limestone formations.*

Model village ££ *Hampton Avenue, Babbacombe; tel: 01803 315315; www.babbacombemodelvillage.co.uk. Open daily 0900–1700 (1000–1600 in winter; some late openings).*

Paignton Zoo £££ *Totnes Road, St Michael's; tel: 01803 697500; www.paigntonzoo.org.uk. Open daily.*

Compton Castle ££ *Marldon, 1 mile NW; tel: 01803 875740. Open Apr–Oct Mon, Wed–Thu 1000–1215, 1400–1700; NT.*

Ⓟ Paignton & Dartmouth Steam Railway £££ *Queen's Park Station, Torbay Road; tel: 01803 553760; www.paignton-steamrailway.co.uk; trips Mar–Oct and Christmas; phone for timetable.*

The three resorts of Torquay, Paignton and Brixham, on the sheltered, sand-fringed shores of Torbay, together form the 'English Riviera'. **Torquay✦✦** is traditionally classy, against a backdrop of palatial Victorian architecture and wind-burned palms. Today it is a busy family resort. **Torre Abbey✦** is a familiar landmark, the medieval gatehouse and Norman tower incorporated into a creeper-covered, mainly 18th-century house. Nearby attractions include **Kents Cavern Showcaves✦** and a **model village✦**.

Paignton✦ caters more for young families, with traditional-style amusements, watersports and large stretches of magnificent red sand. **Paignton Zoo✦✦** and the **Paignton & Dartmouth Steam Railway✦✦** are excellent attractions for children. The working harbour is its prettiest bit. A few older buildings survive – **Kirkham House** was a Tudor merchant's home, and just west of the town is **Compton Castle✦✦**, ancestral home of Sir Humphrey Gilbert, coloniser of Newfoundland.

Brixham✦✦ has kept its original fishing-village character, and is still a bustling port. Quaint, narrow streets pack the hill behind the harbour, where a life-sized reconstruction of Drake's *Golden Hind* sits.

North of Torbay, **Babbacombe✦✦**, **Maidencombe✦✦** and **Watcombe✦✦** are three of the prettiest of an idyllic string of sandy coves in beautiful wooded red-rock settings. All inevitably involve some steep climbs.

Accommodation and food around Torbay

Mulberry House £-££ *1 Scarborough Road, Torquay; tel: 01803 213639.* Tasteful bedrooms and tasty, inventive menus in this exemplary little restaurant-with-rooms a short distance from the seafront.

Tea Rose Tearooms £ *49 Babbacombe Downs Road, Babbacombe; tel: 01803 324477.* Cream teas served with old-fashioned charm in gardens overlooking the sea.

🏛 **Buckland Abbey ££**
*Buckland Monachorum;
tel: 01822 853607;
bucklandabbey@
ntrust.org.uk. Open Apr–Oct
Fri–Wed 1030–1730 and
winter weekends
1400–1700; NT.*

Garden House ££
*Buckland Monachorum; tel:
01822 854769;
www.thegardenhouse.org.uk.
Open Mar–Oct daily
1030–1700.*

Lydford Gorge ££
*Lydford, off A386; tel:
01822 820441;
lydfordgorge@ntrust.org.uk.
Open Apr–Sept 1000–1730
(1600 in Oct; reduced access
in winter); NT. Paths can be
slippery – wear sensible
shoes and supervise
children carefully.*

Below
Dartmoor's Shipley Common

Suggested tour

Total distance: 184 miles (296km). Add 26 miles (42km) for the Exeter detour.

Time: 7 hours.

Links: The A30 is the main spinal West Country road for Cornwall, Dorset and Somerset. Join the M5 at Exeter for points north.

Route: From **DARTMOUTH** ❶, take the A379 south via **Blackpool Sands**••• (a gorgeous, privately owned beach) and the long shingle ridge of **Slapton Sands**••. On the inland side of the road is Slapton Ley, a haunt of wildfowl. The Sherman tank near Slapton village commemorates US troops who died here on a D-Day training mission. Continue through **Kingsbridge**•, detouring on the A381 to see **Salcombe**••. Return to the A379 and head west to **PLYMOUTH** ❷, then north on the A386 for 10 miles. Near the showpiece village of **Buckland Monachorum** lie **Buckland Abbey**••, ancestral home of Sir Francis Drake's family, and the **Garden House**••, a lovely plantsman's garden by a ruined abbey. Turn right on the B3212 and head diagonally on a switchback road through **DARTMOOR** ❸ via **Princetown** (one of the highest towns in England, dominated by its high-security prison), **Two Bridges** and **Postbridge**• (a good starting-point for walks – notice the medieval clapper bridge). **Wistman's Wood**, to the left of the road between these two settlements, is an ancient stunted relic of the oak forests that once covered the moor. A brief right-hand detour near Lettaford takes you to **Grimspound**•, an impressive Bronze Age hut site. Lanes to the right lead through **Chagford**•, a pretty stannary village and a popular walking centre. Turn right on the A382. **Castle Drogo**•• is signed to the right near Easton. Turn left on the A30 through **Okehampton**•, then on to the A386, detouring right to **Lydford Gorge**••, a picturesque scene of waterfalls and whirlpools. Continue south to **TAVISTOCK** ❹. Turn left on the B3357 to see another sector of Dartmoor, taking minor roads through pretty **Buckland in the Moor**•• and **Widecombe in the Moor**• (much visited for its associations with the song *Widecombe Fair*; its church is known as the Cathedral of the Moors),

Powderham Castle
£££ Kenton; tel: 01626 890243; www.powderham.co.uk. Open Apr–Oct Sun–Fri 1000–1730; guided tours. Fortified pile with extensive grounds, fine rose gardens, and Timothy, the world's oldest pet tortoise (believed to be over 160 years old).

Becky Falls*** and **Haytor Vale*****. Continue east on the B3387 to **Bovey Tracey*** (a pleasant centre with crafts and woodland nature reserves), then turn right on the A382 to **TORBAY** ❺ and **Totnes**** before completing the tour at Dartmouth.

Detour: From Bovey Tracey, take the A38 to **EXETER** ❻ and **Topsham***, returning to Torbay via the coastal route past **Powderham Castle**** and **Dawlish Warren*** (an interesting nature reserve of dunes and tidal flats) and the tidy little resort of **Teignmouth***. Cross the Teign at Shaldon and take the coastal road along **Babbacombe Bay****, stopping at some of the pretty red coves *en route*.

Getting out of the car: Dartmoor and the South West Coast Path provide dozens of ways to enjoy life outside the car – on foot (pick up leaflets from local tourist offices), or on horseback (plenty of Dartmoor stables offer horses and ponies for hire). The **Dart Valley Trail** links Totnes, Dartmouth and Kingswear. You can link parts of the 17-mile route with ferry or river cruises, or with the **Paignton & Dartmouth Steam Railway****, which runs through some of the most scenic stretches of the estuary.

Also worth exploring: The dissolved and ruined monastery of **Buckfast Abbey**, on the southeast fringes of Dartmoor, was completely rebuilt from 1882, and is now a thriving Benedictine enterprise selling many monastic products.

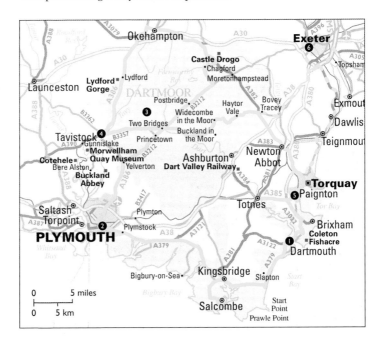

Cornwall

Ratings

Coastline	●●●●●
Seaside resorts	●●●●●
Beaches	●●●●○
Castles and abbeys	●●●●○
Family attractions	●●●●○
Heritage	●●●●○
Villages	●●●●○
Archaeology	●●●○○

Cornwall's principal attraction is its coastline: to negotiate the southern coast, frayed into tatters by deep estuaries, you may have to take expensive car ferries or make lengthy inland detours; road access to the northern coast needs careful map reading too. However, the rewards – idyllic coves and bays, picturesque fishing villages and spectacular headlands – are immense. In contrast, the interior is rather austere, and few of the larger towns are particularly alluring. Sightseeing focuses on dazzling gardens (encouraged by the West Country's mild climate), heritage attractions relating to the tin-mining and china-clay industries, and some smallish archaeological sites. The fairytale setting of St Michael's Mount near Penzance is impressive. Further offshore lie the tantalising Isles of Scilly, the Arthurian lost land of Lyonesse. Cornwall's holiday season is surprisingly short. By October, it can seem forlorn, and many places close for the winter.

FAL ESTUARY❖❖

ℹ️ **Tourist Information** 28 Killigrew Street, Falmouth; tel: 01326 312300.

🏰 **Pendennis Castle** ££ 1 mile E of Falmouth; tel: 01326 316594. Open Apr–Sept 1000–1800, Oct 1000–1700, Nov–Mar 1000–1600; EH.

Right
Falmouth harbour

No fewer than seven rivers debouch into the Carrick Roads, a massive drowned valley that is constantly busy with shipping. **Falmouth**❖ has a pleasant old seafaring quarter around the harbour. The striking **Customs House**❖ is easily recognizable by its chimney, once used for burning contraband tobacco. **Pendennis Castle**❖ was part of Henry VIII's sea-defence scheme. On the opposite side of the estuary, **St Mawes**❖ is a pretty seaside town with another 16th-century fortress. The hinterland peninsula of **Roseland**❖❖ is a mass of quiet hidden creeks and subtropical vegetation. **St Just-in-Roseland**❖❖ has an unforgettable church in a magical setting.

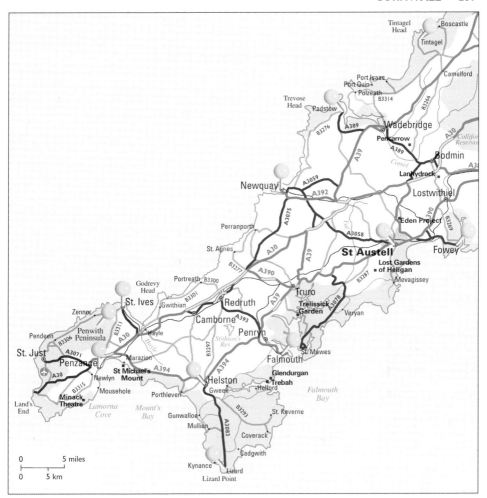

FOWEY✦✦ AND ST AUSTELL✦

ℹ Tourist Information
4 Custom House Hill, Fowey;
tel: 01726 833616.

China Clay Museum ££ Wheal
Martyn, Carthew; tel: 01726
850362; www.wheal-
martyn.com. Open Apr–Oct
daily 1000–1800, Jan–Mar
Wed–Sun 1000–1600.

Fowey✦✦ is a tangle of hilly streets full of flowers and handsome old houses above the estuary. Wooded cliffs line the waterfront, which is a mass of flitting sails and ocean-going ships all summer. Quaint old pubs, intriguing shops and upmarket eating places draw in the crowds. Cliff walks lead to the tranquil scenery of **Gribben Head✦✦**, where Daphne du Maurier's home, Menabilly, was the inspiration for Manderley in her novel *Rebecca*. At **St Austell✦**, pyramidal spoil heaps, the ghostly remains of the china-clay industry, rise like snowy peaks. The **China Clay Museum✦✦** at Wheal Martyn explains the extraction process. Just northeast of St Austell is the celebrated **Eden Project**, a series of huge geodesic domes encapsulating climatic re-creations of all the world's vegetated zones.

Accommodation and food in Fowey

Fowey Hall £££ *Hanson Drive; tel: 01726 833866; www.foweyhall.com.* Grand but unpretentious hospitality in a late Victorian mansion high over the estuary. Splendid cooking. Children welcome.

Marina Hotel ££ *The Esplanade tel: 01726 833315; marina. hotel@dial.pipex.com; www.themarinahotel.co.uk.* Stylishly furnished hotel with magnificent estuary views from the front rooms and restaurant. Car access and parking tricky.

Food for Thought ££ *The Quay; tel: 01726 832221; fax: 01726 832077.* Fine cooking in charming surroundings at the old Customs House overlooking the harbour.

Great Cornish gardens

Cornwall's mild Gulf Stream climate produces some wonderful gardens. A few of the best are listed below. Admission charges and opening times relate to gardens/grounds only.

Eden Project £££ *Bodelva, St Austell; tel: 01726 811911; www. edenproject.com.* Open Apr–Oct daily 1000–1800; rest of year 1000–1630. The story of man's relationship with plants set in the world's largest greenhouses.

Glendurgan ££ *Mawnan Smith; tel: 01326 250906; glendurgan@ ntrust.org.uk.* Open Mar–Oct Tue–Sat 1030–1730; NT. Superb subtropical gardens above Helford River; laurel maze and exotic shrubs.

Lanhydrock ££ *Lanhydrock, Bodmin; tel: 01208 73320.* Open Apr–Oct daily 1000–1800 or dusk; NT. Lovely formal gardens above the Fowey Valley, best in late spring. The house (closed Mon) is as interesting as the gardens.

Lost Gardens of Heligan ££ *Pentervan Off B2373, NW of Mevagissey; tel: 01726 845100; www.heligan.com.* Open Apr–Oct daily 1000–1800; rest of year 1000–1700. Here, an imaginative restoration project has resurrected a neglected Victorian 80-acre site; the walled and kitchen gardens are especially interesting.

Pencarrow ££ *Bodmin; tel: 01208 841369; www.pencarrow.co.uk.* Open Mar–Oct daily 1100–1700 (from 1100 June–Sept). Georgian estate with 50 acres of splendid rhododendrons, conifers and blue hydrangeas.

Trebah ££ *Mawnan Smith; tel: 01326 250448; www.trebah-garden.co.uk.* Open daily 1030–1700. Steep ravine garden with subtropical and water plants, tree ferns and koi carp. Private beach on Helford River.

Trelissick ££ *Feock on B3289 4 miles S of Truro; tel: 01872 862090.* Open Mar–Oct Mon–Sat 1030–1730 and Sun 1230–1730 (dusk off season); NT. Acclaimed woodland park overlooking Fal Estuary. Rhododendrons, camellias, tender plants.

Trewithen ££ *Grampound Road, Probus, off A390 6 miles E of Truro; tel: 01726 883647; www.trewithengardens.co.uk.* Open Mar–Sept Mon–Sat 1000–1630 (Sun Apr–May). Outstanding collection of rare and tender trees in landscaped parkland. Interesting 18th-century house.

THE LIZARD✦✦✦ AND HELSTON✦

ℹ Tourist Information 79 Meneage Street, Helston; tel: 01326 565431.

🏛 Folk Museum £ Market Place, Helston; tel: 01326 564027; www.helstonmuseum.org.uk. Open Mon–Sat 1000–1700.

Poldark Mine £££ Wendron (3 miles NE off A394); tel: 01326 573173; www.poldark-mine.com. Open Apr–Oct daily 1000–1800, Nov–Dec Sat–Thu 1030–1800; underground tours available.

Flambards Village Theme Park £££ Off A394 S of Helston; tel: 01326 573404; www.flambards.co.uk. Open Apr–Oct 1030–1700 (1800 in high season, closed some days – check in advance).

The Lizard peninsula is the most southerly point of mainland Britain. Picturesque fishing villages (**Coverack**✦, **Cadgwith**✦✦, **Gunwalloe**✦) and coves (**Mullion**✦✦, **Kynance**✦✦✦) stud its rocky coastline. **Lizard Point**✦✦ affords an exhilarating view of surf-pounded, shark-fin rocks. The Lizard's interior is rugged and treeless, in sharp contrast to the verdant scenery of the Helford River to the north, which has wooded inlets like **Frenchman's Creek**✦. **Helston**✦ is The Lizard's main town, with reminders of a prosperous tin-mining past in its elegant Georgian architecture. Its **Folk Museum**✦ reveals the background to Helston's famous 'Furry Dance' (*see box*). The **Poldark Mine**✦✦ and **Flambards Village Theme Park**✦✦ are leisure parks re-creating Victorian and wartime periods.

Accommodation and food in the Lizard peninsula

Landewednack House ££ *Church Cove, The Lizard; tel: 01326 290909; fax: 01326 290192; lendewednack-house@virgin.net.* Elegant, characterful rectory in extensive and beautiful gardens. Antiques and imposing bedrooms. Good home-cooking.

Tregildry ££ *Gillan, Manaccan, Helston; tel: 01326 231378; fax: 01326 231561; tregildry@globalnet.co.uk; www.tregildryhotel.co.uk.* Styles and colours of the Mediterranean infuse this gorgeous little place hidden above Gillan Creek. Exceptional cooking.

Furry Dance
Helston's Flora Day (a time-honoured celebration of spring) falls on or around 8 May. The town is decorated with flowers and spring greenery. Traditional dances are held in the streets. Children dressed in white dance at 10 in the morning, then at midday couples in top hats and Easter bonnets perform the Invitation Dance to the famous, repetitive tune.

Right
Trebah Gardens

PADSTOW❖❖ TO TINTAGEL❖❖

Quaint streets and slate houses surround the working fishing harbour of picturesque **Padstow❖❖**, a relative haven on Cornwall's treacherous northern coast. **Constantine Bay❖❖** and **Daymer Bay❖❖** are two of the best of the beautiful beaches around the Camel estuary and its headlands. North of the bridging point of Wadebridge, **Port Quin❖**, **Port Isaac❖❖**, **Trebarwith❖**, **Tintagel❖❖** and **Boscastle❖❖** are all exceptionally pretty and distinctive. **Tintagel**, much hyped for its romantic if spurious Arthurian associations, has a ruined **castle❖** perching over a wall of sheer cliffs. The village **post office❖** is a fine old longhouse, dating back to medieval times. Boscastle's thatched and whitewashed houses straggle along the crumpled slate walls of a winding sea inlet.

ⓘ Tourist Information North Quay, Padstow; tel: 01841 533449.

🏛 Tintagel Castle ££ Tintagel; tel: 01840 770328. Open Apr–Sept daily 1000–1800 (July–Aug 1000–1900), Oct 1000–1700, Nov–Mar 1000–1600; EH.

🍴 Seafood Restaurant £££, St Petroc's Hotel ££, Rick Stein's Café £ Riverside, Padstow; tel: 01841 532700; fax: 01841 532942; www.rickstein.com. Television chef Rick Stein's three very different establishments offer splendid cooking and stylishly unfussy bedrooms. Book well ahead!

Carpenter's Kitchen £ The Harbour, Boscastle; tel: 01840 250595. Excellent home-made cakes and light lunches.

PENWITH PENINSULA❖❖❖

Penwith, better known as the Land's End peninsula, is a typically Cornish landscape of rugged cliffs, sheltered coves and windswept headlands. The hilly, depopulated interior is sprinkled with prehistoric monuments and derelict engine houses. Coastal **Mousehole❖❖** and **Lamorna Cove❖❖** attract swarms of summer visitors. The **Minack Theatre❖❖❖** above Porthcurno is an open-air amphitheatre created in 1929; productions here are unforgettable, in a magical ocean-backed setting. The **Museum of Submarine Telegraphy❖** has a fascinating exhibition on communication systems in secret wartime tunnels. **Land's End❖❖** itself is Britain's most westerly bit of mainland, a wild seascape overshadowed by an inappropriate development of exhibitions, eating places and contrived amusements. Walk around the coastline to enjoy the scenery. The lovely beach of **Sennen Cove❖❖**, northeast of the headland, is well worth seeing.

◐ Minack Theatre and Visitor Centre £££ Porthcurno; tel: 01736 810181; www.minack.com. Performances May–Sept.

🏛 Museum of Submarine Telegraphy ££ Porthcurno; tel: 01736 810966. Open Sun–Fri 1000–1700 (daily July–Aug; Mon–Tue only in winter).

Above Land's End

PENZANCE✦✦✦ AND NEWLYN✦

ℹ **Tourist Information** Station Road, Penzance; tel: 01736 362207.

🧭 Access to the causeway island of **St Michael's Mount** is by boat or on foot over a cobbled causeway at low tide. Check the tide-tables.

🏛 **Penlee House Gallery and Museum £** Morrab Road, Penzance; tel: 01736 363625; www.penleehouse.org.uk. Open May–Sept Mon–Sat 1000–1700 (daily July–Aug); rest of year 1030–1600. Local history and paintings by the Newlyn School.

Trinity House National Lighthouse Centre ££ Wharf Road, Penzance; tel: 01736 360077. Open Easter–Oct 1030–1630.

St Michael's Mount ££ Marazion, 3 miles E of Penzance; tel: 01736 710507. Open Apr–Oct Mon–Fri 1030–1730, and most weekends; limited opening in winter; NT (members asked to pay admission on charity weekends). Ferries do not run in bad weather. No dogs.

Newlyn Art Gallery New Road, Newlyn; tel: 01736 363715; www.newlynartgallery.co.uk. Open Mon–Sat 1000–1700; donation requested.

Palms and giant echiums flourish in the frost-free climate of sheltered Penzance. The town also has historic buildings – including the domed **Market House** and the curious **Egyptian House✦** – good shops, sandy beaches and fine gardens. The **National Lighthouse Centre✦✦** has an excellent exhibition. Penzance is a springboard for trips to the **Isles of Scilly✦✦✦**. Magical **St Michael's Mount✦✦✦** stands on a causeway island in Mount's Bay. Originally a monastery associated with Mont St Michel in Normandy, the abbey was absorbed into a coastal fortress after the Dissolution, and became a domestic residence. South of Penzance, **Newlyn✦** is a bustling fishing port, where the **art gallery✦** keeps up the artistic traditions of the 19th-century Newlyn School.

Accommodation and food in and around Penzance

Abbey Hotel £££ *Abbey Street, Penzance; tel: 01736 366906; www.abbey-hotel.co.uk.* Delightful small hotel overlooking the harbour, with a distinctive interior. Super food and lovely, quirky bedrooms.

Ennys £ *Trewhella Lane, St Hilary, Penzance; tel: 01736 740262; fax: 01736 740055; ennys@ennys.co.uk; www.ennys.co.uk.* Charming farmhouse B&B in lovely setting near St Michael's Mount. Tasteful but imaginative décor. Cream teas, but no dinners served.

Sail Loft £ *The Harbour, St Michael's Mount; tel: 01736 710748.* Cornish cream teas and light lunches in a converted boathouse. Friendly service. *NT.*

Right
St Michael's Mount

St Ives✦✦✦ and Newquay✦

ⓘ **Tourist Information** *The Guildhall, Street-an-Pol, St Ives; tel: 01736 796297; ivtic@penwith.gov.uk; or Marcus Hill, Newquay; tel: 01637 854020; info@newquay.co.uk.*

ⓘ **Tate Gallery St Ives and Barbara Hepworth Museum £££** *Porthmeor Beach, St Ives; tel: 01736 796226; www.tate.org.uk. Open Mar–Oct daily 1000–1730, rest of year Tue–Sun 1000–1630; free to Tate members.*

The clear light and seaside colours of St Ives have attracted artists and craftspeople since the 1920s. The exceptionally pretty fishing village has an outpost of the **Tate Gallery✦✦✦**, and the **Barbara Hepworth Museum✦✦**; the narrow hilly streets around the harbour contain many other galleries and craft studios. Lovely beaches surround the rocky promontory of St Ives Head, extending into a vast dune system all around St Ives Bay. Around the popular family resort of **Newquay✦**, the breakers offer an irresistible challenge to Cornwall's surfers.

Right
Tate Gallery St Ives

Accommodation and food in St Ives

Allamanda ££ *83 Back Road East; tel/fax: 01736 793548; hynd@ allamanda.co.uk; www.allamanda.co.uk.* Delightful B&B in a fisherman's cottage near the beaches and galleries.

Porthminster Beach Café £–££ *Porthminster Beach; tel/fax: 01736 795352.* Bright terrace dining room overlooking Carbis Bay. Cakes and snacks during the day; sophisticated, cosmopolitan evening menus.

Suggested tour

Total distance: 250 miles (400km). Add 10 miles (16km) for the Roseland route.

Time: 10 hours.

Links: Easiest starts for the Devon routes are Bodmin (A38 to Plymouth) or Boscastle (B3263/A39 for Hartland (*see page 242*). The A30 is the main highway to Exeter and points north (*see page 250*).

Route: To get the best out of Cornwall, stick closely to the coast. If you have limited time, omit some of the detours on minor roads. From **FOWEY** ❶, follow signs on the A3082 to **ST AUSTELL** ❷, detouring north to see the Wheal Martyn **China Clay Museum** and the **Eden Project**. Then take the A390 to **Truro**◦, Cornwall's county town with its triple-spired **cathedral**◦.

Detour: A more time-consuming but rewarding drive on tiny lanes takes you round the **Roseland Heritage Coast**◦◦ past the quaint fishing port of **Mevagissey**◦◦, the charming **Veryan**◦ and the fashionable sailing centre of **St Mawes**◦. On the way are the **Lost Gardens of Heligan**◦◦ and the imposing façade of mock-Gothic **Caerhays Castle**◦ at Portholland. Take the vehicle ferry near **Trelissick Garden**◦◦ to pick up the main route south of Truro.

Below
Botallack mine

Take the A39 to **FALMOUTH ❸**, then follow minor roads along the **Helford estuary**✦✦ past the subtropical gardens near Mawnan Smith (**Glendurgan**✦✦ and **Trebah**✦✦), and the seal sanctuary at **Gweek** to **HELSTON ❹**. Head southeast over the Goonhilly Downs on the B3293 to **Coverack**✦✦, **Cadgwith**✦✦ and **LIZARD POINT ❺**. Track down the spectacular coves of **Kynance**✦✦✦ and **Mullion**✦✦ to Gunwalloe (Church Cove) and **Porthleven**. Continue west on the A394 past the surfing beach of **Praa Sands**✦ to **St Michael's Mount**✦✦✦ and **PENZANCE ❻**. Hug the coast roads past **NEWLYN**✦, **Mousehole**✦✦ and **Lamorna Cove**✦✦.

The B3315 leads past the stone circle known as the **Merry Maidens**✦ and the **Minack Theatre**✦✦ near **Porthcurno**. Continue clockwise round **PENWITH ❼** to **Land's End**✦✦, **Sennen Cove**✦✦ and St Just. Tin mines stud the coastline around Pendeen; the **Levant Mine** can be visited. From here the B3306 takes you over rugged, austere moorland with intermittent glimpses of sea; the headlands of Zennor are accessible only on foot from the South West Coast Path. From **ST IVES ❽**, duck inland around Hayle (the Lelant Saltings are a popular place to watch wading birds – RSPB reserve). Take the B3301 past the **Gwithian Towans**✦✦ (a huge sand-dune system) round **Godrevy Head**✦✦, and its lighthouse. From Portreath, rejoin the A30 briefly before heading back towards the coast at **St Agnes**✦ and the **Wheal Coates Mine**✦✦, then follow the coast past **Perranporth**✦ to **NEWQUAY ❾**. Continue north on the B3276 (signed Padstow), detouring to see some of the coastal scenery en route. Near Carnewas (7 miles north of Newquay), look out for signs to a National Trust car park and seasonal visitor centre above the astonishing **Bedruthan Steps**✦✦. Giant pinnacles of granite stud a spectacular beach (take great care if you use the steep steps to the beach, and beware of the cliff edges). **Trevose Head**✦✦ is another magnificent vantage point, fringed by long and lovely surfing beaches. From **PADSTOW ❿** skirt the Camel estuary via Wadebridge, following the coast again via **Polzeath**✦✦, **Port Quin**✦, **Port Isaac**✦ and **Portgaverne**✦ to **TINTAGEL ⓫** and **Boscastle**✦✦. Take the B3266 inland via Camelford turning left just after **Pencarrow**✦✦ on the A389 to Cornwall's former county town **Bodmin**✦. Northeast of the town, **Bodmin Moor**✦ is a bleak stretch of boggy moorland, rising to a maximum altitude of 1400ft. Take the B3269 past **Lanhydrock**✦✦ to complete the tour at Fowey.

Getting out of the car: The South West Coast Path is the best way to

☾ Nare Hotel £££
Carne Beach, Veryan;
tel: 01872 501111; fax:
01872 501856;
www.narehotel.co.uk. Not a cheap option, but a lovely peaceful sea-view location with excellent service and elegant rooms. A choice of restaurants and lots of sports and fitness facilities.

Trengilly Wartha £
Nancenoy, Constantine;
tel/fax: 01326 340332;
trengilly@compuserve.com;
www.trengilly.co.uk. Relaxing pub-with-rooms in quiet position near Helford Passage. Smallish but pretty bedrooms; some larger ones in an annexe.

Above
The Minack Theatre

see much of the coastline, especially around the scenic promontories of **Gribben Head, The Lizard, Penwith, Zennor, Godrevy, St Agnes, Trevose** and **Tintagel**. Penzance is the starting point for trips to the **Isles of Scilly⁺⁺⁺** by boat or (much more expensively) by helicopter. Scilly deserves more than a day; charming **Tresco⁺⁺⁺** is an idyllic retreat of seals and seabirds, where the **Abbey Gardens⁺⁺** are the main place of interest.

Also worth exploring: East of Fowey, Cornwall's southeast coastal strip leads past the classic fishing villages of **Polperro⁺⁺** and **Looe⁺⁺**, and several gorgeous rural beaches (**Lantic⁺⁺, Lantivet⁺** and **Talland⁺ Bays**). The long beaches of Whitsand Bay are popular with surfers, but exposed and dangerous for inexperienced swimmers.

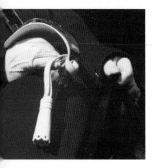

London

Ratings

Art and architecture	●●●●●
Eating out	●●●●●
Historical sights	●●●●●
Museums and galleries	●●●●●
Nightlife	●●●●●
Shopping	●●●●●
Children	●●●●○
Parks and gardens	●●●●○

T wo thousand years of history from Roman times onwards lie stacked on, or under, the pavements of this hugely diverse metropolis. With seven million inhabitants, London is easily Europe's largest and probably its most cosmopolitan city. Whatever you like doing – sightseeing, shopping, clubbing, visiting museums and galleries, dining out – London offers a bewildering choice. Like most capital cities, it can clock up an alarming bill, but there is no charge for wandering through its distinctive, village-like communities, admiring its amazingly varied architecture, or escaping into its parks. Following the River Thames is a great way to get your bearings, and to make sense of the city's geography. As the new millennium dawned, London exploded into an exciting new phase of tourist development, much of it focused around the waterfront areas of the South Bank, Greenwich and the revitalised Docklands in the east.

Getting there and getting around

ⓘ Britain Visitor Centre, 1 Regent Street SW1 (S of Piccadilly Circus); bvccustomerservices@bta.org.uk, offers free transport maps and information, as do London Tourist Board centres at major Underground stations.

Opposite
The British Library

Airports: London's international airports Heathrow, Gatwick, Stansted and Luton (*see page 30*) lie some way outside the city. London City Airport (*tel: 020 7646 0088; www.londoncityairport.com*), mainly for business use, is more central and is connected to Canning Town, Canary Wharf and Liverpool Street stations via shuttle bus services.
Rail: Nine mainline stations in central London serve the rest of the UK. Each has a Underground connection on or near the Circle Line.
Driving: The only sane advice on driving in London is 'don't'. Take public transport, or catch a black cab. Avoid unlicensed minicab firms.
Public transport: The Underground, or 'tube', is one of the most efficient ways of getting around, but not necessarily the most enjoyable. Often you get the best out of London by walking, or taking a bus, or river trip. Good-value one-day Travelcards, cheapest after

0930 on weekdays or any time at weekends, provide unlimited use of the bus, tube, Docklands Light Railway or suburban railway systems within certain zones. All the places in the main tour lie within the central Zone 1 – the nearest tube station is given in each case. Sights in the 'Further afield' section will need a more expensive ticket.

BLOOMSBURY AND MARYLEBONE

British Museum
Great Russell Street WC1; tel: 020 7323 8000; www.thebritishmuseum.ac.uk. Open Sat–Wed 1000–1730, Thu–Fri 1000–2030 (Great Court from 0900). (Russell Square, Tottenham Court Road)

Wallace Collection
Hertford House, Manchester Square W1; tel: 020 7563 9500; www.the-wallace-collection.org.uk. Open Mon–Sat 1000–1700, Sun 1200–1700. (Bond Street)

Madame Tussauds and London Planetarium
£££ Marylebone Road, NW1; tel: 0870 400 3000; www.madame-tussauds.com; www.planetarium.com. Open June–Aug 0900–1730, Sept–May 1000–1730 (Sat–Sun from 0930); Planetarium shows Mon–Fri 1230–1700, Sat–Sun 1030–1700 (1600 in winter). (Baker Street)

London Zoo £££ *Regent's Park NW1; tel: 020 7722 3333. Open daily 1000–1630 (1600 in winter). (Camden Town)*

The Academy ££
17–25 Gower Street, Bloomsbury WC1; tel: 020 7631 4115; fax: 020 7636 3442; res_academy@ etontownhouse.com. Quietly stylish townhouse in the heart of the university quarter.

Renowned for its literary and academic connections, **Bloomsbury's** principal sight is the treasure house of the **British Museum✦✦✦**. **Fitzrovia** is a characterful maze of historic streets, some packed with restaurants, around the sadly inaccessible **British Telecom Tower**. The detective Sherlock Holmes 'lived' in **Marylebone's** Baker Street, to the west. The **Wallace Collection✦✦** has an outstanding array of fine and decorative arts, while **Madame Tussaud's** waxworks museum and the **London Planetarium** are generally identifiable by long queues. **Regent's Park**, home of **London Zoo✦**, has fine rose gardens, and a summer open-air theatre. The **British Library** building lies between the mainline rail stations of Kings Cross and Euston.

Primrose Hill

Regent's Park

London Zoo

PRINCE ALBERT ROAD

PARKWAY

ALBANY STREET

FINCHLEY RD

WELLINGTON ROAD

KILBURN HIGH ROAD

MAIDA VALE

Lords Cricket Ground

ST JOHN'S WOOD RD

EDGWARE RD

Sherlock Holmes Museum

Madame Tussaud's

London Planetarium

BAKER ST

BAKER STREET

ROAD

PORTLAND

BBC Experience

Wallace Collection

MARYLEBONE ROAD

PADDINGTON

MARYLEBONE

WESTWAY

WESTWAY

WESTWAY

Market

PORTOBELLO ROAD

LADBROKE GROVE

BISHOP'S BRIDGE ROAD

EASTBOURNE TERR

PRAED STREET

SUSSEX GARDENS

EDGWARE ROAD

Marks & Spencer

Selfridge's

OXFORD STREET

NEW BOND

Jo Le

BAYSWATER

Whiteleys

London Toy and Model Museum

WESTBOURNE GROVE

QUEENSWAY

MARBLE ARCH

NOTTING HILL

PEMBRIDGE RD

Marble Arch

Speakers Corner

Grosvenor Square

Berkeley Square

HOLLAND PARK

BAYSWATER ROAD

BAYSWATER ROAD

MAYFAIR

NOTTING HILL

LAND PK AVE

Kensington Gardens

Hyde Park

PARK LANE

PARK LANE

PICCADILLY

Gr Pa

Holland Park

KENSINGTON

KENSINGTON CHURCH STREET

Kensington Palace

Serpentine Gallery

The Serpentine

Apsley House Wellington Museum

CONSTITUTION

Bucki Pala

Albert Memorial

KENSINGTON ROAD

KENSINGTON ROAD

KNIGHTSBRIDGE

GROSVENOR PL

KENSINGTON HIGH STREET

EARLS COURT ROAD

Royal Albert Hall

EXHIBITION ROAD

Victoria & Albert Museum

KNIGHTSBRIDGE

Harvey Nichols

BROMPTON ROAD

Science Museum

Harrods

SLOANE STREET

Natural History Museum

ECCLESTON ST

CROMWELL ROAD

CROMWELL RD

WEST CROMWELL RD

OLD BROMPTON ROAD

FULHAM ROAD

CHELSEA

LWR SLOANE S

BUCKINGHAM PALACE RD

EBURY BRIDGE RD

EARL'S COURT

WARWICK ROAD

EARLS COURT RD

REDCLIFFE GDNS

OLD BROMPTON ROAD

KINGS ROAD

PIMLICO ROAD

CHELSEA BRIDGE RD

ROYAL HOSPITAL

Royal Hospital

National Army Museum

GROSVE

0		500 m
0		500 yds

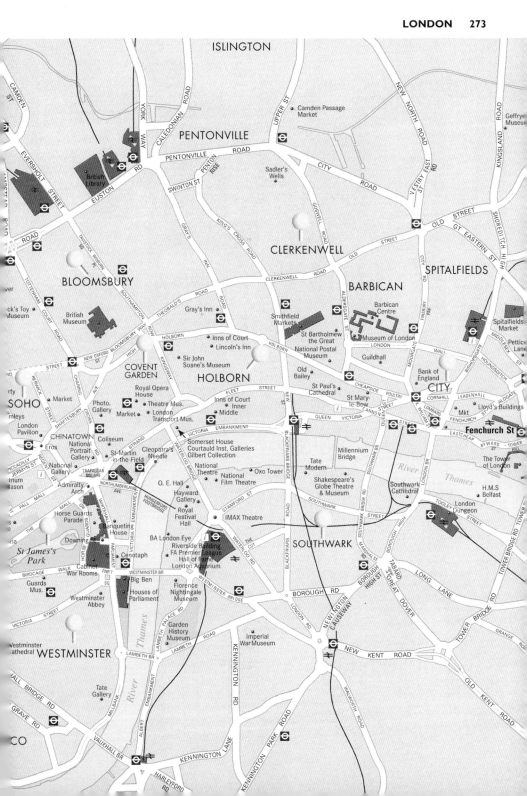

ISLINGTON

PENTONVILLE

• Camden Passage
  Market

Upper St

Camden
St

York Way

Caledonian Road

New North Road

Kingsland Road

Geffrye
Museum

PENTONVILLE   ROAD

SWINTON ST

PENTON RISE

• Sadler's
  Wells

CITY   ROAD

Vestry St East Rd

British
Library

Euston

Gray's Inn Road

King's Cross Road

INN

Goswell Road

Old   STREET   STREET

Gt Eastern St

Shoreditch High St

BLOOMSBURY

CLERKENWELL

CLERKENWELL   ROAD

BARBICAN

Barbican
Centre

Finsbury Pav

SPITALFIELDS

Spitalfields
Market

ck's Toy
Museum

British
Museum

Theobald's   Road

Gray's Inn •

Smithfield
Markets •

St Bartholmew
the Great

Aldersgate St

Moorgate

Museum of London
LONDON

WALL

Bishopsgate

Middlesex

Pettico
Lane

ROAD

New Oxford
St

Bloomsbury Way

High
St

Holborn

HOLBORN

• Inns of Court
• Lincoln's Inn

National Postal
Museum

Guildhall

Houndsditch

i

COVENT
GARDEN

HOLBORN

• Sir John
  Soane's Museum

Old
Bailey

St Paul's
Cathedral

Cheapside

Poultry

Bank of
England

CITY

Leadenhall
St

Lloyd's Buildings

Aldgate

SOHO

Royal Opera
House

• Theatre Mus.

FLEET   STREET

Inns of Court
Inner
• Middle

St Mary-
le-Bow

Cannon St

Cornhill

Lombard St

Fenchurch St

Photo.
Gallery

• Market

London
Transport Mus.

Victoria   Embankment

Queen   Victoria

King William St

Eastcheap

Byward St

Tower Hill

The Tower
of London

CHINATOWN

Coliseum

Cleopatra's
Needle

Somerset House
Courtauld Inst. Galleries
Gilbert Collection

Blackfriars Bridge

Millennium
Bridge

Tate
Modern

London Br

River   Thames

National
Portrait
Gallery

St-Martin-
in-the-Field

National
Theatre

National
Film Theatre

Oxo Tower

Shakespeare's
Globe Theatre
& Museum

Southwark
Cathedral

H.M.S
Belfast

National
Gallery

Trafalgar
Square

Strand

Waterloo Bridge

Q. E. Hall

Hayward
Gallery

Stamford St

SOUTHWARK

Southwark Bridge

Southwark St

Tooley St

London
Dungeon

Tower Bridge Rd

Admiralty
Arch

Northumberland
Ave

Hungerford
Footbridge

Royal
Festival
Hall

IMAX Theatre

The Cut

Southwark Bridge

Borough High

Grange Rd

Horse Guards
Parade

Banqueting
House

BA London Eye

Blackfriars   Rd

Long   Lane

Pall Mall

Whitehall

Downing

Victoria Embankment

Riverside Building
FA Premier League
Hall of Fame
London Aquarium

SOUTHWARK

Waterloo Rd

Marshalsea

Borough
High St

St Great Dover

Tabard St

The Mall

Horse Guards Rd

Parliament St

Cenotaph

BOROUGH   RD

Tower Bridge Rd

St James's
Park

Cabinet
War Rooms

Westminster Br

Big Ben

Houses of
Parliament

Florence
Nightingale
Museum

London Rd

Newington Causeway

NEW   KENT   ROAD

Old Kent Road

Birdcage   Walk

Guards
Mus.

Westminster
Abbey

Westminster Bridge

Garden
History
Museum

Imperial
War Museum

Kennington Rd

Victoria   Street

Lambeth Palace Rd

Lambeth Rd

Kennington Park Road

Walworth Rd

estminster
athedral

WESTMINSTER

Lambeth Br

River   Thames

Tate
Gallery

Millbank

Albert Embankment

Kennington Lane

Harleyford Rd

GRAVE RD

CO

Vauxhall Br

Hall Bridge Rd

THE CITY AND CLERKENWELL

St Paul's Cathedral
£££ *St Paul's Churchyard EC4; tel: 020 7236 4128; www.stpauls.co.uk. Open Mon–Sat 0830–1600 (galleries from 0930). (St Paul's)*

Museum of London ££
150 London Wall EC2; tel: 020 7600 3699; www.museumoflondon.org.uk. Open Mon–Sat 1000–1750, Sun 1200–1750. (St Paul's/Barbican)

Tower of London £££
Tower Hill EC3; tel: 020 7709 0765; www.hrp.org.uk. Open Mar–Oct Mon–Sat 0900–1700, Sun 1000–1700; rest of year Tue–Sat 0900–1600, Sun 1000–1600. (Tower Hill)

The Rookery £££
12 Peter's Lane, Cowcross Street EC1; tel: 020 7336 0931; reservations@rookery.co.uk; www.rookeryhotel.com. Imaginative renovation of a Georgian building. Full of antiques and pictures.

Moro ££ *34–36 Exmouth Market EC1; tel: 020 7833 8336. Not the easiest place to reach in trendy Clerkenwell, but well worth finding for its dazzlingly inventive Spanish–Middle Eastern cooking.*

The **City** is London's square mile devoted to finance and business. The site of the original Roman settlement, it was changed for ever by the Great Plague in 1665 and the Great Fire in 1666. Redesigned by Sir Christopher Wren, the City's greatest monument is **St Paul's Cathedral***, with its massive dome. The City's quaint streets still follow their old medieval layout. Look out for the **Bank of England*** and its museum, the **Royal Exchange***, the **Mansion House***, official residence of the Lord Mayor of London, the innovative **Lloyd's Building***, picturesque **Leadenhall Market***, and the many **guildhalls*** that belong to London's time-honoured livery companies. The **Museum of London*** is the best place to learn more about London's fascinating history. On the waterfront stands the **Tower of London***, the 900-year-old royal palace that houses the Crown Jewels. Spanning the Thames near by is the distinctive **Tower Bridge***. North of the City, historic **Clerkenwell** became fashionably cool in the 1990s, but the earthy markets of Smithfield and Leather Lane keep its feet on the ground.

COVENT GARDEN, SOHO AND HOLBORN

Above
Montage of the City of London and St Paul's Cathedral

These popular central areas are mainly devoted to shopping, eating and nightlife. **Covent Garden**, originally the medieval 'convent garden' of Westminster Abbey, was London's main flower and produce market until the 1970s. Its focal points are now a traffic-free **piazza***,

London Transport Museum £££ *Covent Garden Piazza WC2; tel: 020 7379 6344; www.ltmuseum.co.uk. Open daily 1000–1800 (Fri from 1100). (Covent Garden)*

Sir John Soane's Museum *13 Lincoln's Inn Fields WC2; tel: 020 7405 2107; www.soane.org. Open Tue–Sat 1000–1700 (1800–2100 first Tue of month); donation requested. (Holborn)*

Courtauld Institute Gallery ££ *Somerset House, Strand WC2; tel: 020 7848 2526; galleryinfo@courtauld.ac.uk; www.courtauld.ac.uk. Open daily 1000–1800, free until 1400 on Mon. (Temple)*

and the controversially revamped **Royal Opera House***. The old Victorian Flower Market now houses the family-friendly **London Transport Museum***. West of Covent Garden around Shaftesbury Avenue and Leicester Square lie many West End theatres, and the raffish delights of **Soho**, a district of clubs and porn that is surprisingly fun to explore. London's **Chinatown** occupies the streets immediately west of Leicester Square. **Holborn**, further east, was the location of the first English printing press; Fleet Street subsequently became the heart of the newspaper industry. The 19th-century **Royal Courts of Justice** are in Gothic Revival style; behind is the fascinating judicial quarter known as the **Inns of Court***, where barristers serve before qualifying. Sightseers head for the Tudor **Middle Temple Hall***, the ancient round **Temple Church*** and the eccentric **Sir John Soane's Museum***, home of the architect of the Bank of England. Beyond the Strand, the Renaissance palace of Somerset House contains the Impressionist paintings of the **Courtauld Institute Galleries***, and the **Gilbert Collection*** of decorative silverware.

Accommodation and food in the West End

Covent Garden Hotel £££ *10 Monmouth Street WC2; tel: 020 7806 1000, fax: 020 7806 1100; covent@firmdale.com; www.firmdalehotels. com*. Theatrically themed, beautifully designed bedrooms and a sophisticated atmosphere. Many celebrities guard their privacy here.

Below
Covent Garden busker

The Savoy £££ *The Strand WC2; tel: 020 7836 4343, fax: 020 7240 6040; info@ the-savoy.co.uk; www.savoy-group.com*. Anyone can enjoy afternoon tea or even a light lunch here, recalling the Art Deco glamour of yesteryear. The riverside setting is a great bonus, and the exemplary service is never snobbish.

Cork & Bottle ££ *44–46 Cranbourn Street WC2; tel: 020 7734 7807; www.donhewitson londonwinebar.com*. Popular wine bar in the heart of Leicester Square's bustling entertainment scene, often very crowded. Good wines by the glass. Splendidly 1970s.

Café Fish ££ *36–40 Rupert Street W1; tel: 020 7287 8989, fax: 020 7287 8400; www. cafefish.5pm.co.uk*. Stylish West End fish restaurant in theatreland. Bar-canteen on ground floor; good wines by the glass. Online bookings.

KENSINGTON AND CHELSEA

Victoria and Albert Museum *Cromwell Road SW7; tel: 020 7942 2000; www.vam.ac.uk. Open daily 1000–1745. (South Kensington)*

Natural History Museum *Cromwell Road SW7; tel: 020 7942 5000; www.nhm.ac.uk. Open Mon–Sat 1000–1750 (Wed and last Fri of month until 2200), Sun 1100–1750. (South Kensington)*

Science Museum *Exhibition Road SW7; tel: 0870 870 4868; www.sciencemuseum.org.uk. Open daily 1000–1800. (South Kensington)*

These desirable areas are the haunt of wealthy socialites. Classy shops and restaurants line the streets around Knightsbridge and Sloane Square, while King's Road caters for the trendy. Kensington Gardens and Hyde Park form central London's largest open space, divided by the Serpentine and fringed by the **Royal Albert Hall**✦✦ and the **Albert Memorial**✦, built in memory of Queen Victoria's consort. Well-known department stores like Harrods, Harvey Nichols and Peter Jones exist alongside a complex of huge museums near South Kensington tube. The **Victoria and Albert Museum**✦✦✦ ('the V&A') is an Aladdin's cave of decorative arts. The **Natural History Museum**✦✦ and the **Science Museum**✦✦, also housed in grand Victorian buildings, are both worth many hours of your time.

Accommodation and food in Kensington and Chelsea

Abbey House £ *11 Vicarage Gate W8; tel: 020 7727 2594.* Basic but civilised B&B in an attractive, quiet, period setting near Kensington's best shops. Friendly, courteous service.

Portobello Hotel ££ *22 Stanley Gardens W11; tel: 020 7727 2777; www. portobello-hotel.co.uk.* Delightfully eccentric pad near Notting Hill's famous street market, full of outré charm and romantically styled bedrooms. Watch out for famous faces.

Basil Street ££ *8 Basil Street SW3; tel: 020 7581 3311; fax: 020 7581 3693; info@thebasil.com; www.thebasil.com.* Old world charm a stone's throw from Harrods and the smart shops of Sloane Street. Family-run since Edwardian times, it is a soothing experience, especially for lone women.

Bibendum £££ *Michelin House, 81 Fulham Road SW3; tel: 020 7581 5817, fax: 020 7823 7925; manager@ bibendum.co.uk; www.bibendum.co.uk.* Part of Terence Conran's empire of London restaurants, set in a wonderful turn-of-the-20th-century building. The food is generally as good as the décor, with traditional favourites like steak or fish and chips amid the exotica.

MAYFAIR AND ST JAMES'S

Royal Academy of Arts £££ *Piccadilly W1; tel: 020 7300 8000; www.royalacademy.org.uk. Open Sun–Thu 0900–1800, Fri 1000–2200. (Piccadilly Circus)*

National Gallery *Trafalgar Square WC2; tel: 020 7747 2885; www.nationalgallery.org.uk. Open daily 1000–1800 (Wed and Sat until 2000). (Charing Cross)*

Buckingham Palace £££ *SW1; tel: 020 7321 2233; www.royal.gov.uk. State Rooms open Aug–Sept; Royal Mews Mon–Thu 1200–1600; Changing of the Guard 1130 daily summer; alternate days winter. (St James's Park/Victoria/Green Park)*

Right
Buckingham Palace Guard

The glamorous thoroughfares around Park Lane and Piccadilly are the **Mayfair** domain of bespoke tailoring, discreet gentlemen's clubs, and upmarket hotels. The smart shops around Bond Street and Regent Street are complemented by the more democratic Oxford Street. On Piccadilly, 18th-century Burlington House is occupied by the **Royal Academy of Arts**✤✤, home of world-class art exhibitions. On Trafalgar Square, the **National Gallery**✤✤✤ is London's leading art museum. **St James's** is dominated by Green Park and St James's Park, and **Buckingham Palace**✤, the home of the British monarchy. The Changing of the Guard ceremony is a popular summer spectacle. The Mall is a triumphant formal avenue lined with gracious John Nash Regency terraces.

SOUTH BANK

British Airways London Eye £££ *Jubilee Gardens SE1; tel: 0870 5000 600. Daily from 0900 (closed Jan for maintenance). (Waterloo)*

London Aquarium £££ *County Hall, Westminster Bridge Road SE1; tel: 020 7967 8000. Open daily 1000–1800. (Waterloo)*

Shakespeare's Globe Exhibition £££ *New Globe Walk, Bankside SE1; tel: 020 7401 9919. Open May–Sept daily 0900–1200, Oct–Apr 1000–1700. (Mansion House)*

Left
Royal Albert Hall

A second wave of redevelopment began along this strip of waterfront to greet the new millennium. The first occurred after the Festival of Britain in 1951, when the South Bank arts centre (home of the National Theatre, the National Film Theatre and the Hayward Gallery) grew up around the **Royal Festival Hall**✤✤ in concrete blocks. Today, new attractions enhance this area. The **London Eye**✤✤✤ (*www.ba-londoneye.com*) is unmissable, a 440ft observation wheel offering a vista over most of Greater London. Next to it is the **London Aquarium**✤✤ (*www.londonaquarium.co.uk*), with its breathtaking shark tanks, and on Gabriel's Wharf, the renovated art-deco **Oxo Tower**, with workshop space and a river-view restaurant. The Bankside power station has been imaginatively converted into **Tate Modern**✤✤, housing Britain's leading collection of contemporary art. **Shakespeare's Globe**✤ (*www.shakespeares-globe.org*) is a faithful reconstruction of the Elizabethan theatre where the Bard's plays were first staged. Further east are **Southwark Cathedral**✤, dating back before Chaucer's time, and the modish **Design Museum**✤. Away from the river, the **Imperial War Museum**✤✤ is one of Britain's best-presented accounts of 20th-century war.

Design Museum
£££ Butlers Wharf SE1;
tel: 020 7403 6933;
www.designmuseum.org.
Open daily 1000–1745.

Imperial War Museum
Lambeth Road SE1; tel: 020
7416 5320; www.iwm.org.uk.
Open daily 1000–1800.
(Lambeth North)

HMS Belfast £££ Morgan's
Lane, Tooley Street SE1; tel:
020 7940 6300; www.iwm.
org.uk. Open Mar–Oct daily
1000–1800 (rest of year to
1700). (London Bridge)

Accommodation and food on the South Bank

County Hall Travel Inn £ *Belvedere Road SE1; tel: 0870 238 3300; www.travelinn.co.uk.* Predictable, clean and practical budget accommodation in a superbly convenient South Bank location. Good-value for families.

George Inn £ *77 Borough High Street SE1; tel: 020 7407 2056.* One of the few traditional 17th-century coaching inns left in London, originally dating back to the Middle Ages. Now owned by the National Trust; events are staged in the courtyard in summer.

Oxo Tower £–£££ *Barge House Street SE1; tel: 020 7803 3888; www.harveynichols.co.uk.* There is a mix of eateries in this river-frontage landmark, from a bustling ground-floor sandwich bar to a fashionable (and pricy!) modern brasserie on the 8th floor, with breathtaking views.

WESTMINSTER AND PIMLICO

**Cabinet War
Rooms ££** Clive Steps,
King Charles Street SW1; tel:
020 7930 6961;
www.iwm.org.uk. Open
Apr–Sept daily 0930–1800,
rest of year 1000–1800.
(Westminster)

Banqueting House ££
Whitehall SW1; tel: 020
7930 4179; www.hrp.org.uk.
Open Mon–Sat 1000–1700.
(Embankment/Westminster)

Tate Britain £ Millbank
SW1; tel: 020 7887 8000;
www.tate.org.uk. Open daily
1000–1750. (Pimlico)

Windermere £
142–144 Warwick
Way SW1; tel: 020 7834
5163; fax: 020 7630 8831;
www.windermere-hotel.co.uk.
Great efforts are made to
make your stay agreeable
at this immaculately kept
small hotel not far from
Victoria Station. Small
restaurant downstairs.

Westminster is the powerhouse of the constitution. The **Houses of Parliament**✦✦✦ stand next to the great abbey church after which the area is named. Founded over 1000 years ago, the Gothic masterpiece of **Westminster Abbey**✦✦✦, crammed with monuments and tombs, has witnessed many state occasions. Just off Whitehall is Downing Street – the Prime Minister's London home is at No 10. A few streets away are the underground **Cabinet War Rooms**✦✦, where much of Britain's wartime strategy was planned by Winston Churchill, and the **Banqueting House**✦✦, the only survival of the old royal Whitehall Palace which perished in a fire in 1698. Outside the **Horse Guards**✦✦ building, colourful mounted sentries are popular photographic subjects, especially during the daily **Mounting of the Guard** ceremony, at 1100. Pimlico's key attraction is **Tate Britain**✦✦✦, whose collection features British works from 1550 onwards.

Suggested tour

Total distance: Distances tend to be irrelevant in London. The main part of the tour is based on London Underground's Zone 1, reachable from the Circle Line (tube stations are in *ITALIC CAPITALS*).

Time: If you attempt any exploration of London in a single day, you will become hopelessly exhausted. Seeing even a limited range of sights could take the best part of a week. Be selective, and intersperse major museums or galleries with shopping, or just absorbing the atmosphere by wandering through the streets or parks, or sitting in cafés. Save some energy for the evenings.

Footstool £–££ *St John's, Smith Square SW1; tel: 020 7222 2779; www.sjss.org.uk/restaurant.* Attractive, modestly priced restaurant in the church crypt below the concert hall; civilised surroundings; menus change monthly.

Tate Modern *Sumner Street, Bankside SE1; tel: 020 7887 8000, www.tate.org.uk. Open Sun–Thu 1000–1800, Fri–Sat 1000–2200.*

Vinopolis £££ *1 Bank End SE1; tel: 0870 241 4040; sales@vinopolis.co.uk; www.vinopolis.co.uk. Open Mon 1100–2100, Tue–Fri 1000–1800, Sat 1100–2000.*

Tower Bridge Experience ££ *Tel: 020 7403 3761; enquiries@ towerbridge.org.uk; www.towerbridge.org.uk. Open daily 1000–1830 (0930–1800 in winter).*

Barbican Centre *Silk Street EC2; tel: 020 7638 8891; www.barbican.org.uk; box office open daily 0900–2000.*

Route: The tour in principle follows the Circle Line anti-clockwise from the major coach and rail terminus of Victoria Station. It combines many different options.

From *VICTORIA*, take the Underground east to *WESTMINSTER*. As you emerge from the station, look up at **Big Ben**, Britain's largest clock, and set your watch by it. Right next to the clock tower are the Gothic **Houses of Parliament+++ ❶**, and opposite is **Westminster Abbey+++ ❷**. Next Circle Line stop is *EMBANKMENT*, but it's not far to walk.

Detours: Take a stroll up **Whitehall** past **Downing Street+ ❸** and the **Horse Guards++ ❹** to **Trafalgar Square+++ ❺** past government and civil service buildings. On the way you'll see the **Cenotaph+ ❻**, scene of the Remembrance Day service in November. Walk past the redevelopment behind Charing Cross to return to the Embankment.

Alternatively, cross **Westminster Bridge++ ❼** and admire the riverside on foot from the South Bank's Jubilee Walk past the **London Eye+++ ❽** and the **London Aquarium++ ❾**. You can continue as far as you like along this stretch of the river, returning over a bridge to a handy tube station anywhere between here and **Tower Bridge+++ ❿**. There's masses to enjoy on the revitalised waterfront, including an **Imax Cinema+ ⓫**. Near Blackfriars or Southwark Bridges lie the **Tate Modern++ ⓬** and **Shakespeare's Globe+ ⓭**. Just across from London Bridge lie the imaginative wine exhibition of **Vinopolis+ ⓮** and **Southwark Cathedral++ ⓯**. Further east is the revitalised leisure, shopping and residential warehouse complex of **Hay's Galleria**.

Take the tube, or walk through the Embankment Gardens and past the Savoy Hotel, to *TEMPLE*, best stop-off for **Somerset House++ ⓰** and the **Inns of Court++ ⓱**. *BLACKFRIARS* or *MANSION HOUSE* are the best stations for **St Paul's Cathedral+++ ⓲** and the surrounding historic quarter. True Cockneys are defined by their birthplace, within earshot of the bells of St Mary-le-Bow, off Cheapside. Northwards is the Tudor **Guildhall+ ⓳**, administrative headquarters of the City. *MONUMENT* station is named after Sir Christopher Wren's stone column commemorating the Great Fire of 1666, which started a few paces west in Pudding Lane. Its summit offers a fine view over the City. The **Bank of England+ ⓴** is a few minutes' walk away in Threadneedle Street and the **Lloyd's Building+ ㉑** is in Lime Street by **Leadenhall Market+ ㉒**.

Next station is *TOWER HILL*, where you alight for the **Tower of London+++ ㉓** and **Tower Bridge+++ ㉔**, and where the Docklands Light Railway will take you to the millennial attractions near Greenwich and the Isle of Dogs. Take the Circle Line on to *BARBICAN*, best stop for the **Museum of London++ ㉕** and the **Barbican Centre**. The Smithfield area (site of a colourful Victorian meat market) contains the Central Criminal Court (the **Old Bailey+ ㉖** and **St Bartholmew the Great++ ㉗**, oldest of all the City's churches.

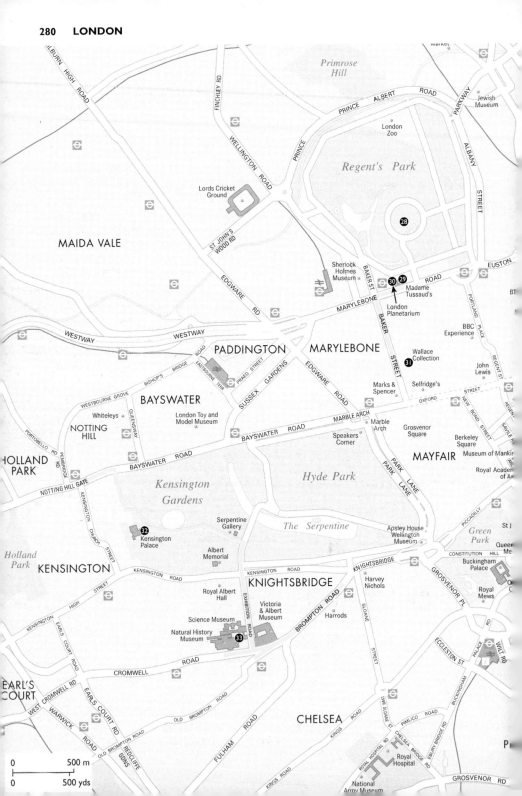

ISLINGTON

PENTONVILLE

Camden Passage
Market

Geffrye
Museum

British
Library

Sadler's
Wells

BLOOMSBURY

CLERKENWELL

SPITALFIELDS

British
Museum

Gray's Inn

Smithfield
Markets

BARBICAN

Barbican
Centre

Spitalfields
Market

Petticoat
Lane

Inns of Court
Lincoln's Inn

St Bartholomew
the Great
National Postal
Museum

㉗

㉕ Museum of London

LONDON

COVENT
GARDEN

Sir John
Soane's Museum

Guildhall ⑲

HOLBORN

Old
Bailey

㉖

Bank of
England

Royal Opera
House

St Paul's
Cathedral

⑱

St Mary-
le-Bow

⑳

CITY

Theatre Mus.
London
Transport Mus.

Inns of Court
Inner ⑰
Middle

CHINATOWN

⑯

Photo.
Gallery

Market

Lloyd's Buildings

㉒ Mkt

㉑

Coliseum

Somerset House
Courtauld Inst. Galleries
Gilbert Collection

Fenchurch St

National
Portrait
Gallery

Cleopatra's
Needle

St-Martin
-in-the-Field

National
Theatre

National
Film Theatre

Eros

National
Gallery

⑤

Admiralty
Arch

Tate
Modern

⑫

Millennium
Bridge

⑬

The Tower
of London

㉓

Q. E. Hall

Shakespeare's
Globe Theatre
& Museum

Southwark
Cathedral

⑭

HMS
Belfast

Horse Guards
Parade

Hayward
Gallery

④

Banqueting
House

⑮

London
Dungeon

⑩

Royal
Festival
Hall

③ Downing St.

⑪

㉔

SOUTHWARK

BA London Eye
Riverside Building
FA Premier League
Hall of Fame
London Aquarium

⑥ Cenotaph

Cabinet
War Rooms

⑨

⑦

Big Ben

② Westminster
Abbey

① Houses of
Parliament

Florence
Nightingale
Museum

WESTMINSTER

Garden
History
Museum

Imperial
War Museum

Tate
Gallery

Pick up the tube again at *FARRINGDON* and continue to *BAKER STREET* for **Regent's Park**•• ➋➑ or **Madame Tussaud's**• ➋➒ and the **Planetarium**• ➌➊. A reasonable walk or bus ride southwards takes you to the **Wallace Collection**•• ➌➊, the tube on to *NOTTING HILL GATE*. The cool glamour of Holland Park's stucco terraces makes it one of London's most fashionable residential areas. Walk through **Kensington Gardens**•• ➌➋, past the former home of the late Diana, Princess of Wales; watch model boats on the Round Pond or see modern art at the Serpentine Gallery. Kensington High Street is a popular shopping area. The closest station to Kensington's main **museums**••• ➌➌ is *SOUTH KENSINGTON*. From here or *SLOANE SQUARE*, the fashionable shops of Knightsbridge lie within easy reach. Another short tube hop takes you back to your starting point at Victoria.

Further afield

Points north: From King's Cross, take the Northern Line to *CAMDEN LOCK*, where the street markets are good for second-hand clothes and antiques. Further north are the fashionably bohemian village suburbs of **Hampstead**•• and **Highgate**•, good for views of London and a bit of interesting nightlife. Have a walk on **Hampstead Heath**•, and track down the Adam mansion of **Kenwood House**••, or **Highgate Cemetery**•, full of famous graves.

Eltham Palace is quite a distance out of town, but accessible by public transport.

The Docklands are accessible and best seen from the Docklands Light Railway.

Points south: In London's amorphous southern suburbs, Forest Hill's **Horniman Museum**•• is an eclectic collection of curios and ethnological items. The renovated **Dulwich Picture Gallery**•• has a long and venerable history. The splendid art-deco house of **Eltham Palace**•• was built for the wealthy Courtauld family on the site of a medieval palace.

Points east: **Greenwich**•••, on the Meridian Line, offers a range of dazzling attractions, including the *Cutty Sark*•• tea clipper, the **National Maritime Museum**•••, the **Royal Naval College**••, the **Ranger's House**• and the **Queen's House**•, and above all the **Royal Observatory**••, where the story of Greenwich Mean Time unfolds. Further east are the **Docklands**•, and the **Thames Barrier**•• near Woolwich.

Points west: The River Thames flows past a number of splendid country houses (Chiswick, Osterley Park, Syon, Marble Hill and Ham). The great royal palace of **Hampton Court**••• was expanded to its present opulent dimensions by successive Tudor and Stuart dynasties. For a breath of fresh air, visit the world-renowned botanic gardens at **Kew**•••, or **Richmond Park**••.

Index

Acknowledgements

Project management (first edition): Dial House Publishing Services
Project management (this edition): Sarah Hudson
Series design: Fox Design
Front cover design: Pumpkin House
Cover artwork: Studio 183
Layout: PDQ Digital Media Solutions Ltd
Map work: Polly Senior Cartography
Repro and image setting: PDQ Digital Media Solutions Ltd
Printed and bound in Spain by: Grafo Industrias Gráficas, Basauri

We would like to thank John Heseltine for the photographs used in this book, to whom the copyright belongs, with the exception of the following:

Front cover: Anne Hathaway's Cottage, Ivan J Belcher/Worldwide Picture Library/Alamy

Back cover: Conwy Castle, Robert Harding Picture Library/Alamy

Britain on View (pages 42, 58B, 59, 92, 105, 160, 243 and 256)

The Devonshire Collection, Chatsworth (page 103)
Reproduced by permission of the Duke of Devonshire and the Chatsworth Settlement Trustees.

Eden Tourism (page 60)

Ethel Davies (pages 23, 271, 275 and 277)

Ffotograff (pages 176B and 198)

Robert Harding Picture Library (pages 114, 208, 210, 260B, 263 and 266)

Caroline Jones (page 257)

Spectrum Colour Library (page 100)

Telegraph Colour Library (pages 43, 72, 73, 74, 80B, 82, 84, 86, 88, 91, 101, 136B, 142, 157, 158, 168 and 254)

Feedback form

If you enjoyed using this book, or even if you didn't, please help us improve future editions by taking part in our reader survey. Every returned form will be acknowledged, and to show our appreciation we will give you £1 off your next purchase of a Thomas Cook guidebook. Just take a few minutes to complete and return this form to us.

When did you buy this book? ....
....

Where did you buy it? (Please give town/city and, if possible, name of retailer)
....
....

When did you/do you intend to travel in England and Wales?...
....

For how long (approx)? ....

How many people in your party? ....

Which cities, national parks and other locations did you/do you intend mainly to visit?
....
....
....
....

Did you/will you:
❑ Make all your travel arrangements independently?
❑ Travel on a fly-drive package?
Please give brief details: ....
....

Did you/do you intend to use this book:
❑ For planning your trip?   ❑ Both?
❑ During the trip itself?

Did you/do you intend also to purchase any of the following travel publications for your trip?
Thomas Cook Travellers: London..
A road map/atlas (please specify) ....
Other guidebooks (please specify) ....

Have you used any other Thomas Cook guidebooks in the past? If so, which?
....
....

Please rate the following features of *Signpost England and Wales* for their value to you (circle VU for 'very useful', U for 'useful', NU for 'little or no use'):

The *Travel Facts* section on pages 14–23	VU	U	NU
The *Driver's Guide* section on pages 24–28	VU	U	NU
The *Highlights* on pages 38–39	VU	U	NU
The recommended driving routes throughout the book	VU	U	NU
Information on towns and cities, National Parks, etc	VU	U	NU
The maps of towns and cities, parks, etc	VU	U	NU

Please use this space to tell us about any features that in your opinion could be changed, improved, or added in future editions of the book, or any other comments you would like to make concerning the book:

....

....

....

....

....

....

....

....

Your age category: ❑ 21-30   ❑ 31-40   ❑ 41-50   ❑ over 50

Your name: Mr/Mrs/Miss/Ms ....

(First name or initials) ....

(Last name) ....

Your full address (please include postal or zip code):

....

....

....

....

....

Your daytime telephone number: ....

Please detach this page and send it to: The Project Editor, Signpost Guides, Thomas Cook Publishing, PO Box 227, Units 19–21, The Thomas Cook Business Park, Coningsby Road, Peterborough PE3 8XX, United Kingdom.

Alternatively you can e-mail us at: *books@thomascook.com,* **or** *editorial@globe-pequot.com* **for the US.**

We will be pleased to send you details of how to claim your discount upon receipt of this questionnaire.